In the generation that followed Martin Luther's protest the evangelical movement in Europe attracted very different levels of support in different parts of the continent. Whereas in Germany, eastern and central Europe the new movement brought a swift transformation of the religious and political landscape, progress elsewhere was more halting: both in the Mediterranean lands and the new nation states of western Europe initial enthusiasm for reform by and large failed to bring about the wholescale renovation of society for which evangelicals had hoped. These fascinating contrasts are the main focus of this volume of specially commissioned essays, each of which charts the progress of reform in one country or region of Europe. Written in each case by a leading specialist in the field, they make available in English for the first time an up-to-date survey based on primary research and a thorough grasp of the vernacular literature. For both scholars and students they will be an invaluable guide to recent debates and literature on the success or failure of the first generation of reform.

D1158538

The early Reformation in Europe

The early Reformation in Europe

Edited by

Andrew Pettegree

*Department of Modern History,
University of St Andrews*

CAMBRIDGE
UNIVERSITY PRESS

Published by the Press Syndicate of the University of Cambridge
The Pitt Building, Trumpington Street, Cambridge CB2 1RP
40 West 20th Street, New York, NY 10011–4211, USA
10 Stamford Road, Oakleigh, Victoria 3166, Australia

First published 1992

Printed in Great Britain at the University Press, Cambridge

A catalogue record for this book is available from the British Library

Library of Congress cataloguing in publication data

The early Reformation in Europe / edited by Andrew Pettegree.
    p.   cm.
    Originated from a course taught by the editor at the University of St Andrews
since 1989.
    Includes index.
    ISBN 0–521–39454-6 (hc). – ISBN 0–521–39768–5 (pb)
    1. Reformation. I. Pettegree, Andrew.
BR309.E37   1992
274'.06 – dc20 91–46844 CIP

ISBN 0 521 39454 6 hardback
ISBN 0 521 39768 5 paperback

Contents

Maps

Notes on contributors

ANDREW PETTEGREE is Lecturer in Modern History at St Andrews University. He is the author of two books on aspects of the international Protestant movement, *Foreign Protestant Communities in Sixteenth-Century London* (1986) and *Emden and the Dutch Revolt. Exile and the development of Reformed Protestantism* (1992).

WINFRIED EBERHARD is Professor of History at the Ruhr-Universität Bochum, and member of the 'Collegium Carolinum' in Munich. He is the author of two monographs on sixteenth-century Bohemia, *Konfessionsbildung und Stände in Böhmen, 1478–1530* (1981) and *Monarchie und Widerstand. Zur ständischen Oppositionsbildung im Herrschaftssystem Ferdinands I.* (1985).

DAVID P. DANIEL, formerly a Professor of Church History at Concordia Seminary in St Louis, serves as Executive Director of the Slovak Academic Information Agency in Bratislava. He is the author of numerous studies of the Reformation in the Austrian Habsburg lands, and in particular among the Czechs and Slovaks.

BRUCE GORDON is a Research Fellow at the Institute for European History at Mainz. He is the author of several articles on aspects of the Swiss Reformation and *Clerical Discipline and the Rural Reformation: the Synod in Zurich, 1532–1580* (1992).

OLE P. GRELL is a Carlsberg Fellow at the Wellcome Unit for the History of Medicine at the University of Cambridge. His publications include articles on the Danish Reformation, and a monograph, *Dutch Calvinists in Early Stuart London* (1989). He is at present completing a study of International Calvinism in the period of the Thirty Years War.

DAVID NICHOLLS is a visiting lecturer at the University of Tours. He has published extensively in periodicals on aspects of the early Reformation in France. He is currently engaged on a full-length study of the French Reformation in the sixteenth century.

ALASTAIR DUKE is Senior Lecturer in History at the University of South-ampton. A collection of his essays on aspects of the Dutch Reformation was recently published as *Reformation and Revolt in the Low Countries* (1990).

DIARMAID MACCULLOCH, until recently Lecturer in Church History at Wesley College Bristol, is now a freelance historian. His publications include *The Later Reformation in England 1547–1603* (1990) and the award-winning *Suffolk under the Tudors* (1986).

EUAN CAMERON is Lecturer in History at the University of Newcastle. He has published two books, *The Reformation of the Heretics* (1984), a study of the Waldensians, and a survey study of *The Reformation in Europe* (1991).

A. GORDON KINDER is a member of the department of Spanish and Portuguese Studies at the University of Manchester. He has published extensively on aspects of Spanish Protestantism, including the only bibliography of the movement, a biography of *Casiorodo de Reina* (1975), and a recent bibliographical survey of sources relating to Michael Servetus (1989).

Preface

This book owes its origins to a course taught to Honours students in the University of St Andrews since 1989. My original intention was to attempt a comparison between the rapid development of Protestantism in Germany and its much more halting progress elsewhere in Europe, but it soon became clear that the sparseness of the literature in English made this difficult to achieve in any full sense. In almost no case was there available an up to date survey dealing explicitly with the period of interest, that is the first thirty years after Luther's protest first ignited the Reformation; sometimes we were faced with an almost complete absence of specialist work in any but the local languages. This volume is intended partly to make good this deficiency; but it is also hoped that by presenting these pieces together in one volume, they may offer some provocative contrasts and comparisons, which may go some way towards answering the question of why the Reformation had so much more impact in some parts of Europe than others.

When I first embarked on this project, kind friends advised me against an edited volume, on the grounds that it was a great deal more trouble than writing a whole book oneself. That this has not been the case is a credit to the contributors, whose generosity of spirit and geniality throughout the production process I have greatly valued. All of those I first approached agreed to take part, and they have borne my editorial interventions with unvarying good temper. Apart from those contributing here I would also acknowledge the help given the project by Tom Scott, who gave me much good advice in the conceptual stages, and proposed the Eastern European contributions which have greatly strengthened the volume as a whole. We have also benefited greatly from the practical advice and efficiency of Richard Fisher of Cambridge University Press. But the project's greatest debt is to the students who first provoked this volume, and have subsequently road-tested much of what follows. I hope they find it useful.

ADMP
St Andrews, 20 October 1991.

xi

Abbreviations

AGKKN	*Archief voor de geschiedenis van de katholieke kerk in Nederland*
ARG	*Archiv für Reformationsgeschichte*
BHR	*Bibliothèque d'Humanisme et Renaissance*
BN	Bibliothèque Nationale, Biblioteca Nacional
BRN	*Bibliotheca reformatoria neerlandicae*, ed. S. Cramer and J. Pijper (10 vols., The Hague, 1903–14)
CD	*Corpus documentorum inquisitionis haereticae pravitatis neerlandicae. Versameling van stukken betreffende de pauselijke inquisite in de Nederlanden* (5 vols., Ghent/The Hague, 1889–1902)
CH	*Church History*
CO	*Calvini Opera*
CR	*Corpus Reformatorum*
DAN I	*Documenta anabaptistica neerlandica I Friesland en Groningen (1530–1550)*, ed. A. F. Mellink (Leiden, 1975)
DAN II	*Documenta anabaptistica neerlandica II Amsterdam (1536–1578)*, ed. A. F. Mellink (Leiden, 1985)
DAN V	*Documenta anabaptistica neerlandica V Amsterdam (1531–1536)*, ed. A. F. Mellink (Leiden, 1985)
DNB	*Dictionary of National Biography*
EHR	*English Historical Review*
HJ	*Historical Journal*
JEH	*Journal of Ecclesiastical History*
NAK	*Nederlands Archief voor Kerkgeschiedenis*
P and P	*Past and Present*
RHPR	*Revue d'Histoire et Philosophie Religieuses*
SCH	Studies in Church History
SCJ	*Sixteenth-Century Journal*
TRE	*Theologische Realenzyklopädie*
WA Br.	*D. Martin Luthers Werke. Kritische Gesammtausgabe* (Weimarer Ausgabe). Briefwechsel

1   The early Reformation in Europe: a German affair or an international movement?

Andrew Pettegree

Viewed in retrospect it is in the years immediately after Luther first came to prominence as a theological writer that the Reformation appears most harmoniously and coherently international. Luther's writings certainly excited the interest of a wide international public: even the briefest glance at the contemporary comment on the 'Luther affair' leaves little doubt of this. Almost from the first months after Luther had begun to achieve notoriety in Germany, reports from across Europe testify to the intense interest aroused in his character, his writings and his fate. Thus, in May 1519, a Swiss student studying in Paris, Peter Tschudi, could note the avidity with which Luther's works were read in the city; even apparently, according to Luther's other correspondents, at the Sorbonne, later the relentless guardian of doctrinal orthodoxy.[1] In Holland and Flanders meanwhile, much of the intellectual community seemed to have been caught up in the new controversies, as the correspondence of Erasmus bears sufficient testimony.[2] It was probably from the Netherlands that numbers of Luther's works were also transported across the Channel to England, where they are known to have been read about this time.[3] The scale of the intellectual interest in Luther's writings is captured in a famous letter to the reformer by the Swiss publisher Johannes Froben, who in February 1519 was in the process of publishing his second collected edition of Luther's Latin works. Froben wrote to Luther that he had despatched some 600 copies of this collection to France and Spain,

---

[1] A. L. Herminyard (ed.), *Correspondance des réformateurs dans les pays de langue française* (9 vols., Geneva, 1866–97), I. 47. Cf. Luther to Lang, April 1519 (a report based on the Froben letter cited in n. 4 below). WA Br. I. 369 (no. 167).

[2] See *Correspondence of Erasmus*, ed. R. A. B. Myers and P. G. Bietenholz (Toronto, 1974 *et seq.*), VI and VII *passim*; Also useful are the documents collected in P. Fredericq (ed.), *Corpus documentorum inquisitionis haereticis pravitatis Neerlandicae* (5 vols, Ghent/The Hague, 1889–1902). Luther's books were reported on sale in Antwerp as early as April 1518. L. Knappert, *Het ontstaan en de vestiging van het protestantisme in de Nederlanden* (Utrecht, 1924), p. 162.

[3] Erasmus to Luther, 30 May 1519: you have people in England who think well of what you write. *Correspondence of Erasmus*, VI, 392 (no. 980).

and further consignments to England, Italy and the Netherlands.[4] Froben's remarks have often been cited to illustrate the scope of Luther's appeal in Western Europe, but it was clear that there was equal interest in the eastern lands. From both Bohemia and Hungary comes evidence of the profound interest in Luther and the German controversies.[5]

A generation later this cheerful unity of purpose – perhaps in any case illusory – would have seemed little more than a distant memory. In Germany itself Luther's movement had proved deeply divisive, but at least it had survived to achieve institutional form in established Lutheran churches. Elsewhere the prospect was much less cheerful. Perhaps the most striking progress had been achieved in the (to western readers) unfamiliar territories of central Europe, where Luther's movement had been able to build on a solid tradition of pre-Reformation dissent, and shield behind the powerfully entrenched local estates. By the 1550s, ironically, the lands of the Austrian Habsburgs played host to some of Europe's best established Lutheran churches.[6] Scandinavia too, had by this time seen the establishment of orthodox Lutheran churches; here, in a different echo of German events, thanks largely to the intervention of a trio of godly princes. But elsewhere the promising beginnings witnessed in countries like France and the Netherlands had not been sustained. In these countries the evangelical movement had proved too delicate a plant to flourish in the face of sustained state hostility. By the time of Luther's death (1546), evangelical groups here were largely fragmented and demoralised. These years also witnessed the collapse of the reform movement in Italy, a surprisingly fertile mission field for the early reformers. Even in Switzerland, an initially powerful evangelical movement had brought conflict and division, its leading figures separated from the German Lutherans by a seemingly unbridgeable chasm of doctrinal misunderstanding. No wonder that the decade after Luther's death saw a mood of almost universal pessimism descend on the battered and dispirited evangelical reformers. Quite apart from the increasingly hostile international climate, the bold hopes of a universal renovation of Christendom raised in the first decade had proved wholly elusive: even in Germany reformers were now increasingly conscious of the apparently intractable problems which they faced if they were to bring about the

---

[4] WA Br. I. 331–5 (no. 146). A partial English version of this important document is in Preserved Smith and Charles M. Jacobs (eds.), *Luther's Correspondence and other Contemporary Letters* (2 vols, Philadelphia, 1913–18), I. 161–2.
[5] Below, chapters 2 and 3. The first translation of Luther into a foreign vernacular was in Czech: a translation of *The Blessed Sacrament and Holy and True Body of Christ*, dated 8 May 1520. J. Benzing, *Lutherbibliographie* (Baden-Baden, 1966), no. 514.
[6] Chapters 2 and 3, below.

moral regeneration which lay at the core of Luther's initial call for reform.[7]

This pessimism was no doubt itself overdone, but it is clear enough that throughout Europe the evangelical movement had failed to live up to the initial promise of the first turbulent years. Why should this have been so? The failure of the evangelicals to convert the early receptivity to calls for reform into a coherent movement will be a common theme in many of the essays which make up this volume, but ultimately it is clear that none of the countries treated here could match the intensity of interest generated in Luther's own homeland. Nowhere was there quite the same potent brew of social, political and religious circumstances which so assisted the cause of the reformers at home. The purpose of this introductory essay will be to sketch these German circumstances; partly by way of context for what follows, but also to point up some of the contrasts and possible points of comparison between German events and the progress of the evangelical movement elsewhere. For it is clear that, for all the problems faced by evangelicals outside Germany, the movement retained throughout this period something of its initial international character. The impact of German events continued to reverberate around the European scene for all of this period, complicating diplomacy and confusing national loyalties. No corner of Europe was entirely safe from the resonance of the German controversies: even in Spain, a stronghold of orthodoxy, the Reformation would have a considerable impact on perceptions of faith and religious orthodoxy.[8]

To understand the reasons why the Reformation movement should have so quickly adopted so many divergent forms, it is necessary to return first to the years of apparent unity: the brief period between the publication of Luther's controversial theses and their official condemnation. It is arguable that even in this period the enthusiasm with which Luther's writings were greeted was owing to a mistaken perception of Luther as a new voice airing the sort of criticisms of church institutions which were common currency in educated circles. Put baldly, many of Luther's first admirers saw him as a humanist, an Erasmian, and as such Luther was able to rely on a sympathetic hearing from many of that loose international fraternity of reform-minded scholars who contributed so significantly to the international climate of the age. This 'constructive misunderstanding' was no doubt a large part of Luther's early international appeal. It was a misunderstanding which Erasmus himself partly

---

[7] See here the debate inspired by Gerald Strauss, *Luther's House of Learning: Indoctrination of the Young in the German Reformation* (Baltimore, 1978). Strauss, 'Success and Failure in the German Reformation', *P and P*, 67 (1975), 30–63.

[8] Chapter 10, below.

shared. The great humanist first became aware of Luther's writings in 1518, at which point he gave them a cautious, if somewhat distant, welcome.[9] Initially at least, his inclination was to defend the young men of Germany, who had as he saw it taken up the cause of liberal studies. Through 1519 and 1520 a stream of German visitors provided further flattering evidence of Erasmus' inspirational role in the evangelical movement. Although Erasmus' cautious encouragement was balanced by a growing anxiety to distance himself from Luther's more intemperate utterances, loyal protestations to Catholic patrons were largely ineffectual, for by this time the two causes, the defence of humanist learning and Luther's affair, had become inextricably linked in the public eye. Those who defended Luther looked to Erasmus as a mentor, and those who sought to damage Erasmus found Luther an increasingly useful pretext.[10] The extent of the confusion was neatly epitomised by Martin Bucer, who, after hearing Luther at the Heidelberg disputation (April 1518), pronounced him the perfect Erasmian.[11]

It was evident that this misunderstanding could not continue indefinitely, and indeed Erasmus' correspondence through 1520 testifies to a growing nervousness in the intellectual community as the church marshalled its defences. When in 1521 the great humanist withdrew from the Netherlands to Basle, it was at least partly to remove himself from the furious theological wrangles in which he found himself engulfed as a result of the Luther affair. Erasmus' reaction indicates that conservative theologians had by now, after a hesitant beginning, succeeded in mounting an effective counter-assault. In 1519 both the universities of Louvain and Cologne formally condemned certain of Luther's teachings, leading in June 1520 to the long expected papal condemnation, the provisional bull of excommunication *Exsurge Domine.*[12] These events, together with the secular condemnation of the Edict of Worms, stimulated a wave of book burnings: at Liège, Louvain and Cologne in October and November, 1520, and the following spring at Paris, and in England at London, Oxford and Cambridge.

The papal condemnation marks the first real break in the movement, for no longer was it possible to present Luther's teaching as part of a

---

[9] Erasmus first mentions Luther's writings (without mentioning him by name) in a letter to Thomas More of March 1518. By the autumn he was confident that Luther was 'approved by all the leading people' and that 'his conclusions satisfied everyone'. *Correspondence of Erasmus*, V. 327, VI. 137 (nos. 785, 872).

[10] *Ibid.*, VI. 313, 350 (nos. 948, 961).

[11] A. Horawitz and K. Hartfelder (eds.), *Briefwechsel des Beatus Rhenanus*, (Leipzig, 1886), 106ff. Smith and Jacobs (eds.), *Luther's Correspondence*, I. 80–3.

[12] Provisional, as Luther was given six months in which to recant. He responded by burning the bull. Scott Hendrix, *Luther and the Papacy. Stages in a Reformation Conflict* (Philadelphia, 1981), pp. 89–120.

theological debate within the normal parameters of scholarly discourse. Of course Luther continued to find support in the international humanist community: many were by now heavily committed, and others shared Erasmus' disapproval that the church authorities had chosen to proceed by threats and ban, rather than by reasoned argument.[13] This, taken with Erasmus' refusal to write against Luther, left enough ambiguity to perpetuate continuing misunderstanding about his position.[14] But others, faced with a clear expression of papal authority and the increasingly fundamental nature of Luther's challenge, drew back. Luther's protest was clearly no longer a movement, if it ever had been, which could be endorsed by the whole international intellectual community. By 1521 the best brains of England, many of them respected humanists, were enrolled into a commission to refute Luther's teachings, a literary campaign which issued in the publication of Henry VIII's famous *Assertio Septem Sacramentorum*, the anti-Lutheran tract which earned Henry the coveted title, Defender of the Faith.[15]

The fact that Luther had now to be seen through a new filter, that of a condemned heretic, inevitably made a profound difference to the way his writings were perceived elsewhere in Europe. Condemnation did not prevent the spread of the evangelical movement, but it certainly put a new and powerful weapon in the hands of conservative forces. Lay rulers could call upon the authority of the church in their suppression of dissent: evangelicals were consequently more guarded in their identification with, and promotion of, Luther's teachings.[16] It was at this point that the movements in Germany and elsewhere begin most obviously to diverge. Whereas in most non-German cultures further evangelical progress became increasingly difficult, in Germany Luther's excommunication ushered in a period of expansive growth. A brief sketch of these German events may perhaps help clarify the reasons for these markedly divergent developments.

[13] The view he put forward in a long consideration of the Luther affair in a letter to Albrecht of Brandenburg of Oct 1519. *Correspondence of Erasmus*, VII. 108–16 (no. 1033).

[14] Well expressed by Albrecht Dürer, who having heard a false rumour of Luther's death after the Diet of Worms, wrote in his diary an anguished entry beseeching Erasmus to take up the struggle in his stead. W. M. Conway (ed.), *Literary remains of Albrecht Dürer* (Cambridge, 1889), 158–9.

[15] Richard Rex, 'The English Campaign against Luther in the 1520s', *Transactions of the Royal Historical Society*, 5th ser., 39 (1989), 85–106.

[16] Most of Luther works translated after this date make no mention of Luther's authorship on the title-page. C.Ch.G. Visser, *Luther's Geschriften in de Nederlanden tot 1546* (Assen, 1969); W. A. Clebsch, 'The Earliest Translations of Luther into English', *Harvard Theological Review*, 56 (1963), 75–86. Useful surveys in J. Fr. Gilmont (ed.), *La Réforme et le Livre* (Paris, 1990); cf. Bernd Moeller, 'Luther in Europe: his Works in Translation, 1517–1546', in E. I. Kouri and Tom Scott (eds.), *Politics and Society in Reformation Europe* (Basingstoke, 1987), 235–51.

6   *Andrew Pettegree*

In Germany papal excommunication was swiftly followed by the secular ban pronounced by the Emperor after Luther's dramatic appearance at the diet of Worms. Although Luther's safe conduct was honoured and he was allowed to depart, the reformer was now an outlaw: to ensure his survival until the political situation clarified it was necessary for his friends to remove him to the protective custody of the Wartburg. Far from thwarting the movement, Luther's temporary isolation in fact prompted a considerable broadening, as other clerical leaders emerged to press the call for church reform. The years 1521–4 would witness a crucial transformation, as Luther's personal controversy was transformed into a widely based popular movement. The catalysing force behind this was a growing band of sympathetic evangelical preachers who boldly associated Luther's cause with a whole range of lay concerns regarding the current state of the church. Luther himself showed the way: both in his period of seclusion and after his triumphant return to Wittenberg in 1522, he addressed himself to a wide range of contemporary issues.[17] The preaching ministers followed with fierce denunciations of clerical immorality, ill-discipline and church privileges, themes which spoke directly to the concerns of their lay audience.

These issues were the subject of an unprecedented polemical campaign, as printers all over Germany took to printing and reprinting the works of Luther and his followers. The economics of the printing industry meant that it was often easier to republish work locally than transport stock long distances, but these frequent reprints also provide eloquent testimony to the extent of public interest in the controversies.[18] For this was the great age, not only of Luther's polemical writing, but of the *Flugschriften*, the short, cheaply produced pamphlets which sought to mediate the church controversies to a wide audience. Recent research suggests that the outpouring of tracts and pamphlets reached a peak during these years that was never again equalled.[19]

Preaching and printed works – in whatever combination[20] – soon began

[17] For the Wartburg writings see Heinrich Bornkamm, *Luther in mid-Career, 1521–1530* (London, 1983), pp. 1–50.
[18] See the list compiled by J. L. Flood, 'Le livre dans le monde Germanique a l'époque de la Réforme', in Gilmont, *La Réforme et le Livre*, p. 40.
[19] Hans-Joachim Köhler, 'Erste Schatten zu einem Meinungsprofil der frühen Reformationszeit', in Volker Press and Dieter Stievermann (eds.), *Martin Luther, Probleme seiner Zeit* (Stuttgart, 1986), pp. 244–65. A useful summary of various compilations of Reformation polemic is Mark E. Edwards, 'Statistics on sixteenth-century printing', in Philip N. Bebb and Sherrin Marshall (eds.), *The Process of Change in Early Modern Europe* (Athens, OH., 1988), pp. 149–63.
[20] For the debate over the respective contributions of verbal and written media to the communication of Reformation ideas see the contributions by Scribner and Moeller in Hans-Joachim Köhler (ed.), *Flugschriften als Massenmedium der Reformationszeit* (Stuttgart, 1981). Also the judicious remarks in Köhler, 'Meinungsprofil', pp. 244–9.

to have their effect on public opinion in the sophisticated German cities. Nuremberg, for instance witnessed what historians have described as a massive outpouring of anticlerical sentiments.[21] Evangelical ministers soon commandeered five of the town's churches, their efforts being ably seconded by the circulation of anonymous slander-sheets, and by monks who abandoned their cloisters to denounce the religious life. Traditional preachers were subjected to public criticism during celebrations of the Mass, and the old rites were openly ridiculed in mock processions. It was therefore little surprise that when the laity presented demands for reform, as for instance in 1523 for communion in both kinds, the civic elite (many of whom had revealed early sympathy for the reform) were forced into a series of measures to rein in the evangelical movement, and pre-empt more radical action. In 1525 the Reformation in Nuremberg was formally adopted. As in Nuremberg, so also in the other towns of Saxony, Franconia and the German south-west. In Strasburg a conservative council was forced to concede ever greater freedoms to a group of evangelical clergy supported by a substantial section of the city population. The reluctant endorsement of Martin Bucer's appointment as minister in August 1523 was followed in December by a decree that the town's ministers should teach nothing but the 'pure Gospel'.[22] The speed of development depended to a large extent on the presence or absence of such charismatic local leaders, but even where there was no figure of stature the movement made steady progress through 1523 and 1524: this was the case at Frankfurt, Ulm and Augsburg, none of which yet formally adopted Reformation measures.[23]

Thus, although it was only towards the end of the decade that the triumph of the Reformation achieved institutional confirmation in most German cities, it was clear that by 1525 the crucial transition towards the emergence of a popular movement had effectively been accomplished. In south Germany at least the movement had moved from its original epicentres, in monasteries and patrician and scholarly circles, towards being a coherent popular movement under clerical leadership. It was already robust enough to survive some heavy blows: necessarily so since the years 1524–5 witnessed the first serious crisis of the Reformation. These years opened badly when at the Diet of Nuremberg (January–April

[21] Günther Vogler, *Nürnberg, 1524–5: Studien zur Geschichte der reformatorischen und sozialen Bewegung in der Reichsstadt* (Berlin-East, 1982). Usefully summarised in his 'Imperial City Nuremberg, 1524–1525: the Reform Movement in Transition', in R. Po-Chia Hsia (ed.), *The German People and the Reformation* (Ithaca, 1988), pp. 32–49.

[22] Thomas Brady, *Ruling Class, Regime and Reformation at Strasbourg, 1520–1555* (Leiden, 1978).

[23] Heinrich Richard Schmidt, *Reichstädte, Reich und Reformation* (Stuttgart, 1986), pp. 68 ff.

1524) the Emperor's agents succeeded in enforcing their demands that the Edict of Worms should be more strictly observed. This represented a serious reverse for the evangelical leadership, which had previously sought with some success to appease progressive forces internally while remaining ostensibly loyal.[24] The Diet represented a distinct hardening of fronts and a retreat from compromise based on a common commitment to reform within the church: a trend dramatically reinforced when in 1525 Erasmus finally bowed to pressure to write against Luther and published his tract on *The Freedom of the Will*. Erasmus' writing and Luther's reply did not end connections between humanism and the evangelical movement – on the contrary, many of the younger humanists would ultimately remain faithful to Luther – but they did demonstrate with stark clarity that the Reformation could no longer be seen as an all-embracing and inclusive movement of church reform.

This, even more so, was the message of the Peasants' War, which erupted through Germany in these same years. The extent to which the rebellious peasants drew their inspiration from Luther was, and remains, a controversial question.[25] It is clear that from one perspective the uprising was part of a long tradition of peasant unrest, which had seen several widespread insurrections over the previous two generations, as peasants banded together to protest economic and social conditions which had deteriorated sharply since the High Middle Ages.[26] But it is equally the case that the evangelical movement unwittingly provided the common man with a new vocabulary and basis of action which allowed long-held grievances against clerical levies and abuses to achieve a much greater cohesion and sharper focus. The most popular of the peasant manifestos, the Twelve Articles, reflected this new confidence in applying the evangelical teaching both to specific grievances and in a more general claim for social justice based on the preaching of the 'pure Gospel'.[27]

The rapid spread of the insurrection through south and central Germany shook the evangelical movement to its core. Luther's denunciation of the rebellious peasants appeared in a poor light after the slaughter at Mühlhausen, but his instinctive response was in fact shared by most of the magisterial reformers, who almost to a man swiftly repudiated the peasants' annexation of evangelical freedom to their own

[24] Schmidt, *Reichstädte*, pp. 130–52.
[25] Peter Blickle, *The Revolution of 1525* (Baltimore, 1981). Henry Cohn, 'Anticlericalism in the German Peasants' War, 1525', *P and P*, 83 (1979), 3–31. See also now Tom Scott and Bob Scribner, *The German Peasants' War. A History in Documents* (London, 1991).
[26] On the *Bundschuh* risings see particularly Tom Scott, 'Freiburg and the Breisgau', in *Town–Country Relations in the Age of Reformation and Peasants' War* (Oxford, 1986), pp. 165–89.
[27] Text in Blickle, *Revolution of 1525*, pp. 195–201.

purposes.[28] The revolt and its aftermath inevitably brought a substantial re-orientation of the Reformation movement. The image of the peasant Karsthans, a stock feature of the early Reformation *Flugschriften*, now disappeared, as reformers opted instead for an increasingly explicit endorsement of the existing social hierarchy. But that the Reformation was ultimately able to survive so severe a crisis was a tribute to the firm roots it had already put down in German soil. The years after 1526 witnessed steady progress for the evangelical movement. Even the Diet of Speyer, held in 1526 in the immediate aftermath of the Peasants' War was much less of a disaster for the evangelicals than might have been expected: in the absence of many conservative representatives the Diet adopted a religious formula which allowed the evangelicals an unexpected degree of licence. The following years saw a further wave of important cities adopt the Reformation, including the previously less deeply penetrated north German towns.[29] Important princely conversions also contributed to the growing strength of the movement. By 1529 the evangelicals were sufficiently entrenched to risk a calculated act of defiance, the 'protestation', when the Catholic majority enforced a strict reaffirmation of the Edict of Worms at the second Diet of Speyer. The further developments of 1530 and 1531, the presentation of the Protestant Confession at Augburg, and the formation of the Schmalkaldic League, in effect confirmed what had already become clear: that the evangelical movement was now so entrenched that only military action could reverse the changes wrought by Luther's movement in Germany.

It was perhaps inevitable that elsewhere in Europe the evangelical movement would take many more years to achieve the same institutional security, even in lands where the Reformation eventually triumphed. In fact the essays which follow testify to the general difficulties faced by evangelicals outside Germany in converting the initial enthusiasm for church reform into a viable popular movement. What was it which made German circumstances so peculiar, and from the point of view of the evangelical movement, so uniquely favourable? Among the whole complex of factors at work, three stand out as of primary importance. Firstly, although the role of printing in the spread of the Reformation is generally acknowledged, it seems in Germany to have had a particular significance. The Reformation from the beginning was accompanied by a flood of printed works. The number of books published in Germany increased sharply from 1519, reaching a peak in the mid-1520s.[30] Equally

---

[28] Robert Kolb, 'The Theologians and the Peasants: Conservative Evangelical Reaction to the German Peasants Revolt', *ARG*, 69 (1978), 103–31.

[29] Schmidt, *Reichstädte*, pp. 268–74. For a detailed study of a northern city Reformation, Rainer Postel, *Die Reformation in Hamburg, 1517–1528* (Gütersloh, 1986).

[30] See the chart in Flood, 'Le monde Germanique', p. 51.

important, the Reformation itself exercised an important transforming influence on the physical shape of the book and the scope of the reading public. At one level the Reformation provided an important impetus for the emergence of the vernacular to challenge the previous domination of Latin. This appeal to a wider public had in effect been sanctioned by Luther himself with the publication of his sermon on Indulgences, *Von Ablass und Gnade*, in a German version as early as 1518. By 1520, this had gone through twenty editions, and in the years that followed Luther revealed himself as a master of this new form of public theological debate.

Countries elsewhere in Europe also developed a popular literature of the Reformation, but the range and depth of the German literature remained exceptional. This is only partly to be attributed to the high state of development of the German printing industry, with over sixty cities possessing functioning presses by 1500; a striking contrast with England, where regional presses were actually in decline in this period.[31] The contrast with England is perhaps an exaggerated one, since the English printing industry was relatively backward by European standards, but even the sophisticated presses of the Netherlands had nothing to compare with the flood of evangelical literature produced in Germany. In the period 1520–46 Dutch presses published some 85 editions of Luther's works; a not inconsiderable quantity considering the perils of evangelical printing.[32] But in Germany some 390 editions of Luther's works appeared in 1523 *alone*, and this was part of a mass of controversial literature published in these years. By 1525 there were possibly as many as 3 million evangelical pamphlets circulating in Germany.[33]

The German passion for such literature was well known: Erasmus commented upon it as something faintly discreditable.[34] But in fact there was little of this sort of pamphlet activity anywhere in Europe before 1517. The work of R. G. Cole, confirmed by the painstaking analysis of Hans-Joachim Köhler's Tübingen project, has demonstrated that the *Flugschriften* were a type of literature largely created by the Reformation.[35] And it

---

[31] The tiny proportion of English books printed outside London can be gauged from the new index volume to the *Short Title Catalogue*: A. W. Pollard and G. R. Redgrave (eds.), *A Short Title Catalogue of Books Printed in England, Scotland and Ireland . . . 1475–1640*, revised Katharine F. Pantzer (3 vols., London, 1976–91), III. 207–12.

[32] Visser, *Luther's geschriften in de Nederlanden*, p. 188.

[33] Flood, 'Le monde Germanique', p. 52; J. Schwitalla, *Deutsche Flugschriften, 1460–1525* (Tübingen, 1983), p. 6.

[34] *Correspondence of Erasmus*, VI. 368–9 (no. 967), VII. 14 (no. 998): 'You know the restless energy of the Germans and their violence of character . . . Look aє the pamphlets with which they cut to pieces anyone who has done them an injury.'

[35] R. G. Cole, 'The Reformation Pamphlet and Communication Processes', in Köhler, *Flugschriften*, pp. 139–61; and his 'The Reformation in Print. German Pamphlets and Propaganda', *ARG*, 66 (1975), 93–102. Köhler, 'Meinungsprofil'.

was a type which never achieved the same importance outside Germany. In France, despite the existence of the small evangelical works identified by Francis Higman, the main pamphleteering movement only began to gather pace in the 1540s, with the emergence of Geneva as the centre of French evangelical propaganda.[36] In the Netherlands it reached its full flood only with the political and religious conflicts of the struggle against Spain in the second half of the sixteenth century. The *Flugschriften* remained a peculiarly German phenomenon: elsewhere, the sheer volume and variety of polemical evangelical writings was never replicated.

The fact that Luther's writings were printed, not only so copiously, but in so many different centres across Germany, highlights the second determining characteristic of the German situation: Germany was a land of towns. The German cities were not necessarily the largest in Europe – the Empire boasted no giants on the scale of Venice or Paris, nor even a city as large as London – but the sheer number of large, prosperous, culturally sophisticated and politically relatively independent cities made the German Empire quite distinct. The towns have long been recognised as the nurseries of the Reformation movement, a primary role not essentially shaken by recent scholarship demonstrating that many countryfolk were also capable of a sincere commitment to the evangelical movement.[37] Towns were important to the dissemination of the movement in a whole number of obvious ways. Their population was disproportionately literate, politically aware and often involved in city government; they were natural centres for intellectual activity and debate; they usually functioned as a communication and trade centre for an extensive hinterland. Thus, when it is possible to follow the pattern of dissemination of evangelical ideas, they are usually found to radiate outwards from a local metropolis to smaller centres and villages.[38] These larger towns were themselves part of an extended network of contacts. Thus many in the German cities knew of Luther even before they read his writings; and Luther's own journeyings in the first years of the Reformation played an important part in reinforcing the network of personal contacts which gave

---

[36] Francis Higman, 'Le levain de l'Evangile', in Henri-Jean Martin and Roger Chartier (eds.), *Histoire de l'édition française. Tome 1. Le livre conquérant* (Paris, 1982), pp. 305–25 and the articles cited in notes 62 and 65 below.

[37] Peter Blickle, *Gemeindereformation. Die Menschen des 16. Jahrhunderts auf dem Weg zum Heil* (Munich, 1987); Franziska Conrad, *Reformation in der Bäuerlichen Gesellschaft. Zur Rezeption Reformatorischer Theologie in Elsass* (Stuttgart, 1984). For a penetrating review of these and other relevant works see Tom Scott, 'The Common People in the German Reformation', *HJ*, 34 (1991), 183–91.

[38] See here the useful study by the geographer Manfred Hannemann, *The Diffusion of the Reformation in southwestern Germany, 1518–1534* (Chicago, University of Chicago Department of Geography research paper, 167, 1975).

him his first support.[39] Neither must one forget the role of the universities, with which Germany was also unusually well supplied.[40] Students showed a strong allegiance to their local university, to which town magistrates also naturally turned when they were looking for an evangelical preacher; a process which enabled the universities to function as informal centres for the placement of surplus evangelical ministers.

If we compare this situation to that of the other countries surveyed here, the contrasts are much more striking than points of similarity. Although in both Scandinavia and England economic contacts with Germany are important in explaining the dissemination of evangelical ideas, the recipient societies were too different to aspire to anything like the German urban Reformation. Denmark had only two towns of any size, Malmø and Copenhagen, both with approximately 8,000 inhabitants, but this was less than half the size of their north German rivals Rostock or Hamburg, and one third the size of Lübeck. In Sweden Stockholm was even smaller.[41] In England, the next largest towns after London were Norwich and Bristol with about 10,000 inhabitants, which put them on a par with Nördlingen, one of 14 towns of similar size in the German south west, and much smaller than the regional metropoles of Strasburg, Augsburg and Ulm.[42]

If we are looking for areas to equate with Germany in terms of such a diverse urban culture, early sixteenth-century Europe seems to offer only two: the Netherlands and northern Italy. Economically the city states of Italy were past their peak, but they still boasted a highly developed urban culture, in a region of good communications and high sophistication. For the Netherlands, in contrast, the Reformation era was a period of economic expansion and growth: the rich industrial provinces of Flanders and Brabant boasted a number of major cities, while Antwerp was fast emerging as the commercial entrepôt of northern Europe. An unusually large proportion of the population lived in towns (around 35 per cent), whereas in Holland, with five cities of 10,000 inhabitants packed into a small area, the proportion was a high as 50 per cent.[43] Here there did exist

39   Thus Luther's contacts with the Nuremberg humanists on his way to and from Augsburg in October 1518, and the excitement that attended his progress to the Diet of Worms in 1521. Philip Bebb, 'Humanism and Reform: The Nürnberg *Sodalitas* Revisited', in Bebb and Marshall (eds.), *Process of Change*, pp. 68–70.
40   By 1508 there were 13 universities in Germany. Data concerning dates of foundation in Gustav Adolf Benrath, 'Die Universität der Reformationszeit', *ARG*, 57 (1966), 32–3.
41   Information supplied by Ole Grell. See Grell, 'The emergence of two cities: the Reformation in Malmø and Copenhagen', in Leif Grane and Kai Hørby (eds.), *Die dänische Reformation vor ihrem internationalen Hintergrund* (Göttingen, 1990), p. 129.
42   Map in Hannemann, *Diffusion of the Reformation*, p. 36. Peter Clark and Paul Slack, *English Towns in Transition, 1500–1700* (Oxford, 1976), p. 83.
43   J. A. van Houtte, *An Economic History of the Low Countries, 800–1800* (London, 1977), pp. 123–6. A. M. van der Woude, 'Demografische ontwikkeling van de noordelijke Nederlanden', *Nieuwe Algemene Geschiedenis der Nederlanden*, V. 135.

the conditions for an urban movement on a par with Germany, and in fact the Netherlands would prove fertile soil for Luther's movement. Nowhere else outside the German-speaking lands does one find evidence of so widespread a groundswell of support for evangelical doctrines: Alastair Duke's article here reveals a genuinely popular Reformation. Italy too, as Euan Cameron makes clear, was by no means as closed to Reformation influences as might be thought. But in neither case did it prove possible to convert the genuine concern for church reform into a Reformation movement on the German model. This was very largely owing to the absence of what we may regard as the third key aspect of the German situation: the unusually favourable political conditions.

Clearly, even by 1520, Luther's movement had ceased to be a purely religious matter. Luther's call for reform struck a deep chord, and not just with those concerned with its spiritual implications. For many Luther became a potent symbol of German nationhood, and in his struggle with the Pope, of German resistance to a resented foreign power.[44] The clumsy attempts of the church to silence him by an appeal to authority rather than engaging the theological issues he had raised only exacerbated this impression. There were many besides Frederick the Wise who had an interest in stressing the German aspect of the affair. Luther swiftly became not only a patriotic icon, but an important pawn in the politics of the estates against the new Emperor. Luther himself was not slow to grasp these political implications, as he demonstrated in his appeal *To the Christian Nobility of the German Nation*. This is recognised as one of the most important of Luther's 1520 writings for its devastating attack on the papacy and recognition of the validity of the temporal power, but contemporaries would have been more struck by the extent to which Luther's criticisms echoed the *Gravamina*, the petition of grievances against the church regularly rehearsed at the German Diet.[45] Luther's writing was a declaration of solidarity with these concerns, and it reaped its reward when the German estates championed his right to a hearing at the Diet of Worms in 1521. The fact that Luther was granted a hearing before his condemnation, against the original intention of the Emperor, was itself a significant victory for the estates.[46] Even after the publication of the ban, Charles' conciliatory behaviour, to Frederick of Saxony in particular, left open the question of whether the Emperor genuinely expected the Edict to be rigorously applied; a fatal ambiguity which provided a breathing space in which a popular movement could put down its roots.[47]

[44] For an introduction to German 'patriotic' humanism, A. G. Dickens, *The German Nation and Martin Luther* (London, 1974), chapter 2.
[45] Wilhelm Borth, *Die Luthersache (causa Lutherani), 1517–1524* (Lübeck and Hamburg, 1970), pp. 75–7.
[46] *Ibid.*, pp. 106–14.   [47] *Ibid.*, pp. 129–30.

These same political factors could obviously not apply elsewhere in Europe: Luther was a potent national symbol only in his homeland. In Italy, to return to one of the countries where the economic and social circumstances might have seemed most favourable to the Reformation, Luther's nationality was rather a barrier than a help to the spread of the movement. While the theological issues raised by Luther merited a hearing, Italian humanists and theologians were reluctant to accept that profound insights were likely to emerge from the barbaric lands north of the Alps. Luther's message would be most effective in Italy where his authorship was not explicitly acknowledged.[48] Elsewhere in Europe it was clear that the effectiveness or otherwise of the central authorities would exercise a decisive influence on the spread of the movement. In France the ambiguous signals emanating from the Court created a decade of confusion which could be exploited by both evangelicals and their conservative opponents; clarity was achieved only when Francis I opted decisively for repression in the mid-1530s.[49] The clearest example of decisive intervention on the part of the secular powers came in the Netherlands, where, as indicated, a popular evangelical movement might have emerged. But here Charles, as hereditary ruler, was untrammelled by the need to co-operate with powerful estates, and the result was a rapid series of repressive measures. This prompt and sustained repression was sufficient to rein in the infant movement, which never as a result developed its full potential.

The evangelical movement was much more likely to flourish in areas of weak or dispersed political control. This was the case in both Switzerland, a confederacy of small independent states, and Scandinavia. Even so, local political factors played a role here too, as for instance in nudging the inner Swiss cantons towards an anti-evangelical stance, a reflection of their suspicion of the imperial ambitions of Zurich as much as any innate hostility to reform.[50] Similarly, the changing loyalties of the noble estates in Denmark had much to do with the shifting balance of political advantage surrounding a disputed royal succession following the deposition of Christian II. The clearest example of local political factors which materially assisted the reform movement would be seen in the eastern Habsburg lands. Here, as in Germany, the Reformation was able to profit by the political aspirations of the powerful estates, for whom their adoption of the evangelical movement was a further expression of their wish for greater autonomy from the Catholic monarch. The fact that these areas

[48] Ugo Rozzo and Silvana Seidel Menchi, 'Livre et Réforme en Italie', in Gilmont (ed.), *La Réforme et le Livre*, pp. 327–74. B. M. Hallman, 'Italian National Supremacy and the Lutheran question', *ARG*, 71 (1980), 134–48.
[49] Below, chapter 6. R. J. Knecht, *Francis I* (Cambridge, 1982).   [50] Below, chapter 2.

also enjoyed close economic and cultural connections with Germany, and the existence, since the Hussite revolution, of a strong pre-existent tradition of independent church reform, all contributed to make these lands the second power-house of the early Reformation.

For all that, Germany was unique in the degree to which all of these circumstances – a vibrant urban and print culture, a dispersed and distant political authority – acted to promote and protect the Reformation. To say this is not to adopt a remorselessly determinist view of the success of the evangelical movement. For all the economic, political and cultural factors that assisted or impeded the spread of the Reformation, its success or failure still depended on individual choices to accept or reject the evangelical teachings. Even in Germany, some lands and cities remained barren territory to the new movement.[51] How important then were the teachings of the reformers in the early progress of the Reformation movement? To pose the question so baldly is not intended to construct a false antithesis, between theology on the one hand and social or political factors on the other. But there is still no real consensus as to the weight that should be given to the doctrinal appeal of Luther's teachings – i.e. theology – in explaining the progress of the evangelical movement. The extent to which the early Reformation was primarily a theological movement is an issue which deserves to be confronted; and here one may once again postulate a distinction between events in Germany and elsewhere in Europe.

To deal first with Germany, one should first perhaps recognise that the question of the importance of doctrine in fact comprises two distinct issues: firstly, to what extent men understood and were motivated by Luther's central theological concerns; and then, to pose an altogether less demanding question, to what extent people's motivation was primarily religious in the broadest sense of the word. Even the narrower issue of the role of Luther's teachings during the period of most rapid evangelical growth (1521–5) has produced some widely divergent assessments. The case for a heavy dependence on Luther is put most strongly by Bernd Moeller, who has argued, on the basis of an analysis of printed sermons, that the teachings of the ministers active in these years reflected a surprising degree of theological agreement. This essentially derived from Luther's basic theological programme, consisting of a demand for Gospel preaching, church reform and communion in both kinds, with Justification as the central theological pivot.[52]

---

[51] Heinrich Richard Schmidt reminds us that as late as 1529 a majority of the Imperial Free cities remained opposed to the evangelical movement. Schmidt, *Reichstädte*, pp. 313–14.

[52] Bernd Moeller, 'Was wurde in der Frühzeit der Reformation in den deutschen Städten gepredigt?', *ARG*, 75 (1984), 176–93.

Moeller's argument is in many respects attractive, not least in recognising the giant status of Luther, but it remains susceptible of criticism. It is arguable that the differences between evangelical preachers were more profound than Moeller recognises. Even in towns which made an early and decisive decision for the Reformation, such as Strasburg and Nuremberg, the first evangelical preachers propounded a wide variety of teachings. Recent research suggests that the same went for the smaller towns of Saxony and Thuringia, Luther's backyard, to an even greater degree: here Gospel preachers expounded doctrines at once more radical and more conservative than are to be found in Luther's developed theology.[53] Thus the Zwickau minister Egranus attacked the cult of saints, but affirmed the validity of communion in one kind; other preachers pursued a similarly individualistic agenda, some denying the real presence or attacking the local magistrate, not views of which Luther could have approved.

This research, which harks back to an older tradition of writing in characterising this period as one of *Wildwuchs*, or wild evangelical growth[54] goes a long way towards undermining Moeller's conclusions, based in any case on a rather restricted sample of generally well-educated town ministers. It is arguable too that both types of work rather miss the point in concentrating exclusively on sermons preached by ordained ministers: this was, after all, a period when lay people involved themselves directly in the great controversies of the day to an extent not equalled before or since. These lay writings exhibit an even greater eclecticism. Rather than dutifully echoing Luther's major themes, lay writers explored a wide variety of different avenues, mixing Reformation theology with aspects of Catholic teaching of which they approved (as for instance the need to perform Christian acts of mercy). These lay works also characteristically exhibit a strong apocalypticism which betrayed their continuing allegiance to earlier, medieval traditions of thought.[55]

Given this evident and increasing theological diversity, where then lay the strength of the early evangelical programme? Two points here seem pertinent. Firstly, to judge from petitions and appeals to city magistrates, perhaps the most reliable expressions of lay thought in these years, lay people were less struck by the implications of Luther's core doctrine of Justification by Faith, than by the appeal of a reform of the church based on pure unadulterated scriptural teaching, or *rein Evangelium*. This

---

[53] Susan Karant-Nunn, 'What was preached in German Cities in the Early Years of the Reformation?', in Bebb and Marshall, *Process of Change*, pp. 81–96.

[54] A word coined by Franz Lau; his view summarised in Franz Lau and Ernst Bizer, *A History of the Reformation in Germany* (London, 1969), pp. 40–41.

[55] Paul A. Russell, *Lay Theology in the Reformation. Popular Pamphleteers in southwest Germany, 1521–1525* (Cambridge, 1986).

phrase crops up again and again in petitions and Council minutes.[56] Second, and closely associated to this, the calls for reform could draw on deep wells of anti-church feeling which amounted to an almost all-pervasive anticlericalism. Hostility to clerical power was undoubtedly unusually intense in Germany; it was also something that could unite all levels of society, from the urban magistrates eager to limit the clergy's civic immunities, to the peasant who despised an oppressive clerical landlord.[57] All of this was ruthlessly exploited by the early evangelicals, who combined their emphasis on pure gospel teaching with a generalised assault on clerical vice, inadequacies and immunities.[58]

Anticlericalism was not of course divorced from theology. Hans Jürgen Goertz has pointed out that both the corner-stones of Luther's theology, Justification by Faith and the Priesthood of all Believers, carried an implicit anticlerical message; the early Reformation writings were also strongly anticlerical in tone, as Luther pursued his own intellectual emancipation from the Papacy.[59] Much of Luther's power in these early years was as a symbol of resistance to church authority, and in particular the external authority of the Pope, a theme presented in hundreds of Reformation tracts and broadsheets.[60] But the generalised resentment of the church went far beyond anything that Luther could approve, or that the mainstream movement could satisfy. Here lay the root of many of the problems that afflicted the Reformation after the first heady days of universal questioning and debate.

Here one can discern a genuine contrast with events outside Germany: elsewhere the Reformation never became in the same way the vehicle for such a potent brew of national, political and social aspirations. Anticlericalism was not of course confined to Germany, but nowhere does it seem quite so widespread, or so easy to mobilise into a generalised movement of church reform. Nor was the church elsewhere so defenceless: in several of the lands treated here such outspoken criticism would simply not have been tolerated, either because the church itself was much better organised

[56] Schmidt, *Reichstädte*. See, for instance, the frank explanation of representatives of the German cities to Charles V in 1523 that repressive measures were bound to fail, since 'den gemaynen man dürstet nach dem evangelio und der bibel'. *Ibid.*, p. 330.
[57] This is the theme of Hans Jürgen Goertz, *Pfaffenhaß und groß Geschrei* (Munich, 1987). In English see also the helpful article of R. W. Scribner, 'Anticlericalism and the German Reformation', in his *Popular Culture and Popular Movements in Germany* (London, 1987), pp. 243–56.
[58] In Thomas Brady's telling phrase, Luther and his followers tried 'to touch every sensitive nerve of his day'. Brady, *Turning Swiss: Cities and Empire, 1450–1550* (Cambridge, 1985), 153.
[59] Goertz, *Pfaffenhaß*, pp. 79–89.
[60] For examples see Max Geisberg, *The German Single Leaf Broadsheet*, (4 vols., New York, 1974), I. 203 (Luther and the Artisans), III. 861 (Luther leading the faithful out of darkness).

18   *Andrew Pettegree*

(as in England or Spain) or because it received timely protection from the state (as in the Netherlands). In such countries the evangelical movement was bound to remain within narrower bonds; indeed one paradoxical result was that by remaining for far longer a movement for renewal within the church, it remained in some senses *more* theological. In this context Luther's central theological preoccupations were widely received and debated. Euan Cameron's contribution in this volume demonstrates the surprising extent to which Italian thinkers continued to interest themselves in Justification, for instance, long after his works were condemned and proscribed.[61]

It was the more theological and pastoral of Luther's works which gained the greatest currency abroad. Surveys of Luther's works in foreign vernaculars reveal a distinct preference for sermons, catechismal works and works of consolation, over the polemical, anti-papal and political tracts so influential in Germany.[62] Undoubtedly this was partly because, as a proscribed heretic, Luther's works were generally published abroad without any acknowledgement of his authorship, often indeed disguised. In this context small works of consolation and christian instruction were more easily smuggled past the censor than major tracts like the *Appeal to the Christian Nobility*.[63] But it was also the case that these major political works were of much less relevance outside the immediate German context.

Nevertheless, surveys of Luther's works in translation do confirm the profound influence exercised by Luther as a writer and teacher throughout Europe. This impression is reinforced by research revealing that, in addition to the obvious translations, numbers of apparently independent vernacular tracts made significant borrowings from Luther's works. Much early Dutch evangelical writing was heavily indebted to Luther's thought in this way.[64] Similarly in France, an early anonymous tract, the *Livre de la subjection des chrestiens* proves on closer inspection to be largely derived from Luther's *Liberty of a Christian Man*.[65] Even in lands where a strong pre-Reformation movement existed, such as

61 Below, chapter 9.
62 See Moeller, 'Luther in Europe', pp. 235–51. Francis Higman, 'Theology for the Layman in the French Reformation, 1520–1550', *The Library*, 6th ser., 9, (1987), pp. 105–27.
63 Translated only once, as was the *Babylonish Captivity*. Benzing, *Lutherbibliographie*, nos. 698, 717.
64 Andrew Johnson, 'The eclectic Reformation: Vernacular Pamphlet Literature in the Dutch-Speaking Low Countries, 1520–1565' (Southampton Univ. Ph.D thesis, 1986); and his 'Lutheranism in disguise: the Corte Instruccye of Cornelis vander Heyden', *NAK*, 68 (1988), 24–9.
65 F. M. Higman, 'Les traductions françaises de Luther, 1524–1550', in J.-F. Gilmont (ed.), *Palestra typographica. Aspects de la production du livre humaniste et religieux au XVIᵉ siècle* (Aubel, 1984), pp. 11–56.

Bohemia, Luther's teachings exercised a profound influence: in Bohemia the increasing dominance of the reform-Utraquists may be traced partly to the fact that they of all the heirs of the Hussite revolution contrived the most harmonious and successful engagement with the new German movement.[66]

One common thread that emerges strongly from the essays collected here is to confirm Luther's pre-eminent stature in the evangelical movement in the first generation of the European Reformation.[67] But this pre-eminence was not monopoly status: on the contrary, several of the evangelical movements treated here were marked by a profound eclecticism. While reformers throughout Europe read and venerated Luther, they just as eagerly read Bucer, Zwingli and Oecolampadius. And perhaps, as time went on, even more: in a number of countries it appears that after around 1530 Luther was losing ground to these other magisterial reformers. The reasons are touched upon in a number of essays, and included the increasing radicalisation of the European movement in the face of mounting persecution. But evangelicals abroad were also capable of exercising an independent theological preference; and here in particular the more rational, less ceremonial, models of ecclesiology emanating from Zurich found a widespread appeal.

Recent work on the German city Reformation has re-emphasised the powerful attraction of Zurich even within the Empire. This was felt particularly strongly in the imperial cities of the German south-west, where there were strong pre-existing cultural and economic ties with the Swiss cantons.[68] The flirtation with Zwingli caused intense nervousness in an orthodox Lutheran town like Nuremberg, and even more so in Wittenberg, where as early as 1525 Luther had publicly identified Zwingli with other fanatics and 'false brethren' for whom he found no place in his movement.[69] The division in the evangelical movement caused increasing difficulties in the years that followed, leading to the final and definite breach at the Colloquy of Marburg in 1529. Marburg revealed Luther's intellectual limitations, since his steady insistence on a Eucharistic theology which commended itself to no other major reformer effectively ruled out all compromise. That the split within Germany was not more

[66] Below, chapter 2.
[67] Thus incidentally answering the question posed by Geoffrey Elton in his provocative short article, 'Die europäische Reformation: mit oder ohne Luther?', in Press and Stievermann, *Martin Luther. Probleme seiner Zeit*, pp. 43–57. It was very much *mit*.
[68] Brady, *Turning Swiss*; Schmidt, *Reichstädte*. Schmidt explains the attractive power of Zurich largely in terms of differences of city constitution, unpersuasively in my view. Zurich's greater radicalism, and the longstanding cultural ties between Swabia and Switzerland, closer than those with Saxony, probably provide the key. See Hannemann, *Diffusion of the Reformation*.
[69] Mark E. Edwards, *Luther and the False Brethren* (Stanford, 1975), pp. 82 ff.

damaging can be largely attributed to Zwingli's untimely death at the battle of Kappel in 1531, which brought a sudden end to Zurich's imperial ambitions within Switzerland and greatly reduced its attractive power in the Empire.[70]

By this time the fortunes of the various European Reformation movements had begun very clearly to diverge. In several western nations, the moment for the planting of an orthodox Lutheran movement had passed; the beleaguered evangelical groups were necessarily driven underground, increasingly a prey to the fragmentation and doctrinal incoherence which followed from their lack of mutual contact and cohesion.[71] In the Netherlands, and to an extent in France and England, the vacuum was partially filled by a variety of radical and prophetic groups, whose tight discipline and strong apocalyptic sense partially inured their followers to the deterrent effects of a continuing and brutal persecution.[72] Germany too, experienced the disturbing effects of Anabaptism, but here the evangelicals were now sufficiently well organised to combine with Catholic forces to eradicate the threat when it emerged most forcefully, at Münster in 1534.[73]

That challenge once successfully negotiated, the 1530s became a decade of consolidation for the Lutheran churches. This was not without a certain smothering effect on the movement as a whole. The wave of princely conversions at the end of the 1520s, followed by the formation of the Schmalkaldic League, had in this respect contrived to alter the nature of the evangelical movement quite considerably. No longer could the evangelical movement aspire to the universal spiritual renovation anticipated in the first naive springtime of reform: the limitations with which they were confronted, both intellectual and territorial, were increasingly apparent, as confessional fronts hardened within the Empire, and the scale of the task of educating a new evangelical people became clear. On the whole Luther and his ministerial colleagues adapted themselves to these changing circumstances with considerable success. Although church organisation had never been at the forefront of Luther's concerns, he now gave dutiful support to the secular rulers as they strove to create an orderly christian society. Luther's large and smaller catechisms (both 1529) were among the most successful works of his mature years. In the

---

[70] A point made by Bruce Gordon, chapter 4 below.   [71] Chapters 6 and 7, below.
[72] On Dutch Anabaptism see especially A. F. Mellink, *De wederdopers in de noordelijke Nederlanden, 1531–1544* (Groningen, 1953); Cornelis Krahn, *Dutch Anabaptism* (The Hague, 1968). Cornelis Augustijn, 'Anabaptism in the Netherlands; another Look', *Mennonite Quarterly Review*, 62 (1988), 197–210.
[73] For an introduction to the enormous literature on the Anabaptist Kingdom of Münster, R. Po-Chia Hsia, 'Münster and the Anabaptists', in his *The German People and the Reformation* (Ithaca, 1988), pp. 51–2.

next generation the catechism became the essential tool of an ambitious programme of christian education designed to embrace the whole population of the new Protestant lands.[74] The uncertain results of such efforts demonstrated the extent to which the first generation of reformers had under-estimated the difficulties of church reform; it also demonstrated how much had changed since the heady days of the first evangelical preaching, as the call for evangelical freedom was replaced by an ever greater stress on social discipline.

The relevance of this area of the German experience is obviously limited, given that the Reformation would not enter this process of consolidation in most parts of Europe in the first part of the century. It does, however, demonstrate the extent to which the further evolution of the reform movement would be dependent on the attitude of the local political power. And the following decade, the 1540s, was a time when the political conjunction was particularly unfavourable to the evangelical movement. The years between 1540 and 1546 witnessed a serious reverse for the evangelical cause in several of the lands treated here: France, England and the Netherlands all witnessed a wave of executions in a conservative clampdown which, in the Netherlands at least, threatened almost to eradicate the intellectual reform movement. It was in this period too that the Italian movement suffered its major and, as it turned out, decisive reverse with the flight of Ochino and Martyr and the collapse of the *spirituali*. Nor must one underestimate the international impact of the failed attempt to introduce reform into the Archbishopric of Cologne by Herman of Wied; several of the leading reformers had involved themselves in this project, and its collapse demonstrated that the territorial limitations of Protestant progress within the Empire were now close to being reached.[75] Indeed, the following years would witness a series of serious reverses for German Protestantism, forced first to absorb the death of Luther in 1546, then face the challenge of Charles V's most determined effort to settle the German problem by military means in the Schmalkaldic War. The exceptionally difficult circumstances faced by evangelicals throughout Europe in these years help explain why the establishment of a Protestant regime in England on the accession of Edward VI (1547) was greeted with such euphoria: in the context of the events of the previous five years this must have appeared as a beacon of light in a perspective of almost unrelieved gloom.

[74] Strauss, *Luther's House of Learning*. For Strauss' considered reaction to the debate set off by this book, see 'The Reformation and its public in an age of orthodoxy', in R. Po-Chia Hsia, *The German People and the Reformation*, pp. 194–214.
[75] On this episode see particularly J. V. Pollet, *Martin Bucer. Études sur les relations de Bucer avec les Pays-Bas, L'Électorat de Cologne et L'Allemagne du Nord* (2 vols., Leiden, 1985), I. 187–234.

B

The widespread interest in these English events towards the end of our period – expressed in numerous letters among the reformers, and more directly in the presence of several in England during Edward's reign – brings us back to our first theme, the internationality of the Reformation movement. For all that the shape and progress of the individual movements treated here was moulded by local circumstances and pressures, the early Reformation never degenerated into parochialism. Evangelicals in one part of Europe retained their concern for the wider picture; news of changes in one country could materially effect events elsewhere. For all the regional and national differences identified in this volume, these national Reformations remained recognisably part of the same movement. It was this sense of common purpose which permitted an Italian like Peter Martyr, or a German like Martin Bucer, to accept invitations to chairs in, respectively, Oxford and Cambridge, where they both performed some of their most signal services to the evangelical movement.[76]

The extent to which, within this context, the individual national movements succeeded in moving out of the shadow of the German convulsions unleashed by Luther is the subject to which these essays are addressed. But for all the variety to which they testify, it is significant that none of these other nations would throw up a figure to challenge the stature of Luther in the first generation; none of the other reformers came close to matching the breadth of his international appeal and reputation. It is no coincidence that the emergence of such a figure – John Calvin – would provide the impetus for the second period of expansive growth in the latter half of the century.

[76] Constantin Hopf, *Martin Bucer and the English Reformation* (Oxford, 1946). Marvin Anderson, *Peter Martyr, a Reformer in Exile (1542–1562)* (Nieuwkoop, 1975).

2 Bohemia, Moravia and Austria

Winfried Eberhard

It is commonly assumed that eastern Central Europe was always a stronghold of Catholicism. This assumption, which rests on the outcome of the Counter-Reformation and the Thirty Years War, ignores the fact that Protestantism was so widespread in the area throughout the sixteenth century that it largely reduced the Catholic Church to a minority. It endangered not only the church, but also the Catholic monarchy, for Protestantism everywhere in eastern Central Europe was rooted in the strong political position of the estates: in Poland, the Bohemian lands (Bohemia itself and the incorporated crown lands, Moravia, Silesia and Lusatia), Hungary and the east Austrian provinces of Upper Austria, Lower Austria, Karinthia, Styria and Krain.[1] On the one hand, the firm representative system of the estates favoured and encouraged acceptance of the confessional alternative to the Catholic monarchy. On the other, Protestantism gave the estates a new and superior (because religious) basis for their self-awareness and their political aim of extending and consolidating their independence.

Throughout the region the estates were in a strong position to restrict the freedom of action of the ruling power. In Bohemia, for instance, the king's military and financial requirements depended on the agreement of the *Landtag* (*sněm*) or diet, and its willingness to raise taxes. So did the election and coronation of his successor. Laws could be passed only with the agreement of all three estates (*curiae*) of the diet: the higher nobility or barons, the lower nobility or knights, and the royal free cities. The supreme court (*Landrecht*) and the provincial government were made up of representatives of the nobility. The leading role of the estates, the powers of the diet and the *Landrecht*, and the independence of the cities had all been strengthened by the Hussite Revolution of

---

[1] R. R. Betts, 'Constitutional Development and Political Thought in Eastern Europe', in G. R. Elton (ed.), *The New Cambridge Modern History, Vol. 2: The Reformation 1520–1559* (Cambridge, 1958), pp. 464–77; also in 2nd edn. (Cambridge, 1990), pp. 526–39. G. Rohde, 'Stände und Königtum in Polen/Litauen und Böhmen/Mähren', *Jahrbücher für Geschichte Osteuropas*, 12 (1964), 221–46.

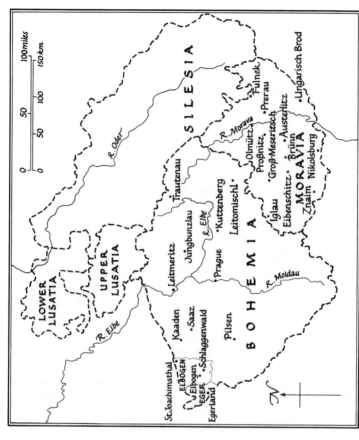

Map 1. The Bohemian Lands
Source: K. J. Dillon, *King and Estates in the Bohemian Lands, 1526–1564* (Brussels, 1976). Studies presented to the international commission for the history of representative and parliamentary institutions, 57.

Key:

Pilsen/Plzeň
Jungbunzlau/Mladá Boleslav
Leitomischl/Litomyšl
Kuttenberg/Kutnáhora
Prague
Eger/Cheb
Elbogen/Loket (District)
St Joachimsthal/Jáchymov
Elbogen/Loket (Town)
Schlaggenwald/Slavkov
Leitmeritz/Litoměřice
Kaaden/Kadaň
Saz/Žatec
Trautenau/Trutnov
Olmütz/Olomouc
Brünn/Brno
Iglau/Jihlava
Znaim/Znojmo
Groß-Meseritsch/Velké Meziříči
Nikolsburg/Mikulov
Prerau/Přerov
Eibenschitz/Ivančice
Proßnitz/Prostějov
Fulnek
Ungarisch Brod/Uherský Brod
Austerlitz/Slavkov

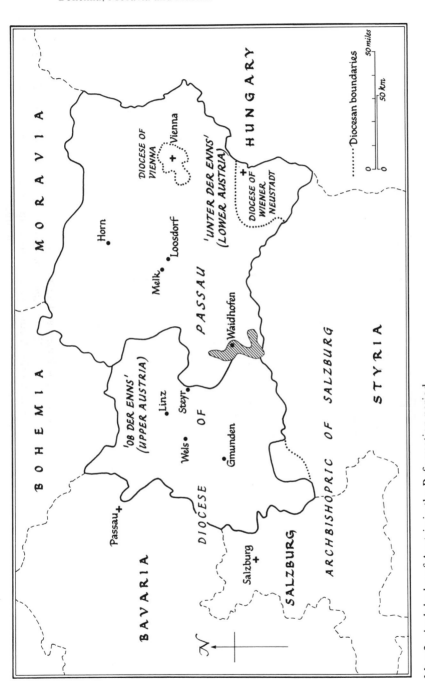

Map 2. Archduchy of Austria in the Reformation period
Source: Die Territorien des Reiches im Zeitalter der Reformation und Konfessionalisierung. Land und Konfession 1500–1650. I: Der Südosten. Ed. by A. Schindling and W. Ziegler.

1419–36.[2] The nobility had acquired the wealth of the church, and a goodly part of the royal patrimony. The clergy, which in the fourteenth century had supported the monarchy, had been eliminated from the diet. The automony of the estates reached its peak under the weak rule of the Jagiellonian kings Ladislas and Louis (1471–1526), when they were credited with the pronouncement, 'You are our king, but we are your masters!'[3]

The Hussite Revolution had also transformed the religious situation in Bohemia. The vast majority of Bohemians had been drafted into the Hussite Utraquist Church (*sub utraque*, Calixtines). Within this church a spiritual consistory headed by an *administrator* exercised jurisdiction and controlled the disposal of offices, discipline and the dogmatic system independently of Rome. But in reality the Utraquist Church was directed by the secular estates of the nobility and the cities: they chose the *administrator* and consistory; at their meetings they set the organisational and theological guidelines for their church; they controlled the property of the parishes and supervised their priests. A committee of *defensores* (the nobles and the council of Prague) represented the interests of the Utraquist Church in ecclesiastical politics.[4] The Catholic Church meanwhile had become a minority, mainly confined to the outlying German-speaking areas in the north, west and south. Catholicism in the east had been reduced to a few small pockets, while in central Bohemia only Pilsen (Plzeň) and a few smaller towns remained Catholic. As for the political estates, of the thirty or so royal free cities only about five still belonged to the Catholic Church. Above all, the nobility, and also the numerous knightly class, had mostly declared for the Hussites.[5]

The nobility also acted as protectors and patrons to a second dissident confession, the Union of the Congregations of Bohemian Brethren (*Brüdergemeinden, Unitas Fratrum*). The Brethren perpetuated the religious beliefs of the left wing of the Hussite movement, the Taborites; but, like the Waldensians, and later the Anabaptists, they refused all use of force, including political coercion (the death penalty, military service and the swearing of oaths). Rather they stressed their status as a voluntary

---

[2] M. D. Lambert, *Medieval Heresy – Popular Movements from Bogumil to Hus* (London, 1977), pp. 314–34. J. K. Zeman, *The Hussite Movement and the Reformation in Bohemia, Moravia and Slovakia (1450–1650). A Bibliographical Study Guide* (Ann Arbor, 1977).

[3] For the position of the estates around 1520, K. J. Dillon, *King and Estates in the Bohemian Lands 1526–1564* (Brussels, 1976), pp. 6–18. For a comparison with the Austrian Estates see W. Eberhard, *Monarchie und Widerstand. Zur ständischen Oppositionsbildung im Herrschaftssystem Ferdinands I. in Böhmen* (Veröffentlichungen des Collegium Carolinum, 54, Munich, 1985), pp. 45–69.

[4] W. Eberhard, *Konfessionsbildung und Stände in Böhmen 1478–1530* (Veröffentlichungen des Collegium Carolinum, 38, Munich/Vienna, 1981), pp. 49–50 and 113–15.

[5] Dillon, *King and Estates*, pp. 71–2.

congregational Church. In complete contrast both to Rome and the Utraquists (who maintained the Catholic sacraments and Mass), they rejected the priesthood, understood the sacraments of baptism and communion in a spiritual sense, and espoused a Christianity that was fundamentally biblical. Their congregations (of which the most important in Bohemia were Jungbunzlau/Mladá Boleslav and Leitomischl/Litomyšl) were led by four chosen elders (*seniores*) and a Council of Twelve; the highest authority for communal decisions was vested in a synod.[6] A royal decree of 1508 allowed the persecution of Brethren, but in practice their noble protectors were usually able to prevent it. The position of the Catholic and Utraquist Churches, on the other hand, was assured and legally recognised, first through the *compactata* agreed with the Council of Basle (1436), to which every king had to swear, and secondly through a religious peace of 1485.[7]

The Lutheran Reformation in Bohemia has to be understood against this complicated and many layered background. There are indeed, essentially two separate Reformation movements in the Bohemian lands: first, the encounter with the Hussite Confessions and the gradual change in their relationship to the German Reformation; but also, no less significant, the spread of Lutheranism in the hitherto Catholic, predominantly German-speaking areas of Bohemia.[8]

It has often been claimed that no country was so predisposed as Bohemia to accept Luther's teaching,[9] meaning of course that the 'first', Hussite Reformation had paved the way.[10] This claim is erroneous for several reasons. Firstly, at the onset of the Reformation the Hussite

---

[6] J. Th. Müller, *Geschichte der Böhmischen Brüder* (3 vols., Herrnhut, 1922–31). P. Brock, *The Political and the Social Doctrines of the Unity of Czech Brethren in the Fifteenth and Early Sixteenth Centuries* (The Hague, 1957). M. L. Wagner, *Petr Chelčický – A Radical Separatist in Hussite Bohemia* (Scottdale, Pa., 1983).

[7] Eberhard, *Konfessionsbildung*, pp. 41–6 and 56–60. W. Eberhard, 'Entstehungsbedingungen für öffentliche Toleranz am Beispiel des Kuttenberger Religionsfriedens von 1485', *Communio Viatorum*, 29 (1986), 129–54.

[8] R. Říčan, *Das Reich Gottes in den böhmischen Ländern. Geschichte des tschechischen Protestantismus* (Stuttgart, 1957), pp. 87–124. K. Richter, 'Die böhmischen Länder von 1471–1740', in K. Bosl (ed.), *Handbuch der Geschichte der böhmischen Länder* (4 vols., Stuttgart, 1967–74), II. 99–412. F. Machilek, 'Böhmen', in A. Schindling and W. Ziegler (eds.), *Die Territorien des Reiches im Zeitalter der Reformation und Konfessionalisierung* (2 vols., Münster, 1989–90), I. 134–52. J. K. Hoensch, *Geschichte Böhmens* (Munich, 1987), pp. 186–229.

[9] G. Loesche, *Geschichte des Protestantismus im vormaligen und im neuen Österreich* (Vienna/Leipzig, 1930), p. 376. E. Winter, *Tausend Jahre Geisteskampf im Sudetenraum. Das religiöse Ringen zweier Völker* (Munich, 1938), p. 146.

[10] For the concept of First and Second Reformations, A. Molnár, 'Husovo místo v evropské reformaci', *Československý časopis historický*, 14 (1966), 1–14. For the Hussite Reformation, A. Molnár, 'Der Hussitismus als christliche Reformbewegung', in F. Seibt (ed.), *Bohemia Sacra, Das Christentum in Böhmen 973–1973* (Düsseldorf, 1974), pp. 92–102 and 565–6.

Czechs were at odds with their Catholic German neighbours, and the country had been officially isolated, being seen as a hotbed of heresy.[11] As a result Luther, who was familiar with both Hus' writings and the Confession of the Bohemian Brethren, considered both as heretical even as late as 1519.[12] Moreover, he had to defend himself against his opponents' attempts to identify him with the Bohemian heretics. In addition, the need for church reform in Hussite Bohemia had been more or less met, and the system of a state church controlled by the secular estates was already established. Further, around 1520 both Hussite Confessions were engaged in a search for identity amongst their own roots, and this made it hard for them to assimilate new stimuli from outside. The Utraquists were divided. The conservative wing held to the letter of the Basle *compactata* and sought unity with Rome, wishing to retain only communion in both kinds, child communion and the secularisation of church property; but the left wing aimed to reform the Utraquist Church on strictly biblical lines, thereby harking back to the earlier Taborite movement and approximating to the theology of the Bohemian Brethren.[13] The Union of Brethren meanwhile, was now in a period of expansion and theological consolidation under the leadership of their *senior*, Brother Lukas of Prague.[14] Thus, in around 1520, the first Hussite Reformation was in no way united, but was seeking its identity in different and incompatible directions. This pre-existing confessional situation, along with the religious policy of the Catholic monarchy, is one of the reasons why the First Reformation in Bohemia gave such a hesitant welcome to the Second, the Lutheran Reformation.

The engagement with Luther did however have the initial effect of strengthening the reform-minded left wing of the Utraquists within the Hussite movement.[15] The major change in Luther's attitude to the Hussites came in the Leipzig Disputation of 1519, when he expressly defended some of Hus' teachings against Eck as being both Christian and evangelical.[16] The delighted Bohemians among the audience put him in contact with the two spiritual leaders in Prague: the pastor of the town church, Jan Poduška, and the provost of the university's Collegium Carolinum,

[11] H. Schenk, 'Die Beziehungen zwischen Nürnberg und Prag von 1450–1500', in I. Bog (ed.), *Der Außenhandel Ostmitteleuropas 1450–1650* (Cologne/Vienna, 1971), pp. 185–203, esp. 193–4.
[12] A. Molnár, 'Luther und die Böhmischen Brüder', *Communio Viatorum*, 24 (1981), 47–67.
[13] Eberhard, *Konfessionsbildung*, pp. 82–5, 98–105 and 125–7.
[14] A. Molnár, *Bratr Lukáš, bohoslovec jednoty* (Prague, 1948). A. Molnár, 'Pasteur dans la tourmente, Luc de Prague entre 1510 et 1515', *Communio Viatorum*, 6 (1963), 276–96.
[15] For this term, in place of the more usual 'New Utraquism', Eberhard, *Konfessionsbildung*, pp. 144–7.
[16] F. G. Heymann, 'The Impact of Martin Luther upon Bohemia', *Central European History*, 1 (1968), 107–30.

Václav Rožd'alovský. Both began a correspondence with Luther, and at his request sent him Hus' most important work, the *De ecclesia*. It reinforced both his new ecclesiological orientation and his reappraisal of the Hussites. Subsequently he even had the work printed. This line of thought culminated in Luther's famous assertion before the Diet of Worms that councils could err, as witness the burning of Jan Hus at Constance. Even before this Luther had spoken several times about co-operation with the Bohemians. Thus in answer to the spiritual leaders in Prague: 'I want, I wish, I request, am thankful and rejoice, that my teachings should please the Bohemians.' Or in the widely disseminated tract *To the Christian Nobility*: 'It is high time that we at last took up the matter of the Bohemians seriously and sincerely, to unite them with us and us with them.'[17]

Luther, then, was interested in unity and co-operation, an attitude which he seldom showed to other reforming trends which diverged from his own. But as regards the Bohemians he was over-optimistic. Rožd'alovský's description of Luther is significant: 'What Jan Hus once was to Bohemia, you, Martin, are now to Saxony.'[18] In other words, the Utraquists saw Luther with Hussite eyes: a fellow-warrior arising in Germany who could at last bring the general reform of the church for which the Hussites had striven in vain for a century, and so deliver Bohemia from its long isolation. In Luther they saw the confirmation of their own tradition.[19] But there was also an active conservative wing of the Bohemian Church, which thought quite differently. In 1522 they even had dealings with Rome over the appointment of an archbishop, for which purpose they were willing to accept a considerable *rapprochement* with the Catholic Church. This prompted Luther to write to the Bohemian estates advising against any union with Rome. The attempt did in fact fail, chiefly because the left-wing Utraquists, with their feeling of solidarity with Luther, were already comparatively numerous among the nobility and the upper classes in Prague.[20]

In 1523 the competition of two noble factions prompted King Louis to change both the government of the province and the city council of Prague. Both now fell under the control of the reformist Utraquists, who

---

[17] K. Oberdorffer, 'Die Reformation in Böhmen und das späte Hussitentum', *Bohemia*, 6 (1965), 123–45, esp. 131–2. The Latin correspondence with the Prague clergy in J. Goll, 'Jak soudil Luther o Husovi', *Časopis českého muzea*, 54 (1880), 60–80, esp. 78–80. WA Br. I. 416–20 (nos. 185, 186).

[18] WA Br. I. 420.   [19] Eberhard, *Konfessionsbildung*, pp. 147–8.

[20] In 1521 this group had even offered hospitality and a stipend in the Collegium Carolinum to Thomas Müntzer, who was hoping through his sermons and his 'Prague Manifesto' to form a new apostolic church, an apocalyptic congregation in Bohemia. A. Friesen, *Thomas Müntzer, a Destroyer of the Godless. The Making of a Sixteenth-Century Religious Revolutionary* (Berkeley, 1990), pp. 100–20.

then altered the leadership of the church in their own favour: the Lutheran scholar Havel Cahera became *administrator*. A synod of February 1524 pointed in the new theological direction. Its resolutions clearly showed agreement with Luther: the absolute authority of Holy Scripture, the restriction of the sacraments to baptism and communion, rejection of the sacrificial idea of the Mass. But it also kept the Taborite rejection of the real presence of Christ in the communion, and the Hussite distrust of the Lutheran principle of salvation through faith alone.[21] Some early and lasting *rapprochement* between the Utraquists and the Lutherans might nevertheless have emerged; but this first encounter between the First and Second Reformations foundered only a year later when the Prague city council was overturned by conservative opponents. The reformist Utraquists were abruptly swept away, and their ministers and followers scattered all over the country.[22]

The conservative reaction was carried further by the new king, the Habsburg Ferdinand I. Since 1526 his religious policy had favoured the Catholics and the conservative Utraquists, whom he hoped to use as a bridge to the confessional unification of the country.[23] Ferdinand did in fact succeed in creating, from among both officials and Prague city councillors, a loyal court party of Catholic and Utraquist royalists, and thence in placing the leadership of the Utraquist Church in conservative hands. Nevertheless, the political and religious opposition grew little by little through the 1530s; finally, in 1539, they laid their demand for religious freedom before the king in the shape of a memorandum by one of the richest and most powerful barons, John of Pernstein.[24] It is worth noting that this gradual advance of reformist Utraquism happened in some of the central and eastern Bohemian towns in the deanery of Kuttenberg (Kutnáhora), and also in Prague.[25] Leading academics from Prague university had established links with Wittenberg (in particular with Melanchthon), and the Prague city council favoured the reform-Utraquists. The 1530s had also seen a sharp increase in the numbers of Bohemian students studying at Wittenberg.[26] In 1539 a meeting of the Utraquist estates elected a new consistory, and thereafter until 1543 it was clear that the reformers were in control of the church. The synod of 1543

---

[21] Eberhard, *Konfessionsbildung*, pp. 136–44.   [22] *Ibid.*, pp. 150–81.

[23] P. S. Fichtner, *Ferdinand I of Austria. The Politics of Dynasticism in the Age of Reformation* (East European Monographs, 100, New York, 1982). A. Skýbová, 'Ferdinand I., der Habsburger, und die Anfänge seiner Regierung im böhmischen Staat', in G. Vogler (ed.), *Europäische Herrscher* (Weimar, 1988), pp. 71–84. For Ferdinand's system of government see also Dillon, *King and Estates*, pp. 33–68. For his religious policy, Eberhard, *Monarchie und Widerstand*, pp. 75, 202–16, 324–8.

[24] This Latin correspondence with Ferdinand is published in *Archiv český*, 20, 82–96. cf. Dillon, *King and Estates*, pp. 85–8, Eberhard, *Monarchie und Widerstand*, pp. 316–34.

[25] *Ibid.*, pp. 155–66, 265–315.   [26] *Ibid.*, pp. 147–50, 306–11.

even took the important step of seeking a *rapprochement* with the Bohemian Brethren, intended to lead to the foundation of a United Reformist Church.[27] This brought them into direct conflict with the king. The church's spokesman Dr Václav Mitmánek was exiled, and the church leadership was purged of its left-Utraquist elements. The opposition among the political estates, however, continued to follow a reformist line.

In the first stages of the Reformation, it was not only with the mainstream Utraquists that Luther made contact, but also with the more radical Bohemian Brethren.[28] However, his discussion with Brother Lukas of Prague during 1522 and 1523 broke down over theological issues: the question of the Real Presence of Christ in the communion, and the Brethren's emphasis on an active life of faith, as opposed to justification by faith alone.[29] Nevertheless, after the death of Brother Lukas in 1528 the Union of Brethren elected *seniores* inclined towards Lutheranism. Prominent among them, and the most active both in church politics and in written output, was Jan Augusta of Prague. There was now great stress on proper theological training in the communities, and more and more of their scholars were sent to study at Wittenberg. Despite their rigid separation from the secular power, which was allowed no ecclesiastical function, in 1530 the Brethren even ventured formally to accept several nobles into their society at a public ceremony. They were encouraged to do this by the example of the German Protestants, who at the Diets of Speyer (1529) and Augsburg (1530) had given their confession a political identity. Imitating the Germans, the Brethren began also to produce religious manuals for secular rulers and thereby moved closer to the fundamentals of Luther's teaching. Their first publication was an *Apology* written at the request of the margrave George of Brandenburg, which Luther had printed in Wittenberg with a preface by himself. To discourage the repression of their congregations, they also presented to King Ferdinand a Justification which developed into the definitive creed of the Union of Brethren and was reprinted repeatedly right up to the seventeenth century. In it they treated Justification through Faith in a thoroughly Lutheran sense as the core of the Gospel, and abandoned rebaptism. The Latin edition of this *Confessio* was also printed by Luther, with his own preface, in Wittenberg in 1538.[30] In the early 1540s the

---

[27] Dillon, *King and Estates*, pp. 84, 98–102.
[28] Molnár, 'Luther und die Böhmischen Brüder', pp. 50–6.
[29] The Hussite Reformers did not, like Luther, take the Gospel as the 'word of God', the mere preaching of which to believers, on Pauline principles, would bring about the salvation of mankind and the transformation of the church. The Hussites, like Wyclif, took it far more as the 'Law of God', laying special stress on the Sermon on the Mount: a direct foundation for the new ordering of the church, society and the world in general.
[30] A. Molnár, 'Bekenntnisse der Böhmischen Reformation', *Communio Viatorum*, 23 (1979), 193–210.

Brethren also made contact with Martin Bucer in Strasburg, and through him had their first personal encounter with Calvin.[31] It is clear that by building contacts with the German Protestants Jan Augusta hoped to win legal acceptance for the *Unitas Fratrum* in Bohemia itself. More ambitiously, he tried through his writings to win over the leftist Utraquists, and with their help to build up an evangelical church in Bohemia. However, the rivalry between Utraquists and Brethren was not to be overcome for many years.

The third area in which the Lutheran reformation began to influence Bohemia, that is among the German-speaking Catholic population, naturally developed not in the centre, in Prague, but in the periphery, especially north and north-west Bohemia. It was in this thriving industrial region, with its silver and tin mines, that the Lutheran Reformation in Bohemia found its first vital, secure and lasting base.[32] At just this time, old mining villages in the Erzgebirge were being revitalised, and mining towns were springing up on the site of newly discovered silver deposits. Miners and mining experts recruited from Saxony brought their Lutheranism along with them. Here, therefore, it was economic growth which fostered acceptance of the Reformation.[33] But this was no Reformation from below: it was brought in by the feudal nobility. Some of these noble families originated from Saxony, but already had multifarious connections with the region: relatives, fiefs, political obligations towards the elector or duke of Saxony.[34]

The importance of the nobility to the spread of the Reformation is epitomised by the family Schlick, whose ancestor, Kaspar Schlick, had risen to be Chancellor in the service of the Emperor Sigismund. The Schlick brothers and cousins held extensive and wealthy estates in the economically thriving region of Elbogen (Loket), east of the Egerland. In 1516, Count Stephan Schlick had founded the silver-mining town of Saint Joachimsthal (Jáchymov): in a few years its population had swollen to some thousands, and it had become an active centre for the Reformation, not least because of its grammar school, which since 1532 had been

[31] A. Molnár, 'La correspondance entre les Frères Tchèques et Bucer', *RHPR*, 1 (1951), 102–56.

[32] Oberdorffer, *Reformation*, p. 130. H. Sturm, *Skizzen zur Geschichte des Obererzgebirges im 16. Jahrhundert* (Stuttgart, 1965).

[33] A. Frind, *Kirchengeschichte Böhmens, vol. 4: Die Administratorenzeit* (Prague, 1878). R. Wolkan, 'Studien zur Reformationsgeschichte Nordböhmens', *Jahrbuch der Gesellschaft für die Geschichte des Protestantismus in Österreich*, 3 (1882), 55–65, 107–19; 4 (1883), 67–95, 145–67. W. Wostry, 'Das Deutschtum Böhmens zwischen Hussitenzeit und Dreißigjährigem Krieg', *Das Sudetendeutschtum, sein Wesen und Werden im Wandel der Jahrhunderte* (Brünn, 1937), pp. 295–370.

[34] Richter, 'Die böhmischen Länder', pp. 124–5. B. Bretholz, *Neuere Geschichte Böhmens* (Gotha, 1920), p. 71.

headed by Johannes Mathesius, a famous associate of Luther.[35] Mathesius remained in constant communication with Luther, and in fact wrote the first biography of him in the form of a collection of sermons. A gifted preacher and popular pastor, he was parish priest of Joachimsthal from 1545 to his death in 1565, always fostering the spread of the Reformation.[36] Indeed, the importance of the grammar and elementary schools in the spread of the Reformation, in Bohemia as elsewhere, can scarcely be overestimated. Another school on the Schlick estates, in Elbogen, became a centre for the Reformation, for as early as 1521 Sebastian Schlick established the first evangelical pastor in Elbogen. Two years later he imposed the first church regulations to give priority to the preaching of the Gospel and abrogate Catholic rites.[37] Another widely influential grammar school was in yet another flourishing mining town, Schlaggenwald (Slavkov). Here, as in their other estates in the region, the barons of the Pflug von Rabstein family brought in Lutheran pastors. Whereas it was mining which stimulated population growth and the spread of the Reformation in the Erzgebirge in the 1520s, the same effect was achieved later in north Bohemia by the rise of glass, linen and textile manufactures.[38]

However, it was to be a long time before the Lutherans of north and north-west Bohemia had a common organisation, unlike the Utraquists and the Union of Brethren. Rather there was a series of disconnected Reformations under individual feudal lords, which gradually extended to certain free cities such as Leitmeritz (Litoměřice), Kaaden (Kadaň), Saaz (Žatec) and Trautenau (Trutnov in east Bohemia). Saaz and Trautenau also had famous schools.[39] It was in the interests of the feudal nobility to

[35] R. Wolkan, 'Die Anfänge der Reformation in Joachimsthal' *Mitteilungen des Vereins für Geschichte der Deutschen in Böhmen*, 32 (1894), 273–99. I. Mittenzwei, *Der Joachims-thaler Aufstand 1525, seine Ursachen und Folgen* (East Berlin, 1968). It was in Joachims-thal that the silver Taler was first minted, in 1521. On Mathesius, G. Loesche, *Johannes Mathesius, ein Lebens- und Sittenbild aus der Reformationszeit* (2 vols., Gotha, 1895). H. Wolf, 'Beiträge zur Mathesius-Bibliographie', *Bohemia*, 5 (1964), 77–107. H. Sturm, *Die St. Joachimsthaler Lateinschulbibliothek aus dem 16. Jahrhundert* (Stuttgart, 1964).

[36] It is striking how many of the pastors and teachers found in north and west Bohemia throughout the century hailed from Joachimsthal (and later on also from Eger). A. Eckert, *Biographisches Handbuch zur böhmischen Reformationsgeschichte* (3 vols., Kirnbach, 1972–77). S. Sieber, 'Geistige Beziehungen zwischen Böhmen und Sachsen zur Zeit der Reformation', *Bohemia* 6 (1965), 146–72; 7 (1966), 127–98.

[37] A. Eckert, 'Fünf evangelische (vor allem lutherische) Kirchenordnungen in Böhmen zwischen 1522 und 1609', *Bohemia*, 18 (1977), 35–50. A. Eckert, 'Evangelische Schulord-nungen und "Lehrverträge"', *Bohemia*, 21 (1980), 15–58.

[38] Wolkan, *Studien*. Bretholz, *Neuere Geschichte*, pp. 69–70. Frind, *Kirchengeschichte*, pp. 397–8, 401–4, 411, 415–17.

[39] K. Kaiserová, 'Zur Frage des Widerhalls der lutherischen Reformation in Nordwestböh-men', in G. Vogler (ed.), *Martin Luther, Leben-Werk-Wirkung* (East Berlin, 1983),

use their right of patronage in order to standardise practice throughout their territories, and to keep control over the clergy, churches and glebes. This reintroduced an old trend towards individual noble control of local churches, which had been repressed in the fourteenth century but revitalised through the Hussite Revolution. Soon the Catholic consistory was lamenting the fact that nobles were appointing and dismissing clergy without reference to the *administrator*, and that tithes were being withheld, clerical assets appropriated and church goods diverted for the use of the local lord.[40] The progress towards unification was made possible by the catastrophic shortage of priests within the Archbishopric: the patrons often had to find priests for their congregations themselves.[41]

All in all, it is clear that this extensive noble patronage did allow the Lutheran Reformation to spread into the German-speaking regions, hitherto loyally Catholic. In 1531 the cathedral chapter complained that 150 parishes had already been wrested from its control. According to the Catholic *administrator*, another hundred or more parishes had followed suit by 1539.[42] Some Catholics blamed the king for not reacting. However, Ferdinand I would have been hard put to devise any opposing strategy without a better supply of young priests and an improvement in the Catholic schools. Mere prohibitions bore little fruit. Above all, the king was dependent on the agreement (and taxes) of the diet for his military undertakings and other financial requirements, and so could not afford to arouse too much opposition in the estates. Until 1545 he was almost constantly involved in expensive wars against the Turks in Hungary.[43]

The spread of Lutheranism in Bohemia gained unexpected political importance through the Emperor's Schmalkaldic War against the Protestants (1546–7). The majority of the Bohemian estates refused to obey the king's order to raise an army against their Protestant neighbours without the agreement of the diet. This infringement by the king of the Bohemian constitution in fact provoked a rebellion among the estates with the aim of reasserting their governmental, legislative and juridical privileges, regaining the confessional and political initiative from the king, and even uniting the Utraquists and the Bohemian Brethren into a

pp. 451–62. Z. Winter, *Život církevní v Čechách* (2 vols., Prague, 1895–96), p. 96: Of the 34 Catholic cities only 15 had accepted Lutheranism by the 1530s.
[40] Consistorial acts, in Latin, German and Czech. *Jednání a dopisy konsistoře katolické a utrakvistické*, Monumenta historiae bohemica, vol. 5, ed. K. Borový (Prague, 1868–69), nrs. 607, 659, 676.
[41] *Nuntiaturberichte aus Deutschland*, I/1, p. 152.
[42] Bretholz, *Neuere Geschichte*, pp. 92–3, 96.
[43] J. Pánek, 'Das Ständewesen und die Gesellschaft in den Böhmischen Ländern in der Zeit vor der Schlacht auf dem Weißen Berg (1526–1620)', *Historica*, 25 (1985), 73–120.

single Hussite party within the estates.[44] This united front briefly brought together leftist Utraquists (nobles and cities), noblemen among the Bohemian Brethren and Lutherans such as the Lutheran nobles of north-west Bohemia, led by the Counts of Schlick and Baron Kaspar Pflug von Rabstein, who were, alongside the cities, the most active in raising armed defiance. However, the majority of the estates saw no further than the defence of their own political rights, and remained undecided. There was never an active struggle for religious freedom, and so the uprising failed.

This failure, however, also had confessional grounds. The number of Lutheran nobles and cities was still too small to form an effective focus for revolt. Here the king's repression of Lutheran influences on Utraquism in the years preceding the uprising proved crucial, together with the alienation of the Brethren's spiritual leaders from Wittenberg, which deprived the opposition of religious leadership, and made it impossible for Lutheranism to act among the non-Catholic estates as a unifying ideological force of active resistance. The legitimation of the rebellion remained in the legalistic limits of traditional political resistance. After the defeat the leaders of the rebellion were condemned to death, exile or confiscation of their property. The cities were hardest hit, by fines, confiscation and political muzzling. The Brethren also suffered, as the king ordered their dissolution.

Nevertheless, this experience of joint rebellious action, and the formulation of a programme of opposition by the estates, formed the basis for a gradual convergence of the non-Catholic estates over the next twenty years. In view of the king's triumph it is quite astonishing how little he was able to stem the further development of the Reformation in Bohemia.[45] Certainly the king's mandate unleashed the first great wave of expulsions of the Bohemian Brethren, so that many of them emigrated to Poland or Prussia. The *senior* Jan Augusta was incarcerated for many years. But the mandate was carried out reluctantly, and in some places not at all. Many Brethren made a mere gesture of submission to the Utraquist Church, or lived on under some nobleman's protection, especially in Moravia, whence many had fled (Moravia having taken no part in the uprising). Even as late as 1555 the governor, Archduke Ferdinand, was forced to insist that the mandate against the Brethren be enforced. This brought a warning from the King against arousing unrest and opposition,

---

[44] Eberhard, *Monarchie und Widerstand*, pp. 399–501. Dillon, *King and Estates*, pp. 111–40.
[45] *Ibid.*, pp. 143–66. J. Pánek, 'The Opposition of the Estates in the Beginnings of the Habsburg Re-Catholicization of Bohemia', *History and Society*, ed. J. Purš and K. Hermann (Prague, 1985), pp. 353–62.

and endangering the religious peace negotiations then taking place at the diet in Augsburg.[46]

The king's attempt to enforce conformity on the Utraquist estates also backfired. Both estates and clergy leaders refused to accept articles of faith adopted by a synod of 1549 under pressure from the king, intended to facilitate a union with the Catholic Church. Later, in 1554, the king arrogated to himself the choice of aristocratic *defensores* and of members for the Utraquist consistory, who had hitherto been elected by the Utraquist estates.[47] But the only effect of this was that the consistory became progressively isolated from the Utraquist clergy, nobles and cities, and lost its authority to the point of total irrelevance. This inclined the reformist Utraquists, whose university teachers and clergy were strongly influenced by Melanchthon and remained in contact with him, to form closer political ties with the Lutherans.[48] Throughout the 1550s and 1560s, nobles and cities in north and west Bohemia increasingly and openly appointed Lutheran pastors.[49] This in spite of a general mandate from the king (1554) ordering the replacement of unconsecrated clergy by Catholic priests. Ferdinand laid extra stress on this by summoning nobles who had been accused by the cathedral chapter to appear, with their pastors, to justify themselves before the governor. It seems that at least two hundred Lutheran pastors were demoted, and fifty rejected, because of this measure.[50] However, the shortage of Catholic replacements meant that they were soon reinstated.[51]

The difficulties King Ferdinand faced emphasised the extent to which he was hamstrung by economic and political constraints. His desire to avoid conflicts with the Protestants in his own kingdom was explained largely by the need to safeguard the Bohemian estates' willingness to raise taxes. The fines and confiscations inflicted on the insurgents had done little to relieve the chronic cash shortage in the royal treasury. Since the Turks had resumed the war in 1551, Ferdinand had been even more dependent on the taxes paid by the Bohemian estates, especially as Bohemia was financially the strongest of all his lands. He felt obliged to

---

[46] *Jednání a dopisy*, nr. 750.

[47] K. Krofta, 'Boj o konsistoř pod obojí v letech 1562–1575 a jeho historický základ' *Český časopis historický*, 17 (1911), 28–57, 178–99, 283–303 and 383–420.

[48] R. Říčan, 'Melanchthon und die böhmischen Länder', *Philipp Melanchthon, Humanist, Reformator, Praeceptor Germaniae* (East Berlin, 1963), pp. 237–60.

[49] Eckert, *Handbuch*. Frind, *Kirchengeschichte*, p. 417.

[50] *Jednání a dopisy*, nos. 707, 711, 713–15, 718–20 and 722–47. Bretholz, *Neuere Geschichte Böhmens*, pp. 256–58.

[51] A good example is the trouble that was caused by the attempt to remove the evangelical pastor of the city of Tachau (Tachov) in west Bohemia, and especially the difficulty of finding him a Catholic successor. Frind, *Kirchengeschichte*, pp. 108 and 383–4. *Jednání a dopisy*, nos. 609, 611, 615, 623–4 and 633.

restrain the over-enthusiastic anti-reformation zeal of his son and governor, Archduke Ferdinand, against the Lutherans in north-west Bohemia,
partly with an eye to the estates and high officials, but also so as not to
hinder the flow of income from the mining towns.[52] This may also have
been why the king soon ceased to take active steps against the reformers
and went over to a policy of active renewal of Catholicism. In 1556 he
summoned the Jesuits to Prague to improve the religious education of
clergy and people; after the Council of Trent, in 1561, he obtained the
Pope's permission to re-establish the archbishopric of Prague, vacant for
over 130 years, with Anton Brus von Müglitz (Antonín Brus z Mohelnice)
as the new archbishop.

These measures prefigure the polarisation which was to mark the
second half of the sixteenth century. For on the other side, opposition
among the estates to the centralising policies of the Habsburgs was also
gathering under confessional auspices. Whereas the king maintained that
the *ius reformandi* which the Peace of Augsburg had accorded to the
estates of the Empire could apply only to the *whole* province of Bohemia,
and thus appertained to the king, the nobles considered it to be their
personal privilege, referring to their 'right to reform' within their own
domains. This makes it easy to understand why the struggle for religious
freedom and recognition of non-Catholic confessions became a key issue
in Bohemia for most of the opposition in the estates, and why that
opposition crystallised more and more into a single evangelical confession
under Lutheran auspices.[53] Nevertheless it was not until 1575 that
Lutherans, reformist Utraquists and Bohemian Brethren could agree on
the text of a common confession, the *Confessio Bohemica*, and submit it to
the Emperor Maximilian II. The text drew heavily on the Confession of
Augsburg. From then on it is possible at least to refer to the Lutherans
and Utraquists together as 'Bohemian evangelicals', while the Union of
Brethren gradually drew closer and closer to Calvinism. But the Evangelicals still did without a common organisation, except that the estates could
now once again choose their *defensores* themselves. Not until the famous
imperial letter of Rudolf II (1609) did they manage to organise themselves
into a common ecclesiastical order.

Although the margravate of Moravia was technically fully incorporated under the Bohemian crown, the religious situation of the province
differed quite significantly. Politically, the Moravian estates jealously
preserved their independence from Bohemia. They had their own local
officials headed by a governor who, while he was appointed by the king as
his representative, was nonetheless bound to represent the interests of his

[52] *Ibid.*, no. 726.   [53] Pánek, 'Opposition', pp. 357–62.

noble colleagues in the estates. The supreme judicial body in Moravia, as in Bohemia, was the aristocratic *Landrecht*, whose judgements were assumed, as customary law, into the *Landtafeln* or legal tables. The Diet, upon whose decisions the king was as dependent as he was in Bohemia, consisted also of the three *curiae* of magnates (barons), knights and royal cities. All institutions were in fact controlled by the magnates, to an even greater extent than in Bohemia. But, unlike in Bohemia, in Moravia the prelates were also represented in the parliament: the Bishop of Olmütz (Olomouc) sat in the noble estate, the lesser prelates or abbots in that of the cities.[54]

Here already we have an indication that the church's situation was different from that in Bohemia. For in Moravia the Hussite Revolution had not forced the Catholic Church into such headlong retreat as it had in Bohemia. The Bishop and cathedral chapter of Olmütz, together with certain monasteries, had kept their hands on a reduced, but still considerable amount of church property. The Catholic congregations were correspondingly larger. Until about 1520 the Catholics held on not only to their church property, but also to certain areas, in particular the German-speaking regions in southern Moravia and on the Bohemian frontier, and also (for the most part) the few, but economically important free royal cities: Brünn (Brno), Olmütz (Olomouc), Iglau (Jihlava) and Znaim (Znojmo). But, apart from two other royal cities, all the rest had fallen into the hands of the nobility in the fifteenth century.

In Moravia, as in Bohemia, the majority of the people, and in the noble estates, adhered to the Utraquist confession. Since the Council of Basle had included Moravia in the *compactata*, the Utraquist Church was legally recognised there. But it lacked a central organisation. Certainly the *administrator*, consistory and Utraquist diets in Prague claimed competence and jurisdiction over the Utraquist priests in Moravia, but in practice they could seldom exercise control over such a distance, leaving the Moravian deaneries largely to their own devices, and the clergy effectively in the charge of their deans and noble patrons. Moreover, the *Landrecht* had enunciated the principle that every man could freely choose his confession, so that under the tolerant eye of the nobility a rather undogmatic, biblical Christianity was developing in the country.[55]

These preliminary remarks explain why the suppression of the leftist

---

[54] Dillon, *King and Estates*, p. 17. O. Peterka, *Rechtsgeschichte der böhmischen Länder in ihren Grundzügen dargestellt* (2 parts, Reichenberg, 1928), here II. 102.
[55] J. Válka, *Přehled dějin Moravy, vol. II: Stavovská Morava (1440–1620)* (Prague, 1987), pp. 60–5.

Utraquists in Bohemia around 1525 did not extend to Moravia, so that exiles from Prague could flee there;[56] they also explain the syncretism visible in the development of reformist Utraquism in Moravia. Thus in 1520 Beneš Optát, Dean of Groß-Meseritsch (Velké Meziříčí), openly espoused leftist Utraquism, following the Taborite traditions of the Bohemian Brethren; but he also made contact with the Lutheran preacher of Iglau. In 1522 he put to him certain disputed questions about the Communion, to which Luther himself finally gave a conciliatory answer. As pastor of Iglau he published sermons and a commentary on the Pauline Letters, in which on the one side he gave a Lutheran emphasis on Justification by Faith and the Priesthood of all Believers, while on the other he stressed the Hussite concepts of faith effective through love and the spiritual concept of the communion.[57] In such ways the Moravian Utraquists must have been strongly influenced by the Union of Brethren and the Lutherans, taking Moravia further than Bohemia down the reformist Utraquist road. This became clear as early as 1526, when a group of reformist Utraquist, Lutheran and Zwinglian ministers met at Nikolsburg (Mikulov) and strove, unsuccessfully as it turned out, for unity.[58]

The Union of the Bohemian Brethren was also very widespread in Moravia, with centres in Prerau (Přerov), Eibenschitz (Ivančice near Brünn), Proßnitz and Fulnek (German congregation in eastern Moravia), together with a printing press in Proßnitz and several schools. The Brethren were protected by the nobility, especially the Barons of Pernstein and Leipa. Prerau, the seat of the Moravian bishop, was generally acknowledged to be the capital of the Moravian Brethren, where repeated synods of the whole Bohemian and Moravian Union took place. The nobles' protection gave the congregations of the Moravian Brethren an even quieter life than in Bohemia: the king could not persecute them so easily here, since King Ladislas' mandate against the Brethren in 1508 had not been implemented by the Moravian diet.[59] Because the Moravian

[56] Above p. 30.
[57] In 1533 he also worked with a minister from Prague on a Czech grammar and a translation of the New Testament. F. Hrejsa, *Dějiny křest'anství v Československu*, (6 vols., Prague, 1946–50), IV, 289–90, V, 8–9, 43, 190.
[58] *Ibid.*, IV, 312–14.
[59] Moravia in fact became a haven for dissidents of all types, including such exotics as Jan Kalenec of the Amosites, a splinter group from the Bohemian Brethren, and Jan Dubčanský, a knight who in the 1520s founded his own faith, the Habrovan or Lultschan Brethren. The Moravian nobles protected their dissident colleague Dubčanský against the king's persecution in 1537. W. Urban, *Der Antitrinitarismus in den Böhmischen Ländern und in der Slowakei im 16. und 17. Jahrhundert* (Baden-Baden, 1986), pp. 21–32. Válka, *Přehled*, pp. 104–5. Müller, *Geschichte*, II, 93–100. Dillon, *King and Estates*, pp. 78–9. Hrejsa, *Dějiny*, V, 67–70.

estates had not taken part in the uprising of 1547, Ferdinand I was also
unable to persecute the congregations of the Brethren there, so that many
Brethren emigrated to Moravia, and in 1548 were even able to found a
new congregation in Ungarisch Brod (Uherský Brod). So great was the
expansion of the Union that in 1553 the great synod of Prerau, which was
attended by clergy from Bohemia, Moravia and Poland, had to enlarge
the high council and the number of ministers in general. The centre of
gravity of the Union shifted gradually towards Moravia, especially after
the dissolution of the leading congregation in the Bohemian Jungbunzlau
in 1555.

In Moravia as in Bohemia, Lutheranism gradually became the
strongest force for Reformation after the Union of Brethren. It had a
considerable power of attraction over the Utraquist ministers. The initiative and energy given to Bohemian Lutheranism by St Joachimsthal was
supplied in Moravia by Iglau (Jihlava).[60] As early as 1522 the Abbot of
Seelau, patron of the town church, had appointed Paulus Speratus,
sometime preacher in the cathedral of Würzburg, as pastor. In Iglau he
won over the citizens of this very socially unstable town to Lutheranism
very rapidly. But only a year later the bishop intervened with King Louis
to have him exiled. He became the first Lutheran bishop of Prussia, but
continued to correspond with the people of Iglau, to strengthen their
Lutheran beliefs, well into the 1530s. Soon most of the citizens, and hence
the majority of the town council, were Lutherans, so that even after
Speratus' departure evangelically minded, and sometimes married,
pastors were appointed, whose influence in the city was essentially more
lasting than his. But because Iglau was a royal city, they had to tread
carefully on the path to reform. In 1543 the council did succeed in turning
ecclesiastical property into a city fund for schools and social undertakings. But when in 1555 they asked Melanchthon for a master from
Wittenberg as pastor, and he planned to abolish the Mass, conflict broke
out. His predecessor, who was also Abbot of Seelau, had given communion in both kinds, but had nevertheless celebrated the Mass. Here,
therefore, Lutheranism was practised through the forms of Utraquism.

Another typical example is Olmütz (Olomouc), where, as in Iglau, the
large influx of German journeymen around 1520 had contributed to the
spread of Lutheranism.[61] Here in 1525 there was an evangelical preacher,
who was protected by the city council, but was soon exiled by the king.

[60] Richter, 'Die böhmischen Länder' in *Handbuch*, p. 124. Válka, *Přehled*, pp. 100–1.
F. Schenner, 'Beiträge zur Geschichte der Reformation in Iglau', *Zeitschrift des
deutschen Vereins für die Geschichte Mährens und Schlesiens*, 15 (1911), 222–55; 16 (1912),
84–102, 374–406.
[61] P. Dedic, 'Die Geschichte des Protestantismus in Olmütz', *Jahrbuch der Gesellschaft für
die Geschichte des Protestantismus in Österreich*, 52 (1931), 148–74.

However, the council appointed another Lutheran preacher to succeed him, a former monk, who was not removed until four years later. In the 1530s not only did he have an evangelical successor, but the council allowed evangelical Passion plays to be publically performed; Jan Olivetský, an evangelical printer, was able to settle in the town. In 1547 he was beheaded, but in 1551 Johann Günther set up yet another evangelical printing house. Moreover, from 1538 evangelical teachers founded several German schools in the town. By 1540 most of the citizens and the council were Lutherans. The council disputed with the bishop and claimed the right to appoint their own pastors, and subsequently regularly appointed Lutheran pastors to the town church, although these were repeatedly exiled by the king. In 1557 this finally goaded the journeymen into revolt.

There is no doubt that Lutheranism also got a grip on the villages and small towns of German-speaking Moravia, but, unlike in Bohemia, it was not the noble estates, but the (predominantly German-speaking) royal towns which were the precursors and centres of the Reformation. Ironically this was to prove disadvantageous to its overall development. For the city estate in Moravia was of limited size and weaker than in Bohemia, so that the king found it easier to interfere in their affairs. However, Ferdinand I lacked obedient tools to carry through his religious politics: the bishop supported them, but the Moravian estates and land-officers did not. Hence for all the king's interference, by the middle of the sixteenth century most of the inhabitants of the Moravian royal cities had gone over to the Reformation.

Under the protection of the Moravian estates another particular circumstance developed within the Reformation of eastern Central Europe: the congregations of Anabaptists.[62] In the German-speaking south Moravian town of Nikolsburg (Mikulov), which belonged to the Barons of Liechtenstein, preachers had been building an evangelical congregation since 1524; preachers influenced not only by Luther, but also and especially by the teachings of Zwingli. In 1526 Balthasar Hubmaier joined this congregation. He had been an outstanding leader and theologian among the south German Anabaptists; he also had connections with Zwingli and had played an ideological part in the Peasants' Revolt. In a short time he won over hundreds of people in and around the town to Anabaptism, which soon founded further congregations in towns like Brünn and Znaim (Znojmo).

However, when the eschatological, spiritualistic Anabaptist preacher Hans Hut arrived in Nikolsburg, a conflict arose in the congregation over

[62] Dillon, *King and Estates*, pp. 71, 74–5. J. Zeman, *The Anabaptists and the Czech Brethren in Moravia. A Study of Origin and Contacts* (Mouton, 1969).

the question of obedience to the secular powers. While Hubmaier's followers accepted political and military authority, the other faction rejected authority of any kind. In consequence Hubmaier's opponents were driven out of the Liechtenstein domains and settled in Austerlitz (Slavkov) under Baron von Kaunitz. At the same time the Anabaptists were scattered by the persecution of King Ferdinand, who in 1527 had issued a severe mandate against them. Hubmaier was an early victim of this persecution, being captured and burned alive in Vienna in 1528. The next year, a group of Tyrolean Anabaptists came to Austerlitz with their preacher, Jakob Huter, who at last managed to unite and organise the Moravian Anabaptists into a pacific kind of primitive Christianity. Characteristic of these 'Huterites' was a kind of communism of production and consumption; they lived in communal houses called *Haushaben*. They were highly valued by noble landowners because of their economic efficiency and the good quality of their products, knives, ceramics and textiles.

In the persecution which followed the annihilation of the militant Anabaptist kingdom of Münster, Jakob Huter returned to the Tyrol and was likewise burned alive (1536). The diet, under pressure from the king, had decided on the expulsion of the supposedly dangerous 'Huterites'. This threat drove some Anabaptists into Austria or into other Moravian domains whose owners were still willing to protect them. However, the repression was only really successful in the royal cities, where the Anabaptists never again found a firm foothold. In 1540 and 1545 the diet defied further expulsion orders from the king. Only in 1547 and 1548 was Ferdinand able to impose a short-lived persecution even in Moravia, forcing Anabaptists to hide or flee into Hungary; but after it most of them soon returned. In the middle of the sixteenth century there were about thirty Anabaptist congregations in Moravia, with approximately 3,000 to 9,000 members. They were cut off from other faiths, and were widespread only among the German-speaking population.[63]

After 1550 both the Anabaptists and the Union of Brethren in Moravia were able to flourish in comparative security until well into the seventeenth century. For at the Diet of Brünn in 1550 the Moravian estates asserted their religious freedom even against King Ferdinand, who, fresh from his victory over the German and Bohemian Protestants, had demanded that Moravia restore the Catholic parishes and go back to the confessional status quo of 1526. The Moravian governor, Wenceslaus Ludanic, stood out openly against this, defending evangelical teaching and reminding the king of his coronation oath to guarantee the religious

[63] Hrejsa, *Dějiny*, V, 61, 90, 122, 127, 167. Válka, *Přehled*, pp. 102–4. Janáček, *Doba předbělohorská*, I, 218–21.

freedom of the Moravian estates. In exchange they had vowed fidelity to the king; but they were ready to lay down their lives for religious freedom. Since an overwhelming majority in the estates backed this vote, the king was unable to press his demands, and religious freedom was effectively guaranteed.[64]

The famous Moravian tolerance, which made the country a paradise for all kinds of religious groups (or as the authorities saw it a notorious hotbed of heresy) was the price the Habsburg king had to pay in religious terms for the greater political loyalty accorded him by the Moravian estates. This, in turn was connected with the economic and family ties binding the Moravian nobility to Austria. In 1526 the Moravian estates, unlike the Bohemians, had willingly acknowledged Ferdinand as their rightful overlord. They were usually readier with their taxes and military aid, since they were more directly threatened by the Turks in Hungary. And finally, with the exception of Iglau they had stood aside from the revolt of the Bohemian estates in 1547. But on the other hand the Moravians laid more stress on the religious freedom of their estates, which was the only ground of their opposition to the sovereign, because the position of the Catholic Church was stronger here than in Bohemia; and because the Utraquist consistory of Prague had lost its influence over Moravia, every noble was able, and indeed obliged, to take responsibility for ecclesiastical matters. Hence a *ius reformandi* had devolved upon the Moravian feudal lords, not *de iure* but *de facto*. The obverse of this religious freedom in Moravia was the fact that the estates cared very little about confessional and organisational unity among non-Catholics. This weakened their opposition to the Counter-Reformation, and later, in 1618–20, to the king.[65]

More clearly than Bohemia, the two provinces 'over the Enns' (Upper Austria, Linz) and 'under the Enns' (Lower Austria, Vienna) legally formed part of the Empire; but in their social and political structures they bore a much closer resemblance to the countries of eastern Central Europe than to the West. One main reason for this is that here, as in Poland, Bohemia–Moravia and Hungary, the Middle Ages had seen the rise of a strong, independent higher nobility alongside the lower nobility, a foundation for a strong representative system. Hence the political institutions of the estates in the eastern Austrian provinces are closer to those of Bohemia than to those in the western Austrian lands.[66] Certainly

[64] Dillon, *King and Estates*, p. 154.
[65] Richter, 'Die böhmischen Länder', in *Handbuch*, pp. 174–5. Janáček, *Doba předbělo-horská*, I, 221–4. Válka, *Přehled*, pp. 153–4.
[66] For a comparison of this nature Eberhard, *Monarchie und Widerstand*, pp. 45–63. V. Press, 'Adel, Reich und Reformation', in W. J. Mommsen etc. (eds.), *The Urban*

the city estate was, as in Moravia, quantitatively weaker, but in Upper Austria it nonetheless included seven feudal cities, some of which (for example Linz, Steyr, Wels, Gmunden) were economically strong, whereas in Lower Austria only Vienna was of much importance. The organisation of the church in both provinces was problematic, a fact which, alongside the strong position of the estates, was to determine the progress of the Reformation. Except for the small and unimportant dioceses of Vienna and Vienna–Neustadt, Upper Austria and most of Lower Austria came under the jurisdiction of the Bishop of Passau, a foreign ecclesiastical overlord. Moreover, the holder of that office during the Reformation came from the rival Bavarian dynasty of Wittelsbach. The ruling Archbishopric of Salzburg similarly escaped the control of the Habsburg provinces. Hence it was the aim of the estates, as of Archduke (later King) Ferdinand, to strengthen secular control over the church against the bishops.

Austrian pulpits had echoed to denunciations of the clergy, of indulgences and of pastoral negligence, for decades before the Reformation, denunciations inspired by the humanism that had taken a hold in the university of Vienna in Lower Austria, and in the monasteries of the sister province.[67] So it is understandable that in around 1520, under the rule of the estates before Archduke Ferdinand's accession to the empire, nobles and townsmen were already making contact with Lutherans. More and more of their sons were being sent to the University of Wittenberg; more and more preachers were being appointed to propagate Luther's ideas. The first centres of evangelical preaching were towns like Vienna and Steyr. Hence it was Upper Austria that became the chief engine of the Reformation. Typical is the course of events in Steyr, an important iron-trading town. First, the monastery, patron of the town church, appointed evangelically minded pastors. Then in 1528 the town council unilaterally assumed the right of appointment. But even when the monastery regained that right, it only furthered the Reformation, because Lutheranism had taken hold in the monastery itself. The first married pastor, in 1548, had been in the monastery; so had the next, who in 1554 introduced evangelical services – and all this with the encouragement and approval of the town council.[68] In 1522 Paulus Speratus, a committed follower of Luther, embarked on evangelical preaching in Vienna. Soon

Classes, the Nobility and the Reformation (Publications of the German Historical Institute London, 5, Stuttgart, 1979), pp. 330–83, here pp. 376–82.
[67] Loesche, *Geschichte des Protestantismus*, pp. 50–2.
[68] G. Mecenseffy, *Geschichte des Protestantismus in Österreich* (Graz/Cologne, 1956), pp. 30–1.

after the towns, the castles and strongholds of the nobles also became centres of Lutheranism in the countryside. The implementation of the Edict of Worms, as ordered by Ferdinand, was impossible in Austria for lack of effective means. The majority of the estates in both provinces, including the two governors, quickly came out in favour of the evangelical movement.[69] All attempts at intervention by the bishop of Passau, such as summons to appear before his foreign ecclesiastical court, were rejected: ecclesiastical matters were to be decided by the secular powers and estates of the province itself; clergy would henceforth be tried by secular courts. Town magistrates and feudal nobles took over spiritual jurisdiction (and church property). The monasteries, already deserted by many of the monks, were further weakened economically in 1529, when Ferdinand ordered them to sell part of their possessions to finance the war against the Turks. At the same time the estates resolutely defied a general mandate from the bishop of Passau; with Ferdinand's approval, as he too resented any such infringements on his legal rights. Indeed, the estates did most to weaken episcopal authority by identifying themselves with Ferdinand's interests in order to construct an ecclesiastical administration controlled by the secular powers. In consequence, no co-operation was possible in Austria between the secular and spiritual authority.

Until 1524 there had been complaints against the clergy, but no more; in 1525, for the first time, the estates of Upper Austria announced their positive demands for religious reform. In an official document they approved of Ferdinand's suppression of the Peasants' Revolt, but demanded that to avoid further disturbances, the gospel pure and simple must be preached, without human accretions. This way of combining political loyalty and religious opposition is typical of the Austrian estates, and very similar to the attitude of their Moravian counterparts. It also explains why in Austria Ferdinand often employed zealous Lutheran nobles as provincial officials and councillors. The political loyalty of the provincial estates can also be seen in their treatment of the Anabaptists, who had been forming congregations in many towns and villages (Steyr, for example) since 1525. From 1527 the estates co-operated with the king to eliminate the Anabaptists, whose congregations were effectively eradicated in Austria in the 1530s. Thereby the estates demonstrated their political obedience to the king and, by obtaining his *de facto* tolerance of

[69] The best summary is still K. Eder, *Studien zur Reformationsgeschichte Oberösterreichs*, vol. 2: *Glaubensspaltung und Landstände in Österreich ob der Enns 1525–1602* (Linz, 1936). W. Ziegler, 'Nieder- und Oberösterreich', A. Schindling and W. Ziegler (eds.) *Die Territorien des Reichs im Zeitalter der Reformation und Konfessionalisierung, Land und Konfession 1500–1650*, vol. 1: *Der Südosten*, (Münster, 1989), pp. 118–33 (with bibliography).

Lutheran preaching, strengthened the monopoly of the Lutherans, which they saw as a stabilising element. Whereas in Bohemia and Moravia the *Unitas Fratrum* and the Anabaptists, at least, had been able to build up their own congregations independently from below, in Austria the initiative and control of the reform movement came from above, from the feudal lords and town councillors.

At almost every diet, the estates reiterated their demand for the pure word of God and for the appointment of preachers equipped to deliver it. From 1526 the Turkish threat loomed large over Austria, and the estates sought to make their military and economic aid conditional on the fulfilment of these demands. Clearly this connection was not wholly successful, for Ferdinand always refused or ignored demands to license the reform movement, and the political loyalty of the estates prevented them from ever seriously opposing the Turkish tax. After the Diet of Augsburg (1530), the estates also accepted the Lutheran dogma of justification *sola fide*. To this acceptance they later (at the diet of 1538) linked a demand for communion in both kinds. At the same time they opposed Ferdinand's attempts to treat the cities as Crown property and govern them by decree. The diet closed ranks and guaranteed the cities their old customary rights as a provincial estate, together with their religious freedom of action. At the general Diet of Prague in 1541–2, which called for fresh aid against the Turks, the Austrian estates presented a single supplication combining all three demands: preaching of the pure Gospel, the Lutheran doctrine of salvation and communion in both kinds. Even after the Emperor's defeat of the Schmalkaldic League they reiterated these demands as the basis of a sought-after Christian Union, but Ferdinand's only answer was to refer them to the Interim and the Council.

While in the first two decades of the Reformation the changes were confined to internal matters of evangelical preaching and Lutheran teaching, from the 1540s onwards nobles and towns added more public religious changes: abolition of the Mass, communion in both kinds, married priests. Only now did the Lutheran congregations become clearly recognisable. Royal visitations in 1528, 1544 and 1556 made no difference: they only demonstrated the collapse of ecclesiastical organisation and the shortage of priests. When a provincial synod in Salzburg in 1548–9 sought once again to extend ecclesiastical jurisdiction, the Upper Austrian estates countered with complaints against the clergy and with the argument that the right to reform lay with the monarch, who had therefore rejected the decisions made by the synod. This stamped the Austrian provinces as unmistakably Lutheran.[70] The estates made this official at a

---

[70] Eder, *Studien*, p. 72.

diet in Vienna in 1556, when they openly adhered to the *Confessio Augustana*. For the rest, in Austria as in Moravia there were no clear theological boundaries, no one confessional text and no one ecclesiastical organisation. The Austrian Lutherans remained entirely dependent for their organisation on individual lords and cities; theologically they depended on the position of Wittenberg, which soon dragged them into the quarrel between Flacians and Philippists.

These though were events that would unfold only in the second half of the sixteenth century; this survey should more appropriately end with an acknowledgement of the extraordinary success of the early Reformation in a region which would subsequently become wholly identified with Counter-Reformation Catholicism. Within the region, we have observed considerable differences in the impact of Protestantism. In Bohemia and Moravia the earlier Hussite Reformation and the comparative religious freedom already established allowed the development of various different sects; in Austria (as in Hungary and Poland) the Reformation in the first half of the sixteenth century was dominated by the Lutherans. But throughout, such progress was made possible by the strong position of the estates and a strong tradition of their political independence. The Reformation was eagerly embraced by the estates, because it reinforced their struggle for autonomy from the king and gave it a religious legitimacy. The leading part was played by the higher nobility, the barons, but also by cities, particularly those of Bohemia and Upper Austria. The linking of the estates' religious opposition with political demands and motivations took on different forms. The Austrian provinces and Moravia bargained political loyalty for religious freedom. In Bohemia, on the other hand, the opposition of the reformist estates more clearly showed political resistance to progressive Habsburg centralisation. Hence it is no coincidence that the first politically motivated estate rebellion triggered by the Reformation broke out in Bohemia. 1547 was the prelude to the greater revolt of 1618–20.

SELECT BIBLIOGRAPHY

Betts, R. R. 'Constitutional Development and Political Thought in Eastern Europe', in G. R. Elton, (ed.), *The New Cambridge Modern History, vol. 2: The Reformation 1520–1559* (Cambridge, 1962), pp. 464–77.
Bretholz, B. *Neuere Geschichte Böhmens, vol. 1: Der politische Kampf zwischen Ständen und Königtum unter Ferdinand I. (1526–1564) und Maximilian II. (1564–1576)* (Gotha, 1920).
Brock, P. *The Political and Social Doctrines of the Unity of Czech Brethren in the Fifteenth and Early Sixteenth Centuries* (The Hague, 1957).
Daniel, D. P. 'Ecumenicity or Orthodoxy: The Dilemma of the Protestants in the Lands of the Austrian Habsburgs', *CH*, 49 (1980), 387–400.

48   *Winfried Eberhard*

Eberhard, W. *Konfessionsbildung und Stände in Böhmen 1478–1530* (Munich/
Vienna, 1981).
*Monarchie und Widerstand. Zur ständischen Oppositionsbildung im Herrschafts-
system Ferdinands I.* in *Böhmen* (Munich, 1985).
Frind, A. *Kirchengeschichte Böhmens im Allgemeinen und in ihrer besonderen
Beziehung auf die jetzige Leitmeritzer Diöcese*, IV: *Die Administratorenzeit*
(Prague, 1878).
Heymann, F. G. 'The Hussite–Utraquist Church in the Fifteenth and Sixteenth
Centuries', *ARG*, 52 (1961), pp. 1–26.
'The Impact of Martin Luther upon Bohemia', *Central European History*, 1
(1968), pp. 107–30.
Hoensch, J. K. *Geschichte Böhmens* (Munich, 1987).
Hrejsa, F. *Dějiny křest'anství v Československu* (6 vols., Prague, 1947–50).
Janáček, J. *Doba předbělohorská 1526–1547*, České dějiny I/1,2 (2 vols., Prague,
1968–84).
Loesche, G. *Geschichte des Protestantismus im vormaligen und im neuen Öster-
reich*, 3rd edn. (Vienna/Leipzig, 1930).
Machilek, F. 'Böhmen', A. Schindling and W. Ziegler (eds.) *Die Territorien des
Reichs im Zeitalter der Reformation und Konfessionalisierung. Land und
Konfession 1500–1650*, vol. I: *Der Südosten*, (Münster, 1989), pp. 134–52.
Molnár, A. 'Der Hussitismus als christliche Reformbewegung', in F. Seibt (ed.),
Bohemia Sacra. Das Christentum in Böhmen 973–1973 (Düsseldorf, 1974),
pp. 92–109 and 565–6.
'Aspects de la continuité de pensée dans la Réforme tchèque', *Communio
Viatorum*, 15 (1972), pp. 27–50 and 111–25.
Müller, J. Th. *Geschichte der Böhmischen Brüder* (3 vols., Herrnhut, 1922–31).
Pánek, J. 'Das Ständewesen und die Gesellschaft in den Böhmischen Ländern in
der Zeit vor der Schlacht auf dem Weissen Berg (1526–1620)', *Historica*, 25
(1985), pp. 73–120.
Rhode, G. 'Die Reformation in Osteuropa. Ihre Stellung in der Weltgeschichte
und ihre Darstellung in den "Weltgeschichten"', *Zeitschrift für Ostforschung*,
7 (1958), pp. 481–500.
Richter, K. 'Die böhmischen Länder von 1471–1740', in K. Bosl (ed.), *Handbuch
der Geschichte der böhmischen Länder* (vol. 2, Stuttgart, 1974), pp. 97–412.
Schramm, G. 'Polen – Böhmen – Ungarn: Übernationale Gemeinsamkeiten in der
politischen Kultur des späten Mittelalters und der frühen Neuzeit', *Przegląd
Historyczny*, 76 (1985), pp. 417–37.
Seibt, F. 'Renaissance in Böhmen', in F. Seibt (ed.), *Renaissance in Böhmen*
(Munich, 1985), pp. 10–26.
Válka, J. *Přehled dějin Moravy*, II: *Stavovská Morava* (1440–1620) (Prague, 1987).
Zeman, J. K. *The Hussite Movement and the Reformation in Bohemia, Moravia and
Slovakia (1350–1650). A Bibliographical Study Guide* (Ann Arbor, 1977).
Ziegler, W. 'Nieder – und Oberösterreich', in A. Schindling and W. Ziegler (eds.)
*Die Territorien des Reichs im Zeitalter der Reformation und Konfes-
sionalisierung. Land und Konfession 1500–1650*, I: *Der Südosten*, (Münster,
1989), pp. 118–33.

3   Hungary

David P. Daniel

The crucial event for Hungary's early Reformation, indeed for its whole history, occurred some nine years after Luther's protest first ignited the Reformation. On 29 August 1526, near Mohács,[1] in south-western Hungary, the army of Louis Jagiello, the twenty-year-old King of Bohemia and Hungary, confronted what appeared to be a modest detachment of Turks. Some magnates advised the king to withdraw. Several bishops urged him to attack. They argued that Suleiman's main army was some distance away and, moreover, 'God willed a Magyar victory'.[2] The king ordered the charge. By five o'clock the battle was over. The small contingent of Turks had been joined by the Sultan's army of nearly two hundred thousand. Strewn across the battlefield were the wounded and the dead, among them the King, the archbishops of Esztergom and Kalocsa, five bishops, twenty-eight magnates, five hundred nobles and sixteen thousand troops; more than three-quarters of the Hungarian army.

Mohács was a disaster for the Hungarians. But it also changed the political and military balance in east Central Europe.[3] With the death of Louis, the crowns of Saint Stephen (Hungary) and Saint Václav (Bohemia) were claimed by the Habsburg Archduke of Austria, Ferdinand, born and raised in Spain. In accord with the treaties of Bratislava (1491) and of Vienna (1515) Ferdinand had married Anna, the sister of Louis, while his sister, Mary, had wed the Hungarian king. Ferdinand was thus able to claim the crowns of Hungary and Bohemia by right of inheritance and alliance.

[1] Place names used in the text are those currently employed in order to make it possible to use contemporary maps. During the sixteenth century a place might have a Latin, Hungarian, and German name, and one in the respective Slavic language. In addition, the names employed by recent scholars reflect their own national language. Thus, the Archdiocese of Strigonensis (Latin) is Esztergom in Hungarian, Gran in German and Ostrihom in Slovak. See appendix. Personal names have also been Anglicised.
[2] G. Farkas (ed.), *Ungarns Geschichte in Dokumenten* (Wiesbaden, 1955), pp. 46–8.
[3] S. Fischer-Galati, *Ottoman Imperialism and German Protestantism, 1521–1555* (2nd edn., New York, 1972). V. Kopčan, *Turecké nebezpečenstvo a Slovensko* (Bratislava, 1986).

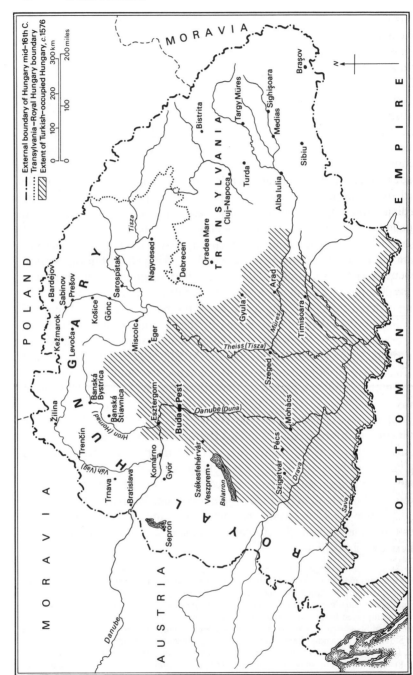

Map 3. Sixteenth-century Hungary

His claim, however, did not go uncontested. In both Hungary and Bohemia, the principle of royal election was vigorously maintained by the diets in which many nobles opposed the Habsburg claims. In Hungary, John Zápolya, Count of Spiš was elected and crowned king in November 1526 at Székesfehérvár. One month later, a smaller assembly of nobles including several influential magnates, elected Ferdinand monarch in Bratislava. For more than a decade, Ferdinand and Zápolya were bitter foes. Yet neither was able to eliminate the other in what became a three-way struggle for control of Hungary after the Turks besieged Vienna in 1529. Eventually, in 1538, Zápolya agreed to the treaty of Oradea Mare. In exchange for a recognition of his position in the eastern third of the kingdom (Siebenbürgen, or Transylvania) he agreed that Ferdinand would succeed him. Shortly after, Zápolya married Isabella Jagiello who, just before his death in 1540, bore him a son and heir. This dashed Ferdinand's hopes of obtaining control of the Siebenbürgen. His royal authority extended only to northern and western Hungary. In Siebenbürgen and in the so-called *partium*, the counties of the east bank of the Theiss river, Isabella served as regent for her infant son, John

TABLE OF PLACE NAMES

Contemporary	German	Hungarian	Slovak	Latin
Albu Iulia (R)	Weissenburg	Gyulafehèrvár		
Ardud (R)	Erdöd	Erdöd	Erdöd	Erdöd
Banská Štiavnica (S)	Schemnitz	Selmecbánya	Banská Štiavnica	Schemnitzium
Banská Bystrica (S)	Neusohl	Besztercebánya	Banská Bystrica	Neosolium
Bardejov (S)	Bartfeld	Bártfa	Bardejov	Bartpha
Bistrita (R)	Bistritz	Beszterce	Bystrica	Bistrice
Brasov (R)	Kronstadt	Brassó		Corona
Bratislava (S)	Pressburg	Pozsony	Bratislava	Posonium
Budapest (H)	Ofen	Buda	Budín	Buda
Cluj-Napoca (R)	Klausenberg	Kolozsvár		Claudiopolis/Colosvarium
Eger (H)	Erlau	Eger	Jáger	Agriensis
Esztergom (H)	Gran	Esztergom	Ostrihom	Strigonium
Győr (H)	Raab	Győr	Ráb	Jaurinum
Kežmarok (S)	Käsmark	Késmárk	Kežmarok	Caesareopolis/Kesmarkium
Košice (S)	Kaschau	Kassa	Košice	Cassovia
Kremnica (S)	Kremnitz	Körmöcbánya	Kremnica	Cremnitzium
Levoča (S)	Leutschau	Löcse	Levoča	Leutschovia
Ljubljana (J)	Laibach			
Medias (R)	Mediasch	Megyes		Megyes
Oradea Mare (R)	Grosswardein	Nagyvárad	Várad	Varadinum
Poprad (S)	Deutschendorf	Poprád	Poprad	Villa Teutonicalis
Prešov (S)	Eperies	Eperjes	Prešov	Eperiessinum
Sabinov (S)	Szeben	Kisszeben	Sabinov	Cibinium
Sibiu (R)	Hermannstadt	Nagyszeben		Cibinium
Siebenbürgen (R)	Siebenbürgen	Erdélyi	Sedmohradsko	Septemcastri (Transylvania)
Sighişoara (R)	Schässburg	Segesvár		Segesdvar
Spiš (S)	Zips	Szepes	Spiš	Scepusia
Spišská Ves (S)	Zipser Neudorf	Igló	Spišská Nová Ves	Nova Villa
Székesfehérvár (H)	Stuhlweissenberg	Székesfehérvár		Alba Regalis
Trenčin (S)	Trentschin	Trenscény	Trenčin	Trenchinium
Zvolen (S)	Altosohl	Zólyom	Zvolen	Veterosolium
Žilina (S)	Sillein	Zsolna	Žilina	Zolna

(R)umania; (H)ungary; (S)lovakia (Czecho-Slovakia); (J)ugoslavia

Sigismund. The central basin of the Danube, meanwhile, remained under Turkish control, a situation which continued for the next one and a half centuries.

This three-way partition of the kingdom established the political geography of Reformation Hungary. The lack of a strong central controlling power undoubtedly assisted the spread of the Reformation in south-east Central Europe, as it did in Germany. So too did long-standing political, ethnic and economic conflicts. Hungary was a multi-national state. The Magyars or Hungarians were the most numerous, especially in the central basin of the Danube. Upper Hungary, modern-day Slovakia, was largely inhabited by Slovaks. In the south-west, Slovenes, Croats and Serbs predominated. The descendants of German settlers, who had come to Hungary during the thirteenth and fourteenth centuries, made up a sizable proportion of the population in the cities and major market towns, especially in northern and western Hungary and Siebenbürgen. Their economic significance was considerable. They maintained contacts with market centres throughout western and northern Europe, and Hungary's prosperity depended upon its delivery of cattle, wine, copper and other raw materials to these markets.[4]

But foreign trade brought foreign influences. In the royal court, Italians had played important roles during the reign of Matthias Corvinus Hunyadi in the fifteenth century. German influence grew with the arrival of Louis Jagiello's bride, Mary of Habsburg, and her retinue. Despite the dictum of Saint Stephen of Hungary that foreigners were to he 'held in honor, for they bring fresh knowledge and arms ... for a country where only one language and one custom prevails is weak and fragile',[5] by the dawn of the sixteenth century many of the lesser Magyar nobles believed that foreign influences were a prime source of the nation's economic and political troubles. They felt threatened by the economic power of the cities and the market towns, by the changing market conditions and economic organisation, and by the inflation which gripped Hungary during the first decades of the sixteenth century.[6] They argued that foreigners were robbing Hungary of her resources. One target of their criticism was George of Brandenburg, one of the original subscribers to the Augsburg Confession, who by his marriage to the widow of the son of Matthias Corvinus controlled a large number of estates in Hungary, in addition to

[4] V. Zimányi, 'Economy and Society in Sixteenth- and Seventeenth-Century Hungary (1526–1650)', *Studia Historica Academiae Scientiarum Hungaricae*, vol. 188 (Budapest, 1987).

[5] R. W. Seton-Watson, *History of the Czechs and the Slovaks* (Hamden, CT, 1965), p. 252.

[6] C. A. Macartney, 'Eastern Europe', in *The New Cambridge Modern History, I. The Renaissance, 1493–1520* (Cambridge, 1957), pp. 386–7. L. Neustadt, *Ungarns Verfall und Maria von Ungarn* (Budapest, 1885).

his possessions in Bohemia, Silesia and Germany. Ladislas had appointed George to serve as the military tutor or *morum formator* of Louis and he was also an advisor to Mary.[7] The Hungarian nobles also attacked the growing economic and political influence of the Fugger–Thurzo Company which had begun its operations in the mining cities of north central Hungary during the last decade of the fifteenth century.[8] The lesser Magyar nobles further resented the influence exerted by the small group of magnate families who held vast estates throughout the kingdom.[9]

The peasants and cottagers, mine workers and other urban day labourers also had grievances. Their economic situation had grown worse owing to increased exploitation, taxation and inflation which they blamed on royal officials, the nobles and the urban oligarchy. During the last decades of the fifteenth and the first decades of the sixteenth century, their discontent erupted in two revolts. In 1514, a peasant army assembled by the Archbishop of Esztergom for a crusade against the Turks and led by George Dozsa revolted and ravaged estates throughout much of central and eastern Hungary.[10] A dozen years later a calculated if callous devaluation of the coinage used to pay day labourers led to a revolt of mine workers in northern Hungary. During the revolt, its leaders were accused of holding 'heretical' religious views.[11]

In the new political circumstances of the 1520s these political and social tensions attained a new importance. The anti-foreigner faction among the lesser Magyar nobility rallied behind Zápolya and Stephen Werbőczy. Zápolya, who held extensive estates throughout eastern and northern Hungary, first emerged as a leader when he crushed the rebellion of peasants in 1514. Werbőczy, a legal scholar who served briefly as Palatine or viceroy during the miners' rebellion, prepared a compilation of Hungarian laws and customs, the *Opus Tripartium*.[12] It provided the legal foundations and justifications for resolving the grievances of the lesser nobility. It maintained that all nobles in Hungary were equal under

[7] L. Neustadt, *Markgraf Georg von Brandenburg als Erzieher am ungarischen Hofe* (Breslau, 1883).

[8] G. Frhr. von Probszt, *Die alten sieben niederungarischen Bergstädte im Slowakischen Erzgebirge* (Vienna, 1960).

[9] D. Sinor, *History of Hungary* (London, 1959), pp. 123–38.

[10] S. Marki, *Dózsa György* (Budapest, 1913).

[11] P. Ratkoš, *Povstanie baníkov na Slovensku roku 1525–1526* (Bratislava, 1963) and 'Banícke povstanie 1525–1526 a reformačna ideológia na Slovensku', *Československý časopis historický*, 2 (1954), 400–15; G. Frhr. von Probszt, 'Die sozialen Ursachen des ungarischen Bergarbeiteraufstandes von 1525/26', *Zeitschrift für Ostforschung*, 10 (1961), 430–2.

[12] G. Illes, 'Stefano Werbőczy', *Corvina*, 5 (1942), 231–43; J. Hegedüs, 'Werbőczy, ein moderner Mensch an der Schwelle der Neuzeit', *Litteraria Hungarica*, 1 (1943), 149–152.

C

the law and that they alone had the right to elect the monarch. At the same time, the former free peasants were condemned to perpetual serfdom. While the *Tripartium* rectified many of the political grievances of the lesser nobles it did little to remedy their economic distress. They continued their attempts to reduce the political and economic influence of both the magnates and the cities, which, like the magnates, enjoyed many privileges and governed themselves by law codes based upon German models. One of their privileges was the right to elect their own pastors.

After the battle of Mohács and the occupation of central Hungary by the Turks, the Magyar nobles fled their ancestral homes. They entered the service of the rivals for the Hungarian crown. In return for their services and loyalty they sought new estates as compensation. Not infrequently these were the secularised former benefices of clerics, the lands of smaller or dissolved monasteries, and estates seized from nobles who had supported the 'false' king.

These social, political, economic and ethnic struggles which disrupted Hungarian society during the first half of the sixteenth century were crucial for enabling the Reformation to take root in Hungary. In a divided and decentralised society, it was all the more easy for heretical ideas to circulate, and for dissident individuals to find a secure refuge. But the way for Reformation was also prepared by widespread discontent with clerical abuses, the influence of late medieval piety and, especially, by the spread of Renaissance humanism.[13]

As in Germany, the Reformation in Hungary profited from widespread discontent with the influence, wealth and power of the higher clergy. Many in the region sought to transform the relationship between ecclesiastical and secular authorities. Already during the late fifteenth century, secular leaders, especially in the cities, had attempted to bring churches and schools under the supervision of local authorities and to secularise religious societies of laymen. They justified their actions by citing the patronage right possessed corporately by free towns and individually by nobles. These prominent laymen, urban oligarchs, members of the humanist intelligentsia and a few of the higher nobility were among the first to adhere to the Reformation. They used the theological justifications for reformation advanced by Martin Luther, especially as enunciated in his three great treatises of 1520, for their own purposes.

The higher ecclesiastical authorities in Hungary had earned the enmity of many laymen in Hungary by their worldliness, wealth and political machinations. It was said that nowhere, except perhaps in England, were

[13] M. Bucsay, *Geschichte des Protestantismus in Ungarn* (Stuttgart, 1959), pp. 15–20; D. P. Daniel, 'The Lutheran Reformation in Slovakia, 1517–1618', (doc. diss., The Pennsylvania State University, 1972), pp. 144–54.

the bishops as rich as in Hungary.[14] High ecclesiastical and secular offices were bestowed upon foreigners or non-nobles despite measures enacted by the diet. During the reign of Corvinus the Archbishopric of Esztergom was held by two Italians, Andreas Scolari and Giovanni Milanesi de Prato, while, during the reign of Ladislas, Hippolyte d'Este was named the Archbishop of Esztergom at the age of 7, and made a cardinal at 14.[15] On the eve of the Reformation, Thomas Bakócz, a peasant, rose to become Bishop of Györ, then of Eger and finally of Esztergom. Laszlo Szalkai took holy orders only after his nomination to the same see. Bakócz attempted to utilise his great wealth to bribe his way to the papal throne.[16] The higher clergy enjoyed the income from multiple benefices to which they appointed miserably paid vicars to perform their required pastoral responsibilities and used their wealth and spiritual power to increase their political influence.[17]

The secularised attitudes of these higher clergy were also shaped by the influence of the Italian humanists. The Bohemian Bohuslav Lobkowitz observed that, in Hungary, ecclesiastical dignitaries were more preoccupied with Plato and Vergil than with the Gospel.[18] During the fifteenth century scores of Hungarian students studied at Padua and Bologna while after 1450 humanist influences also entered Hungary via the universities in Vienna and Cracow.[19] Between 1458 and 1490, 951 students from Hungary enrolled at Vienna, where Conrad Celtis founded the *Litteraria sodalitas Danubiae*; a further 1263 studied at Cracow.[20] Matthias Corvinus established one of the great libraries of manuscripts in Buda and in Bratislava the short-lived *Academia Istropolitana*, where the spirit of humanism and the *Devotio Moderna* reigned.[21]

Despite the often deplorable administrative abuses in the Hungarian church and the secularising influences of Italian humanism, the religion of the intellectuals and the masses was far from moribund. From Vienna and Cracow the *Devotio Moderna* and Erasmian humanism penetrated Hun-

---

[14] S. Klein, *Handbuch der Geschichte von Ungarn und seiner Verfassung* (Kaschau, 1833), p. 418.

[15] E. Révész, Stephen Kováts, and Ladislaus Ravasz, *Hungarian Protestantism: Its Past, Present and Future* (Budapest, 1927), p. 2.

[16] D. Sinor, *History of Hungary*, pp. 138–41.

[17] L. Neustadt, *Ungarns Verfall und Maria von Ungarn*, (Leipzig, 1833) pp. 19–20.

[18] W. Toth, 'Highlights of the Hungarian Reformation', *Church History*, 9 (1940), 141–56.

[19] M. D. Birnbaum, 'Humanism in Hungary', in A. Rabil (ed.), *Renaissance Humanism, Foundations, Forms and Legacy* (3 vols, Philadelphia, 1988), II. 298–302; M. Bucsay, *Geschichte des Protestantismus* (Stuttgart, 1959), p. 17.

[20] Bucsay, *Geschichte des Protestantismus*, p. 18.

[21] T. Kardos, 'Devotio Moderna na Academii Istropolitana,' in L. Holotik and A. Vantuch (eds.), *Humanizmus a renesancia na Slovensku v 15.–16. storočí* (Bratislava, 1967), pp. 25–36.

gary.[22] They emphasised simplicity of faith, humility, trust in the gracious will and mercy of God, moral reform and education. The spirituality of the Franciscans was also a significant force throughout Hungary while the scattered remnants of Hussitism, brought to the region by Hussite warriors during the first half of the fifteenth century, indirectly helped to prepare the way for the Reformation.[23] Throughout the region, moreover, lay religious associations were a common feature of the popular religious landscape.

It is not surprising, therefore, that the German Reformation movement soon found supporters throughout south-eastern Europe. Nevertheless, the Reformation in Hungary proceeded much more slowly and was theologically more eclectic and moderate, at least until mid-century. It was first supported by Germans in the cities of upper Hungary and among the German court circle of Mary of Habsburg. After Mohács, as the number of students from Hungary attending Wittenberg and other universities in Germany increased, the Reformation spread to other cities and market towns, then, as some of the leading magnates and some of the lesser nobility supported and accepted reform, to the smaller towns and villages inhabited by Magyars, Slovaks, Slovenes and Croats. The Reformation was first disseminated by means of imported publications, then by preachers who were engaged for short, specific terms of service or who wandered throughout the country, and finally by regularly called clerics and schoolmasters. By mid-century, it had reached most of the regions and the diverse population of the divided kingdom.

The first reports about Luther and his earliest printed works were brought to Hungary by merchants who regularly travelled abroad, to Poland, Bohemia, Silesia and the German states. Thomas Preisner of Lubica near Kežmarok read Luther's *Ninety-five Theses* from his pulpit in 1521. By 1522 the broad outlines of Luther's thought were known in the mining cities of upper Hungary. In August of that year, the prior of the monastery of Königsstein near Dresden sent some pamphlets of Luther to the pastor of Banská Štiavnica who was involved in a struggle with the Dominicans in the city; George Eysker and Bartolomew Frankfordinus, the notary of Banská Štiavnica, expressed sympathy with the stance of Luther in their private correspondence, and George Baumheckel from Banská Bystrica became the first student from Hungary to matriculate at Wittenberg. In Banská Bystrica, the mayor, Valentine Schneider, and the

[22] L. Nyikos, 'Erasmus und der böhmisch-ungarische Königshof', *Zwingliana*, 7 (1937), 364–74.
[23] J. Špirko, *Husiti, Jiskrovci a bratríci v dejinach Spiša, 1431–1462* (Spišská Kapitula, 1937); B. Varsik, 'Husiti a reformácia na Slovensku,' *Historický štúdie*, 14 (1969), 217–22 and *Husitské revolučne hnutie a Slovensko* (Bratislava, 1965).

church warden, his brother-in-law Henrik Kindlinger, were already in 1521 advocates of reform and attempted to secure Simon Bernhard from Opava in Silesia to preach in the city. This first attempt to call an evangelical preacher to Banská Bystrica initiated a controversy with Nicolaus of Sabinov, the city pastor and Matthias Foyt, his assistant, which lasted until the end of the decade.[24] Nicolaus attacked the councillors for interfering with his rights and responsibilities as city pastor. He wrote a stern letter to Bernhard who subsequently asked the council to release him from his promise to come to the city, indicating that he had no intention of creating conflict. Schneider, Kindlinger and their supporters did not give up their attempts to introduce reform into the city, however. They invited evangelicals to preach in the town for specific terms or for special festivals. Among these were Dominic Hoffmann from Silesia, John Kressling and Conrad Cordatus.

At the same time that the Reformation entered northern Hungary, it also found supporters at the court in Buda: Simon Grynaeus, then curator of the Corvina library in Buda, Viet Winsheim, John Kressling, pastor of St George's and Conrad Cordatus, an early and ardent supporter of Luther from Austria who served as the chaplain of Queen Mary. Equally ardent in his support of the Wittenberg Reformer was George of Brandenburg-Ansbach, who defended Luther before his wards, the youthful king and queen.[25] In a letter to Luther in 1523 he outlined the substance of his defence and posed several theological questions.[26] George had recommended Cordatus as a chaplain for Mary and continued to defend Cordatus after the latter's dismissal and imprisonment. Following the publication of the papal bull *Decet Romanum* in Hungary, Mary was forced to dismiss Cordatus in 1522 because of his passionate support for reform. He was succeeded by John Henckel of Levoča who had studied at Cracow and in Italy before returning to Hungary. Henckel's Erasmian views were similar to those of the queen herself. He weathered the storms of controversy and the growing anti-reform attitudes of the Magyarist

[24] A. Göllnerová, 'Počátky reformace v Banské Bystrici', *Bratislava*, 4 (1930), 580–612; G. Hammann, 'Johannes Kresling', *Jahrbuch für schlesische Kirchengeschichte*, 44 (1965), 7–12; and his 'Bartholomeus Francfordinus Pannonius; Simon Grynäus in Ungarn', *Zeitschrift für Ostforschung*, 14 (1965), 228–42; and his 'Magister Nicolaus von Sabinov, ein Beitrage über den Humanismus und die frühe Reformation in der Slowakei', *Zeitschrift für Ostforschung*, 16 (1967), 25–44.

[25] Neustadt, *Markgraf Georg von Brandenburg*; L. von Sacher-Masoch, *Ungarns Untergang und Maria von Österreich* (Leipzig, 1862); J. de Iongh, *Mary of Hungary, Second Regent of the Netherlands* (London, 1958), pp. 61–65.

[26] WA Br. III. 8–10 (no 568). See also L. Neustadt, 'Zur Luthers Breifwechsel', *Zeitschrift für Kirchengeschichte*, 7 (1886), 466–76 and T. Kolde, 'Der Briefwechsel Luthers und Melanchthons mit den Markgrafen Georg und Friederick von Brandenburg', *Zeitschrift für Kirchengeschichte*, 13 (1892), 318–87.

party at court which forced many of the reformist humanists to flee Buda after 1523. Henckel served Mary until she was appointed Regent of the Netherlands by her brother, the emperor Charles V.[27]

The spread of the Reformation into the economically significant mining cities and among the German circle in Buda alarmed the Catholic hierarchy and the lesser Magyar nobility. They initiated measures to exterminate the German heresy. On April 24, 1523 the Hungarian Diet approved a decree that 'all Lutherans and those favoring them ... should have their property confiscated and themselves punished with death as heretics and foes of the most holy Virgin Mary.'[28] In a letter of 23 March 1524, the Pope commended Stephen Werböczy for his attempt to dissuade Luther from his heretical course during an interview he had with the Reformer, and for the criticisms of Luther he had made at the Diet of Nuremberg.[29] The Pope also dispatched to Hungary his legate, Cardinal Campeggio, with a plea for sterner measures against the heretics. In August 1524 John Horvath de Lomnitz, Provost of Spiš county, issued an anti-Lutherian injunction.[30]

Cardinal Szalkai, Archbishop of Esztergom, sent a commission to the mining cities in April 1524 to search for and destroy publications by Luther and other reformers. The magistrates of the cities were forewarned, however, by Bernhard Beheim, administrator of the Fugger–Thurzo company. The commission was thwarted and at Easter of 1525, Conrad Cordatus and John Kressling preached in Banská Bystrica, Kremnica and Zvolen.[31] Subsequently, the Hungarian diet, meeting at Campo Rákos in May, passed a provision that the king expel all foreigners from court since they offended God and the Apostolic See by holding Lutheran ideas. In Article 54 it also decreed that all Lutherans should be purged from the land, pursued, imprisoned and burned by both the secular and the clerical authorities.[32]

In the Spring of 1525 the mine workers in the mining or *montana* district of central upper Hungary went on strike to protest payment in debased coinage and the rising prices which were a natural result. John Pullemis, the papal nuncio to Buda, and Werböczy blamed the discord

[27] A. Hudak, 'Der Hofprediger Johannes Henckel und seine Beziehungen zu Erasmus von Rotterdam', *Kirche im Osten*, 2 (1959), 106–13 and G. Bauch, 'Dr. Johann Henckel der Hofprediger der Königin Maria von Ungarn', *Ungarische Revue*, 4 (1889), 599–627.
[28] Article 54, 1523. *Corpus Juris Hungarici*, vol. 1 (Budae, 1844).
[29] J. Kvačala, *Dejiny reformácia na Slovensku* (Liptovský sv. Mikuláš, 1935), pp. 41–4.
[30] J. Ribini, *Memorabilia Augustanae Confessionis in regno Hungariae*, vol. 2, (Posonii, 1789), p. 636; J. P. Tomasik, *Andenken an die 300-jährige Jubelfeier der evangelischen Gemeine (sic) in der k. Freistadt Leutschau* (Leutschau, 1844), pp. 18–19.
[31] Hammann, 'Magister Nicolaus von Sabinov', pp. 39–41.
[32] J. Irinyi, *Geschichte der Entstehung des 16. Gesetzartikels von 1790/1 über Religionsangelegenheiten* (Pest, 1857), pp. 2–3; Article 54, 1525, *Corpus Juris Hungarici*.

upon heretical influences. A commission was sent to investigate and the Archbishop of Esztergom wrote to Nicolaus requesting a report on the activities of the miners and the preaching of Cordatus and Kressling. Nicolaus was granted the authority to imprison the leaders of the rebellion even though a local commission had found many of the grievances of the miners just.[33] Cordatus and Kressling were imprisoned. However, they were freed in 1526. Cordatus went to Wittenberg. Kressling returned to Kremnica and from 1541 to 1549 was German preacher in Banská Štiavnica.

While the forces opposing reform thus enjoyed some success in 1525, the events of 1526 provided new opportunties for the spread of the Reformation throughout Hungary. Mohács decimated the ecclesiastical hierarchy of Hungary. The feud between the claimants of the crown of St Stephen and the presence of the Turks made it difficult to enforce anti-reform legislation and edicts. The number of students from Hungary at Wittenberg and other German universities grew steadily while preachers from Silesia, Bohemia, Germany and other lands of the Austrian Habsburgs fanned out across the kingdom.

In upper Hungary and Transylvania most of the major cities called and installed evangelical reformers as preachers or city pastors during the 1530s and 1540s. In north-eastern Hungary, where the influence of humanists from Cracow was especially strong, the Reformation was spread throughout the towns of Spiš, Šariš and Zemplin counties which had substantial German populations. Wolfgang Schustel, a native of Košice who had studied at Cracow, worked in Prešov, Košice and after 1524 in Bardejov. He preached there during the pastorate of Matthew Binder who remained a Catholic. Although influenced by Luther, Schustel adopted a more uncompromising position concerning public piety which brought him into conflict with the city council.[34] In 1531 he departed the city for Silesia and was succeeded by Esaias Lang, who seems to have been influenced by Moravian Anabaptists. Opposed by the bishop of Eger, he was forced to leave by the city council and threatened with loss of property in a royal mandate of June 1534. Finally, in 1540 Michael Radašin, a Croatian who had studied in Wittenberg and had served briefly in Hainburg was called as the town pastor although he had hoped to go to Banská Bystrica. In 1546 he became the evangelical Senior of the royal free cities of north-eastern Hungary.[35]

[33] Göllnerová, p. 591; Ratkoš, *Povstanie baníkov*, p. 321; A. Ipolyi, *Geschichte der Stadt Neusohl; eine kulturgeschichtliche Skizze* (2 vols., Pest, 1857), II. 119.

[34] V. Jankovič, 'Dve postavy zo začiatok reformácie v Bardejove', *Historický časopis*, 38 (1990), 339–50.

[35] D. P. Daniel, 'Bardejov during the era of the Reformation', *Narodný Kalendár* (National Slovak Society), 98 (1990), 29–34.

Alongside Radašin worked Leonard Stöckel, the rector of the so-called humanist school in Bardejov. A native of Bardejov (his father was a goldsmith and served on the council), Stöckel had gone to Wittenberg in 1530 and was joined there by his brother John. During his stay in Germany Stöckel developed close ties to Luther and Philip Melanchthon. He remained in regular correspondence with the latter until their deaths in 1560. Returning home in 1539 Stöckel became one of the leading pedagogues and theologians of the early Reformation in northern Hungary. From his pen came theological studies, polemical works, textbooks, school plays and the first evangelical confession in Hungary, the *Confessio Pentapolitana* of 1549.[36] In nearby Sabinov, Matthew Ramašin initiated the Reformation, while in Košice the humanists Leonard Cox and John Henckel had prepared the way for the introduction of the Reformation by a number of preachers including Matthias Dévai Biró.

In Spiš county, where numerous small German market towns and villages existed,[37] the fraternity of the pastors of the twenty-four cities of Spiš formally accepted the Reformation in 1544 after the senior, George Moeller of Levoča, finally abandoned his first opposition to religious innovations. The first trace of Lutheran influence in the county was the reading of Luther's *Theses* by Thomas Preisner in 1520. Yet, the reform movement only slowly gained adherents among influential segments of the population. Their support was crucial for its success. While in Banská Bystrica some of the leading citizens lent their support to the reform movement from an early stage, in Levoča the council was divided. George Mild, a furrier, wanted to inaugurate reform but was adamantly opposed by Conrad Sperfogel. Despite the opposition of Sperfogel and George Moeller, interest in the cause of reform was growing. Students at Wittenberg from Levoča included Martin Cyriacus, who matriculated in 1522, John Sigler (1527) and a certain Francis who enrolled in 1536.[38]

Considerable difficulties for the spread of the Lutheran reform movement were created by the appearance of the Sabbatarian Anabaptist, Andrew Fischer in Spiš county. Fischer received his Master of Arts degree from the university of Vienna in 1505. Subsequently converted to Anabaptism and influenced by the views of Oswald Glaidt, he travelled through upper Hungary in 1529. He called for the thorough reform of

[36] A. Hajduk, 'Philipp Melanchthon und Leonhard Stöckel', *Communio Viatorum*, 20 (1977), 171–80; D. Škoviera, 'Epistulae Leonardi Stöckel', *Zborník filozofickej fakulty univerzity Komenského, Graecolatina et Orientalia*, 7/8 (1975/6), 265–359 and 'Leonard Stöckel – humanistický rektor bardejovskej školy', *Jednotná škola*, 428 (1975), 339–51.
[37] G. Bruckner, *A reformáczió és ellenreformáczió a Szepességen* (Budapest: 1922) provides the most comprehensive treatment of events in this region where the Germans made up a major proportion of the population.
[38] M. Suchý (ed.), *Dejiny Levoče* (Košice, 1974), I. 149–64.

church and society and a strict adherence to the Decalogue. He gained the support of some of the artisans in the city including George Mild, Peter Münzer and Peter Guttlich. He was soon forced from the city and preached in several villages around Levoča and then in Spiška Nová Ves and Švedlar. Fischer and his wife were captured by the royal commander in the county. Both were condemned to death but Fischer escaped from the gallows and continued his activities through north-eastern Hungary until his departure for Moravia in 1523. In 1540 he returned to the region where he was recaptured and executed by Francis Bebek.[39]

Meanwhile, more and more individuals in north-eastern Hungary were accepting Lutheranism. In 1531 George Leudischer introduced Lutheranism in Kežmarok, and by 1541 Moeller noted that it was almost impossible to find a Catholic priest to serve in the vacant parishes in the region. Alexius Thurzo, the *locum tenens* or viceroy of Ferdinand became a supporter of reform. When the provost of Spiš county converted and married in 1544, Moeller gave up his opposition to reform. Bartholomew Bogner from Brassó in Transylvania was called to implement Lutheran reforms in Levoča and Daniel Türck was called from Košice to serve as the Lutheran schoolmaster of the town. Finally, in 1547, Moeller himself converted to Lutheranism. During the 1540s Laurence Quendel and Anton Toppertz became the reformist pastors of Béla and Poprad respectively. By mid-century, the pastoral fraternities of Spiš county and of the five royal free cities of north-east Hungary were controlled by Lutheran reformers.[40]

In Banská Bystrica, despite the strong Lutheran element in the council, only after the death of Nicolaus of Sabinov in 1529/30 was the way open to call an evangelical city pastor. Andreas Philadelphia was called in 1530 and remained until 1538. The city also attempted to obtain George Leudischer from Kežmarok, but neither he nor Ambrose Mibon, Aegidus Fáber or Michael Radašin accepted calls to the city. Bartholomeus Francík who came from Silesia stayed only to 1540. He was succeeded by Martin Hanko who had become a follower of Luther during the first years

---

[39] D. Liechty, 'Andreas Fischer: A brief biographical sketch', *Mennonite Quarterly Review*, 58 (1984), 125–32 and *Andreas Fischer and the Sabbatarian Anabaptists* (Scottdale, Pa., 1989). See also W. Urban, 'Andreas Fischer, ein radikaler Anabaptist und Spiritualist aus der Slowakei,' in M. Steinmetz (ed.), *Der deutsche Bauenkrieg und Thomas Müntzer* (Leipzig, 1976), pp. 179–82 and *Der Antitrinitarismus in den Böhmischen Ländern und in der Slowakei im 16. und 17. Jahrhundert*, in the series Bibliotheca Dissidentium, scripta et studia, no. 2 (Baden-Baden, 1986), pp. 119–28 as well as his 'Eine Theologische Ausein-andersetzung um den Slowakischen Täufer und Spiritualisten Andreas Fischer', *ARG*, 71 (1980), 149–59. P. Ratkoš, 'Die Anfänge des Wiedertäufertums in der Slowakei', in K. Obermann and J. Polišensky (eds.), *Aus 500 Jahren deutsch-tsechoslowakischer Geschichte* (Berlin, 1958), pp. 41–59.
[40] Tomasik, *Andenken*, pp. 28–35.

of the Reformation in Prague. The city had difficulty with its first evangelical pastors and preachers because of their reluctance to pay a regular salary. The pastor was to support himself through managing potentially profitable properties which belonged to the pastorate of the city. However, until the city agreed to exchange them for a regular salary, the husbandry of these estates demanded much time and energy and proved more a burden than a benefit. Only after 1544 were all three city churches, St Mary's or the Castle Church, St Elizabeth's and Holy Cross of the Slovak Church, served by evangelical clerics and remained in the hands of the Lutherans until 1650.[41]

In the towns of Siebenbürgen (Transylvania) and the *partium* the Reformation spread in a similar manner and pace. By 1547 a considerable proportion of the population, German, and Magyar, had accepted the Reformation. The strongholds of the movement were Sibiu, Brassó and Sighişoara. As in upper Hungary, the inhabitants of Transylvania were first introduced to the Reformation by publications brought by merchants from abroad and by individual preachers. Individual advocates of reform emerged in the early 1520s, among them an Ambrosius from Silesia, Conrad Weich and George, a former Dominican monk who had studied in Wittenberg, all active in Sibiu. George was supported by the councillor John Hecht and Markus Pempflinger, the 'Saxon Count' or leading administrative figure of the Germans in Transylvania.[42]

While Archbishop Szalkai sought to halt the spread of the Reformation by edicts and by dispatching commissions into the region, it continued to spread slowly but surely throughout Transylvania. In 1929 the city pastor of Sibiu, Martin Huet, an opponent of reform, was forced by Pempflinger and the city council to resign his position. Shortly after, the members of the Dominican order were ordered out of the city. The following year, Pempflinger's secretary, Martin Sydonius, and John Fuchs, a member of the council in Brassó, attended the Diet of Augsburg. The latter became one of the most ardent supporters of the work of John Honter. In 1530 Simon Siebenbürger became the first student from Transylvania to sign the matriculation register in Wittenberg. He returned in 1535 to become rector of the school in Brassó. As in other towns of Hungary, the council of Brassó provided students from the city with financial assistance so that

---

[41] Góllnerová, 'Počátky', 601–10.
[42] H. Pitters, 'Luther und die Anfänge der Reformation in der Siebenbürgisch-Sächsischen Kirche. Siebenbürgische Beziehungen zu Wittenberg in der 1. Hälfte des 16. Jahrhunderts', in H. Pitters and G. Schullerus (eds.), *Gefördert und Gesegnet: Die Kirche der Siebenbürger Sachsen und ihr lutherisches Erbe* (Beihefte der Kirchlichen Blätter, 4, 1983), pp. 37–57. L. Binder, 'Die Reformation', in K. Göllner (ed.), *Geschichte der Deutschen auf dem Gebiete Rumäniens* (Bucharest, 1979), pp. 127–37; K. Reinerth, *Die Gründung der evangelischen Kirchen in Siebenbürgen* (Studia Transylvanica, 5, 1979).

they could study at Wittenberg or other evangelical universities in Germany.[43]

However, during the 1530s and early 1940s, dedicated and capable evangelical preachers were as difficult to obtain in Transylvania as in upper Hungary. Paul Benkner, the city pastor in Brassó, resigned in 1535 and was succeeded by Lucas Plecker who previously appeared to support reform. Unfortunately, once he had become pastor Plecker indicated his Catholic sympathies. His term was brief, however. He died the following year and was replaced by Jeremias Jekel who was clearly an evangelical reformer. In the same year Matthias Ramser, who had been the first evangelical pastor in Sabinov, became the city pastor of Sibiu.

The leading reformer among the Germans in the region was John Honter, the epitome of an evangelical humanist and magisterial reformer. He had studied in Vienna and Cracow and worked in Basle for several printers. There he became acquainted with the views of Oecolampadius and other Swiss and upper German reformers. During the early 1530s he adopted the views of the Wittenberg reformer and returned to Brassó. Here he established a press, worked for school reform and, with the support of Fuchs, embarked upon the reform of the church. In October 1542, the first evangelical mass was held by Jeremias Jekel. However, Jekel and Honter disagreed on the role of the magistrate in guiding the reform of the church. In 1542 Honter issued a church order for the region, the *Formula reformationis Coronensis ac Barcensis totius provinciae* (Coronae, 1543) and two years later became the city pastor.[44] Honter's church order was used as the basis for one prepared for all of the Germans of the region, the *Reformatio ecclesiarum Sazonicarum in Transylvania* (Coronae, 1547). The committee which prepared it included the pastors Matthias Glatz and Valentine Wagner, Caspar Helth of Cluj, where the Magyars formed a considerable proportion of the evangelical community, Albert Kirchner from Bistriţa, Lucas Roth from Sighişoara, and Bartholomew Altenberger from Medias who, in 1547 succeeded Ramser as pastor of Sibiu. The adoption of this church order in 1547 indicates the widespread acceptance of the Lutheran reform movement in Transylvaina.

[43] Pitters, 'Siebenbürgische Beziehungen zu Wittenberg', pp. 42–7. H. Scheible, 'Melanchthons Beziehungen zum Donau-Karpaten-Raum bis 1546', in G. and R. Weber (eds), *Luther und Siebenbürgen* (Siebenbürgischen Archiv, 19, 1985), pp. 36–67. W. Toth, 'Luther's Frontier in Hungary', in F. H. Littel (ed.), *Reformation Studies, Essays in Honor of Roland H. Bainton* (Richmond, Va., 1962), pp. 75–91.

[44] L. Binder, 'Johannes Honterus und die Reformation im Süden Siebenbürgens mit besonderer Berücksichtigung der Schweizer und Wittenberger Einflüsse', *Zwingliana*, 13 (1973), 545–587; E. Roth, *Die Reformation in Siebenbürgen, Ihr Verhältnis zu Wittenberg und der Schweiz* (Siebenbürgisches Archiv, 2, 4, 1962, 1964); O. Wittstock, *Johannes Honterus, Der Siebenbürger Humanist und Reformator* (Göttingen, 1970); G. Nussbächer, *Johannes Honterus, Sein Leben und Werk im Bild* (Bucharest, 1971).

The Reformation in Hungary was not, however, just a German movement. During the 1530s and 1540s it began to spread among the Slavs, the Slovaks, Slovenes, and Croats, and also among the Magyars. Here the support of individual members of some of the leading magnate families in the nation was crucial. Among the leading supporters of reformation were members of the Nádasdy, Perényi, Kostka, Révai, Drágffy and Thurzo families. They called evangelicals to serve them as their court preachers and used their patronage rights to install evangelicals as pastors in churches on their estates or in villages and towns under their control. In northern Hungary the Slovaks were drawn to the Reformation by 'windisch' or Slovak preachers appointed by the councils of the cities or by local nobles, for example Stanislaus Koskossinus in Zvolen, John Faber in Žilina and Sulova in north-western Hungary, Paul Kyrmezer, who worked in both upper Hungary and Moravia, Basilius Modenus, George Bohemicus and Paul Huničova who worked in Trenčin county, as well as Caspar Kolarik, Jaroslav Urbanovic and Michael Marček who worked in Orava county.[45]

By the mid 1540s, the Reformation had also begun to attract a few adherents among the Slovenes and Croats in the south-western region of Habsburg Hungary. Bishop Urban Textor of Ljubljana attempted to halt the spread of the Reformation in 1547. Primus Truber was forced to flee to Germany, and Paul Wiener from Ljubljana was imprisoned in Vienna and permanently exiled to Transylvania the following year, 1548, where he eventually became a Senior of the Transylvanian Lutheran clergy. However, while Truber and Hans Ungnad of Sonnegk sought to spread the Reformation among the south Slavs by sending books in their language printed in Germany, their success was limited by the determined opposition of the hierarchy and the political geography of the region.[46]

Many Magyars, including those living in the territory occupied by the Turks, accepted the Reformation, but it made slower progress among them than elsewhere in Hungary. Among the earliest Magyar supporters of reform were the humanist Benedict Komjáthy, the Erasmian Gabriel Pesti Mizsér and John Sylvester, who studied at both Cracow and Witten-

---

[45] D. P. Daniel, 'Highlights of the Lutheran Reformation in Slovakia', *Concordia Theological Quarterly*, 41 (1978), 21–34.
[46] R. Trofenik, *Abhandlungen über die Slowenische Reformation* (Munich, 1968). F. Bucar, *Poviest hrvatske protestantske književnosti za reformacije* (Zagreb, 1910). R. Olesch, 'Südslawische protestantische Drucke des 16. Jahrhunderts', *Zeitschrift für slawische Philologie*, 25 (1956), 381–3. V. Filipović, 'Kroatische Humanisten des 15. und 16. Jahrhunderts', *Südostforschungen*, 17 (1958), 31–41. W. Hočevar, 'Die Anfänge der Reformation auf dem Gebiete des heutigen Jugoslavien', *Zeitschrift für Kirchengeschichte*, 55 (1936), 615–33. B. H. Zimmermann, 'Hans Ungnad, Freiherr von Sonneck als Forderer reformatorischer Bestrebungen bei den Slawen', *Südostforschungen*, 2 (1937), 36–58.

berg. Sylvester returned and taught at schools on the estates of Thomas
Nádasdy until he became professor of Hebrew at Vienna in 1554. In 1541
he published a Hungarian translation of the New Testament at Sárvár.[47]
The careers of other leading figures of Magyar reform, such as Matthias
Dévai Biró, Michael Sztárai and Stephen Szegedi Kis, also demonstrate
the theological eclecticism of the movement. Like so many of the other
first generation of reformers in Hungary, Dévai was influenced principally
by Luther and Melanchthon. Born in Transylvania, he studied at Cracow
and became a member of the Franciscan order. In 1529 he enrolled at
Wittenberg and, after his return to Hungary in 1531, preached in Buda
and in Košice. He published 52 theses defending the theology of the
Reformation as well as an attack on the cult of the saints. Arrested and
taken to Vienna, he defended his views before Bishop John Faber. After
an appeal on his behalf was made by the citizens of Košice he was
released. Years of wandering throughout Hungary followed. Dévai
worked on the estates of Thomas Nádasdy and, after another stay in
Wittenberg, as court preacher for Peter Perényi and then as rector of
Szikszó before returning again briefly to Germany. Then he went to
Miskolc and subsequently lived on the estates of Gáspár Drágffy. His last
home was Debrecen, which became the centre of Hungarian Calvinism,
where he died in 1544.[48]

Dévai was typical of many of the early evangelical reformers in the
eclecticism of his theology. Although he took much from Luther and
Melanchthon, he placed less emphasis on the reality of the physical
presence of the Christ in the sacramental elements of bread and wine
because of his strong opposition to the Mass and the doctrine of transubstantiation. Moreover, because his theology seemed similar to those of the
Helvetic or Sacramentarian reformers, he was criticised by Leonard
Stöckel of Bardejov. In 1544 Luther wrote to the troubled citizens of
Prešov that Dévai had not learned such views at Wittenberg.[49]

Like Dévai, Michael Sztárai was influenced by Luther and
Melanchthon, but was more concerned with practical matters of reform
than with theological formulations. He had been trained in Padua and
had joined the Franciscan order before converting to the cause of the
evangelical Reformation sometime during the 1530s. He worked in the
western half of the region occupied by the Turks where, by his own
account, he founded at least 120 congregations. He was subsequently
elected senior in Laskó and then in Tolna. Because of his conservative

[47] Bucsay, *Geschichte des Protestantismus*, pp. 35–6.
[48] Bucsay, *Geschichte des Protestantismus*, pp. 27–9. J. Sólyom, 'Dévai Mátyás tiszántúli mukodéses', *Egyháztörténete*, 2 (1959), 193–217.
[49] WA Br. X. 555–6 (no. 3984).

liturgical views on the one hand, and his less than precise formulations concerning the presence of the Christ in the Lord's Supper on the other, Sztárai was attacked by the followers of the Swiss reform movement as a Lutheran, by the Lutherans as a Sacramentarian.[50] Stephen Szegedi Kis studied at both Vienna (1535) and Cracow (1537) and worked briefly in Hungary before matriculating at Wittenberg in 1543 where he received his doctorate in theology the following year. Upon his return to Hungary he worked as a schoolmaster before his ordination as pastor for Laskó by Sztárai in 1554.[51] By his death in 1572 he had produced several works (published posthumously) which indicate his affinity for the theology of Heinrich Bullinger, an affinity which was shared by many of his younger contemporary Magyar reformers.[52]

The controversies over the theological positions taken by Dévai and Sztárai and other evangelical reformers in Hungary led to the first evangelical synods held at Oradea Mare in July 1544, at Ardud in 1545 and in Prešov in 1546. The synods indicate that by 1545, as the Reformation clearly had established a foothold in the region, important theological differences among the evangelicals were emerging. They represent the first attempts by the evangelical reformers in Hungary to deal with the problems of theological diversity as they sought to establish basic principles of faith and practice. The participants indicated their agreement to the confession of faith presented at Augsburg in 1530, but they disagreed on the precise formulation of that faith.

After 1548, circumstances in Europe as a whole, and in Hungary in particular, accentuated the differences among the evangelical reformers and provided Ferdinand with an opportunity to halt the Reformation in Hungary. The defeat of the Protestant Schmalkaldic League in Germany at Mühlberg in 1547, the end of the first sessions of the Council of Trent, the passage by the Hungarian diet in 1548 of laws against religious innovations, the growing tensions between Lutherans in Germany as a result of the controversies surrounding the Augsburg Interim, the growing influence of the Swiss Reformation and the Peace of Augsburg in 1555 all contributed to the growth of theological controversies and

[50] Bucsay, *Geschichte des Protestantismus*, pp. 29–30.   [51] *Ibid.*, pp. 30–2.
[52] J. E. Choisy, 'Les relations spirituelles entre Genève et la Hongrie', *Nouvelle Revue de Hongrie*, 2 (1940), 94–100 and 'Genève et la Hongrie protestante', *Revue d'Histoire Comparée*, 5 (1949), 219–22. I. Schlégel, 'Die Beziehungen Heinrich Bullingers zu Ungarn', in W. Hubatsch (ed.), *Wirkungen der Deutschen Reformation bis 1555* (Darmstadt, 1967), pp. 351–9. B. Nagy, 'Geschichte und Bedeutung des Zweiten Helvetischen Bekenntnisses in den Osteuropäischen Länder', in H. Staedtke (ed.), *Glauben und Bekennen, Vierhundert Jahre Confessio Helvetica Posterior. Beiträge zu Ihrer Geschichte und Theologie* (Zürich, 1966), pp. 109–204. S. Juhász, 'Von Luther zu Bullinger. Der theologische Weg der Reformation in den protestantischen Kirchen in Rumänien', *Zeitschrift für Kirchengeschichte*, 81 (1970), 308–33.

ecclesiastical divisions among the evangelicals in Hungary. In 1548, Ferdinand summoned the Diet to meet in Bratislava. Although he did not attend in person (he went instead to the imperial diet in Augsburg), his representatives were able to obtain approval of the first anti-Protestant laws since 1525. The Lutheran party, fearing the influence of both Anabaptism and the Swiss Reformation, joined with the Roman Catholic party to enact an article which decreed the expulsion of Anabaptists and Sacramentarians from the kingdom. Some of the Lutheran cities and magnates, who considered their faith to have been recognised by Ferdinand at the Diet of Augsburg in 1530 (*de facto*, if not *de jure*), did not consider that this law affected them. However, the Roman Catholic hierarchy interpreted the law as ordering the expulsion of all innovators from the kingdom, and prepared to enforce it against the Lutherans as well as against Sacramentarians and Anabaptists. They created commissions of inquiry to conduct visitations to root out the evangelical heresy wherever and in whatever form it appeared, even though Ferdinand had specifically recognised the privileges of the cities in a Diploma of September 11.[53]

In response, the various reformist communities prepared confessions of faith in which they indicated their doctrinal agreement with the Augsburg Confession. They hoped not only to avoid prosecution, but to obtain the toleration extended to the Lutherans in Germany by the Peace of Augsburg of 1555. But, as the evangelicals defined their faith, and sought to establish their identity and integrity, the Lutherans criticised those whose views they considered to be Sacramentarians or Helvetic for not adhering to the unaltered Augsburg Confession, while the latter argued that their views were those expressed by Melanchthon in the modified version of the Confession prepared in 1541. Both groups dissociated themselves from more radical reformers, the Anabaptists and the Antitrinitarians.

Thus by mid-century the evangelical phase of the Reformation in Hungary was over; the era of confessionalisation had just begun. The separation of the evangelicals into distinct denominational groups was only a matter of time. During the second half of the sixteenth century, the reform movements in Hungary continued to be influenced by developments in Germany. Contacts between the second generation of reformers in Hungary and their German and Swiss counterparts increased, and with them the theological differences between Protestant groups in Hungary. To this extent the Reformation in Hungary remained, as it had always been, heavily influenced from Germany. The impetus for reform came from Germany; the first to be attracted to the reform cause were Germans

[53] D. P. Daniel, 'The Lutheran Reformation in Slovakia,' pp. 190–6.

resident in the region, including merchants and smaller entrepreneurs and also younger entrepreneurs influenced by the Renaissance humanism already well established in the region. These advocates of reform acquired the works of Luther and Melanchthon and other German reformers, and sought to establish personal contacts with them. The methods and justifications employed to effect ecclesiastical reform were quite similar to those of the German Reformation.

On the other hand, the Reformation in Hungary should not be considered merely a derivation or extension of the German reform movement. The pressures for reform, the political and ecclesiastical circumstances which shaped its development, and the theological attitudes and formulations of the evangelical reformers in Hungary all contributed to the uniqueness of ecclesiastical reform in sixteenth-century Hungary. In this sense what transpired in Hungary and Germany were inter-connected manifestations of the broader, European-wide Reformation.

SUPPLEMENTARY BIBLIOGRAPHY

Adriányi, G. 'Geschichte und Quellen der ungarischen Kirchengeschichtsschreibung', in G. Adriányi and J. Gottschalk (eds.), *Festschrift für Bernhard Stasiewski, Beiträge zur ostdeutschen und osteuropäischen Kirchengeschichte* (Vienna, 1975), pp. 147–63.

Barton, P. F. *Die Geschichte der Evangelischen in Österreich und Südostmitteleuropa, 1. Im Schatten der Bauernkriege, Die Frühzeit der Reformation*, Studien und Texte zur Kirchengeschichte und Geschichte, 2nd series, X, (Vienna, 1985).

Benda, K. 'La reforme en Hongrie', *Bulletin de la Sociéte de l'Histoire du Protestantisme Français*, 122 (1976), 1–53.

Binder, L. *Die Kirche der Siebenbürger Sachsen* (Erlangen, 1982).
    'Neuere Forschungsergebnisse zur Reformation in der siebenbürgisch-sächsischen Kirche – Darstellung und Kritik', in G. and R. Weber (eds.), *Luther und Siebenbürgen, Ausstrahlungen von Reformation und Humanismus nach Südosteuropa*, Siebenbürgisches Archiv, no. 13 (Cologne, 1985).

Bucasy, M. *Der Protestantismus in Ungarn 1521–1978/ Ungarns Reformationskirchen im Geschichte und Gegenwart. 1. Im Zeitalter der Reformation, Gegenreformation und katholischen Reform* (Vienna, 1977).

Daniel, D. P. *The Historiography of the Reformation in Slovakia*, Sixteenth-Century Bibliography, no. 10 (St Louis, 1977).
    'Výskum obdobia reformácie na Slovensku', *Historický časopis*, 37 (1989), 572–95.

Evans, R. J. W. *The Making of the Habsburg Monarchy, 1500–1700. An Interpretation* (Oxford, 1977).

Fabiny, T. *Hope Preserved. The Past and Present of Hungarian Lutheranism* (Budapest, 1984).

Glettler, M. 'Probleme und Aspekte der Reformation in Ungarn', *Ungarn-Jahrbuch: Zeitschrift für die Kunde Ungarns und verwandte Gebiete*, 10 (1979), 225–39.

Hajduk, A. 'Luther's and Melanchthon's Participation in Theological Disputes in Slovakia', *Communio Viatorum*, 27 (1984), 153–60.

Kann, R. A. *A History of the Habsburg Empire, 1526–1918* (Berkeley, 1974).

Kovács, E. 'Melanchthon und Ungarn', in Melanchthon-Kommittee der Deutschen Demokratischer Republic (ed.), *Philipp Melanchthon 1497–1560. I. Philipp Melanchthon, Humanist, Reformer, Praeceptor Germaniae* (Berlin, 1963), pp. 263–9.

'Die Wirkung der deutschen Reformation auf die Entwicklung der ungarischen Sprache und Literatur', in B. Brentjes and B. Thaler (eds.), *Reformation und Nationalsprachen* (Halle/Saale, 1983), pp. 128–55.

Macartney, C. A. *Hungary: A Short History* (Edinburgh, 1962).

Mészáros, I. *XVI századi városi iskolánik és a 'studia humanitatis'* (Budapest, 1981).

Molnár, A. 'The Riddle of Conrad Cordatus', *Communio Viatorum*, 30 (1987) 23–32.

Pindor, J. *Die evangelische Kirche Kroatien-Slavoniens in Vergangenheit und Gegenwart* (Essig, 1902).

Revész, I. *History of the Hungarian Reformed Church*, transl. by A. F. Knight (Washington, 1956).

Rupel, M. *Primus Truber* (Munich, 1965).

Sólyom, J. *Luther éz Magyarország. A Reformátor kapcsolata hazákkal hálálág* (Budapest, 1924).

Sugar, P. F. *Southeastern Europe under Ottoman rule, 1354–1804* (Seattle, 1977).

Szabo, J. *Der Protestantismus in Ungarn*, transl. by B. Horvath (Berlin, 1927).

Székeley, G. 'Gesellschaft, Kultur und Nationalität in der Lutherischen Reformation in Ungarn', in L. Stern and M. Steinmetz, M. (eds.), *450 Jahre Reformation* (Berlin, 1967).

Szlávik, M. *Die Reformation in Ungarn* (Halle, 1884).

Teutsch, F. *Geschichte der evangelische Kirche in Siebenbürgen* (2 vols., Hermannstadt, 1921–2),

Toth, W. 'Stephen Kis of Szeged, Hungarian Reformer', *ARG*, 44 (1953), 86–103.

Vajcik, P. *Školstvo, študijné a školské poriadky na Slovensku v 16. storoči* (Bratislava, 1955).

Varsik, B. *Husiti a reformácie na Slovensku do žilinskej synodi* (Bratislava, 1932).

Zoványi, J., *A reformáczió Magyarországon 1565-ig* (Budapest, 1922).

4   Switzerland

Bruce Gordon

Reflecting upon the course of the Reformation in 1557, Heinrich Bullinger, successor to Zwingli and leader of the reformed church in Switzerland from 1532 until 1575, presented a gloomy and pessimistic assessment. God had revealed his truth to the German nation in these times and his people had proved themselves ungrateful.[1] The immediate consequence of this infidelity, Bullinger believed, were the dreadful wars between the Emperor and the Protestants ravaging Europe. France, Germany and Italy were engulfed in battles, and Swiss soldiers, despite the persistent opposition of the reform movement to mercenary service, continued to die on foreign territory. Within the Confederation the Protestant cities of Basle and Berne pursued their protracted quarrels with Calvin's Geneva over matters of doctrine and church polity, whilst the Catholics, strengthened by the Council of Trent, were everywhere resurgent.

The despair of the aging reformer at his desk in Zurich accurately reflects the general disappointment among Swiss reformers that the soaring hopes of the first generation had not been fulfilled. The Reformation had not, as Zwingli had originally anticipated, culminated in a unified alliance of evangelical states under the leadership of Zurich. Instead half the Confederation remained defiantly loyal to Catholicism, and even those states which had eventually followed Zurich into the Protestant camp pursued their own models of reform with a stubborn and, at times, cantankerous independence. Any survey of the Reformation in Switzerland should reflect this enduring diversity, a phenomenon which has to some extent been masked by the subsequent success of Zurich and Geneva in impressing their reforming ideals on a wider European movement later in the century. Despite the undoubted success of the later Reform movement, and the important impact of the Zurich reform in southern Germany in the 1520s, it remains the case that nearer home the Swiss Reformation achieved only a very partial victory. The

---

[1] E. Egli (ed.), *Heinrich Bullingers Diarium (Annales vitae) der Jahre 1504–1574*, (rpt. edn., Zurich, 1985), 54.

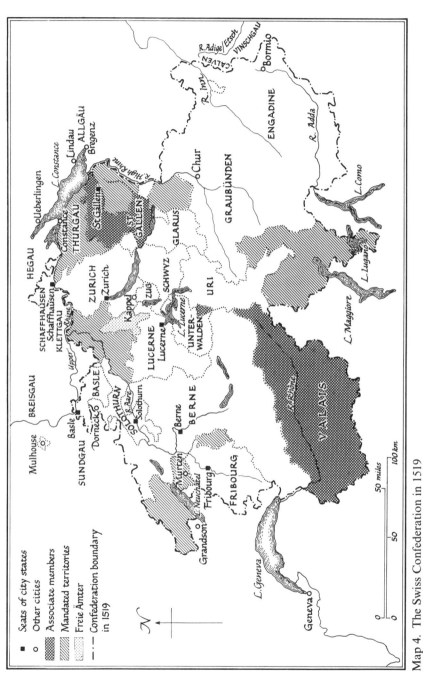

Map 4. The Swiss Confederation in 1519
Source: Thomas Brady, *Turning Swiss* (Cambridge University Press, 1985)

reasons for this lay partly in the unique make-up of the Swiss Confederation, an unusually complex matrix for a great movement of social and religious change. The protracted historical evolution of the Confederation in fact provides many essential clues to explain the course of the Reformation in Switzerland.

The Swiss finally won recognition as a nation with the peace of Basle in 1499, which brought an end to the Swabian War, Emperor Maximillian's disastrous attempt to subdue the recalcitrant confederates.[2] The victory meant for the Swiss the successful conclusion of a struggle against their arch-enemies, the Habsburgs, which had defined the growth of the Swiss Confederation over two centuries. During the fourteenth and fifteenth centuries the Confederation had grown as rural territories and city states had come together for mutual protection against Habsburg hegemony. The fifteenth century had been the golden age of the Swiss soldier as foreign rulers learned the wisdom of eschewing military conflict with the confederates in favour of paying for their mercenary service. Yet this period of expansion, which ended with the defeat of the Swiss mercenaries at Marignano in 1515, masked serious internal weaknesses. Little was accomplished, for example, to consolidate with central institutions the web of alliances which developed as territories entered the Confederation. The Swiss Confederation at the end of the Middle Ages presented two faces: the rural leagues devoted to principles of communal rule free from feudal overlordship, and the increasingly powerful urban oligarchies desirous of extending their control over the rural hinterlands. It was an uneasy alliance in which the rural territories, composed mostly of peasant farmers and mountain villagers, resented the encroachment of the urban powers with their plans for a more centralised alliance.[3]

This collision of interests within the alliance was manifested in the Old Zurich War of 1436–44, as Zurich attempted, as it would again in the 1520s, to counter the expansion of Berne in the west by subjugating the rural areas of eastern Switzerland. On this occasion soldiers from Schwyz, Uri and Unterwalden outmanoeuvred the Zurich army and brought a humiliating defeat upon the city.[4] Nevertheless, Zurich's imperial aspirations remained an enduring feature of Swiss politics for the next hundred years; the reactions of Zurich's weaker rural neighbours to the Reformation were in part conditioned by a fear that Zwingli's evangelical overtures concealed deeper political purposes.

[2] Still the best history of Switzerland in English is E. Bonjour, H. S. Offler and G. R. Potter, *A Short History of Switzerland* (Oxford, 1952).
[3] From 1513 until the French Revolution there were thirteen states: Uri, Schwyz, Unterwalden, Zug, Glarus, Appenzell (rural): Lucerne, Berne, Zurich, Basle, Schaffhausen, Friborg, Solothurn (urban).
[4] Bonjour, *Short History*, p. 113.

If the absence of coherent political institutions was an impediment to concerted action, so too was the condition of the ecclesiastical structures within the Confederation. Late medieval Switzerland was divided into six dioceses: Basle, Chur, Constance, Geneva, Lausanne and Sitten. Of these Sitten was the only purely Swiss; the rest were a mixture of foreign and Confederate territories. Not all of the bishops of the pre-Reformation and Reformation period were averse to reform: Christoph von Utenheim of Basle, Hugo von Hohenlandenberg of Constance, and Aimon von Mont-falçon and his nephew Sebastian in Lausanne attempted to effect reforms by means of revisions of liturgical books and a series of synods intended to root out the endemic evils of pluralism, sexual immorality and the neglect of duties among the clergy.[5] Yet these pre-Reformation efforts at reform failed, largely, it seems, as a result of resistance by the lower clergy. The breakdown in the discipline of the church manifested itself in refusal to pay taxes, non-attendance at the synods, clerical concubinage,[6] and a rejection of the jurisdiction of episcopal courts. That many of the bishops were not themselves Swiss only aggravated the problems. The scope of the bishops for action was greatly diminished where they were under the control of secular rulers (Lausanne and Geneva), or were locked in conflict with powerful civil governments (Constance, Chur and Basle). The 'revolutions' which transformed the Swiss cities in the fifteenth century brought in governments drawn from the guild classes which resented the separate authority of the church.[7] Distant church courts, canon law, and religious orders which appealed to foreign authorities were anathema to the new civic order based upon the idea of the sacral community. There were several means by which a ruling council could break the control of the church within its walls: the abolition of clerical exemptions from its legal jurisdiction, the prohibition of marriage appeals to episcopal courts, the absorption of religious houses and, importantly, the acquisition of the rights of presentation to benefices. Religious houses were particularly vulnerable by virtue of the serious decline in their spiritual life in this period.

[5] For an overview of the Swiss bishoprics, G. May, *Die deutschen Bischöfe angesichts der Glaubensspaltung des 16. Jahrhunderts* (Vienna, 1983). Basle pp. 19–29, Lausanne pp. 29–36, Chur pp. 261–70, Constance pp. 299–313, Sitten, pp. 599–609.
[6] Although this was an endemic problem of the pre-Reformation church, in Switzerland this practice received semi-official sanction through the payment of concubinage fees. The practice became so general that these fees made up an important part of the bishops' income. See O. Vasella, *Reform und Reformation in der Schweiz* (Münster, 1958), pp. 26–32. Heinrich Bullinger was himself the offspring of such a clerical union: his father was organist and priest in the rural town of Bremgarten. F. Blanke and I. Leuschner, *Heinrich Bullinger. Vater der reformierten Kirche* (Zurich, 1990), pp. 11–33.
[7] B. Moeller, *Imperial Cities and the Reformation* (Philadelphia, 1972); for Zurich, G. R. Potter, *Zwingli* (Cambridge, 1976), pp. 47–52.

Over against the malaise of the institutional church was the vitality of traditional lay piety.[8] Altars, shrines, relics, indulgences, church-building and pilgrimages abounded in Switzerland. Devotion directed towards relics was particularly strong. In 1488 the council of Zug sent a request to Peterborough, Northamptonshire, for a relic of St Oswald in order to consecrate its own church to the saint.[9] Pilgrimages were a central spiritual exercise of communities and individuals; if travel to the Holy Land was not possible, there were important locations for the Swiss in their own lands, such as the 'Black Virgin' at the Benedictine house at Einsiedeln. Until 1524 there was an annual pilgrimage from Zurich to Einsiedeln at Pentecost, and Notre Dame de Grâce in Geneva remained a place of pilgrimage in the west for women who had given birth to still-born children.[10] The enduring hold of these forms of piety helped to secure the rural peasantry of the inner states against the Reformation and complicated the implementation of reforms in the countryside of the Protestant territories. Interestingly such lay piety was frequently accompanied by intense anticlerical sentiments; there are fascinating examples of this conjunction in the *Fastnacht* festivals held on the eve of Lent, with their sharp criticisms of abuse in the church.[11]

Balancing this lay piety was a powerful commitment to the new learning. Basle, having entered the Confederation in 1501, with its university (1459) and printers stood among the foremost humanist centres of Europe. As the only university in the Confederation, almost all Swiss students seeking education in theology, arts or jurisprudence came to the city for at least part of their studies. This had the effect of creating a scholarly network throughout Switzerland which partook, in varying degrees, in the humanist programme, and later in reformed humanism. The focal point of this network was Erasmus, for whom Switzerland was almost a second home.[12] Erasmian humanism, with its interest in the recovery of patristic works, in establishing the true text of scripture and its criticisms of ecclesiastical corruption, greatly influenced a whole generation of men who became leaders of the Reformation in Switzerland.[13] Many of these men were non-Swiss drawn to Basle by Erasmus, and they continued to esteem their master well after his break with their movement.

[8] A. Hauser, *Was für ein Leben. Schweizer Alltag vom 15. bis 18. Jahrhundert* (Zurich, 1988), esp. pp. 119–32.
[9] Hauser, *Schweizer Alltag*, p. 121.   [10] *Ibid.*, p. 123.
[11] On the important role of festivals in the Reformation see R. W. Scribner, 'Reformation, Carnival and the World turned Upside Down', in his *Popular Culture and Popular Movements in Germany* (London, 1987), pp. 71–101.
[12] Erasmus first came to Basle in 1514, when he began his celebrated association with the publishing house of Johannes Froben. After returning to the Netherlands in 1517, he settled in Basle once more in 1521, and again in 1534, shortly before his death.
[13] R. Pfister, *Kirchengeschichte der Schweiz* (3 vols., Zurich, 1963–85), II. 15–18.

Yet humanism took another form in the Confederation which likewise exerted a formative influence upon the Reformation. This was the patriotic humanism which sought to develop in Switzerland an intellectual utopia, or *respublica litteraria*, in which the muses might flourish in peace, free from war.[14] Flushed with optimism after the Swabian War, this movement took several forms. Among the most important was the development of historical writing in the service of formulating a national consciousness. There were strong traditions, particularly in Berne, of local histories extolling the liberties of the city and portraying the growth of the urban guild classes in Renaissance terms of nation building and individualism. Heinrich Brennwald (1478–1551), with his account of the Confederation from earliest times, was perhaps the most important exponent of employing historical writing to express the distinctiveness of the Swiss from the Germans. Also of note is Valerius Anselm (d. 1547), who was among the foremost historians who brought the historical craft into the Reformation cause by detailing Swiss history in terms of the unfolding divine will. These humanists did much to enhance a sense of self-identity among the Swiss in a period of political and religious upheaval, and the overtly political nature of their work, including the rejection of mercenary service and of foreign pensions, accorded well with the increasingly influential middle classes governing the cities.

The serenity of this humanist world in Switzerland was shattered by the tumult unleashed by Martin Luther. The relationship between Luther and the Swiss Reformation remains a controversial issue.[15] The publication of Luther's works in Basle, where the Ninety-Five Theses were printed in 1517 and other Latin works followed in 1518, ensured the widespread dissemination of his ideas in the Confederation; Vadianus, the reformer of St Gall, and Michael Eggenstorfer, the abbot of All Saints in Schaffhausen, were both early and prominent supporters. Even the bishop of Basle, Christoph von Utenheim, under the influence of Jakob Wimpfeling of Strasburg, believed that the Wittenberg professor ought to be treated with mercy. The proclamation of the Edict of Worms in 1521 thus placed the rulers of many Swiss territories in a quandary; on the one hand they had to distinguish between the Gospel preaching, which many were

---

[14] K. Maeder, *Die Via Media in der Schweizerischen Reformation. Studien zum Problem der Kontinuität in Zeitalter der Glaubensspaltung* (Zurich, 1970), pp. 37–54. G. W. Locher, *Die Zwinglische Reformation in Rahmen der europäischen Kirchengeschichte* (Göttingen, 1979), pp. 42–54. L. von Muralt, 'Renaissance und Reformation in der Schweiz', *Zwingliana*, 11 (1959), 1–23. Von Muralt gives the most comprehensive account of the forms of humanism in Switzerland.

[15] Maeder, *Via Media*, 54–68. For an examination of the difficult question of Zwingli's relationship with Luther see J. Stayer, 'Zwingli and the "Viri Multi et Excellentes"', in E. J. Furcha and W. W. Pipkin (eds.), *Prophet, Pastor, Protestant. The Work of Huldrych Zwingli after Five Hundred Years* (Allison Park, Pa., 1984), pp. 137–54.

prepared to sanction, and on the other, overtly 'Lutheran' doctrines. In the end they refused to accept the edict, but at the same time they also shied away from condoning Luther.

To the ruling councils, the distinction between true preaching from the Bible and heresy was extremely murky. It was in Zurich that this ambiguity was first resolved, largely through the activity of Switzerland's great reformer, Huldrich Zwingli. Zwingli played a pivotal role in shaping and guiding the Swiss Reformation.[16] It was his theological clarity and political acumen which advanced the reforms in Zurich and propelled the city into the front ranks of the Reformation. Zwingli understood 'reformation' to mean the reform of the community or congregation. The agents of reform were the magistrates. Since human communities reformed by the Word of God were to reflect the divine law by which they were governed, there could be no distinction between the religious and political life of the community; to belong to the state was to belong to the church. Thus political authority was accorded a divine function as the magistrates were charged with administering justice in accordance with Scriptural authority, and further, they were responsible for the spiritual welfare of their people. The end of society in Zwingli's terms was continual self-renewal and service on earth rather than a preoccupation with individual salvation. It was an appealing manifesto for the godly magistrate.[17]

The most decisive events of the early Reformation in Switzerland were the disputations or synods held in Zurich in 1522–3.[18] With the magistrates of the council presiding, Zwingli debated questions concerning legitimate preaching, the role of religious images and the competence of civil magistrates to rule on doctrinal questions. These disputations were crucial to Zwingli's developing theology, since it was during the course of the debates that Zwingli discovered his model of church government in which ruling councils could render decisions on questions previously reserved for general church councils and universities.[19] The disputations did not yet mark Zurich's break from Rome which came officially with the new liturgy for the Lord's Supper celebrated at Easter in 1525, but the direction of events was clear. With the establishment of a legitimate basis for reformation, Zwingli and the council could proceed towards the

[16] On Zwingli and the early Swiss Reformation G. R. Potter, *Zwingli* (Cambridge, 1976) remains the best source of information in English.
[17] Robert Walton, *Zwingli's Theocracy* (Toronto, 1967). On Zwingli's theology, G. W. Locher, *Zwingli's Thought. New Perspectives*, (Leiden, 1981), pp. 142–232. A more detailed treatment is W. P. Stephens, *The Theology of Huldrych Zwingli* (Oxford, 1986).
[18] Potter, *Zwingli*, pp. 97–104.
[19] H. A. Oberman, *Masters of the Reformation. The Emergence of a New Intellectual Climate in Europe* (Cambridge, 1981), pp. 210–39. Oberman provides the most provocative and convincing interpretation of the disputations.

replacement of the Mass (1525) and the introduction of evangelical institutions.[20]

These events in Zurich had a profound effect throughout the Confederation. In the first decade the Reformation made rapid progress throughout Switzerland, as Zwingli's message was carried far afield by evangelical preachers and laymen. Evangelically minded ministers were active in Berne (George Brunner and Berthold Haller), St Gall (Johannes Kessler and Balthasar Hubmaier), Appenzell (Johannes Dörig), Glarus (Fridolin Brunner), Schaffhausen (Sebastion Hofmeister and Michael Eggenstorfer) and Basle (Johannes Oecolampadius).[21] Yet the other urban cantons did not immediately follow Zurich in a formal declaration for the evangelical cause. In Basle and Berne the reform party was frustrated by the presence of strong elements within the councils hostile to the Reformation. It was therefore in the rural areas that the Reformation made some of its most startling early advances. Most notable were Appenzell, Glarus, the Thurgau and Graubünden, into whose remote valleys individual preachers travelled and won over such communities as Flasch, Malans and Davos.[22] The disruption of the delicate balance of the Swiss Confederation caused by the spread of the Reformation in the first years is evident from events in the Thurgau, a mandated territory.[23] The Zwinglian preachers found receptive audiences in the region, feeding off the local anti-clerical and anti-feudal sentiments. Gospel preaching was embraced, and it was interpreted as supporting non-payment of tithes and iconoclasm. Zwingli's teachings on the right of individal communities to choose their own minister also accorded well with aspirations for local autonomy. The evangelical agitation reached its climax with the sacking of the monastery at Ittingen in July 1524 by peasant farmers, a blatant act of iconoclasm for which the Catholic territories held Zurich responsible.[24]

All of this was of course deeply disturbing to traditional forces within the Confederation. The initially hesitant reaction of the Catholic states to

[20] Potter, *Zwingli, passim.* Other useful works on the progress of the Reformation in Zurich are Locher, *Zwinglische Reformation,* pp. 123–96. Walton, *Zwingli's Theocracy;* and his 'The Institutionalization of the Reformation at Zurich', *Zwingliana,* 13 (1972), 497–515. H. C. Rublack, 'Zwingli und Zurich', *Zwingliana,* 16 (1985), 393–423.
[21] For brief summaries of the development of the Reformation in each of the Swiss territories see Pfister, *Kirchengeschichte,* II, pp. 70–168.
[22] An outline of the Reformation in the Graubünden can be found in B. R. Barber, *The Death of Communal Liberty. A History of Freedom in a Swiss Mountain Canton* (Princeton, 1974), pp. 50–4.
[23] These were territories within the Confederation governed jointly by the Catholic and Evangelical states. Naturally this joint governance became a sore point in the Reformation as both parties strove to bring these lands within their sphere of influence. The territories were the Freie Ämter, Thurgau, Baden, the Rheintal, Gaster, and the Italian regions Lugano, Bellizona and Locarno.
[24] Potter, *Zwingli,* pp. 144–9.

the spread of the Reformation partly reflected the weakness of its central institutions. The diet (*Tagsatzung*) had little power to enforce its decisions upon individual states, and when the Catholic states attempted in 1524 to have Zurich, Schaffhausen and Appenzell excluded from their meetings on grounds of their heresy, Berne and Basle argued that the alliance was legal and political and did not extend to religious matters. Doctrinal questions had never before been debated by the Swiss states, and it was clear that the diet was an inadequate forum for the resolution of the crisis. Yet ultimately the Reformation failed to capitalise on this institutional stalemate. From 1525 it was increasingly clear that, despite the strong lead from Zurich, the Reformation would not carry all before it.

The strongest opposition came from the inner rural members, Uri, Schwyz, Unterwalden, Zug and from Lucerne. A number of reasons for this have already been suggested, notably the strength of Catholicism in the rural areas and the traditional fear of Zurich hegemony. The rulers in these territories were not uninterested in church reform. In 1525 the Catholic states signed an agreement (*Glaubenskonkordat*) outlining proposals for clerical reform and the improvement of the peasants' lot. There was even talk of a general council to be held in Switzerland to resolve the religious question. Nevertheless, these initiatives alone do not suffice to explain the inability of the Reformation to penetrate the inner states.[25] Rather, in the years 1525–6, the Reformation in Switzerland, as in Germany, entered a period of crisis which placed evangelicals on the defensive and gave traditional forces a chance to focus their opposition to Zurich-led change.

The Peasants' Revolt in Switzerland was relatively bloodless in comparison with events in southern Germany and Alsace. Although the unrest in 1525 was unusually widespread, peasant revolts were part of a long established tradition in Swiss lands, and the political authorities were therefore sufficiently experienced to be able to deal with the disturbances peacefully.[26] In January of 1525 the Swiss Diet decided to investigate the complaints of the poor, and a mandate was drafted in order to defuse the economic, political and religious agitations behind the revolt. Thus it was clear fairly early on that there was not going to be a bloody uprising. The peasants of the Basle countryside marched to the city walls expecting support from the guilds only to be turned away disappointed; likewise, the activities of peasants in other areas soon ceased. In general,

[25] Neither can one readily accept Peter Blickle's thesis that communal control over the Reformation in these areas was so complete that the evangelical movement was rendered unnecessary. See the penetrating criticism of the Blickle thesis in Tom Scott, 'The Common People in the German Reformation', *HJ*, 34 (1991).

[26] T. A. Brady, *Turning Swiss: Cities and Empire 1450–1550* (Cambridge, 1985), pp. 29–33. Brady argues that the alliance of urban and rural communities in the Confederation produced around sixty rural uprisings between 1336 and 1525.

the lot of the Swiss peasant compared favourably to that of his German neighbours, and the disintegration of the feudal order in the Confederation during the Middle Ages had removed the noble class, so much the focal point of peasant hatred in Germany.[27] Nevertheless, the unrest posed serious questions for Zwingli as his name was frequently invoked by the rebellious peasantry. He counselled the Zurich magistrates to be compassionate but firm on questions of the payment of tithes and the care of the poor. On the tithes question he could not allow antinomian behaviour and advocated obedience to established authorities. Change could only be effected by the godly magistrates.

The revolt also brought into sharp relief the relationship between the Reformation in Switzerland and events in Germany. Swabia and the Upper Rhine were the natural trading partners of the Swiss, and from an early stage the religious events in the Confederation had a considerable resonance within the Empire. The regions along the Swiss–German border were particularly sensitive as the peasant armies of Hegau and the Black Forest looked to their southern neighbours for support.[28] Zurich, Basle and Schaffhausen could not risk a war with the Habsburgs, and confined their role to that of mediators attempting to negotiate peace treaties in the hope of avoiding further massacres. In the end, the Peasants' War proved two points: that the reformers had no intention of altering the structures of society, and that, while the Swiss had become the effective religious leaders in southern Germany, they could not hope to expand their influence without an effective political alliance with the other opponents of the Habsburgs, the free imperial cities. The revolt had also inflamed relations between the Lutheran and Zwinglian theologians in southern Germany, with the Lutherans attempting to link 'sacramentarianism' with the rebellion in order to heighten the princes' fear of the Swiss model.[29]

The advent of religious radicalism in Switzerland in 1525 underscored the danger that the reformers working with the magistrates might lose control of the movement, a danger all the more apparent with the first

[27] P. Blickle, *The Revolution of 1525. The German Peasants' War from a new Perspective* (Baltimore, 1981), pp. 66–7.
[28] For an excellent case study which draws out the complexity of the relationship between the Swiss and developments in Upper Swabia during the revolt, T. Scott, 'Reformation and Peasants' War in Waldshut and Environs: A Structural Analysis', *ARG*, 69 (1978), 82–102; and *ARG*, 70 (1979), 140–69. A very different interpretation is found in P. Blickle, 'Zurichs Anteil am deutschen Bauernkrieg. Die Vorstellung der göttlichen Rechts im Klettgau', *Zeitschrift für die Geschichte des Oberrheins*, 133 (1985), 81–101.
[29] This pejorative tag 'sacramentalist' was employed by Luther and his followers to denote those reformers who denied Christ's corporeal presence in the elements of bread and wine. Luther lumped together the radical Karlstadt with both Zwingli and Oecolampadius as fanatics (*Schwärmer*). H. A. Oberman, *Luther, Man between God and the Devil* (New Haven, 1989), pp. 232–45. On the Swiss model see Brady, *Turning Swiss*, pp. 191–9.

stirrings of Swiss Anabaptism.[30] Although the first adult baptism took place in Zurich only in January 1525, the roots of dissent extended back to the disputations of 1522–3. A group of humanist-minded former priests had then gathered around Konrad Grebel; they objected that Zwingli had compromised the Reformation by bowing to the will of political authorities. They sought to carry through the full logic of the reforms begun in Zurich by freeing the movement from the contamination of worldly authorities. Although expelled from Zurich in 1525, the influence of these radical reformers spread quickly, penetrating into St Gall, Berne, Basle, Appenzell, and further into the Empire. The radicals made headway particularly in the towns and rural areas of north-eastern Switzerland where the Peasants' Revolt had shaken the traditional structures of authority.[31] Swiss Anabaptism was by no means uniform. Although the movement led by Konrad Grebel was essentially pacifist, others, such as Wilhelm Reublin in Schaffhausen and Hans Krüsi in Appenzell and St Gall, linked the cause with peasant unrest by rebaptising communities and supporting anti-tithe riots. The Schleitheim Confession of 1527 marked an important stage in the consolidation of the movement, and emphatically reaffirmed the Anabaptist rejection of civil authority over the church.[32]

The radical challenge forced Zwingli and other reformers to delineate more clearly their vision of the Christian society. Most notably, there was a greater urgency to formulate sacramental theology and define the role of the magistrates. In this respect the radicals' rejection of political authority provided the reformers with a useful pretext to unleash against them the full authority of the civil power. In 1527 the first Anabaptist martyrs were put to death in Zurich.[33] Nevertheless, the enduring strength of the radicals in the rural areas ensured that they remained a thorn in the side of the urban reformers throughout the sixteenth century.

The Reformation in Zurich survived this dual crisis comparatively unscathed, but inevitably this evidence of the radicalism and disorder which followed evangelical reform was a further encouragement to conservative forces to harden resistance to religious change. The Colloquy of Baden in 1526 demonstrated that Catholic forces in Switzerland were increasingly effectively marshalled in opposition to the Reformation.[34] Zurich was the enemy, and Zwingli was the heretic: the Catholic states

[30] Potter, *Zwingli*, pp. 160–97. J. M. Stayer, *Anabaptists and the Sword* (2nd edn., Lawrence, Kan., 1976), pp. 91–132. M. Mattmüller, 'Die Basler Täufer', *Zwingliana*, 12 (1967), 511–21. D. L. Gratz, *Bernese Anabaptists* (Scottdale, Pa., 1953), pp. 1–29. On Conrad Grebel, see Harold S. Bender, *Conrad Grebel c. 1498–1526, The Founder of the Swiss Brethren* (Goschen, Ind., 1950).
[31] Stayer, *Anabaptists*, pp. 108–9.   [32] *Ibid.*, pp. 118–22.
[33] A. Snyder, 'Biblical text and Social Context: Anabaptist Anticlericalism in Reformation Zurich', *Mennonite Quarterly Review*, 65 (1991), 169–91.
[34] On the Baden Colloquy see Potter, *Zwingli*, pp. 230–9.

argued for the connection between faith and the political structure of the Confederation, and from 1524 they refused to meet in the same diet with Zurich or its supporters. The neutral positions of the powerful states Berne and Basle became untenable in a dispute which was tearing Switzerland apart.

During the 1520s the government in Berne had pursued a cautious policy. The slow pace of the Reformation in the city reflected the divergence of Bernese interests from those of Zurich. For Berne, it was the French-speaking lands in the west, particularly the Vaud, which were its natural sphere of influence. Berne had retained a pro-French policy, an alliance especially favoured by the patriciate, who reaped the financial rewards of mercenary service. In addition, Berne controlled a large area of German-speaking territory known as the Oberland, full of rustic peasants in remote valleys, who would forcefully resist imposition of the new faith.[35] The Bernese council attempted to tread the path between the two camps in the religious dispute; its mandates on church matters reflected a desire to adopt certain aspects of the Reformation without abandoning the Catholic faith. Consequently, the council pleased no one.[36] Within Switzerland it defended Zurich's right to remain part of the Confederation, but it had little taste for any religious alliance dominated by its rival. The major problem for the Reformation was that Berne lacked a reformer of the stature of Zwingli or Oecolampadius. Berthold Haller was a fine man, but he did not possess the forcefulness to overcome resistance in the church and council. It was not until the Easter elections of 1527 returned a majority of councillors favourable towards the Reformation that action was possible.[37] A disputation was arranged in order that the Bernese magistrates might rule on the introduction of reforms.

The Disputation of Berne, held from 6–26 January 1528, was the high point of the early Swiss Reformation.[38] By facilitating the transfer to the evangelical camp of this, the most powerful of the Swiss city states, it effectively secured the evangelical cause in Switzerland. Zurich could not stand alone forever; now with the acceptance of the Reformation in Berne many of the lesser cities and rural territories, in which there were significant reform movements, were carried in its wake. In those rural territories not under the jurisdiction of urban councils, a slightly different pattern emerged. In Glarus, Appenzell and the Graubünden the religious situation was settled by allowing individual communities to choose their

---

[35] P. Bierbauer, *Freiheit und Gemeinde in Berner Oberland, 1300–1700* (Berne, 1991), pp. 245–80.
[36] K. Guggisberg, *Bernische Kirchengeschichte* (Berne, 1958), pp. 84–9.
[37] Guggisberg, *Bernische Kirchengeschichte*, pp. 97–100.
[38] D. L. Hendricks, 'The Berne Disputation: Some Observations', *Zwingliana*, 14 (1978), 565–73. Potter, *Zwingli*, pp. 253–62.

confessional allegiance. The missionary work of itinerant evangelical preachers, supported by Zurich, was crucial to the success of the Reformation in these areas.[39]

With the victory at Berne the question of Basle's hesitation came to the fore. Zwingli's colleague and good friend, Johannes Oecolampadius, had begun in 1523 to set down the challenge for reform.[40] Basle was always the Swiss city most receptive to influences from Germany, and Oecolampadius' links with Müntzer, Karlstadt, Hubmaier and others confirmed him in Luther's mind as one of the fanatics. Nevertheless, he won a strong following in the city, but, like Haller in Berne, he shied away from leading a strong attack on the Catholic forces gathered around the bishop and the inner core of the council. In Basle, unlike in Zurich and Berne, there was no political shift within the council allowing pro-reform magistrates to take over and see through the introduction of the Reformation.[41] Instead the council desperately tried to placate both sides with endless compromises, such as the division of churches, in order to avoid strife. The influence of Erasmian humanism was everywhere in evidence. It was only the relentless pressure exerted by the guilds and the real danger of popular unrest which finally forced the council to a decision. Many of the humanists fled the city as images were burnt in February 1529. The prospect of bloodshed and insurrection propelled the magistrates to adopt the Reformation and end Catholic worship on the first of April.

The Catholic states knew that they could not overcome the combined forces of Zurich, Berne and Basle. They were, however, determined to prevent the spread of the Reformation into the mandated territories whose governance they shared with the evangelical states. It was in these mandated territories that the explosive activities leading to the First Kappel War took place. The Thurgau was effectively evangelised by Zurich, which supervised its reforming synod of 1529. The activities of Zwinglian ministers in the Freie Ämter, a small piece of land wedged between Zurich and Berne, led to sporadic acts of iconoclasm which exacerbated an extremely tense situation. On the one side the evangelical states attempted to usurp Catholic authority in these mandated territories by denying them their turn to appoint governors, whilst on the other the Catholic states severely punished ministers who attempted to spread evangelical ideas among their people.

[39] On the Reformation in the Graubünden see W. Klaasen, *Michael Gaismair Revolutionary and Reformer* (Leiden, 1978).

[40] G. Rupp, 'Johannes Oecolampadius. The Reformer as Scholar', in *Patterns of Reformation* (London, 1969), pp. 3–48. The standard work on Oecolampadius remains E. Staehelin, *Das theologische Lebenswerk Johannes Oekolampads* (2 vols., Leipzig, 1939).

[41] R. Wackernagel, *Geschichte der Stadt Basel*, III (Basle, 1924). H. R. Guggisberg, *Basel in the Sixteenth Century* (St Louis, 1982), pp. 19–25. Again, Rupp's *Patterns* provides a useful account of the early Basle Reformation. Locher, *Zwinglische Reformation*, p. 367.

In the end, it was the burning of an evangelical minister, Jakob Kaiser, by the Catholic authorities in Schwyz and Glarus which prompted the long expected war within the Confederation. Zurich declared war against the Catholic states on 8 June 1529 and commenced a campaign which lasted less than three weeks. The First Kappel War, as it became known, did not evolve into a protracted civil war because Zurich's allies, principally Berne and Basle, had little enthusiasm for military action designed to establish its supremacy, because the Catholic states received no assistance from the Habsburgs, and because Berne played a mediating role, successfully heading off any conflict by negotiating the First Peace of Kappel.[42] The terms of the treaty are important: the Catholics were forced to allow the mandated territories to choose their faith, and they had to abandon their alliance with the Habsburgs; the Catholic and evangelical states were no longer to meet in separate diets, and there was to be no coercion of faith. The resolution amounted to a surrender by the Catholic states, who were overpowered by their adversaries, but it was not a complete defeat. Zurich had clearly wanted to force these lands to adopt the evangelical faith, and the acceptance of a treaty recognising a division within the Confederation between the two religions was a blow to Zwingli's ambitions. Further, Zurich was only to receive minimal war compensation. Instead of waging war on the inner states, the Reformed cities chose to impose an economic blockade in the hope of forcing them to submit.

The First Kappel Peace was a bitter pill for Zwingli and the leaders of Zurich, not least because it thwarted their plans for a reformation of the whole Confederation and an alliance with Protestant movements within the Empire against Charles V. This idea of a united Protestant front was not wholly unreasonable given the pervasive influence of Zwingli's urban theology in southern Germany.[43] Against the threat of Habsburg hegemony Zwinglianism represented, in contrast to the negative politics of Luther, a coherent political and religious order appropriate to the needs of the urban classes. 'Wherever the political struggle between old and new wealth, between entrenched patricians and guilds, had not yet reached a final settlement', writes Thomas Brady, 'Zwinglianism went hand-in-hand with anti-patrician, anti-aristocratic sentiments and provocations – thus tying the age of the guild revolts to that of the Reformation – and sometimes ended in a wholesale flight of the urban aristocracy'.[44] For the

---

[42] Potter, *Zwingli*, pp. 368–9.
[43] An influence highlighted by much of the recent literature on the German urban Reformation. See particularly Brady, *Turning Swiss*, Blickle, *Gemeindereformation*, Goertz, *Pfaffenhaß und groß Geschrei* (Munich, 1987).
[44] T. H. Brady, *Ruling Class, Regime and Reformation in Strasburg 1520–1555* (Leiden, 1978), p. 238.

German cities the Swiss Reformation represented an ideal of republicanism and the sacral community. Zwinglian preachers moved north into the major cities of Germany and established parties which did much to counter Lutheran influence. From 1524 Strasburg began looking for an alliance with the Swiss. The period before the First Kappel War saw the formation of an alliance of evangelical cities in Switzerland known as the Christian Civic Union. When in 1529 the Strasburgers joined the Christian Civic Union there was great hope that they would be followed by Ulm, Memmingen, Nördlingen, Biberach and others.[45]

Within the Empire the idea of a grand alliance with the Swiss was championed by Philip of Hesse following his union of Saxony, Ulm, Strasburg and Nuremberg at the Diet of Speyer in 1529.[46] But a political alliance between the German and Swiss parties also required doctrinal agreement between the Lutherans and Zwinglians. The sticking point was, of course, the difference between Luther and Zwingli on the matter of the Lord's Supper. The famous confrontation between the two reformers at Marburg in 1529 effectively scuttled hopes for a political alliance.[47] The attempts of Bucer and Capito to foster concord were in vain as they failed to appreciate that Luther and Zwingli essentially regarded one another as heretical on this point.[48]

The failure of Marburg had serious implications for the Swiss. The German cities, faced with mounting political pressures, were increasingly forced to take refuge in the Lutheran camp. From a purely political viewpoint, a Swiss alliance had limited attractions: the Swiss could not provide them with military protection, and crucially, such an alliance could never be very firm as the inner states would not agree to the German cities joining the Confederation. Berne, too, had demonstrated a distinct lack of interest in German affairs. Such an alliance would thus be dependent upon Zurich, and Zurich had shown herself incapable of subduing the relatively weak Catholic states. Thus even before the disastrous Second Kappel War (1531) the Swiss were being moved increasingly to the periphery of German affairs.

The immediate cause of the Second Kappel War was the economic blockade of the inner states by the evangelical states.[49] In truth, however,

[45] Locher, *Zwinglische Reformation*, pp. 452–501. On the negotiations between the Strasburgers and the Swiss, Brady, *Ruling Class*, pp. 236–45.
[46] R. Hauswirth, 'Landgraf Philipp von Hessen und Zwingli. Ihre politischen Beziehungen 1529/30', *Zwingliana*, 11 (1962), 499–551.
[47] The classic study of Marburg is in W. Köhler, *Zwingli und Luther* (Gütersloh, 1953), pp. 1–163. C.f. Potter, *Zwingli*, chs. 12 and 13.
[48] J. Kittelson, 'Martin Bucer and the Sacramentarian Controversy: The Origins of his Policy of Concord', *ARG*, 64 (1973), 166–83.
[49] H. Meyer, *Der Zweite Kappeler Krieg Die Krise der Schweizerischen Reformation* (Zurich, 1976), pp. 15–67, 111–39.

Zurich was humiliated by the first treaty and was determined to crush the Catholics. By September 1531 the inner states had decided to fight rather than starve, and by 10 October a combined force was moving north towards Zurich. Glarus declared itself neutral and Berne announced that it would only participate in a defensive action. Zurich, always the aggressor, seemed strangely caught unawares, and its leaders were slow to grasp the urgency of the situation. An army was belatedly sent out from the city and made its way towards Kappel. Zwingli accompanied this motley group which was surprised and beaten in a nocturnal rout in which the reformer was killed. A further skirmish between the Catholic forces and troops from Basle, Schaffhausen and St Gall similarly ended in disaster for the evangelical forces.

The defeated Protestants were now forced to sue for peace. The Second Kappel Treaty, signed on November 24 1531, had far-reaching importance for the shaping of the Reformation and modern Switzerland. The most significant provision was the declaration that each state was to decide upon its confession and was forbidden from attempting to force it on another. The evangelical states were prohibited from promoting evangelical ministers in Catholic lands, and the mandated territories of Gaster, Weesen, Sargans, Bremgarten, Mellingen and the Freie Ämter were returned to the Catholic fold.[50] The first treaty was annulled and the Christian Civic Union abolished, thus severing the Swiss evangelical cities from Germany. In the Thurgau, which had been so much in the centre of controversy, individual communities were to be allowed to choose their confession. This principle was also employed in Toggenburg, Appenzell and Glarus. Constance, the German imperial city closest to the Confederation, was later to be returned to Habsburg rule with the inevitable consequence that it was lost to the Reformation.

Zurich was shattered by the defeat. Zwingli was dead, and so too were its ambitions of pre-eminence in Switzerland and southern Germany. The crisis of the Swiss Reformation had been reached, after only ten years of restless expansionist activity. The next twenty years were dominated by the need to come to terms with Kappel: first shoring up the Reformation in the Protestant states, then gradually re-establishing its international role and forming a new alliance with the emerging power of Geneva.

It is arguable that this process was only made possible by the appointment of a man of exceptional stature, Heinrich Bullinger, as Zwingli's successor in Zurich. It was Bullinger who guided Zurich and the rest of reformed Switzerland through the desperate years of the 1530s.[51] This

[50] Meyer, *Zweite Kappeler Krieg*, pp. 232–54.
[51] For an outline in English of Bullinger's life and work, R. C. Walton, 'Heinrich Bullinger', in J. Raitt (ed.), *The Shapers of Religious Traditions in Germany, Switzerland and Poland,*

D

was no easy matter, because the shock of defeat had unleashed strong forces which had not been eliminated during Zwingli's time: Catholicism, Anabaptism and anticlericalism all rose to the surface in the reformed states.[52] In Zurich, Bullinger was forced to accept a number of important restrictions on the minister's role. Although ministers were to continue preaching as before, they were to swear an oath of allegiance to the council and submit to the discipline of the synod, which was under the joint control of the magistrates and the chief minister. This arrangement was given formal expression in the church ordinances of October 1532.[53] The new regulations made clear the extent to which the ministers were henceforth to be regarded as salaried employees of the state.

Although Zurich suffered the brunt of the defeat in the Kappel Wars, there were also major consequences for relations between the Reformed states.[54] There was bad blood between Zurich and Berne following the failure of the Christian Civic Union to act (Berne had taken no part in the second war). This was not alleviated by the arrival of Wolfgang Capito in Berne; his goal was to assist in the reconstruction of the church and to revive plans for unity with the Lutherans.[55] Like so many before and since, Capito ended up satisfying neither party. The confession of faith he drew up for the Berne Synod of 1532, which was later used for the First Basle Confession, stressed a spiritualist understanding of the sacraments unacceptable to the Lutherans.[56] However, in 1537, when he and Bucer returned to Berne, they attempted to win over the Bernese Church to the Wittenberg Concordat (reached between the Lutherans and the southern German cities in 1536). Berne was engulfed in a bitter dispute between the Zwinglian ministers of the rural areas and the Lutheran sympathisers in the city. While in Berne the Strasburgers attempted to overturn the Zwinglianism of the church as adopted in the Berne Disputation by having the catechism drawn up by Kaspar Grossmann (Megander), a committed follower of Zwingli, withdrawn. Bucer rewrote the catechism himself and presented it to the Bernese council for approval. The bitter

1560–1600 (New Haven, 1981), pp. 69–88. For Bullinger's theology, J. W. Baker, *Heinrich Bullinger and the Covenant* (Athens, Ohio, 1980).

52 H. U. Bächtold, 'Bullinger und die Krise der Zürcher Reformation in Jahre 1532', in U. Gäbler and E. Herkenrath (eds.), *Heinrich Bullinger, 1504–1575. Gesammelte Aufsätze zum 400. Todestag* (2 vols, Zurich, 1975), I. 269–89. J. W. Baker, 'Church, State, and Dissent: The Crisis of the Swiss Reformation, 1531–1536', *Church History*, 57 (1988), 135–52.

53 H. U. Bächtold, *Heinrich Bullinger vor dem Rat. Zur Gestaltung und Verwaltung des Zürcher Staatswesens in den Jahren 1531 bis 1575* (Zurich, 1982), esp. pp. 24–36.

54 Basle, Berne, Schaffhausen, St Gall and Mülhausen also had to pay war reparations to the inner cantons. Meyer, *Zweite Kappeler Krieg*, pp. 301–14.

55 J. K. Kittelson, *Wolfgang Capito. From Humanist to Reformer* (Leiden, 1975), pp. 143–70.

56 E. Saxer, 'Capito und der Berner Synodus', in G. W. Locher (ed.), *Der Berner Synodus von 1532* (2 vols., Neukirchen-Vluyn, 1988), II. 150–66.

controversy between Zwinglian and Lutheran supporters led to the departure of Megander and his replacement by Simon Sulzer and Simon Grynaeus, who collaborated to introduce modifications consonant with Lutheran practices. It is interesting that Lutheran teachings did not really take hold in Berne as they did in Basle, for Sulzer and Grynaeus were not able to overcome the strong Zwinglianism of the rural clergy, and their position remained precarious. When the ever pragmatic Berne council began to detect the weakness of German Protestantism in the period leading up to the introduction of the Interim in 1548, it dismissed the two men and appointed Johannes Haller, Bullinger's assistant in Zurich, to lead the church. Haller's position was strengthened by the arrival of Wolfgang Musculus. The Bernese leaders had decided that in dangerous times it was wiser to return to the Zwinglian camp.

In Basle the situation was somewhat different. While Oecolampadius lived there was a close relationship with Zurich. However, the intellectual climate of Basle was quite distinct, since its location made it much more open to German influences.[57] Basle was also at this time (before the rise of Geneva) the principle centre for refugees fleeing religious persecution in France.[58] The connections between France and Basle, established through the *émigré* community and the book trade, ensured a greater diversity of religious ideas. The divergent strain of reformed humanism in the city was represented by Bonifacius Amerbach, the distinguished professor of law in the university, with his Bucerian ideas of religious concord.[59] Despite this eclecticism (or perhaps because of it), Basle played a crucial role in formulating the first combined Swiss evangelical confession, known as the First Helvetic Confession, in 1536.[60] The Confession sought to pick up the pieces after Kappel and provide a way forward to unity among the evangelical churches. It was essentially faithful to Zwingli's teachings on church, ministry and sacrament, but Lutheran elements are detectable. Although Oswald Myconius was elected Oecolampadius' successor, Simon Grynaeus was the theological force behind the Basle church, and his commitment to unity with the Germans was manifested in his presence, representing Basle, at the religious colloquies in the early 1540s between Lutherans and Catholics. Grynaeus was also a friend of Calvin and, despite his Lutheranism, was influential in the Frenchman's

[57] H. R. Guggisberg, 'Das reformierte Basel als geistiger Brennpunkt Europas im 16. Jahrhundert', in H. R. Guggisberg and P. Rotach (eds.), *Ecclesia semper reformanda. Vorträge zum Basler Reformations-Jubiläum 1529–1979* (Basle, 1980), pp. 50–75.
[58] P. G. Bietenholz, *Basle and France in the Sixteenth Century. The Basle Humanists and Printers in their Contacts with Francophone Culture* (Geneva, 1971), pp. 55–164.
[59] On Amerbach see P. G. Bietenholz (ed.) *Contemporaries of Erasmus* (3 vols, Toronto, 1985–87), I. 42–6.
[60] Pfister, *Kirchengeschichte*, pp. 197–9.

return to Geneva in 1541. When Simon Sulzer succeeded Myconius, Basle's relations with the other evangelical cities became quite strained. In 1549 Myconius and Sulzer objected to the *Consensus Tigurinus*, the agreement on the Eucharist reached between Bullinger and Calvin, on the grounds that they had not been consulted. In the early 1550s the rift widened as the Basle church under Sulzer quarrelled with Calvin over questions of excommunication, predestination, the execution of Servetus and the ideas of toleration current in Basle as expounded by Sébastien Castellio.[61]

The events in Berne and Basle emphasised the delicate nature of the alliance of evangelical churches in Switzerland in the post-Kappel period. Zwingli, like Luther, was variously interpreted by his successors. In Germany his doctrines remained a potent religious force and continued to cause disquiet in the Lutheran camp. This is evident from the invective directed by Luther towards the churches in Frankfurt and Augsburg in 1532 and 1533 regarding their conflation of Zwinglian and Lutheran forms of the Lord's Supper. The Württemberg Concord of 1534, instituted by the restored Duke Ulrich to bring about reform in his territory, was clearly a mixture of the two confessions. Nevertheless, the isolation of the Swiss meant that Bucer, and not Bullinger, became the spokesman for the evangelical party in southern Germany. This isolation was underscored in the formation of the Schmalkaldic League in 1531.[62] Although it was the natural successor to the Christian Civic Union, the necessity of doctrinal agreement precluded the inclusion of the Swiss. Finally, a reconciliation between the Swiss and the Germans was rendered impossible by the continuation of the personal bitterness between Luther and Bullinger.[63]

Although the Second Kappel Peace ended the possibility of growth for the Reformation in eastern Switzerland, the situation in the west was more fluid. It was the Bernese who instigated the major expansion of the Swiss Reformation after Kappel by taking over the lands north of Lake Geneva known as the Pays du Vaud. Berne was allied with the cities of Lausanne, Solothurn, Fribourg, Neuchâtel and Geneva, and its principle rivals were the Habsburg vassals the bishop of Lausanne and the Duke of Savoy. Berne effectively ended the rule of these vassals in the Vaud during the late 1520s, and when it adopted the Reformation in 1528 it began to

---

[61] U. Plath, *Calvin und Basel* (Zurich, 1974). On Castellio, S. E. Ozment, *Mysticism and Dissent. Religious Ideology and Social Protest in the Sixteenth Century* (New Haven, 1973), pp. 168–202.

[62] T. A. Brady, Jr., 'Phases and Strategies of the Schmalkaldic League: A Perspective after 450 years', *ARG*, 74 (1983), 162–81.

[63] M. U. Edwards, *Luther and the False Brethren* (Stanford, 1975), pp. 194–6, 202–3.

support the evangelical preachers active in the region.[64] The most important of these preachers in the French-speaking regions was Guillaume Farel.[65] Farel had come to Basle in 1523 as a French refugee. He became acquainted with both Oecolampadius and Pellican, and later Zwingli, before moving to Strasburg. Farel's first triumph, achieved with the support of the Bernese, was in winning the ruling council of Neuchâtel over to the Reformation in November 1530. This was crucial to the expansion of the Reformation in the west of Switzerland.[66]

The imposition of the Reformation by the Bernese in the Vaud was slow and methodical.[67] Although it was in control of the region by 1530, the official acceptance of the evangelical faith was not proclaimed until 1536, following the Disputation of Lausanne. Berne's tardiness did not belie a lack of conviction, but rather an overriding concern that the transition be as smooth as possible. Also, the evangelising of the rural parishes was delayed by the shortage of French-speaking ministers. Nevertheless, events began to overtake Berne's plans as acts of iconoclasm erupted. The Bernese council was forced to act, and reform was introduced according to the Zwinglian model by the holding of a disputation in Lausanne from 1–8 October 1536.

The Lausanne Disputation marked the consolidation of French-speaking Protestantism, in the way that the disputation in Berne had done for German-speaking Switzerland.[68] The disputation was largely a symbolic affair, held in the most important centre of the medieval church in the Vaud, the cathedral in Lausanne, and intended to mark the transition from the old faith to the new. Until the rise of Geneva Lausanne served as the centre of French-speaking Protestantism in Switzerland; its Academy, founded to provide the region with trained ministers, was the premier educational institution in the French-speaking territories until the establishment of the Academy in Geneva in 1559.[69]

The Lausanne Disputation also marked the entry of John Calvin into Swiss religious affairs. The relationship between Geneva and Berne was extremely volatile, and its complexities are beyond the scope of this

[64] On the Reformation in western Switzerland and Geneva, Feller, *Geschichte Berns*, pp. 354–83. Pfister, *Kirchengeschichte*, pp. 139–68.
[65] On Farel see articles in *TRE*, XI. 30–6, *Contemporaries of Erasmus*, II. 11–13.
[66] Pfister, *Kirchengeschichte*, pp. 139–47.
[67] See E. Junod, 'De la conquête du Pays de Vaud à la Dispute de Lausanne' in his *La Dispute de Lausanne (1536). La théologie réformée après Zwingli et avant Calvin* (Lausanne, 1988), pp. 13–22.
[68] F. Higman, 'La Dispute de Lausanne, carrefour de la Reformation française', in Junod, *Dispute de Lausanne*, pp. 23–35.
[69] H. Meylan, *La Haute école de Lausanne, 1537–1937* (Lausanne, 1937). *L'Academie de Lausanne au XVIe siècle: Leges Scholae Lausannensis 1547. Lettres et Documents inédits*, ed. L. Junod and H. Meylan (Lausanne, 1947).

chapter.[70] Geneva did not become fully part of the Confederation until the nineteenth century, but its fate was dependent upon its Swiss neighbours. It was the expansion of the Bernese into the west which secured and preserved Geneva's independence, and it was from Bernese territory that Farel and his fellow ministers launched their missions to Geneva.[71] Yet the arrival of Calvin in Geneva, and his friendship with Farel, gave rise to a movement in the French-speaking lands away from Zwinglianism towards Calvin's positions. Farel carried many ministers with him when he adopted Calvin's ideas, but not all. Berne retained control over the appointment of ministers to parishes in the Vaud, and Zwinglianism was upheld. The differences between Berne and Geneva led to bitter quarrels which marked much of Calvin's later life.[72]

Although Geneva under Calvin would later eclipse Zurich, Basle and Berne as the leading evangelical city, Calvin was initially heavily dependent on the support of his Swiss colleagues in order to establish himself.[73] The fracturing of Lutheranism in Germany and the strength of the Council of Trent necessitated doctrinal agreement between German and French-speaking Protestantism, which meant between Zurich and Geneva. The sore point continued to be the Lord's Supper; Calvin did not wholly ascribe to Bullinger's revision of Zwingli's eucharistic theology. Nevertheless it was Calvin who was adamant that an agreement be reached, and in 1549, after he and Bullinger had committed their views to paper, Calvin and Farel travelled to Zurich to resolve in person the final difficulties. The agreement became known as the *Consensus Tigurinus* and it did much to seal the bond between French- and German-speaking Protestantism in Switzerland.[74] Most scholars allow that Calvin gave more than he received in the debates, and that he deferred to Bullinger on some points for the sake of agreement. It also paved the way for the more comprehensive Second Helvetic Confession of 1566, which was written by Bullinger to provide a basis for a wider confessional unity among the evangelical churches of Europe.

The urgency with which Zurich and Geneva pursued an agreement reflected the precarious state of the Reformation in Switzerland. This was

[70] See particularly Plath, *Calvin und Basel*, pp. 252–68.
[71] U. Gerber, 'Elèves de Zwingli en terres romandes', in Junod, *Dispute de Lausanne*, pp. 104–14.
[72] Feller, *Geschichte Berns*, pp. 384–9.
[73] For a survey of Calvin's relationship with Bullinger see J. W. Baker, 'Christian Discipline and the Early Reformed Tradition: Bullinger and Calvin', in R. V. Schnucker (ed.), *Calviniana. Ideas and Influence of Jean Calvin* (Ann Arbor, 1988), pp. 107–20.
[74] On the Consensus, Paul Rorem, *Calvin and Luther on the Lord's Supper* (Nottingham, 1989). O. Strasser, 'Der Consensus Tigurinus', *Zwingliana*, 9 (1949), 1–16. U. Gäbler, 'Das Zustandekommen des Consensus Tigurinus im Jahre 1549', *Theologische Literaturzeitung*, 104/5 (1979), 321–32.

a result in part of the marked resurgence of Catholicism beginning in the 1540s which threatened to undo much of the evangelical achievement. Following the failure of the Regensberg Colloquy, Pope Paul III renewed his plans for a general council, and through the Swiss legates, Giralamo Franco and Albert Rosin, the papacy waged a vigorous campaign to ensure Swiss participation. Although the confessional divisions within the Confederation precluded a unified response, by 1548 there were suggestions that the evangelical governments might send representatives to the Council of Trent.[75] This proved a shrewd move as many prominent evangelical political leaders were attracted by the offer. Bullinger, Haller and others found themselves pushed onto the defensive, as they scrambled to produce tracts denying that the Council of Trent was in any way a true general council.[76] The Catholic forces had assumed the upper hand, and this was further demonstrated by the expulsion of the Italian Protestant community in Locarno, and the removal of evangelical ministers from Glarus in 1556. By the end of the century new orders, particularly the Jesuits, were active throughout the Confederation; new seminaries were founded, liturgies revised and traditional practices against which the reformers had rebelled were established as binding.

To end this outline something should be said concerning the importance of religious refugees in the Swiss Reformation. In much of the general literature Switzerland is presented as a second power-house of the Reformation, but it is clear from the foregoing survey that its domestic success was never more than partial. The powerful initial impulse for reform had been turned back by a combination of determined resistance and fear of Zurich, whose aggressive proselytising proved in this respect a distinctly mixed blessing. Yet for all that the Swiss Reformation exercised an enduring influence over the wider European movement, not least through the constant flow of refugees into and out of the Confederation, which ensured the dissemination of Swiss theology throughout Europe. The settling of the religious question for most of the Confederation after Kappel, together with Switzerland's security from the hand of the Emperor, produced a haven to which persecuted Christians might come to study, consult or simply live in peace. The Peasants' War in Germany had brought thousands of rebels into Switzerland seeking protection from the sword. Later came further major influxes from all over Europe. From Italy Hieronymous Bolsec, Celio Curione and Bernardino Ochino; from Spain Francisco Enzinas and Doña Briceño. From the east came the Hungarians. Important groups of French, English and Scottish refugees in mid-century played an equally decisive role in the Reformation move-

[75] Pfister, *Kirchengeschichte*, p. 262–8.
[76] Bullinger, *De conciliis* (Zurich, Froschover, 1561). Pfister, *Kirchengeschichte*, pp. 269–78.

ments of their homeland. The refugees were by no means only theologians; large numbers of farmers, artisans and craftsmen and their families lived outside the walls of the evangelical cities and depended upon their social welfare. The relations between the Swiss churches and the refugees were equivocal. On the one hand the Swiss naturally saw themselves as the guardians of the Reformation, obliged to promote reform and care for those persecuted for the truth. Nevertheless, on the other hand, the experience of persecution and dislocation often led to a radicalisation of religious thought, and the plethora of beliefs imported by these refugees, who looked to the Swiss for guidance, was a seriously destabilising force. It was Calvin, a refugee himself, who understood and articulated a faith for those seeking refuge in God.

The evangelical faith did not, in the end, provide the Swiss with the ideological adhesive to bring together the loose collection of territories. The internal and historical tensions within the Confederation militated against the complete success of the Reformation. The unhappy resolution of 1531 is to some extent responsible for the continuation of religious wars in Switzerland until the nineteenth century. The Reformation asked the Swiss a very difficult question: could an alliance exist between semi-autonomous states of widely differing religious convictions? The Swiss found an answer in an external policy of neutrality and an internal order constituted by a complex web of local jurisdictions. The Swiss Reformation was largely about the reform of the community, and the Swiss knew that as long as their communities were secure the alliance could survive. The conjunction of forces which constituted the Swiss Reformation produced not only the first Protestant order, which exercised tremendous influence upon fledgling reform movements throughout Europe, but it established the first political and religious structures in which Protestant and Catholic states, albeit uneasily, could live together. Bullinger, brooding at his desk in Zurich, would certainly have regarded this as a failure, but it may well have secured the Reformation.

SELECT BIBLIOGRAPHY

PRIMARY SOURCES

Bullinger, Heinrich. *Heinrich Bullingers Briefwechsel*, ed. U. Gäbler *et al.*, (Zurich, 1973-ff).
Dürr, Emil and Roth, Paul (eds.) *Aktensammlung zur Geschichte der Basler Reformation in den Jahren 1519 bis Anfang 1534*. (6 vols. Basle, 1921–50).
Egli, Emil. *Actensammlung zur Geschichte der Zürcher Reformation in den Jahren 1519–1533* (reprint edn., Zurich 1970).
Staehelin, Ernst. *Briefe und Akten zum Leben Oekolampads*. (2 vols., Leipzig, 1927–34).

Steck, Rudolf, and Tobler, Gustav (eds.) *Aktensammlung zur Geschichte der Berner Reformation* (2 vols. Bern, 1923).
Zwingli, Huldrych. *Huldrych Zwinglis sämtliche Werke*, ed. Emil Egli *et al.*, (Berlin, 1905–91).

SECONDARY LITERATURE

Baker, J. Wayne, *Heinrich Bullinger and the Covenant. The Other Reformed Tradition* (Athens, Ohio, 1980).
Biel, Pamela, *Doorkeepers at the House of Righteousness. Heinrich Bullinger and the Clergy in Zürich, 1534–1575* (Berne, 1991).
Bietenholz, Peter G. 'Édition et Réforme à Bâle', in Jean-Francois Gilmont (ed.) *La Réforme et le Livre* (Paris, 1990), pp. 239–68.
Blickle, Peter. *Gemeindereformation. Die Menschen des 16. Jahrhunderts auf dem Weg zum Heil* (Munich, 1985).
Bonjour, E., Offler, H. S. and Potter, G. R. *A Short History of Switzerland* (Oxford, 1952).
Brady, Thomas A. Jr. *Turning Swiss: Cities and Empire, 1450–1550* (Cambridge, 1985).
Guggisberg, Kurt, *Bernische Kirchengeschichte* (Berne, 1958).
Hauser, Albert, *Was für ein Leben. Schweizer Alltag vom 15. bis 18. Jahrhundert* (Zurich, 1988).
Helbling, Hanno (ed.) *Handbuch der Schweizer Geschichte* (2 vols., Zurich, 1972–7).
Junod, Eric (ed.). *La Dispute de Lausanne (1536). La théologie réformée après Zwingli et avant Calvin* (Lausanne, 1988).
Locher, Gottfried W. *Die Zwinglische Reformation im Rahmen der europäischen Kirchengeschichte* (Göttingen, 1979).
Zwingli's Thought. New Perspectives (Leiden, 1981).
Muralt, Leonard von, 'Renaissance und Reformation' in *Handbuch der Schweizer Geschichte* (2nd edn., Zurich, 1980), I. 389–570
Pfister, Rudolf, *Kirchengeschichte der Schweiz*. II (Zurich, 1974).
Potter, George R. *Zwingli* (Cambridge, 1976).
Rupp, E. Gordon. *Patterns of Reformation* (London, 1969).
Scott, Tom. 'Reformation and Peasant's War in Waldshut and Environs: A Structural Analysis', *ARG*, 69 (1978) and 70 (1979).
Stayer, James. M. *The Anabaptists and the Sword* (2nd edn., Lawrence, Kansas, 1976).
Stephens, Peter, *The Theology of Huldrych Zwingli* (Oxford, 1986).
Walton, Robert, *Zwingli's Theocracy* (Toronto, 1967).

5   Scandinavia

Ole Peter Grell

The Reformation in Scandinavia seems at first sight to have been a rare example in Europe of a relatively painless transition to a Lutheran state church. This, however, is a misleading impression, born of hindsight and an insufficient comprehension of the political and social complexities of this vast, if sparsely populated, area of northern Europe. The Reformation, in fact, took place within an unusually complex situation. Political and social instability dominated the period. The defeudalisation process of the late Middle Ages had brought lay and ecclesiastical aristocracy into conflict with peasants, burghers and the Crown. The 1520s and 1530s saw a succession of civil wars and revolts, some social or political in origin, others either in defence of Protestantism or specifically to oppose the new teaching. Only in the duchies of Schleswig and Holstein was the Reformation relatively unproblematic; in Denmark and Sweden its birth-pangs were significantly more painful.

The Union of the three Scandinavian kingdoms created in 1397 by the Danish Queen, Margrethe I, was by the sixteenth century on the point of collapse. This unwieldy entity, which included Denmark, Norway and Sweden, along with Finland and the duchies of Schleswig and Holstein, was finally brought down by the rebellion of the Swedish nobleman Gustav Vasa, which established Sweden as an independent kingdom in 1521. The revolt was a crushing blow for the Danish king, Christian II, whose arbitrary behaviour (including the execution of more than 80 leading members of the Swedish lay and ecclesiastical aristocracy in Stockholm in November 1520) had largely provoked the revolt.[1] Christian II's simultaneous attempt to weaken the political influence of the Danish aristocracy eventually led to his deposition by the Danish Council

---

[1] N. Skyum-Nielsen, *Blodbadet i Stockholm og dets juridiske maskering* (Copenhagen 1964); C. F. Allen, *De tre nordiske Rigers Historie under Hans, Christieren den Anden, Frederik den Første, Gustav Vasa, Grevefeiden 1497–1536* (5 vols. Copenhagen, 1835–72), vol. II–V. The Reformation in Norway and Finland will not be treated in what follows. For these, in Reformation terms, less significant countries, see *The New Cambridge Modern History*, II (2nd edn.), G. R. Elton (ed.), *The Reformation 1520–1559*, (Cambridge University Press, 1990), pp. 152–4 and 164–7.

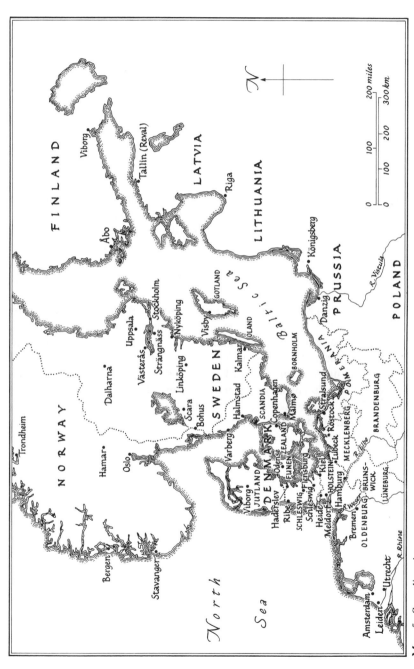

Map 5. Scandinavia

(*Rigsrådet*) in early 1523. Legally, the Council justified its action by referring to the principles of elective kinghip, pointing out that Christian had broken his coronation charter and consequently forfeited the crown. In his place the Council elected Christian's uncle, Duke Frederik of Schleswig and Holstein, who had supported the Council's rebellion.

Although deposed, Christian II continued to threaten the delicate political balance in Scandinavia for a decade or more. His repeated attempts to reverse the decision of 1523 necessitated constant vigilance and the raising of considerable (and expensive) military forces. Most of all Christian did not scruple to use the divisions created by the Reformation to further his cause. Christian's interest in reform seems to have predated his expulsion, though again this may have owed more to opportunism than principle. For a while, at least, he might have contemplated some form of Reformation of the church, aimed at curtailing the power of the bishops and creating a national Catholic Church outside papal influence. To this end he had invited to Denmark not only the learned Wittenberg humanists, Martin Reinhardt and Matthias Gabler, but also Andreas Karlstadt. Gabler spent a couple of years teaching at the University of Copenhagen, while Reinhardt, who was probably the first Protestant to preach in Denmark, left Copenhagen after a year's stay, at the beginning of 1521. Andreas Karlstadt, however, returned to Wittenberg after having spent less than a month in Copenhagen. This was allegedly because he was convinced that Christian II had no serious intention of breaking with Rome, but perhaps more significantly he seems to have been seriously worried about his own safety.[2] Likewise, it was undoubtedly Christian II's interest in humanism and church reform which in 1519 caused him to have a Carmelite College attached to the University of Copenhagen under the guardianship of the learned Erasmian theologian, Paulus Helie, many of whose colleagues, such as Peder Laurentsen and Frants Vormordsen converted to Protestantism in the mid-1520s.[3]

Even in exile, Christian II retained a considerable following among parts of the peasantry, the lower gentry and the citizenship of the major cities, such as Copenhagen, Malmø and Stockholm. In 1523 the exiled king had moved to Wittenberg where he met regularly with Luther and Melanchthon and lodged with Luther's friend, the painter, Lucas Cranach. It was here that he finally converted to Protestantism, addressing his letters 'from the holy city of Wittenberg'. One consequence of

[2] A. Heise (ed.), *Skibykrøniken* (Reprint edn., Copenhagen, 1967), 73–4, and M. Venge, *Christian 2.s fald. Spillet om magten i Danmark januar-februar 1523* (Odense, 1972).

[3] J. O. Andersen, *Paulus Helie*, I, (Copenhagen, 1936) and M. Schwarz Lausten, 'Die Universität Kopenhagen und die Reformation', in L. Grane, *University and Reformation* (Leiden, 1981), 99–113.

Christian II's conversion was the first translation of the New Testament into Danish by his secretaries, Christiern Winter and Hans Mikkelsen. It was printed in Wittenberg in 1524 and was intended as a political as well as a religious propaganda ploy against Frederik I and the Danish Council: along with the translation it included a letter from Hans Mikkelsen encouraging rebellion in the name of the deposed king.[4]

Christian II's continuing ability to exercise influence over events in Scandinavia owed much to his dynastic connection with the house of Habsburg (he was the brother-in-law of Emperor Charles V, having married his sister, Elizabeth, in 1515). The possibility of an invasion with Habsburg backing remained a constant threat to the Scandinavian kingdoms during this period. In the autumn of 1523 Christian II had managed to raise a sizeable army at the river Elbe, just south of the border of the duchies of Schleswig and Holstein. It quickly dissolved, however, owing to the king's shortage of capital. It was only in 1532, when a new military adventure ended in total failure (and Christian's capture) that the threat from Christian was finally neutralised.[5]

For the decade that Christian remained at large he continued to exercise a considerable influence on events in the Nordic kingdoms. One immediate consequence of Christian's deposition had been to reunite Frederik's duchies of Schleswig and Holstein with his new Danish kingdom, comprising Denmark, Norway, Scania, Halland and Blekinge (now southern Sweden). With Frederik's election in 1523 these lands once again came under a single ruler, at the same time as Gustav Vasa became king of Sweden. The circumstances of Christian's deposition also tended to draw together the rival rulers who had profited by Christian's discomforture. The 1520s and 30s, the decisive period for the Reformation in Scandinavia, saw a close co-operation between the two kings and Frederik I's son, Duke Christian, who became stadtholder over Schleswig and Holstein in 1526. Mutual fear of Christian II and opposition to the Hanseatic cities of north Germany (rivals for the trade of the Baltic) underpinned this joint approach.

Nevertheless the Reformation in the Nordic countries did not proceed to a common pattern. The reactions of the three rulers to the new evangelical ideas differed substantially, and there were important local differences in political and social conditions. The three Reformations, in Sweden, Denmark and Schleswig/Holstein, proceeded at a very different pace. In Schleswig/Holstein (or at least Haderslev/Tønning, that part of the duchies given to Duke Christian in 1525), the Reformation was a *fait accompli* by 1528; in essence it was a purely princely Reformation with

---

[4] J. O. Andersen, *Overfor Kirkebruddet* (Copenhagen, 1917).
[5] A. Heise, *Kristiern den Anden i Norge og hans Fængsling* (Copenhagen, 1877), pp. 98 ff.

only few, localised examples of real popular involvement. Similarly, Sweden, where only Stockholm and possibly a few coastal towns can be seen to have developed any significant popular support for the Reformation, was very largely a princely Reformation, directed or halted by a monarch who had serious religious and political doubts about how far to carry the changes in religion. It was only in 1539–40 that Gustav Vasa finally took full control of the Swedish Church, and a further thirty years would elapse before a Protestant church order was introduced in 1571. Denmark, on the other hand, experienced a Reformation which included what can be termed the three classic elements: first the popular, then the magisterial and finally the princely stage in its Reformation. This was the most thoroughgoing of the Scandinavian reformations, but a more detailed survey should begin with Schleswig/Holstein, for it is here that one finds not only some of the inspiration for events elsewhere in Scandinavia, but also one of the earliest examples of an evangelical–Lutheran territorial church in Europe.

Schleswig and Holstein

In 1525 Frederik I made over the administration of Haderslev and Tønning, parts of his duchies of Schleswig/Holstein, to his son Christian. Within three years the young Duke Christian had managed to bring a halt to Catholic services and to introduce a Protestant church order in his fief. Duke Christian's evangelical sympathies derived in part from his youthful experience in Germany. As a member of the delegation of his uncle, Duke Joachim of Brandenburg, Christian had attended the Diet of Worms in 1521 and been moved by Luther's bold defence. His Saxon tutor Wolfgang Utenhof, and his travel-companion and advisor Johann Ranzau were also important evangelical influences.[6] Yet evangelical preaching had already begun in some of the towns in the south-western part of Schleswig and Holstein some years before Duke Christian took control of Haderslev/Tønning. The priest Hermann Tast, a former student at Wittenberg, had begun preaching in Low German in Husum in 1522. His evangelical sermons generated considerable popular support, obliging him to move them from a private house of a wealthy merchant and town-councillor, Mathias Knutzen, out of doors to the local churchyard. By 1525 he was joined by two of his former Catholic colleagues, one of whom, Franz Hamer, had also studied in Wittenberg.[7]

---

[6] H. V. Gregersen, *Reformationen i Sønderjylland* (Aabenraa, 1986), pp. 54–9, and M. Schwarz Lausten, *Christian den 3. og kirken 1537–1559* (Copenhagen, 1987), pp. 9–12. Duke Christian eventually succeeded his father as king of Denmark and Norway in 1536.
[7] Gregersen, *Sønderjylland*, pp. 49–53.

These developments were not allowed to go forward without opposition from the local church authorities. In December 1524 Heindrichs van Zutphen, the only Protestant preacher to suffer martyrdom in the duchies (indeed in the whole of Scandinavia) was executed in Heide. Van Zutphen was a former Augustinian monk, a friend and colleague of Luther's in the monastery in Wittenberg, and an important figure in the early Reformation in his native Netherlands. From Antwerp he had withdrawn to Bremen, and it was from there that he had accepted the invitation to preach in Holstein.[8] Zutphen's case was unique, in so far as it was the only example of a serious attempt by the civil authorities to halt the new teaching in the duchies. Yet considerable opposition to the evangelical movement undoubtedly existed, especially among the upper echelons of society in Schleswig and Holstein, for whom the Bishop of Schleswig, Gottschalk Ahlefeldt, proved an articulate spokesman. This may account for the fact that Duke Christian, whose Lutheran sympathies were well known by 1525, was only given the relatively small fief of Haderslev/Tønning to rule, rather than the whole of Schleswig and Holstein.[9]

However, a diet of the duchies at Rendsburg in May 1525, revealed that the tide was beginning to run in Christian's favour. The previous solidarity of the higher orders now began to break down, since the lay aristocracy wanted their colleagues among the clergy to carry a greater share of the increased tax-burden, and they attacked them for introducing uneducated clergy in the parish churches who only preached nonsense, such as omens and miracles. The diet decided that in future the Gospel should be preached purely and in the vernacular. Apart from the decision's evangelical overtones this represented a direct, lay interference with Catholic jurisdiction.[10]

Duke Christian now moved to take control of church affairs in Haderslev/Tønning. Among his first acts was the dismissal of Johann Wulf, the influential Dean of the collegiate chapter. As in the rest of Scandinavia, the practical and economic aspects of Protestantism also helped promote the new teachings in the Duke's fief. The possibility of marriage proved popular among Catholic priests and monks, in many cases providing them with a much wanted opportunity to regularise hitherto illegitimate relationships. The peasantry, meanwhile, used the opportunity to avoid paying the traditionally unpopular part of the tithe which went to the bishops.[11] It was this development which moved Bishop Ahlefeldt to

---

[8] R. Hansen, 'Die geschichtliche Bedeutung Heinrichs von Zütphen, des Märtyrers der Reformation in Dithmarschen', *Dithmarschen*, 1 (1990), 1–17.

[9] Gregersen, *Sønderjylland*, pp. 54–8.

[10] Lausten, *Christian den 3.*, p. 17 and Gregersen, *Sønderjylland*, pp. 59–62.

[11] Gregersen, *Sønderjylland*, p. 64, and *Skibykrøniken*, p. 111.

protest to the Duke, referring to the guarantees given the church at the recent diet. Faced with a complex and perilous political situation, Frederik urged caution: the need to avoid open conflict at this time was pre-eminent, given the double anxieties caused by the deposed king Christian's renewed military threat, and the implications of the Peasants' War in Germany. At such a time Frederik might have felt particularly ill at ease with actions likely to encourage disobedience among the peasants in Haderslev/Tønning.[12]

But Duke Christian was not to be put off. The following years saw further initiatives towards reform, matched by further obstruction from the bishops. In 1526 the Duke succeeded in introducing two experienced reformers to assist administration of the church in place of the dismissed clerics, Eberhard Weidensee and Johann Wenth. Weidensee, an Augustinian monk who had studied at the University of Leipzig before becoming Dean to the monastery in Halberstadt in 1513, had previously played an important part in reforming initiatives both in his native Halberstadt and in Magdeburg. In Holstein he became the first superintendent of the duchies' churches.[13] He was shortly joined by Johann Wenth, a younger man and another capable Wittenberg-educated scholar.[14]

The timing of their arrival could hardly have been more propitious. The Diet of Kiel in February 1526 had further weakened the Catholic Church, since it was forced to defray most of the costs of Frederik's armament against a possible invasion from Christian II, under the ill-disguised threat that Frederik would otherwise abandon it in favour of the Lutherans.[15] These developments encouraged Duke Christian to accelerate the process of reform in Haderslev/Tønning. On his return from the diet he summoned all the ministers in his fief to a Synod in Haderslev in late April. This brought him into conflict with Iver Munk, the Danish Bishop of Ribe, whose bishopric and jurisdiction included Tønning and with whom he was already engaged in an extensive epistolatory debate, ranging over issues such as fasting, the importance of faith as opposed to works, the right of the clergy to marry, the obligation of the clergy to preach the Gospel unadulterated and in the vernacular. Munk now objected to the duke's interference with clergy who belonged to the bishopric of Ribe and were under his jurisdiction. Here his position as a member of the Danish Council proved invaluable. Frederik I had no wish to cause any disruption to the tentative unity between the Crown and the

[12] H. F. Rørdam, 'En theologisk Brevvexel mellem Christian i Haderslev og biskop Iver Munk', *Kirkehistoriske Samlinger*, 2. R., 2, (1860–2), 1–20. Gregersen, *Sønderjylland*, pp. 80–93.
[13] For Weidensee, see *Schleswig-Holsteinisches Biographisches Lexikon*, (8 vols., Neumünster, 1970–87), V. 276–7.
[14] *Ibid.*, VI. 299–301.   [15] Gregersen, *Sønderjylland*, pp. 76–9.

lay and ecclesiastical aristocracy in Denmark, and accordingly he instructed his son not to interfere in the affairs of the see of Ribe.[16] Thus it was only clergy from the area in and around Haderslev who attended the synod of 1526. They were presented with new evangelical articles of faith, written by Weidensee and Wenth, which were probably more or less identical to the later Haderslev Church Ordinance (1528).[17] Duke Christian's initiative received further encouragement on 27 May 1526 when he was made stadtholder and regent of the whole duchies. By the end of 1527 evangelical ministers had taken over most of the parish churches in the towns of Schleswig and Holstein.

The most important of these were Flensburg, Haderslev, Kiel and Schleswig. In Flensburg Hermann Tast from Husum had begun preaching in private houses during 1526. By December, when a friend and collaborator of Eberhard Weidensee, Gerhard Slewart, had arrived from Magdeburg to take over the ministry at St Nicolai Church, Lutheran services had been introduced in all churches.[18] In Haderslev, where Weidensee and Wenth personally supervised the Reformation, all ministers were evangelical by late 1526, preaching in either Low German or Danish. The collegiate chapter-school was turned into a training academy for Lutheran ministers under the guidance of Johann Wenth (the first of its kind in Scandinavia).[19] Likewise Kiel appears to have seen a total Reformation by the end of 1526, since in January 1527 Frederik I thought fit to appoint the town's leading evangelical theologian, the Wittenberg-educated Marquad Schuldorp, as minister in the cathedral-town, Schleswig.

The king's installation of Schuldorp was evidently intended as a move to get the evangelical movement in Schleswig under control. Thus far it had demonstrated some disturbing signs of a radical nature. Until Schuldorp's arrival, the Protestant party had been led by a former Franciscan monk, Friedrich, who had proved extremely popular with the lower orders, attacking the luxurious living of the clergy while emphasising their obligation to imitate the simple lives of the Apostles. When he and his followers interrupted Mass for a dead canon in the cathedral during Chrismas 1526, the disturbances which followed made the magistracy join the Catholic clergy in complaining to the king. Schuldorp had only been in Schleswig for a couple of months when Friedrich went a step further

---

[16] *Ibid.*, pp. 80–92.
[17] The Ordinance is reprinted in Gregersen, *Sønderjylland*, pp. 244–9.
[18] *Ibid.*, pp. 95–9, 147–8.
[19] *Ibid.*, pp. 167–73. The town's Dominican monastery was closed in January 1527. It was probably done on the instigation of Weidensee who, while in Magdeburg, had published a pamphlet which encouraged the magistracy to prevent the activities of the medicant orders.

and publicly reproached the Duke's Chancellor, Wolfgang Utenhof. He immediately paid the price for his audacity and was expelled from the town. Apart from the cathedral, which remained under Catholic control until Christian succeeded his father as Duke of Schleswig and Holstein in 1533, the town of Schleswig appears to have been under Protestant control by the end of 1527.[20]

Thus, when in 1528 Duke Christian called another Synod in Haderslev of the clergy of Haderslev/Tønning, only the full and practical Reformation of the villages still needed further attention. All village clergy (including those who were under the jurisdiction of the Bishop of Ribe) were given copies of what has become known as the Haderslev Church Ordinance. The Ordinance, written by Weidensee and Wenth, was intended to guide the village clergy in their pastoral activities. It was issued in the administrative language of the duchies, Low German, but stipulated that the Gospel should be preached in both German and Danish. The ministers were obliged to swear an oath of allegiance to the Duke repudiating the teachings of the sacramentarians and Anabaptists. By 1528 the Duke and his advisors, like their friends and family in Germany, were primarily concerned with the dangers presented by the 'left wing' of the Reformation.[21]

The Haderslev Ordinance, together with those of Saxony and Braunschweig from the same year, was the first Lutheran Church Ordinance. Its dependence on Wittenberg is obvious. Among other things it advised the ministers to preach the Gospel as spelled out by Luther in his Kirchenpostille from 1527. Evidently the village clergy in Haderslev/Tønning were expected to own this work. The Ordinance's didactic form indicates that it was intended primarily for the many uneducated ministers in the countryside, whose commitment to Protestantism was necessarily still extremely vague. At the same time the Synod instituted a new system of supervision under a number of rural deans, empowered to inspect how local ministers discharged their office, including preaching, learning and moral behaviour.[22]

Retrospectively, one wonders whether Duke Christian's fear of sacramentarians and Anabaptists, expressed in the oath demanded at the Synod, had been included because of developments in Germany since the mid-1520s, or whether the arrival of Melchior Hoffmann in Kiel in February 1527 had made the Duke specifically aware of such dangers closer to home. Hoffmann had arrived in Kiel after a period of wandering

---

[20] *Ibid.*, pp. 116–17.
[21] Lausten, *Christian den 3.*, p. 19. Gregersen, *Sønderjylland*, p. 120.
[22] B. Kornerup, 'Fra hertug Christians reformation', *Kirkehistoriske Samlinger*, 6. R., 5, (1945–7), 547–8. Gregersen, *Sønderjylland*, pp. 122–35.

in the northern lands, since his expulsion from Livonia two years earlier.[23] The fact that he was appointed minister in Kiel by King Frederik I is somewhat paradoxical, since Frederik I cannot have been unaware of Hoffmann's activities in Stockholm during 1526 where he had preached regularly to the German inhabitants. Here he had been supported by those citizens who were dissatisfied with the hesitant and lukewarm reforms of the Swedish King, Gustav Vasa, and who wanted to carry the Reformation further. The aggressive and eschatological preaching of Hoffmann had caused considerable anxiety within the Swedish government which had forced him into exile in January 1527.

Hoffmann's appointment may have been intended to bring an end to the activities of the prominent reform Catholic minister in Kiel, Wilhelm Pravest. In this it was successful, but Hoffmann's aggressive ministry proved impossible to control and brought him into collision with several Lutheran ministers, among them his predecessor in Kiel, Marquard Schuldorp. Schuldorp attacked Hoffmann both for his obsession with Revelation and his 'rationalist' interpretation of the Communion, for Hoffmann had by then adopted the sacramentarian position, denying both Catholic transubstantiation and Lutheran consubstantiation. Subsequently, when Hoffmann published his view of the Communion in a pamphlet, *Beweiss das M. Schuldorp im seinem Inhalte vom Sacramente und Testament Christi ketzerisch und verfürisch geschriben*, matters came to a head. Luther, who had already been involved in the confrontation obliquely now felt the need to interfere directly. He wrote to Duke Christian, requesting him to bring a halt to Hoffmann's preaching urgently.[24]

The story reached its climax in a disputation between the Duke's Lutheran advisors and Hoffmann at Flensburg in April 1529, in the presence of several hundred people, including some of the leading members of the duchies' nobility and several prominent Lutheran theologians such as Johann Bugenhagen. The result was never in doubt and Hoffmann, who refused to budge, was condemned and expelled.[25] This brought an end to Hoffmann's Scandinavian career. If not as dramatic as his later engagements in Emden and Strasburg, Hoffmann's two year stay in Kiel created the only radical ripple in the otherwise smooth, princely Reformation of Schleswig and Holstein.

---

[23] Klaus Deppermann, *Melchior Hoffmann* (Edinburgh, 1989), pp. 86–152.
[24] Deppermann, *Hoffmann*, pp. 95–137. M. Schwarz Lausten, 'Melchior Hoffmann og de lutherske prædikanter i Slesvig-Holsten', *Kirkehistoriske Samlinger*, 7. R., 5, 237–85.
[25] Lausten, 'Melchior Hoffmann', 264–82. Deppermann, *Hoffmann*, pp. 126–37.

Denmark

For obvious reasons the Reformation in Denmark had to follow a different route from that of Schleswig and Holstein. Any early and decisive steps by Frederik I to introduce a princely Reformation on a par with his son's initiatives in Haderslev/Tønning would have been extremely risky. The king owed his crown to the lay and ecclesiastical aristocracy in Denmark which had rebelled against his nephew. He had been obliged to sign a coronation charter which was more or less identical to the political programme of the aristocracy. Only if he could engineer a split between the bishops and their family and friends within the Council (*Rigsrådet*) could he hope to introduce changes in religion, a consideration which Frederik I constantly had to balance against the ever-looming threat of invasion from his predecessor.

Frederik I's coronation charter placed the responsibility for having introduced the new evangelical teachings into Copenhagen on Christian II. The charter affirmed that many simple people had been led into error by Christian's promotion of 'heretical' preachers. Consequently, Frederik I was forced to promise:

not to allow any heretics, disciples of Luther or others to preach and teach, either openly or secretly, against God, the faith of the Holy Church, the holiest father, the Pope, or the Catholic Church, but where they are found in this Kingdom, We promise to punish them on life and property.[26]

This paragraph is difficult to understand unless evangelical preachers were already active in the kingdom. It probably referred to itinerant preachers who, like Melchior Hoffmann, had arrived via the Hanseatic cities of the Baltic. In Copenhagen and Malmø they would have found a receptive audience not only among the sizeable, resident German merchant communities, but also among the considerable number of Danish citizens who mastered German.[27]

Yet notwithstanding the king's ostensible support, the Catholic Church in Denmark was badly equipped to counter the approaching challenge by the growing evangelical movement. The church had few theologically trained bishops and the archbishopric of Lund had been in a state of confusion since the death of its last confirmed archbishop, Birger Gunnersen, in 1519. Five candidates occupied the see between 1519 and 1536, primarily because of interference by the Crown and, to a lesser extent, by the Pope. At the time of Frederik I's accession the archbishopric had no

[26] Coronation charter in *Aarsberetninger fra Geheimearchivet*, II (Copenhagen 1856–60), 67, 71.
[27] O. P. Grell, 'The City of Malmø and the Danish Reformation', *ARG*, 79 (1988), 329–30.

less than three elected candidates. One of these, Jørgen Skodborg, managed to obtain papal confirmation only to find that he had lost the support of the king. Instead the internal candidate, the canon Aage Sparre, was able to occupy the see with the support of king and council. Sparre was in a weak position, lacking papal recognition and the support of one of his most important episcopal colleagues, Lauge Urne, Bishop of Zealand, who urged him to vacate the see for Skodborg. His attempts to halt the Reformation, which were in any case restricted to the locality of Scania, failed. In 1532 he finally acknowledged defeat and resigned in order to make room for another senior member of the chapter, Torbern Bille, whose attempts to restrict the progress of the evangelical movement fared no better.[28]

By 1526 evangelical preachers were active in most of the towns in Jutland. According to the Erasmian, Paulus Helie, 'the poison of Lutheranism was sneaking through the whole of Jutland' that year, and its leading proponent was the 'most obstinate of all heretics, Hans Tausen'. Tausen, who had studied at several foreign universities, while a member of the Order of St John of Jerusalem, had taken both his BA and MA from the University of Rostock and subsequently continued his biblical studies at Louvain in 1522 and Wittenberg between 1523 and 1524. He had spent the academic year 1521/2 at the University of Copenhagen, probably as a member of Helie's Carmelite College, which helps to explain his former master's bitterness towards him.[29] His Lutheran preaching in the monastery of Antvorskov in Zealand had initially caused the Prior to send him to Viborg in Jutland where his continued preaching led to his expulsion from the order in 1526. He was able, however, to carry on in private residences until October of that year, when he was given a royal letter of protection on the request of the magistracy in Viborg. The civic leaders had no doubt been encouraged by Frederik I's refusal to suppress the evangelical preachers in Schleswig and Holstein at the Diet of Kiel earlier in the year. At the same time they would have found further positive signs of the king's growing attraction to Protestantism in the approaching marriage of his daughter Dorothea to a recent Protestant convert, Duke Albrecht of Prussia; not to mention that the king and his chancellor had started to eat meat on Fridays and take communion in both forms.[30]

With royal backing Tausen was able to preach in one of the smaller

[28] G. Johannesson, *Den Skånska Kyrkan och Reformationen* (Lund, 1947), pp. 23–61.
[29] For Hans Tausen, see *Dansk Biografisk Leksikon* (3rd. edn., 16 vols., Copenhagen, 1979–87), XIV. 378–85. *Skibykrøniken*, p. 111.
[30] *Skibykrøniken*, pp. 113–14. O. P. Grell, 'The Emergence of two Cities: The Reformation in Malmø and Copenhagen', in L. Grane and K. Hørby, *Die dänische Reformation vor ihrem internationalen Hintergrund* (Göttingen, 1990), 133.

churches in Viborg, assisted by Jørgen Jensen Sadolin, another who had recently returned from Germany. They quickly generated considerable popular support for the evangelical cause. Sadolin was given a royal letter of protection in December 1526, which permitted him to open a school for evangelical ministers in Viborg. Evidently Frederik I considered the model from Haderslev worth imitating. Meanwhile, the multitude who wanted to hear Tausen's sermons forced the preacher to move out into the churchyard to accommodate his congregation.[31]

In December 1526 a Danish Parliament (*Herredag*) gathered in Odense. The meeting turned the Catholic Church in Denmark into a national church, declaring that bishops in future should not seek confirmation in Rome and that all fees which had hitherto been paid to the *Curia* should now fall to the Crown. The time for a religious solution limited to reform of abuse within the Catholic Church had passed. The main exponent of this solution, Paulus Helie, had tried to gain a hearing when he preached to the Court in Copenhagen in June 1526, only to find himself ridiculed by the courtiers and pursued by the Chancellor's jester through the castle-gate.[32] The following parliament, which met in Odense in August 1527, proved a turning point for the Reformation in Denmark. Frederik I seized the opportunity to inform the bishops that 'the Holy Christian Faith is free' and that he only governed 'life and property, but not the soul'. This was no less than a declaration of faith by the king. No mention was made of the evangelical preachers in the statute produced by parliament. They were able to continue preaching under royal letters of protection, which in effect excluded them from episcopal jurisdiction.[33]

These events in Odense served further to encourage the evangelical movement. In Viborg the evangelical party took over the large Franciscan monastery by force, not only for the use of the growing Protestant congregation, but also for Jørgen Jensen Sadolin's training school for evangelical ministers. By the end of 1528 only the cathedral remained under the control of the Catholic Church, and the magistracy was given permission by the king to tear down twelve redundant parish churches and to appropriate the Franciscan and Dominican monasteries. That year the Viborg reformers were also able to begin their production of Protestant propaganda printed on the recently arrived printing-press of Hans Weingarten. Under such pressure the Catholics were only able to hold out

[31] For Jørgen Jensen Sadolin, see *Dansk Biografisk Leksikon*, XII. 564–66. For Sadolin's royal letter of protection, see K. Erslev and W. Mollerup (eds.), *Kong Frederik den Forstes danske Registranter* (Copenhagen, 1879), 124.
[32] *Skibykroniken*, pp. 116–17.   [33] Grell, 'Malmø', 316–22.

in the cathedral for another year before disturbances brought an end to their services.[34]

The importance of the evangelical movement in Viborg for the kingdom as a whole, however, diminished after 1527. Thereafter it was the strength of the evangelical party in the much larger, and commercially far more important cities of Copenhagen and Malmø, which mattered. Here, as in the towns of Jutland, anticlericalism was rife. The Catholic Church owned or shared ownership of about one third of all plots and houses in the cities where expansion was restricted by the walls. Bearing in mind that the church was exempted from tax, this provided fertile soil for a growing anticlericalism.[35] The magistracy of Malmø under the leadership of its energetic mayor, Jørgen Kock, had managed to secure the service of the preacher, Claus Mortensen, in the spring of 1527, after the Bishop of Zealand, Lauge Urne, had prevented him from preaching in the churches in Copenhagen. Mortensen was to be the first in a series of evangelical ministers recruited by the magistracy of Malmø from Copenhagen, where the evangelical movement was severely constrained by Bishop Lauge Urne and the collegiate chapter of Our Lady's Church until the Bishop's death in 1529.[36]

Initially Jørgen Kock and his colleagues within the magistracy took a careful approach. Mortensen was only allowed to preach outside the city walls in a disused chapel in order to gauge the support for the Reformation. Only when his sermons had proved popular was he moved inside the walls. Towards the end of the year he attracted such multitudes that a considerably larger church was needed. Backed by the magistracy, he managed to obtain royal permission to transfer his sermons to the Church of Sts Simon and Judas in early 1528. There he was assisted by another recent convert to the evangelical cause, Hans Olufsen Spandemager, formerly of the Order of the Holy Spirit.[37] Together they introduced a more regulated evangelical service, where the congregation 'sang their songs and according to the fashion of the Lutherans held their services in Danish'.[38]

Like in Viborg the magistracy in Malmø wanted to close down the mendicant monasteries in the city. Jørgen Kock, who had the king's ear, managed to obtain royal permission to take over the monasteries of the Franciscans and the Brethren of the Holy Spirit in October 1528,

---

[34] L. Helweg, *Den Danske Kirkes Historie til Reformationen* (Copenhagen, 1870), pp. 795–800. Anne Riising, 'Le livre et la Réforme au Danemarke et en Norvège, 1523–1540', in J. F. Gilmont (ed.), *La Réforme et le livre* (Paris, 1990), 442–73.
[35] Grell, 'Two cities', 130–1.   [36] *Ibid.*, 135–6.
[37] H. Heilesen (ed.), *Krøniken om Gråbrødrenes fordrivelse fra deres Klostre i Danmark* (Copenhagen, 1967), pp. 37–8. *Skibykrøniken*, p. 121.
[38] Heilesen, *Krøniken*, 37–8. Grell, 'Malmø', 318.

108   *Ole Peter Grell*

provided that the magistracy could negotiate a peaceful settlement with the remaining monks. As later developments were to demonstrate, the magistracy showed scant regard for this proviso.[39]

By the autumn of 1528 the danger to the Catholic Church posed by the evangelical movement in Malmø had dawned on the Archbishop in Lund. On 18 November Aage Sparre arrived in the city accompanied by some of the leading conservative members of the Council, all belonging to the Scania aristocracy. After the Archbishop's attempts to discipline the evangelical preachers had failed, he threatened their protectors, the magistracy, with a heresy trial. The civic leaders bowed to the pressure, evidently realising that nothing could be gained from a confrontation at this point. They decided to send the preachers, Claus Mortensen and Hans Olufsen Spandemager, into temporary exile. Their choice of Haderslev in Schleswig–Holstein was hardly a coincidence. The town had, as shown above, recently experienced a full Reformation and offered excellent educational opportunities for the two preachers at Johann Wenth's academy. They may indeed have been badly in need of additional training, if Paulus Helie's low opinion of their learning can be trusted. He described Mortensen as 'an uneducated fellow totally ignorant of all good scholarship', while referring to his collaborator, Spandemager, as 'only slightly more learned'.[40]

The success of Aage Sparre's intervention was limited and short-lived. Some time during 1528 the magistracy in Malmø had managed to attract the former priest turned printer, Oluf Ulriksson, who had hitherto served Hans Brask, the Catholic Bishop of Linköping in Sweden. His printworks were now put at the disposal of the evangelical theologians in Malmø and turned out a number of Protestant pamphlets during the early 1530s.[41] Among these evangelical authors was the preacher, Frants Vormordsen, a Carmelite monk of Dutch origin who arrived in Malmø during the first months of 1529. Once again an invitation appears to have been issued by the magistracy in Malmø to a Copenhagen activist. Considering the negative response Vormordsen's sermons had elicited from the canons in Copenhagen, it is surprising that the Archbishop authorised him to preach in the city. If Aage Sparre had hoped to be able to contain the evangelical movement in Malmø through a man whom he considered to be an Erasmian Catholic, later events would have forced him to acknowledge that he had been misguided, and had helped Malmø to another, far

[39] O. P. Grell, 'Jørgen Kock – En studie i religion og politik i reformationstidens Danmark', in S. E. Green-Petersen, *Festskrift til Poul Enemark. Profiler i Nordisk Senmiddelalder og Renæssance*, (Århus, 1983), pp. 113–26. Grell, 'Two cities', 135–45.
[40] Grell, 'Malmø', 319. For Paulus Helie's observations, see *Skibykrøniken*, p. 121.
[41] Johannesson, *Skånska Kyrkan*, pp. 107–8. Riising, 'Livre et Réforme', p. 443.

more gifted, evangelical preacher. Vormordsen was soon joined by another Carmelite convert, Peder Laurentsen, who like him had been a colleague of Paulus Helie in the Carmelite College at the University of Copenhagen. Laurentsen became the most important apologist of the Reformation in Malmø or, as Paulus Helie put it, 'the city's appointed scribbler'.[42]

As had been the case the previous year, the magistracy interceded with the king in order to secure further privileges for the growing evangelical movement. Since they had 'embraced the Holy evangelical faith', the king allowed them to take over the properties which belonged to altars, vicariates and confraternities within the city walls. The royal letter guaranteed the economic foundation of the new Protestant congregations in Malmø, and provided for the establishment of a lectureship, a school and an academy for ministers. As in 1528 a restraining clause instructed the magistracy not to use force against the Catholic incumbents. Yet, in clear defiance of the two royal provisos, the magistracy in Malmø not only tolerated the use of violence, but actively engaged in it, in order to rid the city of a restive Catholic minority. An autumn of violence and street brawls commenced with iconoclasm in the main church of St Petri under the guidance of the newly returned preacher, Claus Mortensen, while the mayor, Jørgen Kock, led the way in harassing the remaining monks in the monasteries. At the end of the year the Reformation had triumphed in Malmø under the guidance of the city's magistracy.[43]

While Malmø had seen a total Reformation by the end of 1529, Copenhagen could hardly lay claim to an evangelical movement of any significance before 1529. Here the Catholic Church had benefitted from the presence of a collegiate chapter and a strong bishop. Yet when Bishop Lauge Urne died in April 1529 his successor Joachim Ronnow was forced to sign a letter of obligation to Frederik I, promising not to obstruct evangelical preaching in Copenhagen. Having achieved this opening, the king must have decided that the evangelical movement in the city needed further royal guidance and he transferred Hans Tausen from Viborg to Copenhagen. This initiative quickly transformed the situation and the evangelical movement began to prosper. By May 1530 Copenhagen had at least four evangelical preachers, while the magistracy had taken over most of the monasteries within the city walls. A political and religious split, however, occurred among the civic leaders of Copenhagen, between

---

[42] Grell, 'Malmø', 316–22. In January 1530 Peder Laurentsen published *Malmøbogen*, in which he described all the changes which had taken place, for instance how Mass had been abolished and the properties of the Catholic churches and altars now provided the economic basis for an evangelical community.

[43] P. Laurentsen, *Malmøbogen*, ed. H. F. Rørdam (Copenhagen, 1868).

a group of latent supporters of the deposed king, Christian II, who favoured a faster and more radical Reformation, and those who supported Frederik I and adopted a more careful approach. After a violent iconoclastic attack headed by the mayor Ambrosius Bogbinder, the leader of the radical faction, Frederik I found it necessary to purge the magistracy of disloyal radicals. Consequently, Copenhagen remained a partly Protestant, partly Catholic city, until its rebellion and the beginning of the civil war known as *Grevens Fejde* in June 1534.[44]

Frederik I, when calling a parliament which met in Copenhagen in July 1530, had evidently intended to deal comprehensively with the religious question. He had invited twenty-one evangelical preachers to participate in a disputation with the Catholic bishops, who had enlisted the support of Paulus Helie and two German theologians. This debate was clearly intended as a preamble to a full Reformation of the kingdom, on a par with what had already taken place in several places in Germany. However, when the participants met in Copenhagen, developments abroad had forced the religious issue off the agenda. The renewed threat of an invasion by Christian II made it necessary for parliament to concentrate on foreign policy and defence. The willingness of the burghers to contribute to extra taxes was rewarded by the king. They received a charter which, among other things, gave them *carte blanche* to introduce evangelical services in the towns and cities.[45] This charter was the last act of Frederik I to promote the Reformation before his death in April 1533. It represents the final and most important step in a sequence of moves which served to undermine the jurisdiction of the Catholic Church in Denmark while flagrantly disregarding the promises made in the king's coronation charter of 1523.

In strictly confessional terms, the evangelical message of the preachers in Zealand and Scania was of a more radical and Scripture-based nature than that in Jutland, which was basically Lutheran. This difference is easily explained by the dissemination of ideas. The mercantile centres of Malmø and Copenhagen were in close and regular contact with the Hanseatic cities of the Baltic from where they were influenced by the more radical, evangelical theology emanating from the south-German cities of Strasburg and Nuremberg.[46] In Jutland the evangelical movement received its inspiration through the duchies of Schleswig and Holstein which were totally dominated by Lutheran theologians, not to mention the duke's close personal relations with Luther and Bugenhagen. Perhaps too much significance should not be attached to these theological vari-

---

[44] Grell, 'Two cities', 140–5.   [45] Grell, 'Malmø', 322–5.
[46] N. K. Andersen, *Confessio Hafniensis. Den københavnske Bekendelse af 1530* (Copenhagen, 1954).

ations. Such theological differences also characterised the evangelical movements of the 1520s in Germany, and exactly what constituted Lutheran, evangelical and 'according to Scripture' was ill-defined and ambiguous in this period.

In June 1533 a parliament met in Copenhagen to elect Frederik I's successor. A conservative and Catholic majority led by the bishops wanted to avoid the election of the Lutheran Duke Christian, who had already succeeded his father as Duke of Schleswig and Holstein. The conservatives managed to have the election postponed to the following year, while leading Protestant members of the Council left Copenhagen in disgust. The government remained for the time being in the hands of the reactionary majority of the Council. During the first half of 1534, pressure was applied by members of Council to the towns of Scania to expel their evangelical preachers and to restore ecclesiastical control to the elected Archbishop of Lund. Consequently, the city of Malmø rebelled forcing a reluctant magistracy in Copenhagen to join it in an alliance with the Hanseatic cities of the Baltic. The civil war, *Grevens Fejde*, which ensued was, however, not fought over religion, but over political and social issues. A month later, in July, the aristocracy in Jutland and Funen found it necessary to back down and elect Duke Christian king. From then on, both sides championed the Protestant cause and a total reformation of the kingdom was only a question of time.[47]

When Copenhagen surrendered in July 1536, Duke Christian, the later King Christian III, had emerged from the civil war victorious. He immediately imprisoned the Catholic bishops and summoned parliament to meet in Copenhagen in October. This gathering, which comprised a much larger number of representatives of gentry, burghers and peasants than was customary at such occasions, put its seal of approval on the creation of a Lutheran territorial church in Denmark. This full Reformation of the whole kingdom was finally achieved in 1537 under the guidance of Johann Bugenhagen when the king signed the Church Ordinance and Bugenhagen ordained the seven new Lutheran superintendents.[48]

Thus a Lutheran state church was finally established in Denmark a decade after the evangelical movement had begun to make an impact. Its birth had been arduous, linked as it was with political and, to a lesser degree, social issues. It proved an ideal solution for an increasingly absolutist monarchy. It also served the interests of an emerging group of influential burghers in the major towns and cities. By contrast the con-

---

[47] M. Schwarz Lausten, 'Weltliche Obrigkeit und Kirche bei König Christian III. von Dänemark (1536–1559)', in Grane and Hørby, *Dänische Reformation*, 91–107.
[48] Lausten, *Christian den 3.*, pp. 20–31.

servative majority of the nobility were forced, for political reasons, to accept it, after their reactionary coup of 1533 had failed.

Sweden

In 1523 Gustav Vasa succeeded to the Swedish throne after a long and expensive war of independence. Part of the kingdom, including Finland and the island of Gotland, remained under Danish control for some time to come. Most of the Swedish bishoprics were vacant, including the archbishopric of Uppsala. The incumbents, who more often than not had been promoted by Christian II, had found it in their best interest to flee Sweden in the wake of Christian's defeat. Gustav Vasa used this opportunity to weaken the Catholic Church further through direct interference in the election of the new bishops. Thus only one of the bishops managed to obtain papal confirmation, while the rest, who owed their election to the king (including the Archbishop Johannes Magnus, a firm supporter of the old church), had very limited scope for independent religious and political action. When Johannes Magnus decided to go into exile whilst on a diplomatic mission to Poland in 1526, the leadership of the increasingly embattled Catholic Church fell to the Bishop of Linköping, Hans Brask.[49]

There is no evidence at this stage that Gustav Vasa was disposed to favour Protestantism for its own sake, but he quickly came to appreciate the potential of the new evangelical teachings in his attack on the wealth and influence of the Catholic Church in Sweden. Like Malmø and Copenhagen, Stockholm had not only a sizeable, resident German population, but a majority, whose attraction to the new evangelical ideas had been evident for some time. Itinerant German preachers had already helped spread Protestantism in the town, before Gustav Vasa decided to employ the archdeacon of the chapter in Strängnäs, Laurentius Andreae, a leading evangelical churchman, as his Chancellor. In 1524 the king promoted another recent convert to the evangelical cause, the lecturer of the chapter school in Strängnäs, Olaus Petri. He became clerk and minister to the town of Stockholm, a position which offered him an excellent platform from which to launch his evangelical preaching. Together, these two men were to become the leading exponents of the Reformation in Sweden.

Both Andreae and Petri had been educated in Germany, Andreae at the conservative University of Rostock, the most popular university among

---

[49] H. Holmquist and H. Pleijel (eds.), *Svenska Kyrkans Historia* (4 vols., Uppsala, 1933–41), III. 89–102, 129–30. See also H. Schück, *Ecclesia Lincopensis. Studier om Linköpinskyrkan under Medeltiden och Gustav Vasa* (Stockholm, 1959), pp. 134–56.

Scandinavian clergy before the Reformation, and Olaus Petri initially at the University of Leipzig and later, between 1516 and 1518, at Wittenberg. Both had reached their Protestant belief via biblical humanism. They were both to co-operate closely with Gustav Vasa during the 1520s, but their efforts in promoting the Reformation differed substantially. Andreae as chancellor made his contribution in the political and administrative realm, while Petri promoted the evangelical cause through preaching and publishing.[50] The chancellor provided Gustav Vasa with the theological rationale for the national church he wanted to establish in a programme enunciated in his famous letter to the monastery of Vadstena in February 1524. This maintained that the church consisted of all believers and that its resources had been given for public ends: in other words the church's wealth belonged to the nation. It was a useful justification of the accelerating secularisation of monastic lands which had already been initiated by Gustav Vasa.

Olaus Petri, on the other hand, concentrated on expounding the new faith, primarily through publishing. In 1526 he published *Een nyttwgh wnderwijsning*, which in parts is a translation of Luther's Betbüchlein of 1522, and a couple of months later this was followed by his celebrated translation of the Gospel into Swedish. Initially, Petri seems to have faced some problems in generating support for the evangelical cause among the native Swedish population in Stockholm, but he must have had considerable backing among the citizenship by 1525, for in that year he married in a highly public ceremony. The large German population in Stockholm had already been won over to Protestantism, and had received its first Protestant minister, Nicholas Stecker, from Eisleben, in 1524.

Petri, however, was not alone in putting the printing-press to good use. The Catholic bishop, Hans Brask, had established his own printworks in Linköping, run by Oluf Ulriksson, from where he attacked both Lutheranism and Olaus Petri. In November 1526 Gustav Vasa intervened on the side of Petri and forced Brask to close his press. To add insult to injury, Ulriksson then moved the print-works to Malmø where, in 1528, he had established himself as the evangelical printer *par excellence*. This was undoubtedly part of the same strategy which had made the king resurrect the old printing-press in Uppsala and recruit the printer, Jörgen Richlhoff, from Lübeck. Later, Gustav Vasa secured full evangelical control over this press by moving it to Stockholm and placing it under Andreae's supervision.[51]

[50] K. B. Westman, *Reformation och Revolution: en Olavus-Petristudie* (Uppsala, 1941).
[51] R. Murray, *Stockholms kyrkostyrelse intill 1630-talets mitt* (Lund, 1949), and his *Olavus Petri* (Stockholm, 1952), pp. 28–53. Remi Kick, 'Le livre et la Réforme dans le royaume de Suède, 1526–1571', in Gilmont, *La Réforme et le livre*, 460–63. For *Een nyttwgh*

114   *Ole Peter Grell*

Possibly inspired by events further south, Gustav Vasa attempted to accelerate the pace of the Reformation in Sweden during 1526. The ten questions he had forwarded to the Catholic clergy and the evangelical leaders towards the end of 1526 indicate that the king planned a religious disputation as a precursor to some sort of Reformation, having witnessed the success of similar, earlier disputations in Germany. Olaus Petri presented the evangelical position verbally to the king and council while the Catholics had the questions answered in writing by Peder Galle, the learned canon of the chapter in Uppsala.[52] At this stage Gustav Vasa does not seem to have been unduly concerned with the mounting protests from the Swedish peasantry, who objected to increased taxation and evangelical changes. Neither do the developments over the summer of 1526 in Stockholm appear to have worried him. Here the arrival of Melchior Hoffmann had generated iconoclastic disturbances. Hoffmann's type of radical/popular Protestantism had found fertile soil among the German residents. His eschatological preaching received the backing of leading merchants and supporters of Christian II, such as Gorius Holste, the former mayor, Kurt Druvenagel, Hans Bökman, and Jöran von Sottern, several of whom were also active in the later disturbances of 1529 and 1534. In spite of admonitions from the king, Hoffmann proved unwilling to temper his activities. Consequently, he was expelled from Sweden in January 1527, and left for Holstein.[53]

In early 1527 dissatisfaction among the peasants finally spilled over in the *Daljunkern's* revolt. Gustav Vasa, who had called a parliament (*Riksdag*) to meet in Västeras in June suspected that the prelates secretly supported the rebellion in order to prevent him from weakening the secular power of the church. If this was so, their efforts failed. At this parliament the Catholic Church in Sweden lost most vestiges of political and economic power, since it was forced to return all its fiefs to the Crown. The king took over the administration of all lay properties belonging to the monasteries and the church, while the lay nobility, who had deserted their family and friends among the Catholic hieracy, could reclaim all properties donated to the church since 1454. Meanwhile parliament accepted Gustav Vasa's disingenuous claim that he knew of no Lutherans, and that he had only protected and promoted preachers who preached the Gospel. In consequence the evangelical preachers were

wnderwijsning, see B. Hesselman (ed.), *Olavus Petri Samlade Skrifter* (4 vols., Uppsala, 1914), I. 1–129.
[52] Holmquist, *Svenska Kyrkans*, III. 131–40.
[53] M. Roberts, *The Early Vasas. A History of Sweden, 1523–1611* (Cambridge, 1968), 70–1. See also Deppermann, *Hoffmann*, 35–94 and E. Schieche, *Die Anfänge der deutschen St. Gertruds-Gemeinde zu Stockholm im 16. Jahrhundert* (Münster/Köln 1952).

able to continue their activities.[54] The economic decisions from Västeras were put into effect immediately. Gustav Vasa needed every penny he could raise in order to repay his debts to Lübeck and the other Hanseatic cities of the Baltic, incurred in the war of independence against Christian II. Realising defeat, Bishop Hans Brask fled to Danzig in 1528 rather than face humiliation.

Despite the king's skilful handling of the parliament the need for religious uniformity was becoming increasingly urgent. In January 1529 a national synod was convened in Örebro under the chairmanship of Laurentius Andreae. Despite conciliatory words from Olaus Petri hardly anything was achieved. A few Catholic holy days were abolished, but the Synod decided to continue with a modified Latin Mass supplemented with sermons in the vernacular.[55] As a compromise, this solution satisfied no-one. The vanguard of the Reformation, which primarily consisted of German residents in Stockholm, was strongly opposed to the Synod's decision. The magistracy, after having warned the German residents and their minister, Tielemann, not to cause any disturbances, was eventually forced to imprison leading members of the community. In April 1529 another peasant revolt broke out, this time in south-west Sweden. Once more it was a political rebellion with strong anti-evangelical overtones. The rebels complained about the unchristian government and the new Lutheran heresies, and on this occasion they were supported by representatives from other social groups such as the gentry and the nobility, who provided cohesion and leadership. In the event Gustav Vasa managed to contain the danger by promising to retain the status quo in religion. At the ensuing parliament in Strängnäs in June, the king emphasised that changes in ceremonies and discipline, such as services in Swedish, had neither been forbidden nor enforced by him.[56]

Despite this delicate balancing act, political reality, if not religious inclination, forced Gustav Vasa to adopt a far less evangelical church policy from the spring of 1529. When, in 1531, he wanted to fill the archbishopric which had remained vacant since Johannes Magnus' flight to Poland in 1526, he avoided appointing the leading reformer, Laurentius Andreae. Instead, the position was given to the brother of Olaus Petri, Laurentius Petri. Andreae was clearly out of favour by 1531. That year he lost his chancellorship, which was given to Olaus Petri, who in the event would hold the Royal Seal for only two years. By 1533 both reformers had been marginalised.

Olaus Petri's dismissal was part of a general shift in Gustav Vasa's

[54] H. Yrwing, *Gustav Vasas, kröningsfrågan och Västerås riksdag 1527* (Lund, 1956).
[55] Roberts, *The Early Vasas*, pp. 85–6. Holmquist, *Svenska Kyrkans*, III. pp. 190–4.
[56] Holmquist, *Svenska Kyrkans*, III. pp. 196–8.

church policy. The first seeds of change had undoubtedly been sown back in 1529 when the revolt had forced the king to re-think his church policy. His misgivings were reinforced by the brief Catholic reaction in Denmark following the death of Frederik I. The radical Reformation which had just taken place in Lübeck can only have added to the king's anxieties regarding the loyalty of the evangelical movement in Sweden, which of course had its strongest support among the German population of Stockholm. These anxieties seemed to be justified when a conspiracy to blow him up and hand over Stockholm to the Hansa – a Swedish Gunpowder Plot – was discovered in 1536. The protagonists included the mint-master, Anders Hansen, and most of the German merchants who had been involved in the disturbances in 1526. Olaus Petri was suspected of having been among the conspirators and his plea for mercy for those arrested did nothing to improve his standing with the king.[57]

In the event, the setback to the Reformation in Sweden proved only temporary. Victory for the Reformation in Denmark encouraged Gustav Vasa to re-start the process of reform in Sweden. Once again the king allowed a national Synod to take the initiative. The Synod of Uppsala under the guidance of Archbishop Laurentius Petri introduced the first significant changes to the order and ceremonies of the Swedish Church. The Synod decided that all services should be conducted in Swedish and that Swedish manuals should be used for baptisms and marriage. The king, however, had no intention of allowing the ministers to seize the initiative in a reorganised church. The strong reactions and protests from the peasants against the changes in religion served to convince him that the Crown had to take full control of the church. Royal directions were issued which referred to the decision reached at Västeras in 1527, pointing out that the clergy were not empowered to introduce any changes in ceremonies. During 1539 Gustav Vasa repeatedly attacked Laurentius Andreae and Olaus Petri for failing to teach obedience towards secular authority.

These tensions finally came to a head at the parliament in Örebro in December 1539, where Gustav Vasa took the necessary measures to guarantee full royal control over the Swedish Church. On 8 December the king issued instructions for a new church government. They were heavily influenced by the Wittenberg theologian, Georg Norman, who, on the recommendation of Luther and Melanchton, had been recruited by the king to advise him on church matters. Norman, who had arrived together with Finland's reformer, Michael Agricola, had been counselling the king since the summer. Gustav Vasa used his *cura religionis* as 'protector of the

---

[57] Murray, *Stockholms kyrkostyrelse*. For the reformation in Lübeck, see W. Jannasch, *Reformationsgeschichte Lübecks 1515–1530* (Lübeck, 1958).

Holy Christian faith in the whole kingdom' to introduce a new church structure parallel to the episcopal system which it would replace when the incumbents retired or died. It consisted of a 'superintendent' (Georg Norman), assisted by an 'adjunkt' and a religious council, while a 'konservator' (a layman), and two 'seniorer' (both clergy) should be appointed in each diocese in order to create uniformity. As if to emphasise royal supremacy Laurentius Andreae and Olaus Petri, who had been so closely associated with the independence of the emerging evangelical church, were accused of treason and condemned to death by parliament, only to be pardoned by the king a few days later.[58]

By 1540 the Swedish Church had finally experienced a princely Reformation, even if only in church government. It still had to wait another thirty years before it received a full Protestant church order in 1571. The long drawn-out and (in comparison with Denmark and Schleswig–Holstein) tortuous course of the Reformation in Sweden, was rooted in two specific characteristics of the local situation. Firstly, Gustav Vasa never appears to have been a particular religious man, and certainly not a committed Protestant. Of the three Scandinavian rulers in the Reformation period he was the least influenced by religion; instead his church policy was determined by political and economic considerations. His counterparts in Denmark and Schleswig–Holstein, Frederik I and Christian III, were both dedicated Protestants, not only politically, but also personally. Secondly, Gustav Vasa's constant change of pace and direction in church policy was facilitated by the lack of any significant popular support for the evangelical cause in Sweden. Only Stockholm, with its large German population, offered significant backing for the Reformation, and here, as in Copenhagen, the evangelical movement became hopelessly enmeshed in the political game surrounding the deposed king, Christian II.

It also has to be recognised that Gustav Vasa was not able to feel secure on the Swedish throne before 1540. Personally he nurtured the doubts of the *parvenu*, and politically the not infrequent rebellions against him served to underline the fragility of his rule. A princely Reformation on a par with that of Schleswig–Holstein was never within his reach, depending as it did on political stability and a strong ruler. Neither could he model his church policy on that of Frederik I in Denmark: the political freedom of action on offer to the Danish king from 1526 onwards, due to the growing popular support for the Reformation in the towns and cities in Denmark, was totally lacking in Sweden. Thus politics, in the person of the deposed king Christian and unresolved social tensions, cast a long

[58] Roberts, *The Early Vasas*, pp. 107–23.

E

118   *Ole Peter Grell*

shadow over the Reformation in Scandinavia. Sweden, for all its later fidelity to the Lutheran cause, had made a curiously hesitant beginning in the first generation, and evangelicals were consistently indebted to the promptings and example of the kingdoms further south.

SELECT BIBLIOGRAPHY

SOURCES

Heilesen, H. (ed.), *Krøniken om Gråbrødrenes fordrivelse fra deres klostre i Danmark* (Copenhagen, 1967).
Heise, A. (ed.), *Skibykrøniken* (Reprint edn., Copenhagen, 1967).
Hesselman, B. (ed.), *Olavus Petri Samlade Skrifter* (4 vols., Uppsala, 1914–17).
Kristensen, M. and Andersen, N. K. (eds.), *Skrifter af Paulus Helie* (7 vols., Copenhagen, 1932–48).
Rørdam, H. Fr. (ed.), *Skrifter fra Reformationstiden* (5 vols., Copenhagen, 1889–90).

LITERATURE

Andersen, J. O. *Overfor Kirkebruddet* (Copenhagen, 1917).
Paulus Helie, I (Copenhagen, 1936).
Andersen, N. K. *Confessio Hafniensis. Den københavnske Bekendelse af 1530* (Copenhagen, 1954).
Andrén, Carl-Gustav (ed.), *Reformationen i Norden. Kontinuitet och Förnyelse* (Lund, 1973).
Bergendoff, C. *Olavus Petri and the ecclesiastical transformation in Sweden, 1521–1552* (2nd edn., Philadelphia, 1965).
Deppermann, Klaus. *Melchior Hoffman* (Edinburgh, 1989).
Dunkley, E. H. *The Reformation in Denmark* (London, 1948).
Grane, L. and Hørby, K. (eds.), *Die dänische Reformation vor ihrem internationalen Hintergrund* (Göttingen, 1990).
Gregersen, H. V. *Reformation i Sønderjylland* (Aabenraa, 1986).
Grell, O. P. 'Jørgen Kock – En studie i religion og politik i reformationstidens Danmark', in S. E. Green-Petersen et al. (eds.), *Festskrift til Poul Enemark. Profiler i Nordisk Senmiddelalder og Renaessance*, (Århus, 1983).
'The City of Malmø and the Danish Reformation', *ARG*, 79, (1988).
'The Emergence of two Cities: The Reformation in Sweden and Copenhagen', in Grane and Hørby, *Dänische Reformation*.
Holmquist, H. and Pleijel, H. (eds.), *Svenska kyrkans Historia. III. Reformationstidevarvet, 1521–1611* (Uppsala, 1983).
Ingebrand, S. *Olavus Petris reformatoriske åskådning* (Lund, 1964).
Johannesson, G. *Den skånska Kyrkan och Reformationen* (Lund, 1947).
Murray, R. *Stockholms kyrkostyrelse intill 1630–talets mitt* (Lund, 1949).
Roberts, M. *The Early Vasa. A History of Sweden, 1523–1611* (Cambridge, 1968).
Schwarz Lausten, M. *Christian den 3. og kirken 1537–1559* (Copenhagen, 1987).
Schück, H. *Ecclesia Lincopensis. Studier om Linköpinskyrkan under Medeltiden och Gustav Vasa* (Stockholm, 1959).

Schwaiger, G. *Die Reformation in den nordischen Ländern* (Munich, 1962).
Skyum-Nielsen, N. 'Ærkekonge og Ærkebiskop. Nye træk i dansk kirkehistorie, 1376–1536', *Scandia*, 23 (1955–6), 1–101.
Svalenius, I. *Georg Norman. En biografisk studie* (Lund, 1937).
Westman, K. B. *Reformation och Revolution: en Olavus-Petristudie* (Uppsala, 1941).

6   France

David Nicholls

The questions posed by the Reformation in France are different from those involved in countries that experienced a state Reformation. With the exception of Béarn (Navarre), which cannot be considered as fully a part of France during the sixteenth century, Protestants were only rarely in a position to try and impose their religion and way of life upon an uncommitted or hostile population. For the most part their periods of domination in a particular city or region, dependent on the protection of the powerful and the fortunes of religious war, were too short to allow a sustained effort at the 'Protestantisation' of the populace. Instead we are dealing with the growth, at first slow then spectacular, of an initially clandestine and unorganised movement, all of whose adherents, however mixed their motives, were Huguenots because they wanted to be, in conscious opposition to the existing church and implicitly, whether they liked it or not, the state. In so doing they developed not only a new ecclesiastical organisation, eventually channelled by Calvinism, but also new political theories and an original morality and mentality. To this extent a recognisable French Protestantism was being forged during the period considered here, from the 1520s to the 1560s, although it was only from about 1555 onwards that French Protestantism would find a secure base and organised church structure.

Equally important to the fate of the first tentative reforming initiatives of the first generation was the fact that French Catholicism was neither static nor monolithic. Both Reformation and Counter Reformation were relative latecomers in France, and the boundaries of orthodoxy were porous on both sides. Reform within the church, which had been proclaimed loudly, but only realised in a patchy, almost haphazard manner before the Reformation, was now diverted by the range of possible reactions to the Protestant menace. The Gallican tradition of independence from papal control and interference ensured that if a French king had attempted a Henry VIII-style break with Rome, as may have been possible in 1551, a considerable number of the clergy would have followed happily.[1] And the reactions to Protestantism from clergy at all levels ranged through conversion to the new religion, the adoption of aspects of it while rejecting others, and attempts at compromise and reconciliation, to violent hostility, usually accompanied by internal reform and the revival or re-creation of a militant Catholic piety. The notions of reform and Reformation in France have so many facets as to be, if we are not careful, positively bewildering, but at the same time they can help us towards a critical assessment of the labelling and rigid characterisations inherent in Reformation history.

Reform and Reformation were primarily urban phenomena. This may seem surprising at first glance because the only heresy existing in France on the eve of the Reformation was overwhelmingly and prototypically rural. Recent work on the Waldensians of the Alps and Provence, however, has revealed them as adherents or guardians of a peasant religion, based as much as anything on proverbial wisdom and a strict morality, with a skeletal organisation provided by their wandering holy men or *barbes*.[2] Persecution of the Waldenses seems to have been inspired by economic greed, the desire of cliques drawn from local elites to get their hands on land owned by the supposed heretics, and in Provence by the desire to convert or eliminate a dangerously independent population in a strategically vital region. Certainly the Waldensians viewed themselves as the only true church, but when they presented a petition complaining about persecution to King Louis XII in 1502 their ideas were only marginally heterodox and a slow process of rehabilitation proceeded. Eventually, under the prompting of their *barbes*, the Waldenses were to adhere to Swiss reform, but without apparently giving up their old attitudes. Their small numbers and geographical position on the periphery of the kingdom makes them a fascinating case study of religious change in isolated communities, but marginal to the history of the French Reformation. It seems that when Erasmus made his famous statement in 1517 that France was 'the purest and most prosperous part of christendom', free of heretics and Jews, he was wrong about Jews but right about heretics.[3]

The problem of determining what exactly was heretical, however, did not go away for many years, at least until Protestant churches were properly organised on a national level in the late 1550s. In the first

[1] See M. Venard, 'Une réforme Gallicane? Le projet de concile national de 1551', *Revue d'histoire de l'Eglise de France*, 67 (1981), 201–25.
[2] E. Cameron, *The Reformation of the Heretics: The Waldenses of the Alps, 1480–1580* (Oxford, 1984); G. Audisio, *Les Vaudois du Luberon: Une minorité en Provence (1460–1560)* (Gap, 1984). M. Venard, *L'Eglise d'Avignon au XVIe siècle* (Service de Reproduction des Thèses, Universitaire de Lille III, 1980), pp. 366–505.
[3] M. Mann, *Erasme et les débuts de la Réforme Française* (Paris, 1934), p. 23.

generation the variety of reformist opinion within the church made it difficult to define whether any particular individual had overstepped the bounds of acceptability; and there again, the very awareness of the existence of a new and challenging heresy, the extent of which was almost invariably exaggerated by worried clerics, caused ecclesiastical and civil authorities to look askance at what may have been accepted or unnoticed in the relatively open, multivalent and complacent atmosphere of pre-Reformation Catholicism. The machinery for dealing with heresy varied in different parts of France, but was everywhere unclear: bishops, the king, the sovereign courts, town councils, inquisitors in the south, and the theology faculty of the University of Paris (known as the Sorbonne) were all involved, and the possibilities for the kind of conflicts of jurisdiction beloved of civil and canon lawyers were almost endless. Cases could drag on endlessly, and acute suspects could create more confusion by moving from one area of jurisdiction to another. For example, in 1538 a certain Jean du Rez managed to procure his release from heresy charges by exploiting jealousies between the Parlement of Paris and local courts in Amiens.[4] The periodic royal attempts at simplification had only limited success. Henry II's creation in 1547 of a new chamber in the Parlement of Paris to deal with heresy cases, which became known as the *chambre ardente*, was resented by churchmen, who lost jurisdiction over heresy cases involving lay suspects, and by the other magistrates of the Parlement, some of whom resented the increased authority given to their colleagues, others of whom were opposed to the death penalty for heretics. This lasted until 1551, when the Edict of Châteaubriand tried to return heresy prosecution to local courts, civil for cases involving sedition, ecclesiastical for simple heresy. But the definition of seditious heresy was inevitably difficult to establish and bickering continued. Finally in 1560 the Edict of Romorantin gave all jurisdiction over simple heresy to church courts, while secular courts dealt with disorder or treason arising from heresy. This system remained in force for the rest of the century, but complaints, especially from the clergy, never ceased.[5] Add to this the fact that in many towns arguments were still going on between municipalities and ecclesiastical bodies about areas of jurisdiction within cities, and it becomes clear that the only people sure to gain from heresy trials were lawyers. The church was a house divided, faced with intermittent but serious demands from the laity that it put itself in order. The lay desire to keep the church in its place, which was to emerge forcefully in the Estates General of 1560 and 1561, was yet another facet of reform.

---

[4] D. Nicholls, 'The Nature of Popular Heresy in France 1520–1541', *HJ*, 26 (1983), 263.
[5] English summaries of the relevant edicts are to be found in N. M. Sutherland, *The Huguenot Struggle for Recognition* (New Haven and London, 1980), pp. 333–72.

All these problems appeared around 'the cradle of the French Reformation', the diocese of Meaux under Guillaume Briçonnet in the early 1520s.[6] Briçonnet was far from being the first reformist bishop in France, but the intensity of his effort in a diocese near Paris, the court, the Parlement and the Sorbonne, and at a time when Protestant ideas were beginning to circulate among intellectuals and churchmen, turned the Meaux reform into a springboard of Reformation. Bishops were, of course, members of the elite, the vast majority of them concerned more with politics and family advancement than with the spiritual matters, and the Briçonnet family, which had risen spectacularly from the financial and mercantile milieu of Tours, had been no exception to this rule. Guillaume Briçonnet, after pursuing a classic career as pluralist and diplomat, became abbot of St-Germain-des-Prés, then bishop of Lozère and then of Meaux, where, excluded from the highest political elite in 1517, he made the startling move of taking his episcopal duties seriously. This was bound to tread on a number of sensitive toes. Reform of religious life could only be carried out properly if the power and authority of bishops within their dioceses were strengthened and extended. Other ecclesiastical bodies, most notably cathedral chapters and religious orders, would not take kindly to the inevitable erosion of their traditional rights and privileges. Briçonnet survived harassment by the Sorbonne because of his powerful connections at the royal court, especially Marguerite of Navarre, sister of Francis I. In a society based on clientage and protection, patronage from the powerful allowed humanists and writers to flirt openly with heretical ideas. But this was a dangerous game, and when unorthodox ideas began to spread outside restricted intellectual or courtly circles the price of survival became dissimulation or silence.

The basis of the Meaux reform was preaching. The standard of preaching, and the fact that the higher clergy did so little of it, was a major target for humanist and Protestant criticisms of the church. The major burden in the fifteenth century had fallen onto the shoulders of the mendicant orders, and the emotional revivalist preaching of the Franciscans in particular had struck a strong popular chord.[7] And, the obvious importance of printing in spreading new ideas notwithstanding, the astonishing capacity of early-modern people to sit or stand listening to sermons for hours on end, and a positive desire and curiosity to hear what preachers had to say, was to attract large numbers to Protestantism, even if only

[6] The latest and fullest study of Briçonnet is M. Veissière, *L'évêque Guillaume Briçonnet (1470–1534)* (Provins, 1986).

[7] See in particular H. Martin, *Les ordres mendiants en Bretagne, vers 1230–vers 1530* (Paris, 1975), and his 'La prédication et les masses au XVe siècle. Facteurs et limites d'une réussite', in J. Delumeau (ed.), *Histoire vécue du peuple chrétien* (2 vols., Toulouse, 1979), II. 9–41; A. J. Krailsheimer, *Rabelais and the Franciscans* (Oxford, 1963).

temporarily. Briçonnet attempted to meet the demand by a reform of preaching root and branch throughout his diocese, and this inevitably upset the Franciscans who saw their privileges under attack. In 1521 he invited his old friend, the noted scholar and teacher Jacques Lefèvre d'Etaples, whose brand of mystical Christianity and humanist biblical studies made him a victim of the climate of suspicion in Paris, to reside in Meaux, which was just far enough away from the capital to ensure his safety. Other younger evangelicals soon followed, some of whom, most notably Guillaume Farel and Pierre Caroli, were quickly to embrace a form of Protestantism. The diocese was divided into thirty-two 'stations', with preaching duties shared between parish priests and specialist itinerant preachers, either Franciscans or members of the Meaux group of evangelicals. However, doctrinal deviations soon crept into sermons, causing Briçonnet twice to revoke the powers of preachers with 'Lutheran' tendencies and to preach himself against Lutheranism.[8]

Briçonnet and Lefèvre continued to enjoy the protection of Marguerite of Navarre and good relations with the court, but in 1525 the Franciscans were able to take advantage of the absence of Francis I, in captivity after the battle of Pavia, to drag Briçonnet and so-called *bibliens* before the Parlement of Paris, initially over orders to stop the Franciscans preaching, but widening to include accusations of heresy against the preachers. The trial became a tussle between the Parlement, the newly created *juges délégués*, who were supposed to try clerics accused of heresy, and the queen mother, Louise of Savoy, and the whole affair eventually petered out after the king's return from his Spanish prison. However, it put an end to the Meaux group, most of whom fled either abroad or to some powerful protector to avoid arrest. Furthermore, the Parlement's gathering of information through agents sent to various parts of the diocese revealed alarming evidence of heresy among the people, thus apparently proving Briçonnet's opponents right about the consequences of his reforms. Briçonnet's reforming ambitions had placed him in the position of having constantly to defend his own orthodoxy and seemed to have weakened the church instead of strengthening it. Old and tired, he continued as bishop of Meaux until his death in 1534, still devoting some effort to reforming the monasteries of the diocese, but avoiding anything that might have any effect in society at large.[9]

Two distinct issues had scuppered the Meaux reform: internal ecclesiastical politics and the growth of popular heresy. The former had more to do with power than with doctrine, the fundamental issue being the extent and nature of episcopal authority. Far away from Meaux, the contempor-

---

[8] Veissière, *Briçonnet*, pp. 224–30, 263–76.   [9] *Ibid.*, pp. 313–73, 411–33.

neous efforts of the very orthodox Robert Cenalis to reform the small south-eastern diocese of Riez also ran into bitter opposition, this time from the cathedral chapter, causing him to transfer to Avranches in 1532.[10] Briçonnet had always insisted strongly on the affirmation of his powers, but ran up against the self-interest, usefully boosted by Gallican ideas, of the various *corps* that made up the church in France, principally here the mendicant orders and the Sorbonne. This problem was to remain unsolved throughout the sixteenth century, hindering the efforts of those bishops who wished to apply the decrees of the Council of Trent in their dioceses.

Unorthodox ideas, meanwhile, could be discussed in intellectual and courtly circles as long as they remained confined there. Individual suspects became the unfortunate objects of power struggles between the Crown, the Parlement and the Sorbonne. The most prominent of these in the 1520s was the humanist and printer Louis de Berquin, who Francis I, jealous of his authority and his image as father of letters, managed to save until 1529. But the apparent growth of popular heresy, 'the Lutheran plague', was an altogether much more worrying matter, which united the king with the guardians of orthodoxy. As yet the numbers involved were only small, but any public manifestation, such as the smashing of an image of the Virgin in the rue du Petit-Saint-Antoine in Paris in 1528, was both subversive of public order and apparently indicative of the existence of an organised and clandestine sect of who knew what proportions. The official response in the form of expiatory processions and rewards for information about the guilty had to be swift, public, and involving all civil and ecclesiastical authorities, headed by the king himself.[11]

The guardians of orthodoxy had a vested interest in exaggerating the Lutheran threat, reformists in playing it down. When René du Bellay, administrator of the diocese of Paris and protector of humanists, tried to take a calm view in 1533, saying that the danger was over-estimated and that there were fewer Lutherans than in previous years, his words seemed to be contradicted by the Affair of the Placards, when notices containing a violent attack on the Mass were posted in Paris and other cities.[12] In the inflamed atmosphere following this outrage the papal nuncio, Aleander,

[10] F. J. Baumgartner, *Change and Continuity in the French Episcopate: The Bishops and the Wars of Religion, 1547–1610* (Durham, N.C., 1986), pp. 102, 145.

[11] See the contemporary accounts in V.-L. Bourilly (ed.), *Le journal d'un bourgeois de Paris sous le règne de François Ier (1515–1536)* (Paris, 1910), pp. 290–4, and G. Fagniez (ed.), *Livre de raison de Me Nicolas Versoris, avocat au parlement de Paris, 1519–1530* (Paris, 1885), pp. 112–14.

[12] R. Hari, 'Les placards de 1534', (with text and reproduction of surviving copy), in G. Berthoud *et al.*, *Aspects de la propagande religieuse* (Geneva, 1957), pp. 79–142. The fullest account of the affair is in G. Berthoud, *Antoine Marcourt* (Geneva, 1973), pp. 157–222.

could state that there were 30,000 Lutherans in Paris, a patently absurd notion but one which could not be refuted.[13] And what were these heretical hordes up to? According to the English ambassador, Francis I seriously believed that the Lutherans 'had determined, among other things, to burn all the churches in Paris on Christmas Eve', and the urban rumour mill caused all English and Germans to be seen as Lutherans.[14]

Reality was more sober, but in the long run more threatening. Appreciable numbers of artisans in large and small towns gradually became detached or semi-detached from the full panoply of Catholicism during the 1520s and 1530s.[15] Coherence and order developed more slowly: heresy was still individual and individualist, defined by what it was against rather than by positive doctrinal content. People did not suddenly convert to a form of coherent Protestantism. They heard preachers, read if they were literate or listened to reading if they were illiterate, talked and argued in inns, workshops and their homes. The Reformation was first an upsurge of interest in fundamental religious matters by a sizeable minority of all classes, but principally the bourgeois ruling groups of the towns and established artisans, some of whom still had a voice in urban politics. Catholicism's weakest points were the most obviously venal aspects of its practice, those which wounded the pocket as well as the conscience. At Meaux in the early 1520s the difficult economic situation had undoubtedly made people unwilling or unable to dispense money for saints' cults or to ease souls through purgatory, especially when the preachers of the Meaux groups were asserting that such beliefs were unfounded in Scripture and imposed by the avarice of corrupt clerics.[16] Gradually the alternatives, presented in little books of protestantising doctrine, became available elsewhere, carried far and wide by itinerant peddlers or *colporteurs*.[17] The individuals involved were mostly charged with publicly attacking one aspect or another of Catholic practice, and there was often confusion about whether specific propositions were in fact heretical. During the 1530s, however, and particularly after the Affair of the Placards, the acid test of heresy came to be the Mass and the doctrine

[13] P. Imbart de la Tour, *Les origines de la Réforme* (4 vols., Paris, 1905–35), III. 414.
[14] *Calendar of Letters and Papers, Foreign and Domestic, of the Reign of Henry VIII*, vol. 8 (1885), no. 165.
[15] See Nicholls, 'The Nature of Popular Heresy'.
[16] H. Heller, *The Conquest of Poverty: The Calvinist Revolt in Sixteenth-Century France* (Leiden, 1986), ch. 2, and his 'Famine, Revolt and Heresy at Meaux, 1521–25', *ARG*, 68 (1977), 133–57.
[17] On the role of printing see F. Higman, 'Le levain de l'Evangile', in R. Chartier and H.-J. Martin (eds.), *Histoire de l'édition française. Vol 1: Le livre conquérant. Du moyen âge au milieu du XVIIe siècle* (Paris, 1989), pp. 372–403, and his 'Le domaine française, 1520–1562', in J.-F. Gilmont (ed.), *La Réforme et le livre* (Paris, 1990), pp. 105–86.

of the Eucharist. Rejection of the 'sacrament of the altar' became the high road to the stake for martyrs whose conduct at their execution still aroused curiosity and sympathy and gave them an impact on popular perceptions out of all proportion to their numbers.[18] Such organisation as existed before the mid-1540s consisted of small groups discussing Scripture in inns or private houses, and leaders were those with the prestige attached to reading ability or ownership of books.

Although the mostly lower-class *sacramentaires* burnt at the stake in the 1530s would not have appreciated the fact, the situation with regard to repression and compromise remained complicated. In court and intellectual circles, in universities and colleges, and indeed within the church it makes little sense to talk of Protestants as opposed to Catholics, only of patrons and clients, with the result that the consistency historians look for is not to be found. Patronage from humanistically inclined members of a prominent political and ecclesiastical dynasty, such as the du Bellays, could keep the Sorbonnard wolves at bay. René du Bellay and his brother Jean, bishop of Paris, protected the indisputably unorthodox Gérard Roussel, one of the Meaux preachers, who in 1536 obtained the bishopric of Oloron through the good offices of Marguerite of Navarre; while even the very orthodox cardinal François de Tournon patronised the law professor, Jean du Boysonné, who was suspected of heresy by the Parlement of Toulouse in 1532.[19] Another du Bellay, Guillaume, seigneur de Langey and patron of Rabelais and many others, was instrumental in the abortive attempt of 1534–5 to bring Philip Melanchthon and other German Lutherans to France to debate the possibility of religious unification with the theologians of the Sorbonne.[20] The reason behind this was political, Francis I's desire for an alliance with the Schmalkaldic League, but it does illustrate that there was no specific date when compromise became impossible, right up to Catherine de Medici's Colloquy of Poissy in September 1561. Religious doctrine could be made malleable, even if the structures of power could not.

Nowhere was this more evident than in the field of education. Although no Protestant or Jesuit academies were founded in France before 1560, municipal colleges, set up by town councils, often against ecclesiastical opposition, became the medium whereby evangelical ideas and religious controversies were transmitted to the generation destined to attain local

[18] See D. Nicholls, 'The Theatre of Martyrdom in the French Reformation', *P and P*, 121 (1988), 49–73.
[19] Baumgartner, *Change and Continuity*, pp. 122–5; R. A. Mentzer, *Heresy Proceedings in Languedoc, 1500–1560* (*Transactions of the American Philosophical Society*, 74, 1984), p. 132.
[20] See R. J. Knecht, *Francis I* (Cambridge, 1982), pp. 392–4.

prominence during the religious wars.[21] Significantly, although this was a national phenomenon, smaller towns in the south appear to have been more fervent than those in the north in the establishment of colleges, and in a city like Nîmes defence of the local college against charges of propagating heresy could easily become a matter of civil pride.[22] Locally powerful laymen would, as always, defend their rights and privileges against clerical interference, even at the cost of admitting the heretical poison into the urban bloodstream. Some establishments, most notoriously the Collège de Guyenne in Bordeaux, became well known as 'foyers of heresy', simply because the best available regents and schoolmasters, attracted from Paris by salaries and the promise of protection, were proponents of humanist education with an evangelical colouring, determined to instil religious knowledge into their pupils and free them from superstition as the necessary precondition for their living a good life. Florimond de Raemond, an ex-pupil of the Collège de Guyenne who later became a fervent Catholic, wrote of the 1530s and 1540s: 'France was then in such a state that in our colleges it had become customary to point out those who showed no sign of appreciating the evangelical innovations: such boys were considered retarded.'[23] This was exaggerated and somewhat paranoid, a classic example of a conservative blaming progressive education for perceived moral and social ills. Protestantism succeeded very well in establishing itself in cities without a municipal college, as at Tours or Angers, more strongly than in de Raemond's Bordeaux. Nor did students necessarily go along with what their teachers told them, as de Raemond himself shows. But it does indicate an important point about the attitudes of urban elites, humanistically trained at local colleges or far away universities, who would not view Protestantism as the devilish contagion portrayed by its enemies. In the years before the religious wars such people, like their counterparts in the church, were to be squeezed between fervent Protestant and Catholic minorities, but would remain committed to trying to keep the peace, if necessary by religious compromise. It was to be a losing battle, conditioned by the creation of militant minorities and by the behaviour of those more powerful than town councillors or even bishops.

While the urban elites received their humanist schooling a parallel intelligentsia of preachers, pamphleteers and prophets, not as yet as significant as they would become during the religious wars, tried to

---

21 See G. Huppert, *Public Schools in Renaissance France* (Urbana and Chicago, 1984), and his 'Classes dangereuses: école et Réforme en France, 1530–1560', in B. Chevalier and R. Sauzet (eds.), *Les Réformes: Enracinement socio-culturel* (Paris, 1985), pp. 209–17.
22 H. Hauser, 'Nîmes, les consultats et la Réforme', in his *Etudes sur la Réforme Française* (Paris, 1909), pp. 184–202.
23 Quoted in Huppert, *Public Schools*, pp. 99–100.

propagate an apocalyptic interpretation of current events, calling the people to repentance either through strict adherence to Catholic orthodoxy or through radical rejection of a corrupt church and world.[24] On the Protestant side the task of combating such tendencies was the work of Calvinism, but the individualism and prophetic drift of early Protestantism were not suddenly brought under control merely because the French edition of Calvin's *Institution of the Christian Religion* became available after 1542. One would not expect Protestant nobles, whose seigneurial Protestantism was based on their feudal role as protectors and military leaders, to submit happily to discipline enforced by the bourgeois of Geneva. But townspeople, bourgeois and artisans, could be equally fractious: Protestantism in the cities retained something of the nature of a religious debating society. Nevertheless, the history of Protestantism in the 1540s and 1550s is characterised by the progressive imposition of doctrinal unity under the aegis of Geneva, culminating in the foundation of Calvinist churches from 1555 onwards and the creation of Protestant parties at local, provincial and national levels under the ultimate leadership of some of the highest nobles in the land. The acceptance of doctrinal unity, itself by no means unanimous, did not mean that the growing numbers of Huguenots all thought and acted in the same way or that they accepted the views of Calvin and the Genevan theologians on any matter other than religious doctrine, that is on tactics or politics. There were militant prophetic Protestants, some influenced by millenarian ideas, who wished to overthrow the papal Antichrist and impose the new religion on the unregenerate; peaceful Protestants, who merely wanted to be left alone to practice their religion; Protestant sympathisers, who kept their feelings secret, partly through fear and social convention, but partly also for genuine religious reasons; and the Protestant nobility, who never stopped being nobles, with a concomitant mentality and lifestyle. Geneva supplied religious guidance and, most important, pastors and preachers, but was never in a position to control events as they developed rapidly and unpredictably, especially in the late 1550s.

The precise situation was different in every city, small town and province. Rural folk were not immune to Protestantism. The Cévennes, which combined a high level of artisanal activity with geographical isolation from the centres of power, became one of the strongholds of the Reformation, a process which evidence from wills suggests began in the 1530s.[25] Huguenot peasants and rural artisans were to be found else-

[24] See D. Crouzet, *Les guerriers de Dieu: la violence au temps des troubles de religion, vers 1525-vers 1610* (2 vols., Paris, 1990), I, chs. 2, 3.
[25] A. Molinier, 'De la religion des oeuvres à la Réformation dans les Cévennes (1450–1600)', *Revue d'histoire de l'Eglise de France*, 72 (1986), 245–63.

where, in Dauphiné, the Midi and Normandy for example. Villages which enjoyed economic contacts with cities through a putting-out system of manufacture were easily penetrated, and the estates of Protestant nobles became refuges and provided places of worship for Huguenots from surrounding areas. But hatred of an unpopular *seigneur* could override religious differences, as when Catholic peasants joined with Protestants in the murder of the baron de Fumel in the Agenais in 1561, prefiguring similar incidents during the religious wars.[26] For the most part the peasantry stood on the sidelines of religious division, only really being moved to action in self-defence against marauding armies and noble bandits of either persuasion or none. Artisans and village notaries, where they existed, were easily attracted to new ideas, but in general Le Roy Ladurie's distinction between 'cardeurs huguenots et laboureurs papistes' holds good. Peasants maintained and defended their own traditions and 'danced despite the Huguenots'.[27]

Towns and cities were the heart and motor of Protestantism. The intense rhythms of life in a crowded environment provided the breeding ground for divisions nurtured by class, neighbourhood, cultural differences and struggles for local political power, and nourished by propaganda, preaching and rumour. These basic considerations conditioned the progress of Protestantism everywhere, but no city was hermetically sealed from the wider world. Nobles, both petty local *hobereaux* and the greatest in the kingdom, interfered in and exploited urban affairs, while itinerant preachers, both official pastors from Geneva and awkward unofficial disturbers of the religious peace, moved from town to town to the distress as much of respectable Calvinists as of Catholic authorities. The lack of direct evidence of how Protestant ideas spread is unsurmountable: we can only judge by the outcome. It is not even clear what groups of Protestants did during their meetings before churches were constituted, the wilder fantasies of hostile observers being best ignored. One of the reasons for the growing influence of Calvin is that he created a simple form of service which could be followed by clandestine groups, provided that some qualified person was available to assume the role of pastor. It is evident, however, that ideas did not circulate in the same way among urban notables as among the artisan *menu peuple*, and that the process was far removed from the attempted indoctrination we associate with state-sponsored Reformation. Protestantism attracted adherents among all social classes, except for the floating population of the poor and

[26] G. Baum and E. Cunitz (eds.), *Histoire ecclésiastique des églises réformées au royaume de France* (3 vols., Paris, 1883-9), I. 885–7. For an interpretation stressing the Protestant apocalyptic aspect of Fumel's murder, see Crouzet, *Les guerriers de Dieu*, I. 515–23.
[27] E. Le Roy Ladurie, *Les paysans de Languedoc* (2 vols., Paris, 1966), I. 341–4.

indigent, the marginal folk who remained outside all religious structures. It was, with a few exceptions, not so much a question of particular social groups being attracted to Protestantism *en bloc*, more of groupings more likely to take an active interest in religious and political affairs and therefore to be committed to one side or the other as confessions consolidated. Although the majority of the population, even in 1560, probably held to a fluid religious position, or possibly none at all, sizeable minorities among both notables and *menu peuple* were becoming openly committed. The Protestants had the initial advantages of having their organisations in place first and the high hopes engendered by being part of a movement growing in spectacular fashion after 1555; but after 1560 Catholic reform or revival had in turn given birth to a specifically anti-Protestant militancy. This eventually gained more casual followers, not as absorbed by religious questions as the militant minorities, but having in their own eyes good reasons to hate Huguenots.

Although the confessional divide cut across class divisions, certain social groups were of particular significance in their propensity towards active religious commitment. Lawyers, especially from the numerous and burgeoning lower ranks of the legal profession, were actively involved in disproportionate numbers in all religious movements, from early Protestantism to the later Catholic League. The higher magistrates of the Parlements and other sovereign courts remained for the most part faithful to Gallican Catholicism, though their primary concern for social order rather than religious purity could get them into trouble when militant Catholicism gained the upper hand.[28] But more than any other group lawyers of lesser prominence could provide ideological justification for political acts without being hindered by the doubts and hesitations of theologians or the overwhelming desire of higher magistrates and towns councils to preserve the peace until the last possible moment. The 'fourth estate', says Professor Kelly, 'provided a great training-ground for intellectual mercenaries and an inexhaustible source of argumentation and means of legitimization on which governments and interest groups of all sorts could draw'.[29] Their importance in Protestantism before the religious wars is confirmed by the few statistics we possess: at Tours in

[28] *Parlementaires* could be accused of Protestant sympathies when they were simply trying to uphold the law and not to create Protestant martyrs, thus resulting in their being excluded from office where the Catholic party got the upper hand during the first civil war, as in Paris and Toulouse. See D. Richet, 'Aspects socio-culturels de conflits religieux à Paris dans la seconde moitié du XVIe siècle', *Annales E.S.C.*, 32 (1977), 768; J. Estèbe in *Histoire des protestants en France* (Toulouse, 1977), p. 61. Cf. also R. A. Mentzer, 'Calvinist Propaganda and the Parlement of Toulouse', *ARG*, 68 (1977), 268–83; P. Benedict, *Rouen during the Wars of Religion* (Cambridge, 1981), pp. 78–9.
[29] D. R. Kelly, *The Beginning of Ideology: Consciousness and Society in the French Reformation* (Cambridge, 1981), pp. 78–9.

1562 it would appear that about one third of lawyers were suspected of Protestantism, including ten of the twenty judges of the *présidential* court, founded in 1552 to provide a level of justice between the Parlements and the lesser *bailliage* courts, while at Montpellier in 1560 the lower ranks of law and medicine made up 15.4 per cent of those attending Huguenot services, as opposed to 69 per cent artisans but only 4.3 per cent merchants.[30]

That the majority of Protestants should be artisans is hardly surprising, given that they made up the greater part of the urban population. What is more significant is the active role played by people who, while they were not totally excluded from political life in many towns, were not members of the highest urban elite, and the way in which members of particular trades were attracted to religious change. This is a somewhat controversial matter, owing to the temptation of linking adherence to a new religious movement to social discontent and demands on a basis of *post hoc ergo propter hoc*, especially during a period of underlying economic uncertainty, declining real wages and frequent short-term crises. But the relationship between religious commitment and economic resentment will always remain shadowy. The idea that desire for social justice or better economic conditions had to be expressed in reified religious terms certainly does not hold water, as the existence of journeymens' associations and strikes makes clear: if workers wanted more money or shorter hours, then they demanded and fought for them quite overtly. Nevertheless, studies of individual towns suggest two kinds of connection: a distrust of exploitative authority, easily transposed from the secular to the religious sphere, among those with even more reason than most to dislike the holders of power; and a certain social and mental volatility among artisans in newer trades, less enmeshed in the socio-religious web of traditional forms of work and leisure sanctioned by religious observance and the festivals of the Christian calendar. In Meaux wool-workers, whose first moves towards heresy had been conditioned by the economic difficulties of the 1520s, continued to play a leading role, while in Rouen and Amiens the less proletarianised types of textile-workers, more sensitive about the strict regulations imposed by self-perpetuating civic and guild hierarchies, adhered to Protestantism in disproportionate numbers.[31] Among the newer trades printing, where even the lowliest

---

[30] P. Aquilon, 'A Tours entre les "cent jours" et la Saint-Barthélémy: les protestants de la paroisse Saint-Pierre-du-Boille', in Chevalier and Sauzet, *Les Réformes*, p. 81; Le Roy Ladurie, *Paysans de Languedoc*, I. 343.

[31] Heller, *Conquest of Poverty*, ch. 2; Benedict, *Rouen*, p. 80. Heller's work represents the latest and most sophisticated version of the approach, stemming from Henri Hauser, linking social unrest and Protestantism. For discussion of the historiography see Crouzet,

work required a certain level of literacy, and which was organised on precociously capitalistic lines, is obviously a case apart, but other luxury and high-status trades, notably goldsmiths, were also prominent, confirming de Raemond's observation that 'those whose trades contain a certain nobility of the spirit were the easiest to ensnare'.[32] Yet this nobility of the spirit, or higher level of culture as we may express it today, could be a double-edged sword – the printers' journeymen of Lyon, turbulent and strike-prone, eventually came to resent Calvinist discipline as much as they had Catholic corruption.[33] Support among a city's artisanate was vital to the nascent Protestant churches of the 1550s, but with the younger artisans, especially journeymen, it introduced a volatile and uncontrollable element, little concerned with the profuse declarations of pacific submission to the political order made by respectable Protestants.

No class analysis, however, can do justice to the urban atmosphere in which Protestantism spread. Rapidly growing urban populations were crammed into crowded neighbourhoods where everyone knew everybody else's business, privacy was virtually non-existent, gossip and quarrels were the stuff of everyday life, and rumours spread like wildfire. Particular neighbourhoods and streets became identified with Protestantism and could demonstrate their difference with quiet ostentation by refusing to participate in the public festivals which marked the high points of the liturgical year, principally the Corpus Christi processions. In Paris and Toulouse the university quarters were predictably suspect, while artisan quarters in Tours around the *halles*, near the river Garonne in Toulouse, and the parish of St Jean and the rue des Forges in Dijon were all, if not Protestant in majority, well known as centres of heresy.[34] Areas on the outskirts of cities around city gates proved most suitable for Protestant assemblies in the early 1560s, when large crowds would gather in fields outside the gates or wherever there were open spaces, such as the *faubourg* St Germain in Paris. The religious riots and conflicts of 1562–3 were battles between *quartiers* as well as of Protestant minorities against Catholic majorities.

The cement to hold the new religion together had to be provided by organised churches, and this meant their pastors. The eighty-eight men

Guerriers de Dieu, I. 61–75, and D. Nicholls, 'The Social History of the French Reformation: Ideology, Confession and Culture', *Social History*, 9 (1984), 25–43.
[32] Quoted in Benedict, *Rouen*, p. 80.
[33] N. Z. Davis, 'Strikes and Salvation at Lyon', in her *Society and Culture in Early Modern France* (London, 1975), pp. 1–16.
[34] M. Greengrass, 'The Anatomy of a Religious Riot in Toulouse in May 1562', *JEH*, 34 (1983), 367–91; J. G. Gray, 'The Origin of the Word Huguenot', *SCJ*, 14 (1983), 349–59; J. R. Farr, 'Popular Religious Solidarity in Sixteenth-Century Dijon', *French Historical Studies*, 14 (1985), 192–214.

sent from Geneva between 1555 and 1563 did not have an easy task trying
to control their flocks at a time when the numbers of the faithful seemed
to be increasing with astonishing and providential speed.[35] Churches
complained that they had one pastor when they needed three or four. In
1561 the faithful of Chinon wrote desperately to Geneva asking for a
second pastor, even though they were fully aware that 'this so exuberant
fountain of capable men which God has made to rise among you is almost
completely exhausted'.[36] The pastors' provenance from Geneva gave
them great authority, but it was not unchallengeable, and they were in
reality reliant on their own abilities, the most important of which was
holding an audience's attention. The churches demanded above all a good
preacher, demonstrating an inexhaustible desire for sermons which
harried pastors could not always satisfy. Nicolas Parent, who organised
several churches in Dauphiné, simply did not have enough time to meet
the demand: 'for although I preach for two hours, this seems very little to
them, so hungry are they for the Word'.[37] The Protestant mood in 1561–3
was accordingly ambiguous. While Calvin urged patience on the suffering
faithful, waves of iconoclasm and attacks on the clergy spread through
the south-west, leagues of Catholic nobles formed in response, and some
pastors allowed themselves to be swept along by the apocalyptic energies
of lower-class Protestants.[38] The view from the church at Grenoble in
1562 was that 'since Jesus Christ has taken hold of the highest rocks and
valleys of the mountains of this country, I can be sure of the imminent
overthrow of Antichrist and his whore', while Jacques de Saussure in
Champagne was certain that 'soon you will see the papacy defeated in
France'.[39] On the other hand, some pastors, though amazed and delighted
by what was happening, were aware of their own inadequacies in controlling it. Nicolas Le More wrote to Geneva from Bazas bemoaning his
youth and lack of experience, which caused some of his flock to be
dissatisfied with him, a problem compounded in the Midi by language
difficulties. Even in Dauphiné, Jean de la Place in Valence found that the
work among his rapidly growing flock posed great difficulties, not least
because the governor, La Motte Gondrin, largely ignored the tolerant

[35] On the pastors, see R. M. Kingdon, Geneva and the Coming of the Wars of Religion in France, 1555–1563 (Geneva, 1956).
[36] Letter printed in A. Dupin de Saint-André, Histoire du protestantisme en Touraine (Paris, 1885), pp. 277–9.
[37] N. Weiss, 'La fondation de l'église Réformée de Gap: lettre inédite de Nicolas Parent, 29 avril 1561', BSHPF, 40 (1891), 523.
[38] Crouzet, Guerriers de Dieu, I, chs. 7–10.
[39] 'Le protestantisme en Dauphiné. Lettres des églises de Die, de Grenoble et de Valence à Calvin (janvier et mars 1562)', BSHPF, 18 (1869), 532; 'Le protestantisme en Champagne au XVIe siècle. Lettres de Jacques Sorel, Jean Duchat, les fidèles de l'église de Troyes, J. de Saussure, Pierre Fornelet, de Châlons. 1561', BSHPF, 12 (1863), 361.

January edict of 1562, and imposed impossible constraints upon Protestant worship.[40]

In such conditions splits and dissension were all but inevitable. Protestant groups had grown independent of any outside control and this continued to mark their character, even as properly instituted churches, for as long as Protestantism was an expanding movement. Schisms within churches had several sources: non-Calvinist ideas available in print; the educative or 'discussion group' aspect of Protestantism; and patronage, whereby local notables sought control through their preachers and clients. The larger cities of the Loire valley were the most troubled, the smaller towns of the Midi, which came to form the bedrock of Calvinism, much less so. At Poitiers a split was caused by a certain Lavau de Saint-Vertunian, a follower of Sébastien Castellio, the apostle of religious tolerance and fervent opponent of Calvin, while at Tours a local nobleman, Martin Pillabeau, sieur de la Bédouère, patronised the preacher François de Beaupas, *dit* Chasseboeuf, against the 'Genevan' Jacques L'Anglois, causing a division which was only healed by Genevan arbitration and the excommunication of la Bédouère.[41] Also at Tours in 1561 local Protestants instituted an unofficial Academy where, according to a sternly disapproving Calvinist chronicler, even women were allowed to debate religious questions.[42] Such behaviour had to be by-passed by the creation of orthodox Academies, the first of which, soon followed by others, were founded at Nîmes and Orthez in the 1560s, but these could not prevent the final challenge to Calvinist hegemony, articulated by Jean Morély in the 1560s in the name of congregational independence.[43] But Calvinist theology was established as the doctrine of Huguenotism: even Morély deferred to Calvin on doctrinal matters and consistently sought his approval like a rebellious son seeking his father's blessing. The hazards of intermittent war and insecure peace made tight ecclesiastical and military organisation necessary, and Calvinist discipline was revealed as ideal for the needs of an embattled minority.

By the early 1560s the geography of French Protestantism was established, with a strong crescent in the south stretching from La Rochelle and Saintonge beneath the Massif Central to Dauphiné, with strongholds in Montauban, Nîmes and the relatively dense network of small and

[40] N. Weiss, 'L'organisation des églises Réformées de France et la Compagnie des Pasteurs de Genève, 1561', *BSHPF*, 46 (1897), 466–8; *CO*, XIX. 353–7.
[41] Heller, *Conquest of Poverty*, pp. 199–200; Baum and Cunitz (eds.), *Histoire ecclésiastique*, I. 127–9; Kingdon, *Geneva and the Coming*, pp. 49–50.
[42] Baum and Cunitz (eds.), *Histoire ecclésiastique*, I. 835–6.
[43] See Kingdon, *Geneva and the Consolidation of the French Protestant Movement, 1564–1572* (Geneva, 1967) pp. 43–137, and the reprint of Morély's *Traité de la discipline et police chrestienne* (Geneva, 1968).

medium-sized towns where orthodoxy could be readily maintained. But there were Protestant minorities nearly everywhere, in larger towns, Normandy, and Béarn under the protection of Jeanne d'Albret, queen of Navarre. The coping stone of the Huguenot edifice, however, had to be provided by noblemen, who became patrons of the church and made Protestantism into a national political party, magnifying its influence by representing it at court and providing military strength and expertise. The ground had been prepared by noblewomen, benefiting from the education and liberty denied to most of their sex and assiduously cultivated by Calvin and Genevans. Marguerite of Navarre's protection of reformers had been emulated by several of her contemporaries, including Louise de Montmorency, sister of constable Anne de Montmorency, and Jacqueline de Longwy, duchess of Montpensier, while Marguerite's daughter, Jeanne d'Albret, established a virtual Protestant kingdom in Béarn. These were only the most prominent among many like-minded women.[44] Large-scale conversion among their menfolk in all levels of the nobility came after 1555, at the very time when Protestant churches were being founded, and was inspired as much by ambition and desire to get their hands on church possessions and benefices as by conviction. Louis, prince de Condé, the Huguenot political and military leader in the early religious wars, announced his conversion in 1558, and he was soon joined by chiefs from the Montmorency–Châtillon clan, most notably Gaspard de Coligny, admiral of France and with an extensive clientage in Normandy, and François Dandelot, colonel general of the royal infantry. Many lesser lights followed their leaders – even in very Catholic Brittany Dandelot had a considerable number of clients – but by no means all, and the regional pattern was uneven. The large numbers of Huguenot *hobereaux* in lower Normandy or Dauphiné, for example, must be set against the comparatively few in Provence. Greed, anticlericalism, political ambition, a traditional warrior mentality and, in some cases, genuine conviction governed noble actions. As with the artisans in the cities, however, events were to show that petty noblemen could be dangerous allies for magnates and bourgeois.

For urban Huguenots or the peasants of the Cévennes becoming Protestant meant adopting a new mentality, being born again, for, wrote Calvin, 'we cannot be children of God if first we are not reborn'.[45] This meant adhering to a strict moral code and if possible imposing it on the unrighteous, a purification of self and society according to the precepts of godliness, frugality and an individual unmediated relationship with God.

[44] N. L. Roelker, 'The Appeal of Calvinism to French Noblewomen in the Sixteenth Century', *Journal of Interdisciplinary History*, 2 (1972), 391–418.
[45] *CO*, VII. 200.

Huguenots were a self-proclaimed elite, looking down on the superstitious practices of the ungodly, bearing persecution with pride, living by
the Word, and trying to follow the dictates of the Protestant conscience in
obedience to God and the magistrate. This did not apply to the nobility,
as was most graphically demonstrated by the so-called Tumult of
Amboise in 1560, a conspiracy of Huguenot petty noblemen led by one
Jean du Barry, seigneur de la Renaudie, to stage a coup and capture King
Francis II and the Court. La Renaudie's enterprise was supported by
Condé, but not by the other magnates or Calvin, and ended in the
summary executions of several hundred plotters and their followers. But,
like iconoclasm and riots in the cities, it showed the limitations of
Calvinist discipline within such a socially heterogeneous movement.

For all that, however, Calvinist ecclesiastical organisation, with its
pyramidal structure of local, provincial and national synods, did give the
Huguenots a considerable advantage over their adversaries. If synods
could not impose unity and discipline at will, they could make provision
for present and future dangers and work out a considered response to
events. The first national synod, held in Paris in 1559, drew up a confession of faith and a Discipline, both somewhat ambiguous about where
ultimate authority lay, and events moved too fast for the matter to be
settled satisfactorily.[46] Provincial synods and political assemblies (the
distinction was vague) in 1560–2 concentrated on choosing military
leaders and overcoming doubts about the legality of armed resistance to
the state. The third national synod, held at Orléans in 1562, confirmed
Condé as the protector of the Calvinist churches and 'protector and
defender of the house and crown of France', while at the provincial level
other nobles, such as the baron des Adrets in Dauphiné, assumed the
patron's role. Objections from the congregations were rendered invalid by
the rapidly deteriorating political situation.

What Condé claimed to be protecting 'the house and crown of France'
from was the Guise family. The house of Guise, cadet branch of the ducal
family of Lorraine, princes of the blood, and based most strongly in
eastern France, provided militant Catholicism with the protection and
leadership which the Huguenot magnates gave to the Protestant party.
Both parties in the cities could hope to get powerful backing when
required. In Troyes, for example, during the first civil war the ultra-
Catholic faction, protected by Claude de Guise, duc d'Aumale, acting
governor of Champagne and Brie, and supported by committed Catholics
and opportunists, gained control of the council and placed their clients in
local courts, overcoming the Protestant party, whose nearest protector

---

[46] The Confession of Faith and Discipline are printed in *Histoire ecclésiastique*, I. 201–20.

138   *David Nicholls*

was Dandelot. The majority of the population, while Catholic, was not bellicose, but would do nothing to help or protect Protestants.[47] Armed force was now decisive: by 1563 the Huguenot party was dominated by the military nobility, while militant Catholicism, on the national level, had as yet little else to rely on.

When it came to working on the hearts and minds of the population the Catholics had fallen behind in the key areas of printed propaganda and education. Too many anti-Huguenot pamphlets and tracts on the eve of the religious wars portrayed Protestants in the most fanciful terms as devoted to an anarchistic delight in libertine pleasure, whose secret meetings turned into sex orgies, and were probably too much at odds with observable reality to be credible.[48] In the colleges the counter-attack would have to be spearheaded by the Jesuits, but up to 1562 they had only managed to establish themselves in the minor centres of Billom, Touron, Rodez and Mauriac. They finally arrived in Paris in 1563, in Toulouse in 1564 and Lyon in 1565, in these latter places both in the wake of massacres of Protestants.[49] The decline in the main Catholic lay organisations, the confraternities, had been halted, and new specifically anti-Protestant Confraternities of the Holy Sacrament and Companies of Penitents were being founded, but they were only to be mobilised properly later in the religious wars.[50] The real strength of Catholicism in the 1560s lay in the development of popular hatred of Protestants as they came to be identified with social instability and then the miseries of war. In Paris attacks on Protestants began in 1557 after the French defeat at the battle of St Quentin and the discovery of Protestants meeting in the rue St Jacques in the Latin Quarter. After the death of Henry II in 1559, when political instability coincided with grave economic difficulties and subsistence crises, the Huguenots seemed insolent and arrogant, basking in powerful protection while the Crown clearly would not guarantee to maintain public order and food supplies or deal with the religious problem. Catholic preachers bitterly denounced the edicts of 1561 and 1562 granting limited freedom to Protestants, and took every subsequent opportunity during the first religious war, with the assassination of the duke of Guise and rumours of Huguenot atrocities, to portray the enemy in a bad light. By the time of the second civil war in 1567, when a Huguenot army rampaged around the Paris region, apparently attempt-

---

[47] On Troyes see Heller, *Conquest of Poverty*, ch. 5; A. N. Galpern, *The Religions of the People in Sixteenth-Century Champagne* (Cambridge, Mass., 1976), chs. 4 and 5.

[48] G. Wylie Sypher, '"Faisant ce qu'il leur vient à plaisir": The Image of Protestantism in French Catholic Polemic on the Eve of the Religious Wars', *SCJ*, 11 (1980), 59–84.

[49] Huppert, *Public Schools*, pp. 104–7.

[50] R. R. Harding, 'The Mobilization of Confraternities Against the Reformation in France', *SCJ*, 10 (1979), 85–107.

ing to starve the Parisians into submission, the populace had become fanatically anti-Protestant.[51] Riots, disorder and economic crisis elsewhere had created similar hostility throughout the kingdom. The Catholic party, like the Protestant, had gained fanatical but unreliably turbulent supporters, and rather more of them.

The division into two camps now seems inevitable, almost natural, but we should not forget that this was not how it was perceived by contemporaries until reform had become warfare. At the colloquy of Poissy, organised by Catherine de Medici in 1561 in an attempt at religious reconciliation, the formal sessions ended in confrontation and name-calling, but informal discussions between reformist Catholics and Calvinists were more friendly.[52] In the new religious situation, however, the old humanist reformist tradition had splintered. Reform without doctrinal compromise was now identified with the Catholic party. Much of what Charles de Guise, cardinal of Lorraine, introduced in his bishopric of Reims from 1548 onwards was not so very different from what Briçonnet had done twenty-five years earlier at Meaux. He too reformed preaching at the expense of the mendicant orders, recruited suitable priests after examination and obliged them to reside in their benefices. But the purpose now was to stop the advance of Calvinism.[53] A more open attitude towards Protestantism, which had once been a perfectly respectable outlook with widespread support, was now redefined as hesitation, fence-sitting or opportunism, and its adherents were unnatural, neither fish nor fowl, and necessarily untrustworthy.

Antonio Caracciolo, bishop of Troyes, tried desperately and tortuously to preserve the religious unity of his city, asking at one point to be ordained as a Protestant minister while retaining his bishopric. He only succeeded in earning the hostility of both sides, and he was subsequently forced to retire from his post in disgrace.[54] The more theologically consistent Jean de Monluc at Valence, more truly in the line of Briçonnet and Lefèvre d'Etaples, continued to propound a Christocentric religion which sought to spiritualise traditional practices rather than rejecting them. In his own conflicts with the municipality of Valence over episcopal privileges Monluc refused any fundamental concessions, placing him once again in the tradition of Briçonnet. But his tentative overtures to more

[51] B. Diefendorf, 'Prologue to a Massacre: Popular Unrest in Paris, 1557–1572', *American Historical Review*, 90 (1985), 1067–91; J.-P. Babelon, *Nouvelle histoire de Paris: Paris au XVIe siècle* (Paris, 1986), pp. 413–46.

[52] See D. Nugent, *Ecumenism in the Age of the Reformation: The Colloquy of Poissy* (Cambridge, Mass., 1974).

[53] J.-M. Constant, *Les Guise* (Paris, 1984), pp. 35–6.

[54] In addition to references in n. 43 above, see the biography by J. Roserot de Melin, *Antonio Caracciolo, évêque de Troyes: 1515–1570* (Paris, 1923).

moderate Calvinists got nowhere: a combination of party and lay anticlericalism had made him out of date.[55] Two bishops, Jean de Lattes of Montauban and Jean de St-Chamond, archbishop of Aix, did become Protestant, the latter by a spectacular renunciation in 1566, thus throwing in their lots with one of the enduring faces of reform. Monluc's position, designed to forestall the growth of Protestantism, was either forty years too late or had never been realistic in the first place.

The confessonal division against which a Caracciolo or a de Monluc struggled in vain had originated in various aspirations to reform, accompanied by a religious revival and a spirit of curiosity, a new desire to discuss religious matters and to define the meaning of 'living a Christian life'. The mendicant preachers at the beginning of the sixteenth century had preached personal reform; Guillaume Briçonnet had attempted a reform of the church through better churchmen, but ignored the possibility of popular heresy. The impulse for reform, almost universally accepted or at least proclaimed, had led on the one hand to Protestantism, on the other to Catholic reform, itself swiftly divided into a ferociously anti-Protestant wing and others more willing to compromise. Calvinism proposed a new form of personal reform, framed by a rigid doctrine and an effective ecclesiastical structure, both vigorously contested within the ranks of Protestant reform. But it had been hijacked by the nobility, its fortunes becoming inseparable from political ambition, and as a result it became associated in the eyes of the majority with disorder and war. Only those forms of reform compatible with the political and social aspirations of the powerful in state and church proved capable of enduring. The individualism and free debate of the early Reformation were casualties of this inescapable reality, as were all attempts at finding a religious solution neither Huguenot nor papist. The process by which religious ferment became confessional division ensured the survival of Reformation, but buried the original aspirations of reform.

[55] Heller, *Conquest of Poverty*, pp. 230–3.

SELECT BIBLIOGRAPHY

Baumgartner, F. J. *Change and Continuity in the French Episcopate: The Bishops and the Wars of Religion, 1547–1610* (Durham, NC, 1986).
Benedict, P. *Rouen during the Wars of Religion* (Cambridge, 1981).
Cameron, E. *The Reformation of the Heretics: The Waldenses of the Alps, 1480–1580* (Oxford, 1984).
Crouzet, D. *Les guerriers de Dieu: La violence au temps des troubles de religion, vers 1525–vers 1610* (2 vols., Paris, 1990).
Davies, J. M. 'Persecution and Protestantism: Toulouse, 1562–75', *HJ*, 22 (1979), 31–51.

Davis, N. Z. *Society and Culture in Early Modern France* (London, 1975).
'The Sacred and the Body Social in Sixteenth-Century Lyon', *P and P*, 90 (1981), 40–70.
Farge, J. K. *Orthodoxy and Reform in Early Reformation France: The Faculty of Theology of Paris, 1500–1543* (Leiden, 1985).
Galpern, A. N. *The Religions of the People in Sixteenth-Century Champagne* (Cambridge, Mass, 1976).
Garrison-Estèbe, J. *Protestants du Midi, 1555–98* (Toulouse, 1980).
Garrison, J. *Les protestants au XVIe siècle* (Paris, 1988).
Greengrass, M. *The French Reformation* (Oxford, 1987).
'The anatomy of a Religious Riot in Toulouse in May 1562', *JEH*, 34 (1983), 367–91.
Heller, H. *The Conquest of Poverty: The Calvinist Revolt in Sixteenth-Century France* (Leiden, 1986).
'Famine, Revolt and Heresy at Meaux, 1521–5', *ARG*, 68 (1977), 132–56.
Huppert, G. *Public Schools in Renaissance France* (Urbana and Chicago, 1984)
Imbart de la Tour, P. *Les origines de la Réforme* (4 vols., Paris, 1905–35).
Kelley, D. *The Beginning of Iedology: Consciousness and Society in the French Reformation* (Cambridge, 1981).
Kingdon, R. M. *Geneva and the Coming of the Wars of Religion in France, 1555–1563* (Geneva, 1956).
Geneva and the Consolidation of the French Protestant Movement, 1564–1572 (Geneva, 1967).
Lamet, M. S. 'French Protestants in a Position of Strength: The Early Years of the Reformation in Caen', *SCJ*, 9 (1978), 35–55.
Mentzer, R. M. *Heresy Proceedings in Languedoc, 1500–1560 (Transactions of the American Philosophical Society*, 76, 1984).
Nicholls, D. 'The Nature of Popular Heresy in France 1520–1541', *HJ*, 26 (1983), 261–75.
Salmon, J. H. M. *Society in Crisis: France in the Sixteenth Century* (London, 1975).
Sutherland, N. M. *The Huguenot Struggle for Recognition* (New Haven and London, 1980).
Princes, Politics and Religion, 1547–89 (London, 1984).

7   The Netherlands

Alastair Duke

On 29 March 1521 Cornelius Grapheus, the town secretary of Antwerp, finished his introduction to a previously unpublished treatise on Christian liberty by a fifteenth-century critic of monastic vows. Grapheus' words eloquently demonstrated the depth of his commitment to Christian humanism.. Christianity, he asserted, had relapsed for the past eight-hundred years into 'a more than Egyptian servitude', where man-made ordinances had replaced 'Christ's yoke', and 'human fables' his promises of redemption. He deplored the closed-shop mentality of the theologians who denied the laity access to the Scriptures on the spurious grounds that they had no knowledge of the schoolmen and complicated the Gospel with subtleties of their own invention. In language reminiscent of Erasmus, he called for the translation of the Scriptures into the vernacular and for expository preaching so that 'the philosophy of Christ', which was common to all, might be available to all. Grapheus was full of optimism about the present age. Those devoted to Christian liberty could take heart for 'everywhere good letters arise again, the Gospel of Christ has been reborn and Paul has come to life once more'.[1]

Grapheus was emboldened to assail the monkish establishment and scholastic theology because for some years both had been on the defensive. By 1520, Christian humanism had influential advocates in the grammar schools, among the jurists and, in the case of Groningen, among the leading clergy. In the grammar schools the textbooks of Vives and Despauterius were displacing Alexander's *Doctrinale* on the syllabus and Greek made an occasional appearance on the curriculum. The growing popularity of Erasmus' *Enchiridion* provided yet another indicator of the way opinion among the intellectual elite had changed. The foundation in 1517 of the Trilingual College at Louvain seemed to offer tangible proof

---

[1] *BRN*, VI. 35–9. For an English translation of Grapheus' preface see C. Ullmann, *Reformers before the Reformation, principally in Germany and the Netherlands* (2 vols., Edinburgh, 1863), I. 138–41; for the best recent assessment of Grapheus see B. J. Spruyt, 'Humanisme, Evangelisme en Reformatie in de Nederlanden, 1520–1530' in W. de Greef and M. van Campen (eds.) *Reformatie in meervoud* (Kampen, 1991), pp. 31–4.

that the philological approach to the text of the Scriptures, recommended by Erasmus and others, had finally gained acceptance. No wonder such men believed a golden age was dawning. In December 1518 an obscure correspondent of Erasmus gave vent to this sense of anticipation when he ended his letter with this exclamation: 'How blessed we are to live in an age like this, in which with you to guide and lead us and bring us to perfection both literature and true Christianity are being born again.'[2]

It was only natural that many Christian humanists did not appreciate that the *causa Lutheri* had, almost overnight, transformed the theological landscape. In their battle against scholasticism they rather glibly took Luther to be an ally. Erasmus, however, sought to distance himself from the controversy which he feared might damage his own reform programme, though the 'witch-hunt' instigated by conservative churchmen against Luther filled him with foreboding. He knew, as he told Wolsey in May 1519, that his reactionary opponents would seek to 'confound the cause of humanities with the business of Reuchlin and Luther', but his stance was little understood by any of the parties.[3] In Antwerp the Augustinian monastery, which belonged to the Saxon congregation, soon emerged as the seat of the evangelical cause. Several monks from this house matriculated at Wittenberg between 1516 and 1520 and, having witnessed the dramatic course of events there at first hand, came out in support of Luther's theology. Quite probably the Antwerp Augustinians had a hand in the translation of the six works of Luther which appeared in Dutch between September 1520 and March 1521. Despite a local edict in September forbidding the dissemination of Luther's books and the public burning of his writings at Louvain that same autumn, the Antwerp printer Claes de Grave made no attempt to conceal the authorship of these books. Possibly the reformer's notoriety encouraged the printer, with an eye to the main chance, to state that 'the right learned Doctor in divinity Martin Luther, brother of the order of St. Augustine' had written these.[4]

In fact the Augustinians and those humanists who, like Grapheus, continued to taunt the conservatives had gravely miscalculated. The reconciliation between Erasmus and the theologians at Louvain in September 1519 broke down in October when Jacob van Hoogstraten, already infamous in the eyes of the German humanists as the prosecutor of Reuchlin, accused the Rotterdammer of siding with Luther. In November 1519 the University duly condemned Luther and in September 1520, when

[2] R. A. B. Mynors and P. G. Bietenholz (eds.) *Correspondence of Erasmus* (Toronto, 1974 *et seq*), VI. 191, 193 (no. 904).
[3] *Correspondence of Erasmus*, VI. 368 (no. 967).
[4] C. Ch. G. Visser, *Luther's geschriften in de Nederlanden tot 1546* (Assen, 1969), pp. 31–9, 56–60, 152–6; O. Rudloff, *Bonae litterae et Lutherus. Texte und Untersuchungen zu den Anfänge der Theologie des Bremer Reformators Jakob Propst* (Bremen, 1985) 126–7.

Aleander brought the bull *Exsurge domini* to Charles V in Antwerp, Nicholas van Baechem (a Carmelite theologian whom Erasmus nicknamed the Camel) preached there against Luther. Charles signalled his support for the papal bull by attending an *auto-da-fé* at Louvain and in May 1521 he issued a version of the Edict of Worms, with an expanded preamble, for his 'Nidererblanden' (literally, 'hereditary Netherlands').[5] By then the conservatives were in full cry. Further book-burnings accompanied the publication of this edict in the cities of Flanders and Brabant, and the mendicants began an orchestrated campaign against the 'Lutheran impiety' as they preached up and down the country. The central government also moved to silence the Antwerp Augustinians and on 5 December 1521 their prior, Jacob Praepositus, whom Erasmus had two years earlier praised as almost the only cleric in that city to preach Christ,[6] was 'invited' to Brussels for friendly discussions with Mr Frans van der Hulst, a member of the Council of Brabant. The prior succumbed to the pressure and in February 1522 the offensive against the 'Lutherans' claimed its first victim when he abjured his errors in the principal church of Brussels. A few days earlier three humanists from Antwerp, including Grapheus, were also summoned to Brussels and on 23 April 1522, the very day van der Hulst received his commission as the new imperial inquisitor, they recanted. Grapheus' sallies against the clergy and his spirited defence of the laity's right to read the Scriptures, which had not seemed especially daring twelve months earlier, now proved his undoing. Publicly disgraced, dismissed from the secretaryship and declared unfit to hold any office, he found himself incarcerated in Brussels, and deprived of his property.[7]

This hard lesson was not lost on contemporaries. Long before July 1523 when two Augustinians were burnt as obstinate heretics in Brussels, the mood of optimism among Erasmus' friends in Antwerp ebbed away.[8] Those whose reputations had been harmed by incautious remarks in the past either left the Low Countries for a time or tried to cover up their

[5] For the Dutch and (incomplete) French texts see *CD*, IV. 60–76.
[6] *Correspondence of Erasmus*, VI. 393 (no. 980).
[7] *CD*, IV. 105–9. For an English translation see J. Alton Templin, 'Cornelius Grapheus (1482–1558): A Humanist Scholar of the Netherlands who Recanted', *The Iliff Review*, 36 (1979), 18–19. The recanted propositions attributed to Grapheus in April 1522 explicitly mention Luther, though nowhere in the offending preface had he referred to the reformer by name. Compare Grapheus' statement that 'everywhere good letters arise again, the gospel of Christ has been reborn and Paul has come to life once more' (*BRN*, VI. 38) with the retracted proposition: 'Thanks to the writings of Luther and others who adhere to his doctrine and who have given expression to evangelical liberty the gospel has been reborn and Paul has come to life again', (*CD*, IV. 106). For his sentence see *CD*, IV. 147.
[8] Nicholas Daryngton, writing from Louvain to an English acquaintance on 14 February 1522, remarked, 'Bella interim silent, Lutherus dormit.' P. S. Allen, 'Some Letters of Masters and Scholars, 1500–1530', *EHR*, 22 (1907), 747.

tracks.[9] The reverberations alarmed evangelical humanists everywhere. Writing in the first half of 1522, a schoolmaster in Delft, who was also a fervent evangelical, heaped scorn on Erasmus' 'puerile timidity' and on the numerous 'Nicodemuses' in his own circle.[10] A correspondent informed Erasmus in November 1522 that after the recantation of Grapheus and the arrest of others, 'such terror had seized everyone there [Antwerp] who had ever spared Luther a thought that scarcely anyone thought himself safe'.[11]

Given the determination of Charles V to resist heresy, the outcome to this trial of strength between the religious conservatives and their critics, who exhibited a naive enthusiasm for Luther, was never in doubt. Though Charles as the ruler of the decentralised Habsburg–Burgundian state did not exercise the authority of Henry VIII or Francis I, the evangelicals had no powerful patrons to whom they might turn. The misfortunes that befell the evangelicals in the household of the Danish king Christian II, in exile in the southern Netherlands during the 1520s, demonstrate the weakness of their position. The conduct of the 'Lutherans' in the Danish king's entourage in Brabant and Amsterdam certainly vexed Margaret of Austria, but Christian depended too heavily on the support of his brother-in-law, the Emperor, for the recovery of his kingdom to be able to protect these from prosecution when his back was turned.[12] A few minor nobles, more especially in the eastern Netherlands, connived at, even if they did not openly support, heterodox preachers, on their lordships and manors.[13] At this time the only great nobleman to show any curiosity in evangelical theology was Floris van Egmont, the

---

[9] Hinne Rode, the rector of a monastic house in Utrecht, who was dismissed 'propter Luterum' in 1522, went to Germany; Nicolaus Buscoducensis went to Basle for a while after his abjuration; Petrus Aegidius was apparently so fearful of arousing suspicions about his orthodoxy in late 1522 that he declined to forward a letter to his old friend Erasmus through an acquaintance, *Correspondence of Erasmus*, IX. 191–2 (no. 1318).

[10] D. P. Oosterbaan, 'School en kerk in het middeleeuwse Delft' part II, *Spiegel der historie*, 1 (1966), 113–14.

[11] *Correspondence of Erasmus*, IX. 191–2 (no. 1318).

[12] For the complaints of Margaret of Austria about the Lutherans in the king's entourage in 1526 see *CD*, V. 120; G. A. IJssel de Schepper. *Lotgevallen van Christiern II en Isabella van Oostenrijk ... voornamelijk gedurende hunne ballingschap in de Nederlanden*, (Zwolle, 1870), p. 183. In 1527 a member of the king's household was in touch with evangelicals in Brussels, J. Decavele, 'Vroege reformatorische bedrijvigheid in de grote Nederlandse steden: Claes van der Elst te Brussel, Antwerpen, Amsterdam en Leiden (1524–1528)', *NAK*, 70 (1990), 19–20. In July 1528 Margaret had six or seven of Christian's 'serviteurs' 'vivans en la maudite secte luthérane' arrested in their master's absence, including his treasurer, admiral, and steward Willem van Zwolle, *CD*, V. 336.

[13] For example, Joost van Cruiningen, the lord of Heenvliet on Voorne in South Holland, allowed a renegade Augustinian Henrick to preach there before he presented the well-known evangelical Angelus Merula to the living in 1533. A. de Bussy, 'De eerste informatie naar Merula's ketterij (1533)', *NAK*, n.s. 16 (1921), 140.

count of Buren.[14] But this small and unconvincing band of reform-minded patrons could not defy openly the religious policy of the central government. The degree of political pressure which Brussels exerted in the provinces of Brabant, Flanders and Holland, which together with Zeeland and the Walloon towns comprised the heartland of the Habsburg Netherlands, ensured that the Reformation could not survive for long in the open. The relatively large number of persons executed for heresy and related offences under Charles V from these provinces tells its own tale. Between 1523 and 1555 sixty-three were put to death in the Walloon towns of Mons, Tournai, Lille and Valenciennes, 100 in Flanders and 384 in the county of Holland.[15]

On the other hand the central government discovered that, though it had the means to scotch the several dissident movements, it could not altogether eradicate these. For one thing it was not possible to winkle out every suspect cleric. Since neither the secular princes nor the bishops controlled lesser ecclesiastical appointments, the parish churches, collegiate foundations, chantries, chapels, hospitals and religious houses provided many niches where dissidents could nestle, sometimes without even having to celebrate Mass. Secondly, neither Charles nor his son Philip of Spain could reckon on the wholehearted support of the governing classes in their campaign against heresy, even though these were for the most part devout Catholics. The provinces, towns and corporate bodies did not readily accept that the anti-heresy legislation should override privileges which protected property rights and ensured the conduct of trials in accordance with local customs. Sometimes the privileges were set aside, but the ill-feeling such controversies engendered locally distracted attention from the prosecution of 'heretics', especially when these were not considered a threat to public order.

Once the Protestant Reformation achieved a degree of permanence in large parts of Germany and in the Baltic, commercial considerations also persuaded the towns in the Low Countries to oppose measures which might deter Protestant merchants from these parts from doing business there. So Antwerp refused to publish the comprehensive anti-heresy edict of April 1550 because of a requirement that no one might take up residence without first producing a certificate of his Catholic orthodoxy.

14 Floris van Egmond (1469–1539) was certainly not committed to the cause of the Reformation, but he and his family had various associations with evangelicals. A manuscript Dutch translation of Bugenhagen's commentary on the Psalms bears his coat of arms, *Het boek in Nederland in de 16de eeuw* (The Hague, 1986), 61. His wife reputedly patronised evangelical preachers, R. van Roosbroeck, 'Een nieuw document over de beginperiode van het lutheranisme te Antwerpen', *De Gulden Passer*, 5 (1927), 276.
15 These figures have been extrapolated from the sources given in Alastair Duke, *Reformation and Revolt in the Low Countries*, (London, 1990) p. 71 n. 1.

Although the town successfully lobbied to have foreign merchants exempted, it declined to issue the substantially modified version of the edict until it had first received a statement to the effect that publication would not prejudice the city's privileges.[16] Although Groningen was incorporated in the Habsburg Netherlands in 1536, the influence of Brussels remained weak because effective political power still rested with the local magistrates and gentry,[17] who would brook no interference from Brussels in the matter of religion. Here 'protestantising' Catholic priests continued to preach evangelical doctrines from the pulpit with relative impunity until Alba and the Council of Troubles began to purge the local clergy after 1567. Since the inquisition never operated effectively here and few heeded the edicts, a *de facto* 'religious peace' existed in the province.[18] As a result the process of confessionalisation proceeded at a more leisurely pace in Groningen, and indeed in Friesland and Gelderland, than in Brabant, Flanders and Holland. In these 'core' provinces the repressive policies of the central government compelled those 'of the gospel', as the dissidents referred to themselves in the later 1520s, to go underground. It is to the dissidents here and to their incipient organisations that we now turn.

Wherever the Reformation found support in these urbanised provinces, controversy followed and riots occurred in several towns. In the early years it was often clerics, speaking either in favour of or against Luther, who launched the first salvoes in the war of words. The central government and the town magistrates therefore forbade the laity from attending sermons outside the parish churches and mendicant houses, ordered schoolmasters to eschew 'mystical' expositions when they interpreted the Gospel and Epistle of the day to their pupils and sought to moderate the tone of pulpit polemicists.[19] Not surprisingly, unsupervised 'secret assemblies', which first came to notice in Amsterdam in November 1523, were strictly forbidden.[20] Next year conventicles were reported in several other towns in Holland as well as in Utrecht, Flanders and

[16] J. J. Mulder, 'De uitvoering der geloofsplakkaten en het stedelijk verzet tegen de inquisitie te Antwerpen (1550–1566)', *Twee verhandelingen over de inquisitie in de Nederlanden tijdens de zestiende eeuw* (Ghent–The Hague, 1897), pp. 6–7, 9, 13.

[17] F. Postma, 'Regenerus Praedinus (*ca.* 1510–1559), zijn school en zijn invloed', *AGKKN*, 32 (1990), 167.

[18] Abel Eppens, a well-read Calvinist farmer, remarked in his chronicle, begun in 1580, that a sort of 'natural religious peace' existed and no one need fear persecution and tyranny, 'since they left the edicts published by the provincial court on one side', W. Bergsma, *De wereld volgens Abel Eppens, een ommelander boer uit de zestiende eeuw* (Groningen–Leeuwarden, 1988), p. 158. Persecution of religious dissidents was comparatively rare in Groningen; indeed only one Protestant was put to death before 1566. This moderation was the more remarkable given the violence and radicalism of the local Anabaptists in the 1530s.

[19] *CD*, IV. 501, V. 2–5, 17, 120–1, 158–9, 187–8; *cf.* 367–8.   [20] *CD*, IV. 240.

Antwerp[21] and outdoor assemblies took place in the vicinity of Antwerp in 1525 and Leiden in 1530.[22] Usually such meetings took place in private houses attended by between a dozen and twenty people. Numbers depended, of course, on the available accommodation, but small groups could more easily escape detection.[23] Larger gatherings did take place. A raid on a 'secret and illegal' gathering in Antwerp in 1524 led to charges against thirty-seven people,[24] and some fifty heard an evangelical priest preaching in a Brussels' garden in 1527.[25] Though the few open-air meetings never drew the vast crowds which flocked to the 'hedge-services' of 1566, a shearman addressed around 200 near 's-Hertogenbosch on Easter Monday 1533.[26] At the other end of the scale Anabaptists used to go by boat in twos and threes from Amsterdam into the countryside in the summer, reading their New Testaments and singing on the way.[27]

Evangelically minded priests and religious seem to have taken the lead in such groups, at least in the 1520s. This is hardly surprising since the clergy possessed the necessary expertise and authority. At Antwerp, for example, Augustinians and several parish clergy preached the new doctrines in public and in private, and at Tournai a parish priest directed the 'luthériens' until 1535.[28] Nevertheless lay evangelicals did assume prominent positions from the outset. A mysterious professional singer, Georgius die Bascouter, was apparently the first to disseminate the new ideas in Amsterdam and a painter expounded the Scriptures at the conventicle discovered at Antwerp in March 1524. Anna Bijns, a Catholic poet, was then not so far wide of the mark when she asserted that 'carpenters [and] masons have become our theologians' and sneered at the 'Dutch clerks', meaning those without Latin, who thought themselves so much smarter than the scholars.[29]

According to hostile contemporaries those who went to such clandes-

21 *CD*, IV. 255, 258, 259–61, 264, 266–7, 288. Th. Sevens, *Handvesten rakende de wederdopers en de calvinisten der XVIe eeuw in de voormalige kastelnij van Kortrijk* (Kortrijk, 1925), pp. 1–2.
22 *CD*, IV. 378–9, 380, 392; L. Knappert, *De opkomst van het protestantisme in eene Noord-Nederlandsche stad. Geschiedenis van de hervorming binnen Leiden* (Leiden, 1908), p. 119.
23 For that same reason the first Calvinist congregation in Antwerp was broken into house-groups of between eight and twelve members. Duke, *Reformation and Revolt*, p. 116.
24 *CD*, IV. 259–60.   25 Decavele, 'Vroege reformatorische bedrijvigheid', 20.
26 L. J. A. van de Laar, 'De opkomst van de reformatie in 's-Hertogenbosch *c.* 1525–1565', *AGKKN*, 20 (1978), 122.
27 *DAN*, II, pp. 103–4, 105, 128.
28 *CD*, IV. 377–83, V. 63–65; G. Moreau, *Histoire du protestantisme à Tournai jusqu' à la veille de la Révolution des Pay-Bas* (Paris, 1962), pp. 67, 69.
29 *CD*, V. 195, IV. 266.

tine meetings conformed with one of two stereotypes. Either they were ignorant 'furriers and weavers' or melancholic intellectuals and impressionable artists.[30] Conservatives could never make up their minds whether the greater challenge to the authority of the church came from *Herr Omnes* or from the *trahison des clercs*. What little is known about the composition of these early evangelical gatherings, however, lends colour to both these fears. The dozen or so evangelicals who used to meet regularly at a shoemaker's house in Maastricht in the late 1520s were, for example, all artisans,[31] and most of those present at the gathering in Antwerp in 1524 were skilled or semi-skilled craftsmen who had migrated to the town, presumably in search of employment. The involvement, however, of six men who made a living as painters, engravers, silversmiths and girdlers is, perhaps, more surprising. In Brussels, where the fine and applied arts flourished on account of the Court, the artistic elite predominated in the evangelical circle delated to the authorities in May 1527.[32] No fewer than eleven of the forty-eight men then under investigation worked as painters and another twenty-five wove tapestries. Though Bernard van Orley is the best-known of the painters, the group included several notable artists who designed tapestries for the court of Margaret of Austria. In 1543 forty-three inhabitants of Louvain stood trial charged with the possession of forbidden books, the dissemination of heretical opinions and attendance at evangelical meetings.[33] This group too consisted chiefly of independent craftsmen with a significant leavening of artists and clerics.

In the absence of systematic research into the composition of these evangelical gatherings, conclusions about their occupational and social structure should be treated with caution. It is, however, clear that two numerically important social groups were virtually unrepresented, namely the underclass of vagrants and paupers and agricultural labourers.

---

[30] L. van Helten (ed.), *Refereinen van Anna Bijns naar de nalatenschap van Mr. A. Bogaers* (Rotterdam, 1875), 30, 49. See also Duke, *Reformation and Revolt*, pp. 37–38.

[31] W. Bax, *Het protestantisme in het bisdom Luik en vooral te Maastricht, 1505–1557* (The Hague, 1937), I. 77–93.

[32] The following analysis of the evangelical circle meeting at Brussels in 1527 relies on J. Duverger, 'Lutherse predicatie te Brussel en het proces tegen een aantal kunstenaars (april-juni 1527)' *Wetenschappelijke tijdingen*, 36 (1977), col. 221–8; J. Decavele, 'De opkomst van het protestantisme te Brussel', *Noordgouw. Cultureel tijdschrift van de provincie Antwerpen*, 19–20 (1979–83), 25–44, and 'Vroege reformatorische bedrijvigheid', 13–29.

[33] C.-A. Campan (ed.), *Mémoires de Francisco de Enzinas ... 1543–1545* (2 vols., Brussels, 1862–3), I. 206–305. Also R. van Uytven, 'Bijdrage tot de sociale geschiedenis van de protestanten te Leuven in de eerste helft der XVIe eeuw', *Mededelingen van de geschieden oudheidkundige kring voor Leuven en omgeving*, 3 (1963), 5–38; and his 'Invloeden van het sociale en professionele milieu op de godsdienstkeuze: Leuven en Edingen', in *Sources de l'histoire religieuse de la Belgique* (Louvain, 1968), 260–4.

F

150   *Alastair Duke*

Though the evangelicals at Brussels lacked a formal organisation, the routines of work served to integrate the participants into a cohesive and tight-knit group. Painters, tapestry designers and weavers worked closely with one another, apprentices sometimes lived in their masters' households and accompanied them to the sermons. Family ties also underpinned this occupational homogeneity. Almost half the group belonged to eight family clusters and the preacher, Claes van der Elst, was himself related by blood or marriage to at least nine members of the group. Though on average a few years younger than Luther,[34] most of the evangelicals at Brussels belonged to a generation (and to a social elite) whose allegiance to the old order had been shaken by the reactionary response of the scholastic theologians to Reuchlin and Erasmus. Perhaps for that reason they felt an instinctive sympathy with Luther. Though the network of relationships linking the later Louvain dissidents has been less thoroughly explored, bonds of affection and the comradeship of the workplace also ensured a degree of familiarity and stability within the group.[35] If these ties made it harder for outsiders, and therefore for spies, to infiltrate the meetings, they also put the entire group at risk when the authorities were alerted. Fortunately for the Brussels evangelicals, who also had influential patrons, the persecutions had not yet begun in earnest in 1527 and they therefore escaped with nothing worse than a stiff fine. The dissidents arrested at Louvain in 1543 were treated altogether more harshly, and five of them paid for their beliefs with their lives.

Our knowledge of the earliest conventicles derives from a few scattered and fairly laconic reports. They began as Bible study groups, though they followed no set pattern. The painter Adriaen was sentenced at Antwerp in 1524 because he 'had read and interpreted the holy Gospel and other holy Scriptures contrary to His Imperial Majesty's commands' at one such gathering.[36] Sometimes an evangelical cleric would deliver a sermon behind closed doors. The chaplain of a hospital in Den Briel used to preach 'in secret' to a select company of men and women, and Claes van der Elst, a one-time parish priest in Antwerp, gave a series of nine sermons in Brussels during Holy Week in private houses in which he refuted the notion that Christ was objectively present in the eucharistic elements.[37] At Leiden evangelicals attended meetings outside the town in the spring of 1530 at which, the authorities reported, one of their number preached and expounded the Scriptures 'after their fashion' from 'a great

---

[34] The average age of the group in 1527 was around 38 or 39. The age of forty-nine of the seventy-six persons under suspicion is recorded, Decavele, 'De opkomst van het protestantisme', 39–44.
[35] Van Uytven, 'Bijdrage tot de sociale geschiedenis', 28–31.   [36] *CD*, IV. 259, 266.
[37] *CD*, V. 325; Decavele, 'Vroege reformatorische bedrijvigheid', 20–2.

book on his lap'.[38] The meetings held at Veere in Zeeland during 1529–31 were led by both sympathetic local clergy and by visiting preachers. Between ten and fifty attended, and those present listened to the sermon sitting around a table, while one of their number kept watch to see that no one was snooping outside.[39]

These clandestine meetings were commonly described as 'schools'.[40] A conventicle at Maastricht was known as the 'school of this Lutheran sect' while another at Veere was called simply 'de scole'.[41] Though 'schole' in this context has usually been understood as 'a secret gathering', contemporaries also employed the term advisedly to connote a place where heresy was taught. There is an analogous usage in late Middle English. In the fifteenth-century English ecclesiastical authorities called Lollard meetings 'scoles of heresie' where the dissidents 'herd, conceyved, lerned and reported [repeated]' their false doctrines.[42] As the following examples show formal doctrinal instruction was given in some Netherlandish conventicles. In the Flemish countryside Bible-study groups evolved in the early 1530s. After Sunday Mass interested villagers, including some clerics, met in the local tavern where someone read aloud a passage from the New Testament and gave a brief exposition. The meeting then adjourned to give the participants, divided up in pairs, an opportunity to discuss the text together. When they reconvened, each group reported its conclusions to the full company.[43] The early Anabaptists apparently combined open discussion with rote learning. When they held a meeting, someone read from the Bible 'and everyone', according to the statement of an apostate priest, 'says what he has learned and remembered concerning their sect and how they understand the scripture on that score'. Then in the evening they 'came to recite their lesson [huer lesse upseggen]'.[44] If the conventicles indeed functioned as 'schools of heresy' where dissidents were drilled or catechised in the new doctrines, this would help to explain the martyrs' impressive knowledge of the Scriptures as well as the recurrence of certain doctrinal arguments, proof texts and even anticlerical jokes. If the reconstruction is correct, then the conventicle deserves recognition, no less than the 'nieuwe Evangely boecxkens', as an

[38] Knappert, De opkomst van het protestantisme, p. 119.
[39] J. G. de Hoop Scheffer, Geschiedenis der kerkhervorming in Nederland van haar ontstaan tot 1531 (Amsterdam, 1873), pp. 512–16.
[40] CD, V. 32, 149.   [41] Bax, Maastricht, I. 89; De Hoop Scheffer, Geschiedenis, p. 513.
[42] N. Tanner (ed.), Heresy Trials in the Diocese of Norwich, 1428–31 (London, 1977), pp. 140, 146, 153, 165, 179 (English); pp. 93, 94, 176, 207, 217 (Latin).
[43] J. Decavele, De dageraad van de reformatie in Vlaanderen (1520–1565) (2 vols., Brussels, 1975), I. 268–69.
[44] A. L. E. Verheyden, 'De noordvlaamse broederschap binnen de Zeeuwse invloedssfeer (1530–1560)', Doopsgezinde bijdragen, n.r., 2 (1976), 105.

important vehicle for the diffusion of Reformation theology at a popular level and for the cultivation of a lay evangelical idiom.[45] These gatherings often had a convivial side to them. Dissidents at Veere concluded their meetings by eating together; at Louvain they made jolly excursions into the countryside; at Maastricht they 'sang songs which mocked the Pope and the ecclesiastical prelates'.[46] When Anna Bijns complained that 'Scripture is read in the tavern, the Gospel in one hand and the tankard in the other,' she probably had in mind groups like those Flemish villagers who gathered in the local taphouse to study the Bible.[47] In the intimacy of the 'secret fellowship' they discussed and exchanged evangelical literature, exhibited satirical prints and jested about the Mass and purgatory. Gradually these *ad hoc* gatherings began to act collectively. The evangelical circle at Brussels, which came to the attention of the authorities in 1527, gave practical and spiritual support to a monk, sentenced in 1523 to lifelong imprisonment for his beliefs. Members regularly visited him, bringing him food, letters, books and clean linen.[48] The 'luthériens' of Tournai had a common chest by 1535 while the evangelicals at Louvain were required to give alms to help the indigent 'of their own persuasion'.[49]

As a result of this creeping institutionalisation, evangelicals in the Low Countries found themselves drifting into a sort of unintentional separatism. The prospect of schism was abhorrent to those who were concerned for the renewal of the church and for Christian liberty. They went to hear evangelical preachers and attended Bible studies to supplement, not to replace, the services in the parish churches. The unknown evangelical author of the influential *Summa der godliker scrifturen*, first printed in 1523, therefore urged parents to take their children to church on holy days 'and to teach them to hear mass and especially the sermon'.[50] Such counsel made good sense provided evangelicals could seek out sympathetic priests within the established church. We know that clerics of this sort could still be found at Amsterdam in the early 1530s and indeed at Louvain in the early 1540s.[51]

45 See Duke, *Reformation and Revolt*, p. 116; Tanner, *Heresy Trials*, p. 28.
46 De Hoop Scheffer, *Geschiedenis der kerkhervorming*, p. 515; *Mémoires de Francisco Enzinas*, I. 406, 408; van Uytven, 'Bijdrage tot de sociale geschiedenis', 30–1; Bax, *Maastricht*, I. 80.
47 *Refereinen van Anna Bijns*, p. 85.
48 Decavele, 'Vroege reformatorische bedrijvigheid', 16–17.
49 Moreau, *Histoire du protestantisme à Tournai*, p. 255; *Mémoires de Francisco de Enzinas*, I. 350, 394.
50 J. Trapman, 'Le rôle des "sacramentaires" des origines de la Réforme jusq'en 1530 aux Pays-Bas', *NAK*, 63 (1983), 9, 13. In a later edition, a more evangelical vocabulary was employed. This passage then read, 'and teach them [the children] to keep the Lord's Supper and to hear the true Word of God'.
51 In 1534 conservatives denounced several evangelicals among the Amsterdam clergy, some of whom did not celebrate Mass, to the authorities. A. Mellink, *Amsterdam en de*

But what if the authorities refused to appoint 'evangelical preachers'? In 1526 two unknown Dutch disciples of Luther told the evangelicals in Antwerp that, if they could not go where the gospel was publicly preached, they should follow the example of the early church and maintain in their houses 'pious and discerning brethren' to preach the Gospel. In so far they must obey God rather than man, but the Christians at Antwerp were warned that as private individuals they could go no further than to call preachers into their homes.[52] In all other respects they should conform with the religious practices of the church. Evangelicals in Antwerp remained, however, deeply troubled about their relations with the 'papists' as we learn from a letter they sent to Luther in 1531.[53] The brethren sought his advice because they were divided on the question whether or not 'Christians', on the point of death, might call on 'the papists to administer the Lord's Supper' without thereby denying Christ. This had become urgent because, although they had celebrated the 'Lord's Supper' in the past in their conventicles when presumably they had the services of a sympathetic priest, they had stopped this practice. When, however, they had to choose a preacher, they found themselves in a dilemma. Since they believed that 'the choice of preachers belongs to the whole Church of Christ', they thought it would 'smack of the conduct of the monks' to exclude anyone, and only admit those whom they knew. Presumably because such an open-door policy had become impossible in Antwerp, they had reverted to holding Bible-study meetings.

The repressive policy of the central government and of the ecclesiastical authorities reinforced the sectarian tendencies. As early as November 1522 a minor official in a provincial council referred to 'la secte Lutheriane', when indenting for expenses incurred in connection with the Antwerp Augustinians;[54] thereafter descriptions like 'secte vanden Lutranen' frequently occur in administrative documents. Such language,

wederdopers in de zestiende eeuw (Nijmegen, 1978), p. 24. A dissident on trial at Rotterdam in 1529 maintained that in his native town of Delft there were enough clergy 'who were evangelical men and still did not celebrate mass', W. Bezemer, 'Geloofsvervolging te Rotterdam, 1534–1539' *Archief voor nederlandsch kerkgeschiedenis*, 6 (1897), 49.
52 G. Hammer, 'Der Streit um Bucer in Antwerpen: ein rätselvoller Textfund und ein unbekannter Lutherbrief' in G. Hammer and K. -H. zur Mühlen (ed.), *Lutheriana: zaum 500. Geburtstag Martin-Luthers* (Cologne–Vienna, 1984), p. 441. Also discussed at length by B. J. Spruyt, 'Humanisme, evangelisme en reformatie', 38–9. Nevertheless some evangelicals evidently did celebrate the Lord's Supper at their conventicles. Dissidents at Waldfeucht (Jülich), however, explained in 1533 that, since their priest did not give communion in two kinds or preach properly, they met together to read and discuss the gospel and epistle, 'und weiter nit', in other words they did not baptise or hold Communion services. O. R. Redlich, *Jülich-Bergische Kirchenpolitik am Ausgang des Mittelalters und der Reformationszeit, Visitationsprotokolle und Berichte*, II *Jülich, 1533–1589* (Bonn, 1911), p. 520.
53 WA Br. VI. 189–91 (no. 1863).   54 *CD*, IV. 143.

was, of course, natural, but it conferred a specious collectivity on dissent at a stage when this lacked any such unity. Some evangelicals in the Low Countries tried to distinguish between the Roman Church and the Christian Church. Heer Jan van Woerden, burnt at The Hague in 1525, spoke for such when he defined the holy church as 'an invisible and spiritual gathering of all those who will be saved by Christ'.[55] The Roman Church was variously described as 'the gathering of Antichrist', 'the synagogue of Satan', 'the Church of the wicked', the whore of Babylon and the seven-headed dragon, while the Pope appeared as the Antichrist.[56] In making this identification Dutch evangelicals were simply treading in the footsteps of Luther, who used the argument to justify his defiance of the papal condemnation. In the Low Countries this assimilation of the Roman Church with Babylon had far-reaching consequences. The persecution of evangelical clergy and the implacable hostility of the ecclesiastical authorities there to the Reformation brought despair to those concerned for the renewal of the church. Besides, the conduct of the inquisitors contributed to the impression that the local church bore a startling resemblance to 'the congregation of Satan'. Once this notion took hold, it was hard to resist the logic of those who argued that Christians should withdraw from the parish church and from the Mass. The likelihood of separatism increased when the clergy were accused of being 'soul murderers'. When dissidents went beyond indulgences, pilgrimages and monastic vows to denounce the images in the churches as 'wood and stone', the chrism as good only for greasing boots and to deride the notion of the real presence, they moved from the issue of Christian freedom, which was paramount in the early 1520s, to attack, perhaps unwittingly, the immanent theology of the Catholic Church. In the circumstances separatism appeared inevitable.

Yet despite these immense doctrinal pressures driving Dutch evangelicals towards schism, there is no unambiguous evidence for separatist congregations before 1530,[57] although the number staying away from the obligatory Easter Communion seems to have increased during the later 1520s.[58] No doubt Luther's well-known opposition to sectarianism and the fear inspired by persecution held the separatist impulses in check. The

---

55 *CD*, IV. 477.
56 *BRN*, VIII. 77; *CD*, IV. 446, 477; Decavele, 'Vroege reformatorische bedrijvigheid', 21–2.
57 An unknown Dutch evangelical, writing to Bucer from Amsterdam in June 1529, ends his letter with a request for prayers for 'nostras ecclesias', J. P. Pollet, *Martin Bucer. Études sur les relations de Bucer avec les Pays-Bas, l'Électorat de Cologne et l'Allemagne du Nord* (2 vols., Leiden, 1985), II. 6.
58 For evidence of abstention see Duke *Reformation and Revolt*, p. 39. Several Anabaptists at Amsterdam, examined in 1534–5, had not been to Mass for between five and ten years, *DAN*, V, pp. 70, 76, 155; cf. pp. 5, 63, 76.

intervention of Melchior Hoffmann, however, opened the way for a sectarian Reformation, at least in the northern Netherlands. Long before his break with Luther, Hoffmann had stressed the imminence of the Day of Judgement. In this he was not exceptional, but he was unusually specific about the timing. In his commentary on Daniel, published in 1526, he had prophesied that after the Antichrist had reigned for three-and-a-half years, Christ would return in Judgement in 1533.[59] In the summer of 1530 Hoffmann returned to East Friesland from Strasburg, inspired by his encounters with the prophets and with leading Anabaptists in that city, and he promptly began to baptise adults in Emden. According to Hoffmann, those who had 'surrendered themselves to the Lord' should separate themselves from the world and bind themselves to Christ publicly through the 'true sign of the covenant', that is believers' baptism.[60]

When Hoffmann was forced to leave Emden in June 1530, he appointed Jan Volkertsz., a mulemaker from Hoorn, as his successor. Within a few months, however, the Hollander was banished from Emden and he began to baptise in Amsterdam and elsewhere. True to Hoffmann's teaching, those whom he baptised had to promise 'to forsake the Devil, the world and the flesh, to cleave to God and to love their neighbour'.[61] Already in 1531 Hoffmann's followers at Amsterdam commemorated the Lord's Supper, thereby underlining the separatist nature of this Melchiorite congregation.[62] The execution of Jan Volkertsz. and eight other disciples in December 1531, however, so shocked Hoffmann that he ordered baptisms to be halted for two years, until the end of 1533. The effect of this suspension on the *kleyne luyden* (the small people), who proved by far the most receptive to the preaching of Hoffmann and Jan Volkertsz., can only be guessed, but it probably induced confusion, even despair in dissident circles in Friesland and especially in and around Amsterdam. Hoffmann's apocalyptic vision had offered an 'explanation' for their present sufferings and held out the prospect of the Second Coming when the persecution would end and the oppressed would become 'victors'. Moreover this was to be accomplished within a short time span. But as the day appointed for the Last Judgement approached, the ban on baptism became, to use Deppermann's description, 'unbearable'.[63] Jan Matthijsz., a baker from Haarlem, ended the suspense when in November 1533 he bludgeoned the Melchiorite leadership in Amsterdam into recognising

[59] K. Deppermann, *Melchior Hoffmann. Social Unrest and Apocalyptic Visions in the Age of the Reformation* (Edinburgh, 1987), pp. 74–75.
[60] G. H. Williams and A. M. Mergal (eds.), *Spiritual and Anabaptist Writers* (London, 1957), pp. 188–89; 192. For the Dutch text see *BRN*, V. 150, 155.
[61] O. J. de Jong, *De reformatie in Culemborg* (Assen, 1957), p. 33.   [62] *DAN*, V, p. 19.
[63] Deppermann, *Melchior Hoffmann*, p. 334.

him as the true Enoch, one of the two witnesses to the last punishment of the world, mentioned in Revelation 11 v. 4. He proceeded to send out 'apostles' to various parts of the northern Netherlands and to the Westphalian city of Münster and gave orders that believers' baptism should be resumed.

Hoffmann's separatist and apocalyptic theology changed substantially under the influence of Jan Matthijsz., and Bernd Rothmann, the radical preacher in Münster. Hoffmann looked to the magistrates of Strasburg to defend that city, which he cast as the New Jerusalem. The new Anabaptist leaders had no such faith in the established powers, perhaps because the persecuting authorities in the Habsburg Netherlands did not make plausible candidates. The heavenly city, now identified with Münster, would be saved by the saints, who had a duty to take up the sword against the godless. Secondly, Matthijsz. interpreted baptism as the seal put on the foreheads of 144,000 servants of God: anyone without 'the Signum Tau ... will be subjected to the Father's wrath and punished'.[64] This simple yet stark message had an electric effect on the dissidents in Holland, Friesland, Groningen and in Maastricht. When Pieter Houtzager, an apostle of Jan Matthijsz., came to Friesland around New Year 1534, he taught that the Day of Judgement was at hand and therefore everyone should repent and be baptised whereupon, according to a contemporary, many were rebaptised out of dread.[65] Repeatedly Anabaptists maintained under examination that their salvation depended on their undergoing believers' baptism. Brechte Wolfert's account was typical of many: she had been ill when Pieter Houtzager told her 'that she must allow herself to be baptised or she would be damned'.[66]

Münster attracted widespread support among Dutch Anabaptists because their success in gaining control of the city in February 1534 appeared to authenticate Jan Matthijsz.' prophecy in the most extraordinary way. It lent credibility to 'envoys' like Jacob van Ossenbrug who went at this time to the prince-bishopric of Liège to warn the 'common simple man' that between then and Easter:

the world would be fiercely punished and that one in ten would not survive; also that nowhere except in Münster would there be peace and safety, since Münster was the city of the Lord and the new Jerusalem, where the Lord would preserve his [people] and everyone would have enough.[67]

The range of Anabaptist activity, which extended during 1534–5 from

---

[64] Deppermann, *Melchior Hoffmann*, pp. 232, 334.
[65] *DAN*, I, p. 5. Not all dissidents were convinced. Obbe Philips, writing long after events in which he had been closely involved, recalled that Houtzager encountered opposition in Leeuwarden from 'Zwinglians', presumably so-called because they denied the real presence, Williams and Mergal (eds.), *Spiritual and Anabaptist Writers*, pp. 217–18.
[66] *DAN*, V, p. 143; cf. p. 150 and Bax, *Maastricht*, I. 120, 122.
[67] Bax, *Maastricht*, I. 71.

Westphalia to all the northern maritime provinces of the Netherlands and down to Maastricht, is remarkable. The movement, though not always well co-ordinated and sometimes divided on doctrine,[68] nevertheless caused considerable alarm to Charles V and to the territorial princes in north-western Germany. Itinerant 'apostolic messengers', first used by Jan Matthijsz., served to link Münster with the local Anabaptist congregations in the towns of the northern Netherlands throughout the siege of the episcopal city. They it was who brought the summons to the saints to assemble in Münster in March 1534 which galvanised several thousands of Anabaptists in Holland to embark on an exodus across the Zuiderzee. They also distributed the works of Rothmann, printed in Münster, to the local congregations, where they were read attentively. In the last desperate months of the siege, envoys tried to relieve the beleaguered city by mobilising support in many parts of the northern Netherlands and by fomenting diversionary insurrections in, among other towns, Amsterdam.

The Anabaptist congregations which sprang up overnight throughout Holland differed in several important respects from the earlier conventicles. First and foremost the laity set the tone in these separatist 'counter-churches'. While evangelicals in the 1520 had tended to look to sympathetic clerics for leadership, the prophets, teachers and elders of the Anabaptists in Amsterdam and Friesland were craftsmen almost to a man. Even after Münster, the radical Reformation in the Low Countries, in all its manifestations, continued under lay control.[69] Secondly, the apocalyptic expectations gave the local congregations an essentially transitory function: they provided a temporary shelter for the 'covenanters' during the last great persecutions before the Second Coming. Yet notwithstanding their provisional character, the Anabaptists gave their congregations a fairly clear structure. The most important congregations were headed by a 'bishop', an office exercised, for example, by Jacob van Campen in Amsterdam and Jan Smeitgen in Maastricht.[70] These had the authority to baptise and to choose the deacons and they were assisted by 'teachers', who were lay preachers. In several, probably many, congregations a diaconate was established. A needy Anabaptist at Maastricht received money 'from the common purse' to repair his roof, and in Amsterdam the deacons pressed a wealthy convert to contribute once more because 'the house of God is in need'.[71]

[68] For example, the Anabaptists at Amsterdam were at odds concerning hermeneutics, the march to Münster in 1534 and the use of the sword.
[69] G. K. Waite, *David Joris and Dutch Anabaptism, 1524–1543* (Waterloo, 1990), p. 30.
[70] *DAN*, V, pp. 20, 90; Bax, *Maastricht*, I. 135.
[71] Bax, *Maastricht*, I. 98, 116, 118; *DAN*, V, p. 89; *cf.* pp. 90, 111, 222. The Anabaptists at 's-Hertogenbosch had a purse-keeper 'boersdrager' in 1538, A. F. Mellink, *De wederdopers in de noordelijke Nederlanden, 1531–1544* (Groningen, 1953), p. 314.

Faithful to their Melchiorite past, the Anabaptist congregations broke entirely with the Roman Church. When adepts sought entry to the 'covenant' through believer's baptism, they had 'to swear or promise not to go to church any more and to foreswear everything that is done or stands in the church'. They also undertook to abstain from drunkenness and gossip-mongering.[72] The self-awareness of these 'chosen lambs of [the Lord's] pasture' left its imprint on their religious vocabulary. They spoke of themselves as 'the Christian brethren', 'covenant and Christian brethren', 'those of the covenant' and of their church as 'the community of Christians' and 'the godly congregation'.[73] When they met, they recognised one another by using a particular form of greeting.[74] They shunned the world where the 'godless' ruled, even to the extent of appointing their own 'chiefs' to settle disputes within the community without recourse to the law courts.[75] Yet 'the covenanters' of Amsterdam did make distinctions among those outside the community; in particular, they felt some kinship with the sacramentarian dissidents. When the Anabaptists in the city tried to seize control of the city, they called in their hour of need on the others 'of the Lutheran sect and the sacramentarians who favoured the Gospel' to assist in the destruction of the 'godless'.[76] Such sympathies were only to be expected, since many an Anabaptist in the early 1530s had begun his dissident career as a sacramentarian.[77]

The fall of the Anabaptist Kingdom at Münster in June 1535 not only provoked widespread disillusion among whose who had given credence to the apocalyptic claims of Hoffmann, Jan Matthijsz. and John of Leyden; it removed the lynch-pin which had restrained the centrifugal tendencies among the radicals. As a result Dutch Anabaptism lost its coherence for a decade as it fell apart into several splinter groups. Although no love was lost between the leaders of these factions, the rank-and-file could switch their allegiances, partly because each preserved elements of the Melchior–Münsterite legacy.

The Batenburgers, so named because they acknowledged Jan van Batenburg rather than John of Leyden as the new David, stood most

---

[72] *DAN*, I, p. 5; see also p. 20. According to the testimony of Jan Paeuw a promise was not required of those who were considered 'strong enough in the faith', *DAN*, V, p. 90.
[73] Bax, *Maastricht*, I. 74–74, 93 n., 115; *DAN*, V, pp. 20, 30–1, 85, 173.
[74] Bax, *Maastricht*, I. 117 see also 98 n. 2.
[75] Bax, *Maastricht*, I. 75.
[76] *DAN*, V, p. 261. The local authorities and the public also showed a greater ability to draw distinctions between the dissident sects than is sometimes supposed, see *DAN*, V, pp. 45–6, 77.
[77] For the transition from sacramentarian dissent to Anabaptism see De Hoop Scheffer, *Geschiedenis der kerkhervorming*, pp. 618–19; Mellink, *De wederdopers in de noordelijke Nederlanden*, pp. 334–44; Bax, *Maastricht*, I. 97.

directly in the Münsterite tradition.[78] They looked forward to the imminent establishment of the New Jerusalem on earth, in preparation for which they, as God's elect, should take up the sword against the 'godless'. But there were also important differences. Since the 'door to grace' had been closed at Münster, they abandoned believers' baptism: new recruits were admitted, but they were destined to hold inferior positions in the Kingdom. Secondly, the Batenburgers were allowed to conceal their religious beliefs in order to avoid detection and they therefore went to confession and to Mass. On that account they called themselves 'children of Jacob' after the deception the patriarch Jacob had practised on Isaac. They wreaked vengeance against the religious establishment by plundering churches and monasteries, especially in Overijssel and in Westphalia. They also opposed the extension of Habsburg authority into the north-eastern Netherlands and cast the dynasty in the role of Babylon. Despite this apocalyptic terminology, the sect became after 1538 almost indistinguishable from any other tight-knit robber band, save that the members were bound together by their participation in blasphemous, as well as criminal, activities. The introverted and exclusive nature of the sect, which depended on a leader, doomed the Batenburgers to extinction: in this form the radical Reformation had, in effect, retreated into a cul de sac.

The Anabaptist movement led by David Joris seemed to have a more promising future. Indeed Joris is widely regarded as the most influential figure in Dutch Anabaptist circles in the aftermath of Münster. After a series of visionary experiences in 1536, he accepted his vocation as the 'Third David', who had received the 'Key' to the apocalyptic passages of Scripture. Yet Joris also remained true to the separatist tradition of Hoffmann, requiring his followers to distance themselves from the world before it was too late because 'the Lord is coming to pay vengeance'.[79] The route to 'the highest perfection' began with the mortification of the 'old man'; the 'Vergottung' of the individual only took place after he had divested himself of his creatureliness. Believers' baptism lost much of its significance for Joris, who indeed allowed his followers 'to dissemble with the world' and attend any church service. As a charismatic leader Joris exercised an extraordinary personal authority over his followers. These included the 'rich, powerful, experienced and learned',[80] some of whom subsidised the printing of his books and followed him to Basle in 1544,

---

[78] This paragraph is indebted to L. Jansma, 'Revolutionaire wederdopers na 1535', in *Historisch bewogen. Opstellen over de radicale reformatie in de 16e en 17e eeuw ... aangeboden aan Prof. Dr. A. F. Mellink* (Groningen, 1984), pp. 49–66.
[79] Waite, *David Joris*, p. 58.
[80] W. Bergsma and E. H. Waterbolk (eds.), *Kroniekje van een Ommelander boer in de zestiende eeuw* (Groningen, 1986), p. 77.

when he left the Low Countries. Though the faithful received instruction in Joris' esoteric doctrines in assemblies,[81] the organisation remained very loose,[82] and did not long survive the death of the prophet in Basle in 1556. Dissension among his closest disciples and the posthumous disgrace of Joris caused the movement to fall into public disrepute.[83]

In several important respects the fortunes of the Catholic Church in north west Europe revived in the 1540s. During this decade the Counter-Reformation began to bear fruit. In 1544 the theologians at Louvain clarified Catholic doctrine with a short statement of orthodox belief and two years later they published the first detailed *Index* of forbidden books. At the same time the central government overhauled the Inquisition and succeeded in suppressing the printing (but not the distribution) of Protestant literature at Antwerp.[84] The repression removed the last remnants of the Batenburgers, forced Joris to flee and snuffed out the first Reformed congregations in the Walloon towns almost before they had been established. In the Lower Rhine Charles V halted the slide towards Protestantism in Cleves and in the prince-bishopric of Cologne. The balance of advantage did not, however, entirely lie with the established church. Reformed Protestantism strengthened its grip on East Friesland under the direction of John à Lasco and Emden became a sanctuary for Dutch religious dissidents seeking refuge from persecution.

At this time too the influence of Menno Simons began to make itself felt in Holland. Since his conversion to Anabaptism in January 1536 this Frisian ex-priest had worked as an 'elder' in the northern Netherlands as well as in East Friesland and the Lower Rhine. His major work *Dat Fundament des Christelycken leers* (*The Foundation of Christian Doctrine*), first published in 1539, provided 'the first systematic survey' of Anabaptist theology in the wake of Münster.[85] When Obbe Philips apostatised in 1540, having lost his faith in the apocalyptic visions of Hoffmann and others, Menno emerged as the natural leader of all those Anabaptists who rejected both the violent apocalypticism of the Münsterites and the spiritualism of Joris. Although Menno continued to believe in the imminent Second Coming of Christ and accepted Hoffmann's teaching about the doctrine of the Incarnation, he and Dirk Philips, Obbe's

---

[81] A Jorist teacher employed a visual aid, in this case a woodcut from his master's *Wonderboek*, in order probably to explain the doctrine of the New Man, see Duke, *Reformation and Revolt*, p. 105.

[82] Waite, *David Joris*, p. 149.

[83] Joris' spiritualist theology, however, continued to exercise some appeal for intellectuals in the late sixteenth century, who deplored the growth of organised Protestant churches.

[84] A. G. Johnston and J.-F. Gilmont, 'L'imprimerie et la Réforme à Anvers' in J. -F. Gilmont (ed.), *La Réforme et le livre* (Paris, 1990), p. 194.

[85] M. Simons, *Dat Fundament des Christelycken leers*, ed. H. W. Meihuizen (The Hague, 1967), p. xii.

brother, stood in the tradition of the 'evangelical Anabaptists', to use Williams' description.[86] They stressed both the discipleship of the faithful Christian and the maintenance of the unblemished congregation, at odds with the world. The two elements coincided so neatly that it is difficult to argue for the priority of one over the other.

By the early 1540s a 'Mennonite' congregation had come together in Amsterdam under the guidance of Jan Claesz. Several women joined 'the school and secret preaching' held at his house where he expounded the Scriptures.[87] Jan Claesz. himself was sentenced to death in January 1544 for having arranged the publication and distribution of one of Menno's books.[88] The 'testaments' which he addressed to his family while awaiting trial reveal his conviction that the holy church is 'the assembly of the faithful born by the Word of God'. 'Heed not the great multitude, nor long-established tradition', he warned his children, 'but look to the little flock, which is persecuted for the sake of the Lord's Word, for the good do not persecute, but are persecuted'.[89] Though the eschatological element recurs, notably in the testimony of Hans van Overdam, executed at Ghent in 1551, the emphasis among such Anabaptists has shifted to the 'holy congregation'. According to Claes de Praet, 'the true Church, which Christ instituted ... is glorious, holy and blameless, without spot or wrinkle'.[90] At the same time the rebirth of the new man was not neglected. This aspect found expression in the puritan and ascetic exhortations of the elders and teachers.[91] Nor does there seem any reason to doubt the strict morality observed among the Anabaptists: both Catholics and Calvinists acknowledged that they led exemplary lives.[92]

As the immediacy of the Second Coming receded, the Anabaptist congregations acquired a more settled character. For such communities, concerned to uphold their irreproachable reputation, discipline appeared to be indispensable, but who should have the authority to exercise that discipline and how strictly should it be enforced? These issues provoked furious controversies among Dutch Anabaptists in the mid-sixteenth century. In 1557 Dirk Philips eventually prevailed on Menno Simons to endorse the uncompromising position that required a husband or wife to shun an excommunicated marriage partner. Yet within a few years of that decision Dutch Anabaptism began to fragment when moderates resisted

---

[86] G. H. Williams, *The Radical Reformation* (Philadelphia, 1967), p. 853.
[87] *DAN*, II, p. 49.
[88] *DAN*, II, p. 47.
[89] *BRN*, II. 78–88. For an English translation see Th. J. van Braght, *The Bloody Theater or Martyrs Mirror* (Scottdale, 1951), pp. 468–71.
[90] *BRN*, II. 249; van Braght, *Martyrs Mirror*, p., 558; *cf. BRN*, II. 138, 262.
[91] *DAN*, II, pp. 101, 136, 138.
[92] *BRN*, II, 247; J. Decavele, *Dageraad*, I. 335.

what they regarded as the tyranny of the elders and the legalistic moralism, which appeared to contradict the principle of Christian freedom with which the Reformation had begun.

From the outset of the Reformation in the Low Countries religious dissidents had wrestled with the problem of how to realise, in a hostile environment, their divergent ideals of a church renewed, reformed or restored. Luther had made known his opposition to any form of secret house church, which competed with the public church. Christians should either be satisfied with private devotions at home, or be prepared to leave the country.[93] Years later a leading Lutheran from Antwerp still considered secret assemblies to be a species of rebellion.[94] But such advice took no account of the circumstances in which Dutch dissidents found themselves. Despite Luther clandestine gatherings took place spontaneously because evangelicals who wanted to study the Scripture and the fashionable new theologies were denied an opportunity to do so within the Catholic Church. But what began as an informal response to this refusal and to the experience of persecution gradually evolved into a schismatic organisation, whose existence called for doctrinal justification.

A mutually reinforcing process took place: revulsion against the Mass on the one hand and the experience of persecution on the other served to authenticate the belief that the Church of Rome was the 'synagogue of Satan' with which the saints could have no dealings. As a result expressly sectarian congregations emerged to give temporary shelter to 'God's elect' on the eve of the Second Coming. Indeed salvation was only promised to those who had been incorporated into the 'covenant' by means of believers' baptism. When the expectations about Münster as the New Jerusalem were disappointed, some, like Obbe Philips, poured scorn on the Melchiorite preachers who had insisted 'that there must be established a congregation, assembly, ordination, office and order, as though no one could be saved unless he stood in such a congregation'.[95] Joris, too, reacted against this insistence by reducing the significance of the sacraments and permitting his followers to conform with the rituals of the prevailing church, be it Roman or Protestant. Guided by Menno and Dirk Philips, however, most Dutch Anabaptists preferred to reassert the importance of separatist congregations, which were intended to coincide, as far as possible, with the invisible church of the elect. To protect the unblemished character of these congregations the exercise of discipline became at once a necessity and a bone of contention.

93 J. W. Pont, *Geschiedenis van het lutheranisme in de Nederlanden tot 1618* (Haarlem, 1911), pp. 42–3.
94 Pont, *Geschiedenis van het lutheranisme*, p. 54.
95 Williams and Mergal (eds.), *Spiritual and Anabaptist Writers*, p. 207.

These tensions did not slacken after 1555. When Calvin told evangelicals, living like those in the Low Countries among the 'papists', to choose between exile or complete withdrawal from the Roman Church (and probably persecution), his uncompromising advice found approval with the Flemish Reformed leader Petrus Dathenus. He insisted that those 'who have through faith become God's people and who have left Babylon behind in their hearts should also depart in body if they do not want to mock and despise God's commandment'.[96] But many others disagreed. Some shared the viewpoint of the Flemish evangelical who maintained that the Roman Church, for all its corruption, remained 'the Church of Christ';[97] others sympathised with those dissidents in Groningen who refused to attend the Reformed services there 'saying that you can be saved outside the congregation'.[98]

These debates about church organisation were not, of course, confined to the dissidents of the Low Countries. They could be heard wherever the Protestant Reformation made an impact. But in the case of the Netherlands the problems were exacerbated by the repressive policies enforced by Charles V. Dissidents here were obliged to conform outwardly, to seek refuge abroad, or to enter, however reluctantly into some form of sectarianism. There were no easy choices. In so far as the early Reformation in the Low Countries can lay claim to be distinctive, it derives from the prolonged exposure of dissidents in the Netherlands to persecution. It was this experience that drove a wedge between evangelicals in the Low Countries and their counterparts in Germany and helped to mould the structures of dissent.

[96] Quoted by A. G. Johnston, 'The Eclectic Reformation: Vernacular Evangelical Pamphlet Literature in the Dutch-speaking Low Countries' (unpub. Ph.D. Southampton, 1986), p. 239.
[97] Decavele, *Dageraad*, I. 383.
[98] H. Schilling and K.-D. Schreiber (eds.), *Die Kirchenratsprotokolle der Reformierten Gemeinde Emden 1557–1620* (2 vols., Cologne/Vienna, 1989–92), I. 121.

SELECT BIBLIOGRAPHY

PRIMARY SOURCES

Braght, Thieleman J. van. *The Bloody Theater or Martyrs Mirror of the Defenseless Christians* (Scottdale, 1951).
Cramer, S. and F. Pijper, (eds.), *Bibliotheca reformatoria neerlandica. Geschriften uit den tijd der hervorming in de Nederlanden*, (10 vols., The Hague, 1903–14).
Enzinas, Francisco de, *Mémoires de. Texte latin inédit avec la traduction française au XVIe siècle en regard 1543–45*, ed. C. A. Campan (2 vols., Brussels-The Hague, 1862).

164   *Alastair Duke*

Fredericq, P. (ed.). *Corpus documentorum inquisitionis haereticae pravitatis neerlandicae* (5 vols., Ghent-The Hague, 1889–1902).

Grauwels, J. (ed.). *Dagboek van gebeurtenissen opgetekend door Christiaan Munters, 1529–1545* (Assen, 1972).

Mellink, A. F. (ed.). *Documenta anabaptistica neerlandica* I *Friesland en Groningen (1530–1550)* (Leiden, 1975).

Documenta anabaptistica neerlandica V *Amsterdam (1531–1536)* (Leiden, 1985).

Documenta anabaptistica neerlandica II *Amsterdam (1536–1578)* (Leiden, 1980).

Santbergen, R. van. *Un procès de religion à Louvain. Paul de Rovere (1542–1546)* (Brussels, 1953).

Simons, Menno. *The Complete Writings of Menno Simons c. 1496–1561* (Scottdale, 1956).

SECONDARY SOURCES

Augustijn, C. 'Anabaptism in the Netherlands; another look', *Mennonite Quarterly Review*, 62 (1988).

Bax, W. *Het protestantisme in het bisdom Luik en vooral te Maastricht, 1505–1557* (The Hague, 1937).

Boom, H. ten. *De reformatie in Rotterdam, 1530–1585* (n.p., 1985).

Decavele, J. *De dageraad van de reformatie in Vlaanderen (1520–1565)* (2 vols., Brussels, 1975).

'De opkomst van het protestantisme te Brussel', *Noordgouw*, 19–20 (1979–83).

'Vroege reformatorische bedrijvigheid in de grote Nederlandse steden: Claes van der Elst te Brussel, Antwerpen, Amsterdam en Leiden, 1524–1528', *NAK*, 70 (1990).

Denis, P. *Les églises d'étrangers en pays rhénans (1538–1564)* (Paris, 1984).

Deppermann, K. *Melchior Hoffmann. Social Unrest and Apocalyptic Visions in the Age of the Reformation* (Edinburgh, 1987).

Duke, A. *Reformation and Revolt in the Low Countries* (London, 1990).

Frederichs, J. *De secte der Loïsten of Antwerpsche libertijnen (1525–1545)* (Ghent-The Hague, 1891).

Historisch bewogen. Opstellen over de radicale reformatie in de 16e en 17e ... aangeboden aan Prof. Dr. Mellink (Groningen, 1984).

Hoop Scheffer, J. G. de. *Geschiedenis der kerkhervorming in Nederland van haar ontstaan tot 1531* (Amsterdam, 1873).

Johnston, A. G. 'The Eclectic Reformation: Vernacular Evangelical Pamphlet Literature in the Dutch-speaking Low Countries, 1520–1565', Ph.D. dissertation (University of Southampton, 1986).

Kronenberg, M. E. *Verboden boeken en opstandige drukkers in de hervormingstijd* (Amsterdam, 1948).

Mellink, A. F. *De wederdopers in de noordelijke nederlanden, 1531–1544* (Groningen, 1953).

Amsterdam en de wederdopers in de zestiende eeuw (Nijmegen, 1978).

Moreau, G. *Histoire du Protestantisme à Tournai jusqu' à la veille de la Révolution des Pays-Bas* (Paris, 1962).

Pettegree, Andrew 'The Exile Churches and the Churches "under the Cross":
Antwerp and Emden during the Dutch Revolt', *JEH*, 38 (1987).

Emden and the Dutch Revolt. Exile and the Development of Reformed Protestantism (Oxford, 1992).

Postma, F. 'Regnerus Praedinus (*ca.* 1510–1559). Zijn school en zijn invloed',
Archief voor de katholieke kerk in Nederland, 32 (1990).

Sources de l'histoire religieuse de la Belgique. Moyen âge et Temps modernes
(Bibliothèque de la revue d'histoire ecclésiastique, fasc. 47, Louvain, 1968).

Spruyt, B. J. 'Humanisme, Evangelisme en Reformatie in de Nederlanden, 1520–
1530' in W. de Greef and M. van Campen (eds.), *Reformatie in meervoud*
(Kampen, 1991).

'Listrius *lutherizans*: his *Epistola theologica adversus Dominicanos Suollenses
(1520)*', *SCJ* (1991).

Tracy, J. D. *Holland under Habsburg rule 1506–1566. The Formation of a Body
Politic* (Oxford, 1990).

Trapman, J. *De Summa der godliker scrifturen (1523)* (Leiden, 1978).

'Le rôle des "sacramentaires" des origines de la Réforme jusqu'en 1530 aux
Pay-Bas', *NAK*, 63 (1983).

Verheyden, A. L. E. *Anabaptism in Flanders, 1530–1650* (Scottdale, 1961).

Visser, C. Ch. G. *Luther's geschriften in de Nederlanden tot 1546* (Assen 1969).

Waite, G. K. *David Joris and Dutch Anabaptism, 1524–1543* (Waterloo, 1990).

Woltjer, J. J. *Friesland in hervormingstijd* (Leiden, 1962).

8   England

Diarmaid MacCulloch

The English Reformation was the creation of the English monarchy, more an act of state than in any other part of Europe apart from Scandinavia: the result of one man's obsessive quest for a male heir, rather than a nation's search for the way back to the Church of the Apostles. If Henry VIII had not sought a divorce from his first wife at the wrong moment for the Papacy, it is unlikely that he would have been propelled away from Rome, and it is unlikely that anyone else in England would have had the strength to force a break against his will or the will of his successors. Sixteenth-century England was one of the most centralised states in Europe; Henry VII (1485–1509) and Henry VIII (1509–47) had brought it out of a long political crisis to a remarkable degree of subservience to royal wishes. The kingdom which the Tudors controlled so effectively was largely a patchwork of rural societies. Where one can discern urban Reformations in England, they were small-scale and circumscribed by government policy, because English urban centres were nearly all small and limited in initiative by Continental standards. Only London could challenge comparison with the Imperial cities of Germany, and London's weight was never decisively or consistently thrown behind either conservatism or reform; both viewpoints were strongly represented among its clergy and people, but neither side could outface the other without the necessary lead from the Crown up the river at Westminster.[1]

Only occasionally did the English Crown's command of events falter. The governments of Henry VIII and of Edward VI faced risings from conservatives and the government of Mary from Protestants, but in all cases these were crushed, and they strengthened the Crown's commitment to implementing its chosen policies rather than retarding the course of events. What is particularly significant is how few members of the parliamentary peerage, the upper aristocracy, were involved in these risings. Most gentry and noblemen proved reluctant to challenge the monarch's wishes, whatever their private religious sympathies; quiet local obstruc-

---

[1] S. Brigden, *London and the Reformation* (Oxford, 1989).

tion or non-compliance with change was usually the limit of their defiance, and successive governments were generally ready to call the bluff of
this variety of dumb insolence if they felt that the effort was worthwhile.[2]

Because of this direction from the top, more than with most Continental Reformations, discussion of the English Reformation repeatedly turns
to a discussion of royal politics and personalities. One often underrated
feature of the early English Reformation story which makes it unique
among the European Reformations is its debt, not just to the initiatives of
men, but to the influence of one woman: Anne Boleyn (c. 1501–36). Anne
was not merely the catalyst for Henry VIII's efforts to rid himself of an
unloved wife in a legal fashion; she emerged during her brief spell as
Queen Consort from 1533 to 1536 as a major player in her own right.
Well-educated and with first-hand experience of Court life in the Low
Countries and France, she had an informed enthusiasm for the contemporary French reform movement, and she was not afraid to draw Henry's
attention to important early works of Protestantism in English. It may
well have been thanks to her, and was certainly thanks to her family, that
Thomas Cranmer (1489–1556) became Archbishop of Canterbury; it was
on her initiative that England gained its first Protestant bishops, and
among her carefully chosen chaplains were some of the future leaders of
the Protestant Church of England, including her daughter Elizabeth's
first Archbishop of Canterbury, Matthew Parker. Significantly, those
who had known her described her period as Henry's wife as her 'reign';
indeed it was probably her masterfulness which sealed her doom, as
Henry found the qualities which had been fascinating in a mistress
increasingly irksome in a wife.[3]

In addition to Anne, the men who cleared the ground for the English
Reformation were not clergy but laymen: royal ministers and servants at
Court. Under Henry VIII during the 1530s, there was the busy, methodical Thomas Cromwell (c. 1485–1540), pushing forward the work of his
vicegerency of Henry's newly independent church with a sincere commitment to evangelical reform, while walking a tightrope of aristocratic envy
and conservative hatred from which he would eventually fall. After his
execution in 1540, a group of Protestant courtiers and aristocrats fought a
rearguard action against the conservatives who had destroyed him, and

---

[2] A. Fletcher, *Tudor Rebellions* (3rd edn., London, 1983).
[3] On Anne and the Reformation, E. W. Ives, *Anne Boleyn* (Oxford, 1986), pp. 302–34. On
Anne and her 'reign', see J. Foxe, *Acts and Monuments* ..., ed. G. Townshend and S. R.
Cattley (8 vols. London, 1837–41) V. 420; M. Dowling, 'The Gospel and the Court:
Reformation under Henry VIII', in P. Lake and M. Dowling, *Protestantism and the
National Church in Sixteenth-Century England* (London, 1987), pp. 36–77, and cf.,
M. Dowling (ed.), 'William Latymer's Cronickille of Anne Bulleyne', *Camden Miscellany
30* (Camden Society, 4th ser. 39, 1990), 33.

eventually succeeded in the king's last months of illness in gaining the upper hand decisively for the future shape of policy under the boy-king Edward VI (1547–53). For Edward's successive guardians, the Dukes of Somerset and Northumberland, the destruction of what remained of doctrinal Catholicism and subsequent Protestant restructuring were only one aspect of their battles for personal power.

Thus one does not find fiery clerical reformers independently spear-heading the changes which transformed the English Church. There was no Luther to arouse the nation against the Pope, no Zwingli to turn the eating of a sausage into the downfall of a city's traditional faith, and among the rather thin and muted ranks of English religious radicalism, no Thomas Müntzer to face death for a revolutionary new Jerusalem. Most prominent among the clergy who undertook the theological and liturgical engineering for the new church during twenty years' faction and uncertainty was that most reluctant of heroes, Thomas Cranmer: a man whom short sight and a methodical approach to scholarship had pre-disposed to lifelong caution. Catapulted by the urgent needs of the king's divorce in his early forties from a worthy but unspectacular academic career (without the ghost of any pastoral experience as a priest) into the highest office in the English Church, Cranmer did not always come unscathed out of the messy compromises of Henry VIII's political world; it is difficult to find inspiration in his fifteen years' concealment of his illegal marriage or in his frequent subservience to Henry VIII's ego.[4]

However, under Edward VI, Cranmer's remarkable flair for writing balanced, monumental prose was an accidental bonus to his creation of a scholarly and workmanlike Protestant English liturgy; he also allied with Nicholas Ridley, Bishop of London, to keep at bay attempts by more fiery spirits like John Hooper to berth the English Church more closely alongside that of Zurich. The crucial dispute deciding the outcome of this struggle came in 1550–1: the first of many rows within the Church of England where an apparently trivial issue (in this case, what a clergyman should wear) took on significance in deciding the nature and identity of the established church. Offered the bishopric of Gloucester, Hooper took a principled stand against putting on the traditional episcopal rochet and chimer at his consecration: these were 'rather the habit and vesture of Aaron and the Gentiles, than of the ministers of Christ'.[5] Although

---

[4] At present the standard biography of Cranmer is J. Ridley, *Thomas Cranmer* (Oxford, 1962); I am engaged on a new biography. On Cranmer's second marriage, cf. Ridley, *ibid.*, pp. 12, 16, 19, 46–7, 51, 146–51, 165, 188–9, 327, 377, 389.

[5] S. Carr (ed.) *Early Writings of John Hooper D.D. ...* (Parker Society, 1853), 479. A clear account of this dispute is to be found in C. Smyth, *Cranmer and the Reformation under Edward VI* (London, 1926), pp. 190–220. See also J. Opie, 'The Anglicizing of John

Cranmer and his colleagues gave way on Hooper's parallel scruples on the form of oath he should swear, this was too much; Hooper was opposing a decision of authority on the form of episcopal consecration for the sake of a piece of trivial symbolism. Ridley in particular struggled and politicked to such good effect with the Privy Council that Councillors' support for Hooper gave way. Hooper found himself in prison for his defiance, and by February 1551 he had been forced to accept defeat in order to take up his bishopric. Nothing could be more symbolic of the character of the whole English Reformation: the clerical zealot was curbed on the initiative of his more cautious colleagues at the government's behest. Now, in the perilously short time available before King Edward's death, the shaping of the church's liturgy and theological statements was in the hands of Cranmer and his allies: creating a middle way between the conservatism of Luther's Wittenberg and the root-and-branch reform of the Swiss Protestant cities, which gave birth to an English idea of *via media* in religious life. English churchmen of later centuries would redefine this middle way to run between Rome and Reformation, but that is not how the Edwardian reformers would have viewed matters.[6]

It is clear from these Edwardian disputes that early English Protestantism found it difficult to agree on what it was supposed to be: hardly surprisingly, since by the time that an unequivocally Protestant regime was established under Edward VI, the Continental Reformation had already become deeply divided. There were indeed distinctive English theological priorities, but the English added little that was original; indeed, the English lack of capacity for abstract theological invention is so marked through our history as to constitute a dangerously plausible argument for persistent national characteristics. To chronicle the theological story of the English Reformation is largely to chronicle the shifting influences from the Continent, and English assimilation of them or reaction against them. How, then, did the English respond to the religious upheavals in the rest of Europe?

Even before the Reformation, England was affected by the Continental humanist movement: at the end of the fifteenth century the universities of Oxford and Cambridge ended a period of comparative insularity and began to take an interest in the upsurge of classical scholarship in northern Europe, giving prolonged hospitality to the greatest name among Continental humanist scholars, Desiderius Erasmus. Humanist ideals of what constituted useful learning and good teaching would shape

---

Hooper', *ARG*, 59 (1968), 150, and A. Pettegree, *Foreign Protestant Communities in Sixteenth-Century London* (Oxford, 1986), chs. 2–3.
6 For general discussion of the *via media* question, see D. MacCulloch, 'The myth of the English Reformation', *Journal of British Studies*, 30 (1991).

the way in which Tudor England's clerical and lay leadership was educated. However, it is perilous to draw the conclusion from this that the English Reformation was the logical outcome of the growth of humanism in England; those who opposed Henry VIII's schemes and were destroyed by him, John Fisher and Thomas More, and those of Henry's bishops who profoundly distrusted Cromwell's reformist programme, like John Stokesley and Cuthbert Tunstall, had been part of the humanist world as much as the Cambridge-educated clergy and statesmen who helped to shape the churches of Edward VI and Elizabeth I. Humanism was a way of approaching the acquisition and ordering of knowledge, not a coherent movement of thought; we have been far too inclined to lump together the leading figures like Erasmus and More without seeing that even before the Reformation upheaval, there were profound differences of outlook among those who have been classified as humanists. Humanist learning certainly led people to question the assumptions of medieval intellectual systems and to propose schemes of social, political and religious reform, but this did not prevent Englishmen interested in the humanist agenda finding themselves on opposite sides in the struggles of the Reformation.[7]

Moreover, humanism was not the only source of reformist ideas in England, any more than it was for Martin Luther in Wittenberg. English common law had long provided an alternative road to fame and fortune alongside the structures of the church. It had its own training schools, the Inns of Court in London, which could trace nearly two centuries of institutional existence by the dawn of the Reformation, giving its members a powerful sense of professional *esprit de corps*; this did not always bode well for clerical pretensions. One of the most strident English voices calling for reform and the curbing of the church's power in the 1530s was Christopher St German, a lawyer and legal writer already approaching old age; in 1531 he produced a draft scheme for national reform to be presented to parliament which was among the most practical and thorough to emerge in a decade when Thomas Cromwell encouraged much radical thinking on the future shape of the kingdom. However, there was little that was humanist about St German's work; it reflected the pragmatic energy of an expanding legal profession, which had scant interest in the abstract ideas of the humanists. Moreover, in terms of doctrine, St German was a conservative who abhorred the ideas of the Continental reformers; it was structural and not theological reform which

---

[7] A. Fox and J. Guy, *Reassessing the Henrician Age: Humanism, Politics and Reform 1500–1550* (Oxford, 1986), ch. 1. J. K. McConica, *English Humanists and Reformation Politics under Henry VIII and Edward VI* (Oxford, 1965), argued for a consistent humanist impulse to the early Reformation in England; for reviews critical of his thesis, see G. R. Elton, *HJ*, 10 (1967), 137–8, and A. G. Dickens, *History*, 52 (1967), 77–8.

he sought, a preoccupation which matched well the interests of King Henry.[8]

Where a minority of English clergy and lay people did take up the evangelical ideas convulsing northern Europe during the 1520s, it was at first Luther who caught the attention, provoking in turn a burst of English literary attacks on the German Reformation throughout that decade as the universities and senior clergy struggled to fight back; only the king's personal crisis from 1527 turned this polemical energy away from Luther towards the royal need for a battery of arguments on his quest for divorce.[9] Among the early enthusiasts for Luther was a rare Oxford man in a Reformation which would come to be dominated by Cambridge academics, William Tyndale (?1495–1536); his pioneering work of Bible translation went hand in hand with translations of sections of Luther's biblical commentaries presented in discreet anonymity. Although Henry VIII never accepted Tyndale's translation, detesting the Lutheran flavour of the accompanying notes, and indeed collaborated in his betrayal to, and execution by, the Emperor Charles V, this work lay at the heart of successive projects of English biblical translation which eventually achieved official status in 1537, and which represented the most enduring positive achievement of Thomas Cromwell's years in charge of the English Church. At the heart of the English Reformation, as at the heart of Luther's, was the inspiration of a vernacular Bible.

One might indeed think that it would be the Lutheran Reformation, based as it was on the support of a godly prince, which would have made more headway in the kingdom of England than Swiss Reformations deriving their impetus from the support of oligarchies in city-states. However, in practice, Lutheran influence was already on the wane during Henry VIII's last years. Henry had personally detested Luther ever since their literary quarrel of 1521 which had earned the king the title of 'Defender of the Faith', and he took little from the Lutheran example apart from his sponsorship of the vernacular Bible and the central place of the monarch in governing the church.[10] With the exception of various diplomatic manoeuvres, most notably and disastrously the negotiations which led in 1540 to Henry's farcically brief marriage to Anne of Cleves,

[8] On St German, Fox and Guy, *Reassessing the Henrician Age*, pp. 16–18; and on the legal profession E.W. Ives, *The Common Lawyers of Pre-Reformation England: Thomas Kebell: A Case Study* (Cambridge, 1983).
[9] R. Rex, 'The English Campaign against Luther in the 1520s', *Transactions of the Royal Historical Society*, 5th ser. 39 (1989), 85–106.
[10] On Henry, Luther, the Supremacy and vernacular scripture, see J.J. Scarisbrick, *Henry VIII* (London, 1968), pp. 110–16, 246–8, 252–5, 275–81, 326, 366–7, 395–7, 401–2, 406–9, 414–15.

German Lutheran theologians were unwelcome figures in Henrician England, with little chance of spreading their ideas directly. Moreover, the thought of the English reformers came to display certain key themes which clashed with Lutheran theology. Three in particular deserve our attention: a pronounced interest in moral legalism, a detestation of shrines, images and pilgrimages and a scepticism about the idea of real presence in the eucharistic elements. Even Tyndale's thought as revealed in his notes and commentaries on the Biblical text turned increasingly towards an interest in the role of law in the Christian life, and images and shrines began to suffer official attack with Thomas Cromwell's injunctions of 1538, an attack which would continue intermittently with considerable official backing into Elizabeth's reign.[11] In eucharistic discussion, at the opening of the 1530s, Tyndale's assistant and fellow-martyr John Frith (*c.* 1503–33) began developing ideas about the eucharist which would have a leading influence on Thomas Cranmer's published rejections of real presence notions in the eucharist: consequently Frith's thought had great significance for the future of English reformed eucharistic theology.[12] By contrast with these three themes of legalism, iconoclasm and scepticism on ideas of eucharistic presence, the whole basis of Luther's theological breakthrough had been a rejection of the power of law in the Christian life, and he had no particular animus against the world of saints and statues; his insistence on the real presence in the eucharistic elements had been at the heart of his bitter quarrel with Huldrich Zwingli.[13]

When one looks for the origin of this trio of distinctive English theological preoccupations dividing English theology from Lutheranism, it is worth noting both their correspondence with the earlier English rebellion against medieval Catholicism in Lollardy and with the ideas of the Swiss reformers. It is tempting to suggest that the pre-existing themes of Lollard dissent struck chords with churchmen of evangelical sympathies encountering the ideas of Zwingli and his successors; however, the most vital connection to be made for this thesis, the proof of definite links between Lollardy and the English academics who became spokesmen for the Reformation, is the most difficult to substantiate. Lollardy does not give much impression of intellectual energy by the early sixteenth century;

11 On Tyndale, see W. A. Clebsch, *England's Earliest Protestants 1520–1535* (New Haven, 1964); on iconoclasm, M. Aston, *England's Iconoclasts* (Oxford, 2 vols. I, 1988).
12 On Frith and his influence on Cranmer, see Foxe, *Acts and Monuments*, V. 9; G. Burnet, *History of the Reformation of the Church of England* (3 vols. in 6, London, 1820–2) I i. 262–3.
13 On Luther and images, Aston, *England's Iconoclasts*, I. 2, 6, 40–1, 42–3, 243n, 307, 437; on Luther and the Eucharist, H. Bornkamm, *Luther in Mid-Career 1521–30* (London, 1983), chs. 19, 23.

it had become a movement with no base in the universities and no capacity to produce new literature. Nevertheless, it had managed to survive the English Church's efforts at its total destruction, and in at least one case, that of Thomas Bilney the English protomartyr (c. 1495–1531), J. F. Davis has identified a significant conjunction of the possibility of a Lollard background with humanist studies at Cambridge University.[14] This may be a clue to the direction which the English Reformation took. The Swiss reformers were generally much more prepared to acknowledge a debt to humanism and to display humanist presuppositions than was Luther himself; they easily forged friendships with the lively humanist academic community in the English universities at a time when the developing Lutheran humanism of the generation of Philip Melanchthon was increasingly barred from access to England.

Contacts between Swiss reformers and England can be ascertained at least from 1536, when English evangelicals were welcomed in Zurich by reformed scholars, and the friendships formed then led to the visit to Oxford in 1537 of a young Swiss destined to be one of the leaders of Zurich reform, Rodolph Gualter. The sharp conservative government reaction which led to parliament passing the Act of Six Articles in 1539 produced a crop of English exiles who, among other places, made for Switzerland. They multiplied friendly contacts with the Swiss, while under Edward VI, English Protestants could return Swiss hospitality alongside a sudden influx of foreign refugees from the more troubled parts of Europe, prompted chiefly by the Emperor Charles V's victory at Mühlberg in 1547 and his enforcement of the Interim in 1548. Amid this rush of international theological talent ranging from Spaniards and Italians to Poles, turning England temporarily into an international capital of Protestant thought, German Lutherans were notable by their absence; they found themselves under less pressure from the Emperor's policies than others.[15]

Admittedly, the foreign guests most in tune with Archbishop Cranmer's thinking were not Zurich men, but those who sought to bring unity to the divided world of Protestantism, particularly Peter Martyr and Martin Bucer; their readiness to seek for compromise amid Protestant disputes did not always endear them either to the Lutherans or to the Swiss reformers. Cranmer was prepared to use Lutheran precedents in some aspects of his new Prayer Books and also in drawing up the Forty-Two Articles. He had enough respect for Philip Melanchthon, Luther's successor at Wittenberg, to attempt to bring him to England

[14] J. F. Davis, 'The trials of Thomas Bilney and the English Reformation', *HJ*, 24 (1981), 775–90.
[15] Smyth, *Cranmer and the English Reformation*, pp. 80–105.

after the death of Bucer to remedy the loss to Protestant scholarship at Cambridge University, a plan which at the time of King Edward's death had got as far as sending Melanchthon his travel expenses for the trip to England.[16] However, the frustration of this scheme by Mary's accession effectively marked the end of Lutheran influence in England; already more central to the sacramental ideas of the 1552 Prayer Book were the doctrines of Zurich or Berne as modified by Cranmer's own slow progress away from real presence views of the eucharist.

Views of the nature of human salvation and damnation also became significant in the loss of Lutheran influence in England. Mainstream Lutheran thought was increasingly influenced by Melanchthon to move away from Luther's predestinarian emphasis on the irresistible majesty of God, towards the belief of his great adversary Erasmus: human beings are capable of exercising their own free will in turning from evil to good and being justified for salvation in the eyes of God. This change among Lutherans marked a further breach with the theologians of Zurich, and above all of Geneva, where the arch-predestinarian Jean Calvin effectively crushed a variety of opposition during the 1550s to produce a theological orthodoxy for much of Protestant Europe, including a powerful influence in the England of Elizabeth I. By the end of the century, the eclipse of Lutheranism's reputation in England was complete except among a beleaguered minority of anti-Calvinist divines.[17]

The radical Reformation so important in the coastal regions across the North Sea from England (particularly the northern Netherlands) had only a marginal impact among the English. Lollardy had sheltered a number of individuals with eccentric religious views, but the interrogations of Lollards through the fifteenth and early sixteenth century suggest that most of them remained dominated in their thinking by the three themes to which we have already drawn attention: leading a good life according to biblical precepts, iconoclasm and rejection of medieval eucharistic theology. Nevertheless, Continental radicals shared with more mainstream reformers in the network of contacts built up by the Lollards over the previous century, and radical religion's activities in the English

---

[16] J. D. Alsop, 'Philip Melanchthon and England in 1553', *Notes and Queries*, 235 (June, 1990), 164–5. C. Hopf, *Martin Bucer and the English Reformation* (Oxford, 1946); M. Anderson, 'Rhetoric and Reality: Peter Martyr and the English Reformation', *SCJ*, 19 (1988), 451–69. For opinions critical of Martyr and Bucer, H. Robinson (ed.), *Original Letters relative to the English Reformation* ... (2 vols., Parker Society, 1846–7), I. 61, II. 509n, 518, 662; and for criticism of Martyr's eucharistic statements by Bucer himself, *ibid.*, II. 544.

[17] B. Hall, 'The early Rise and gradual Decline of Lutheranism in England (1520–1600)', in D. Baker (ed.), *Reform and Reformation: England and the Continent c.1500–1750* (London: SCH: Subsidia 2, 1979), pp. 103–31.

Reformation were largely confined to the south-eastern area from Kent to the Wash which had formed the main focus of Lollard activity.[18]

The first traceable radicals with definite links to the Anabaptism of the Continent were foreign refugees who found comparative security in England. They caused considerable alarm to Henry's government, and the king caused more of them to be burnt than the total number of Lollard martyrdoms throughout the fifteenth century, but the total of less than twenty deaths was still small compared with the hundreds of executions in the Netherlands and north Germany.[19] As more refugees streamed in under Edward VI, the new Protestant regimes also proved nervous of radicalism and burnt two Anabaptists even after abolishing the heresy laws which had caught so many mainstream evangelicals; one of the victims was a strong-minded Englishwoman, Joan Bocher of Kent. A significant incentive for the establishment of Strangers' Churches for foreign Protestants in the capital and elsewhere was to provide a framework for curbing such beliefs, and when Cranmer drew up Forty-Two Articles of belief for the Church of England in 1553, the statements were designed to combat Anabaptism even more than papistry. Under Mary's reaction, Anabaptists were swept up into the general persecution, which caused John Foxe some problems when he came to glorify the Marian martyrs in his *Acts and Monuments*.[20]

Nevertheless the government's fears of Münster-style anarchy appearing in England were never fulfilled. Anabaptism of the sort familiar in the Low Countries remained largely a movement of foreigners, whose only noticeable success in establishing a long-term English bridgehead, and that on a small scale, was in the form of Hendrik Niklaes' Family of Love. Familists were secretly recruited during Mary's reign, particularly around London and East Anglia by followers of Niklaes, and remained as an underground organisation to alarm the authorities down into the early seventeenth century; with their willingness to practice systematic deception and lead a double life, they can be traced in at least one English parish under James I as the parish officers who ought to have been combatting such religious deviance.[21] The only other radical movement to

[18] For a general survey, see I. B. Horst, *The Radical Brethren: Anabaptism and the English Reformation to 1558* (Nieuwkoop, 1972).

[19] Horst, *Radical Brethren*, p. 31.

[20] W. K. Jordan (ed.) *The Chronicle and Political Papers of King Edward VI* (London and Ithaca, 1966), 37. On the martyrs, J. F. Davis, *Heresy and Reformation in the South East of England 1520–1559* (London and New Jersey: Royal Historical Society Studies in History Series 34, 1983) pp. 143–7, and P. Collinson, 'Truth and Legend: the veracity of John Foxe's Book of Martyrs', in A. C. Duke and C. A. Tamse (eds.), *Clio's Mirror. Historiography in Britain and the Netherlands* (Zutphen, 1985), pp. 31–54.

[21] A. Hamilton, *The Family of Love* (Cambridge, 1981); J. W. Martin, 'The Elizabethan Familists', *Baptist Quarterly*, 29 (1982), reprinted in his collected essays, *Religious*

appear during the early English Reformation was an amorphous and ill-assorted group of clergy and humble unlearned folk concentrated in Kent and Essex known as the Freewillers. Causing anxiety to the Edwardian authorities and irritation to fellow-sufferers from Mary's persecution, their distinctive characteristic was to proclaim the importance of human free will for salvation, resisting the dominant trend in English theology to embrace predestinarian views, but on a wider basis they deplored dogmatic assertions in theological discussion and encouraged individual exploration of the way to salvation. Disappearing more quickly than the Familists, they seem to have no contact with the re-emergence of anti-Calvinist views on predestination among a minority of academics and parish clergy at the end of Elizabeth's reign. Indeed, the links between the radicals of the first half of the century and Elizabethan separatists are tenuous, and later English separatism owes its theological development more to trends within the Puritan movement, part of mainstream Elizabethan Protestantism.[22]

All these Continental influences did not come into a spiritual vacuum or wasteland relieved only by Lollards, humanists and sceptical lawyers. In recent years evidence has accumulated that there was plenty of vigour in the devotional patterns of the traditional church on the eve of the English Reformation: parish life, chantries, soul-masses, gilds and fraternities flourished. How easily did the Reformation sweep aside this spiritual life to impose new priorities? In the past, disagreements about this largely depended on the confessional bias of the historical commentator; but the cooling of passions about the Reformation has not ended controversy. Recent debate centring on the work of self-styled 'revisionist' historians has isolated two pairs of possibilities in describing the Reformation: rapid or slow? Imposed from above or rising from below?[23]

One reason for contrasting answers to the revisionists' questions is that the English response to the Reformation was fragmented by region: one area might indeed provide evidence for a quick Reformation drawing on significant support from below, while another could reveal a very late popular assimilation of religious change: 'slow and from above'. After a lifetime of local research and a survey of the many local studies produced over the last few decades, A. G. Dickens has singled out as the area where the Reformation enjoyed genuine early popular support, the 'great cre-

Radicals in Tudor England (1989); C. Marsh, '"A Graceless and Audacious Companie"': The Family of Love in the Parish of Balsham, 1550–1630', in W. J. Sheils and D. Wood (eds.) *Voluntary Religion* (SCH, 23, 1986), pp. 191–208.

[22] J. W. Martin, 'The first that made separation from the Reformed Church of England', *ARG*, 77 (1986), 281–312, and D. A. Penny, *Free will or Predestination* (London and New York, Royal Historical Society Studies in History series, 61, 1990).

[23] See a bibliographical discussion in C. Haigh (ed.), *The English Reformation Revised*, ch. 1.

scent' of south-east England within a line stretching from Norwich to Hove and extending up the Thames valley, with some outlying regions receptive to reform relating to particular ancient urban centres such as Bristol, Gloucester or Coventry. Outside these areas in lowland southern England, and through most of the highland zone north of a line from the Bristol Channel to the Humber estuary, there was much less enthusiasm for Protestantism, with a heartland of traditionalist survival in Lancashire giving rise in the reign of Elizabeth to the only major centre of Catholic activism with a popular base.[24]

Undoubtedly this distribution reflected a regional predisposition to reform produced by the survival of Lollardy. We have already noted the way in which Lollard preoccupations coincided with the doctrinal concerns of the English Reformers as those concerns moved further away from the initial influence of Luther and Germany towards the Swiss Reform. Beyond the universities, at the level of popular religious practice, there is also a striking coincidence between the areas where Lollardy had been strong and Dickens' 'great crescent' of early popular Protestantism. Another reason for regional variation was the strength or weakness of the parish system and its place in shaping the attitudes of local communities. If Protestant governments were going to win over the hearts and minds of the population, the Reformation would have to prove itself effective at parish level; after all, Protestantism had destroyed the alternative devotional structures of monasticism and shrines, and ended the preaching work of the orders of friars. During the sixteenth century, the parish became a still more fundamental unit of English life, taking on an unprecedented role in local administration through a series of Acts of Parliament which gave ever wider powers over poor relief to parish officers whose duties had previously been centred on maintaining the fabric of the parish church and its round of worship.

The problem for Catholic and Protestant alike was the uneven coverage of the parish network, still frozen through administrative inertia in the geographical pattern of the thirteenth century, and offering absurd contrasts of size and effectiveness 300 years on. On the whole lowland England was provided with a parish system which offered the chance of detailed pastoral supervision either by a pre-Reformation parish priest or the Protestant minister who came after him. In the north of England, however, the situation was different. Some northern parishes consisted of largely empty uplands, but not all northern monster parishes were barren wastes; many included several townships and had large populations. For traditional religious practice, this was not so serious as it was for

[24] A. G. Dickens, 'The early Expansion of Protestantism in England 1520–1558', *ARG*, 78 (1987), 379–410.

Protestantism: the deficiencies of the northern parish system might be compensated for by the continuing important role of the monasteries, and gaps in northern pastoral provision had often been made up by chantry chapels which could stand as independent units, rather than as subordinate structures within an existing parish church building as was more commonly the case in the south.[25] Pre-Reformation north and south therefore had different patterns of devotional life. In some areas of the south, such as East Anglia, the evidence of bequests for church-building in wills suggests a peak of devotional provision in the late fifteenth century, even though the work of furnishing and beautifying churches went on until snuffed out by government changes of policy in the late 1530s and 1540s. In some urban centres like Bristol, and particularly in places like Coventry suffering economic decline, the elaborate round of traditional worship may have seemed more of a burden than a joyful duty to those officers charged with carrying it out, and the Reformation may have come as something of a relief.[26]

However, in the north, the atmosphere and timetable of change were different. The region had been particularly hard-hit by the Black Death, and economic recovery came very slowly; this was reflected in a later expansion of church-building than in the south. The movement to found chantries also took off later: in Cumbria, full-scale chantry colleges were being founded on the eve of their general dissolution, in Lancashire the movement to set up chantries had only gathered momentum in the 1450s, and, in Yorkshire, more chantries were being founded in the early sixteenth century than at any time since the early fourteenth. Here the pastoral care of the living through an extra supply of clergy may have been as important an incentive for founders of chantries as the needs of the dead. Monasteries were also more highly valued in the north than in the south: the explosion of indignation at the closure of the monasteries in Lancashire, Yorkshire and Cumbria expressed in the Pilgrimage of Grace in 1536/7 shows a depth of feeling about the importance and continuing relevance of monastic life which has been underestimated by many modern commentators on the risings and which found little echo south of the river Humber. To add to the problems of enforcing religious change, the dissolution of chantries under Henry VIII and Edward VI weakened the provision of pastoral care: where there was pastoral need, chapel buildings were supposed to be preserved, but in the overwhelming

[25] C. Haigh, *Reformation and Resistance in Tudor Lancashire* (Cambridge, 1975), pp. 1–97.
[26] D. MacCulloch, *Suffolk and the Tudors: Politics and Religion in an English County 1500–1600* (Oxford, 1986); C. Burgess, '"By Quick and by Dead": Wills and Pious Provision in late medieval Bristol', *EHR*, 102 (1987), 857; C. Phythian-Adams, *Desolation of a City: Coventry and the Urban Crisis of the late Middle Ages* (Cambridge, 1979), p. 287.

number of cases, where the government's commissioners could prove that their endowments had 'superstitious' purposes for the provision of soul-masses, their source of financial support would be lost. The combination of these factors goes a long way to explaining why Protestant advance in northern England was so hesitant and patchy: why, indeed, the Reformation hardly affected large areas of the north until the 1570s and 1580s.[27]

Similar circumstances applied in Wales, which was an administrator's nightmare until changes in government during the late 1530s and 1540s brought it more into line with English county structures. The cultural and language barrier between England and most of the Welsh people made things much worse. The bishops of late medieval Wales, faced with some of the lowest incomes on the episcopal bench, tended to be English careerists on the lookout for something better, or English abbots with fairer havens elsewhere; therefore the problems of an absentee leadership which also affected some pre-Reformation English dioceses were here acute. Protestant interest in evangelising this alien culture seems to have been virtually nil in the early Reformation, and the Welsh would have to wait until Elizabeth's reign until remarkably successful initiatives were taken by the government and by a succession of devoted Welsh bishops and devout cultured laypeople to give Protestantism a sound base within Welsh life and language.[28]

There was therefore a real contrast between highland and lowland which affects consideration of the 'above/below, rapid/slow' polarities in assessing the popular base of the Reformation. One should not be too determinist about the geographical divide; there were indeed strong early pockets of popular Protestantism in the north, for instance in the cloth-producing areas of Yorkshire and around Manchester and Kendal: places where industry and commercial movements of cloth encouraged contacts with the south.[29] Nor was the subsequent survival of Catholicism evenly distributed within the North; it concentrated in Lancashire and Yorkshire and had much less purchase on the border areas, north-west Wales or

[27] A. Kreider, *English Chantries: the Road to Dissolution* (Cambridge, Mass., 1979), pp. 90–1; J. T. Rosenthal, 'The Yorkshire Chantry Certificates of 1546: an Analysis', *Northern History*, 9 (1974), 30. On the Pilgrimage, see Haigh, *Reformation and Resistance*, ch. 9, and for a similar emphasis on the role of the monasteries in the Cumbrian part of the Pilgrimage, M. Clark, 'The Reformation in the Lake Counties, 1500–1571' (Council for National Academic Awards Ph.D., 1990), pp. 112–40. Cf. the comments of C. Davies on the Pilgrimage in A. Fletcher and J. Stevenson (eds.), *Order and Disorder in Early Modern England* (Cambridge, 1985), pp. 58–91.

[28] G. Williams, *Recovery, Reorientation and Reformation in Wales c. 1415–1642* (Oxford, 1987), pp. 118–42, 279–304.

[29] A. G. Dickens, *Lollards and Protestants in the Diocese of York 1509–58* (London, 1982), pp. 2, 5, 29–52, 214–35; Haigh, *Reformation and Resistance*, pp. 173–5, 296–9; Clark, 'Reformation in the Lake Counties', pp. 330 ff.

180   *Diarmaid MacCulloch*

Cornwall, despite similar conditions applying across the whole highland area. One cannot simply explain this later growth or stagnation of conservatism by looking at the preconditions: much had to do with the work of Catholic clergy, both survivors from the old established church who resisted Protestantism and new recruits trained on the Continent from the 1570s.

Within the south, too, geography and trade produced differential patterns of religious development within apparently similar areas: for instance, the diocese of Norwich showed more evidence of early reformist activity in its southern half, Suffolk, than in Norfolk to the north. We should be seeking explanations for these differences, and, just as in the north, patterns of trade and contact may provide answers. In the case of Suffolk and Norfolk, it would be worth considering their contrasting patterns of coastal trade: in Norfolk, northwards to Newcastle in an exchange of grain for coal, and in Suffolk, southwards with dairy products to London and the English garrison at Calais.[30] Moreover, no-one should underestimate the general strength of Catholic resistance and survival in the lowland zone, where the system of compact parishes had offered a framework for vigorous Catholic devotional life as much as for subsequent Protestant expansion, and where some of the most obstinate county networks of Catholic gentry households would develop under Elizabeth.[31] Even in the south, there must have been precious few places before the reign of Elizabeth, perhaps just a handful of urban communities, where religious change could command the enthusiasm of a majority of people.

Research which takes the pulse of religious practice in the localities has used two main sources to examine the impact of religious change: parish records, especially churchwardens' accounts, and wills. These tend to give two slightly different pictures. Parish records give an official version of local reaction: the response of parish officers to orders handed down from above. They have the additional complication that the surviving records are heavily weighted to the south and west of England, making it difficult to gain a clear picture of what was happening at parish level elsewhere. Wills reveal something more personal, the response of individuals facing up to the crisis of death: historians have paid especial attention to their religious preambles, which were almost universal in this period, to chart trends in traditional or evangelical sympathies. Admittedly, one must recognise the limitations of this evidence; even wills are not purely

[30] N. Williams, *The Maritime Trade of the East Anglian Ports 1550–1590* (Oxford, 1988).
[31] On pre-Reformation parish life, see J. J. Scarisbrick, *The Reformation and the English People* (Oxford, 1984), chs. 1, 2. For discussion of the origins of recusancy, see D. Mac-Culloch, *The Later Reformation in England 1547–1603* (Basingstoke, 1990), pp. 144–52.

spontaneous expressions of opinion. A testator was unlikely to make open financial provision for activities which a twist in government policy had made illegal, and the testator's religious views might undergo some form of censorship or manipulation at the hands of the person writing his will, often a local clergyman or experienced clerk. Moreover, many individual preambles previously seen as significant have now been recognised as being copied from formulae published expressly to guide will-makers. Nevertheless, when used with due caution and sensitivity, both these sources can be combined with more occasional, anecdotal evidence to build up a detailed picture of the reception of the early Reformation.[32]

Amid the uncertainties of the Henrician Reformation, parish officers seem to have reacted reasonably promptly to the necessity of dismantling the old religious furniture when told to, but rather less eagerly to the prospect of expenditure on new items such as an English Bible. The prime impact of religious change on the parishes seems to have been negative: the destruction of old Catholic habits rather than the creation of Protestant ones – hardly surprisingly, in view of the ambiguities of what Henry was doing. Already in the 1540s the old world was losing its enchantment. Ronald Hutton and Robert Whiting have shown how expenditure on church goods, ornaments and fabrics never regained former levels after 1540, and Whiting observes of surviving decoration and furnishings in west-country churches dateable to the 1530s, that there is already a move towards more secular or abstract subjects.[33] At the same time the gilds, one of the most important expressions of popular religious life, showed signs of rapid decline, with a slump in the number of bequests in wills and a rash of lawsuits about their possessions and endowments, together with those of chantries. The preambles of wills confirm these trends, as a steady, if gradual, shift occurred from traditional formulae in which the testator bequeathed his or her soul not only to God but also to Our Lady and the holy company of heaven, towards formulae more cautiously neutral or even Protestant in tone. Once more we need to notice the different pace of change in north and south, but even in Yorkshire and

[32] One of the most detailed studies of the use of wills alongside other documents is M. Spufford, *Contrasting Communities: English Villagers in the sixteenth and seventeenth centuries* (Oxford and New York, 1974), ch. 13; see also C. Cross, 'Wills as Evidence of Popular Piety in the Reformation period: Leeds and Hull, 1540–1640', in D. M. Loades (ed.), The *End of Strife* (Edinburgh, 1984), pp. 44–51. I am preparing a paper on the influence of the early published will of William Tracey on subsequent Protestant will-making.
[33] R. Hutton, 'The local Impact of the Tudor Reformations' in Haigh (ed.) *English Reformation Revised*; R. Whiting, *The Blind Devotion of the People* (Cambridge, 1989).

Nottinghamshire, the official condemnation of shrines and the cult of the saints in 1538 prompted a decline in the traditional form of preamble.[34]

Under Edward VI, as in the 1530s and 1540s, churchwardens' accounts indicate that, at least in the south, destructive change generally followed quickly on official orders, but that even here, positive provision for the new order came more slowly and patchily. No doubt this reflected widespread uncertainty about Protestantism; Edwardian bishops produced orders about non-attendance at church, which were probably recognitions that many people voted with their feet on the introduction of English services. Once more there is evidence of the differential pace of change between north and south: both anecdotal and more broadly based. Anecdotal scraps include the observations in the diary of the conservative Yorkshire priest Robert Parkyn that the south was much more eager to destroy the old ways than his own countrymen, and an incidental reference in an East Anglian lawsuit to the widespread destruction of Suffolk rood screens by a minority of Protestant activists, to the annoyance and embarrassment of the area's gentry establishment. More systematically, the returns to the various Edwardian commissions inventorying church goods provide clear signs that in the northern counties (unlike the south-east) very few parishes had sold their church plate before the government began its moves towards confiscation, and there was a parallel reluctance to buy ex-chantry lands.[35]

Wills once more reveal very different degrees of positive enthusiasm for Protestantism in different areas. As under Henry VIII, Kent was in the vanguard of change, with 8 per cent of Kentish wills opting for a recognisably Protestant preamble formula in the first two years of the reign alone; in Suffolk, further round Dickens' 'crescent', no less than 27 per cent of lay wills included Protestant preambles during Edward's reign. At the other extreme, before 1550 there are only two traceable Protestant preambles in nearly 900 early sixteenth-century wills surviving for the city of York, and only one amid the admittedly poor survival rate for wills in south-west England. Nevertheless, the Edwardian regime had to face only one major rising which sought to restore the old religion, the Devon and Cornwall rising of 1549, and even here motives other than religion may

[34] For summary discussion on wills, see Dickens, 'Early expansion of Protestantism', 214–17, and for detailed examples, D. Palliser, *Tudor York* (Oxford, 1979), pp. 250–1; A. G. Dickens, *Lollards and Protestants*, pp. 171–2; G. J. Mayhew, 'The progress of the Reformation in east Sussex 1530–1559: the Evidence from Wills', *Southern History*, 5 (1983), 38–67; M. Bowker, *The Henrician Reformation: the diocese of Lincoln under John Longland 1521–1547* (Cambridge, 1981), pp. 176–8.

[35] A. G. Dickens (ed.), 'Robert Parkyn's Narrative of the Reformation', *EHR*, 62 (1947), 68–73; MacCulloch, *Suffolk and the Tudors*, pp. 169–70; Clark, 'Reformation in the Lake Counties', pp. 278, 320, 324–5, and private communication on sales of church plate, in which she particularly cites Public Record Office S.P. 10/3/4.

have been equally important. What was also significant in this conservative rebellion was that its published list of demands never mentioned the Pope; clearly the Holy Father's name was more of a hindrance than a help in rallying people to the old faith even in the south-west. Twenty years of anti-papal propaganda seemed to have done its work; that would not make Mary's task any easier when she sought to harness the kingdom's widespread weariness with religious change to a restoration of papal obedience.[36]

Mary faced a task both of undoing negative work from the previous reign and of building up positive Catholicism. In many parts, especially in the north, the old Latin services were restored with spontaneous enthusiasm, and to rebuild the formal devotional life of the parish churches was the easiest part of the Marian task. Even in Kent, the most recalcitrant part of the country, where Cranmer's administration had been most directly able to encourage change, the job of re-equipping churches for Catholic worship was satisfactorily advanced in four-fifths of parishes within four years. Coupled with this was a massive job of disciplining and redeploying about 2,000 parish clergy who had married: the largest clerical upheaval of the century, although most of those affected seem to have been ready enough to co-operate and take another benefice elsewhere after their reconciliation. All this represented a heroic effort by the bishops to wipe the religious slate clean, but what else could or should be restored? So much of the past seemed to have gone for ever, and the government was either not equipped or not ready to restore the whole of the old system.

Queen Mary was not quite like the later French Bourbons: she may have learnt nothing from the intervening years since the break with Rome, but she seemed to have forgotten much about the old world. Her personal piety centred on the Mass, for which she had struggled and suffered in the reign of her half-brother Edward; other aspects of life in the old church do not seem to have aroused her enthusiasm in the same way.[37] No-one in the government tried to revive the cults at great shrines of the past like St Thomas of Canterbury or Our Lady of Walsingham (although the restored monks of Westminster conscientiously rebuilt the

[36] P. Clark, *English Provincial Society from the Reformation to the Revolution: ... Kent 1500–1640* (Hassocks, 1977), pp. 75–6; D. Peet, 'The mid-sixteenth-century Parish Clergy, with particular consideration of the Dioceses of Norwich and York' (Cambridge University Ph.D., 1980), p. 223; Palliser, *Tudor York*, pp. 250–1; R. Whiting, 'Prayers for the Dead in the Tudor South-West', *Southern History*, 5 (1983), 79, 87; cf. discussion by D. M. Palliser in F. Heal and R. O'Day (eds.), *Church and Society in England* (Basingstoke, 1977), pp. 39–40. J. Youings, 'The South-Western Rebellion of 1549', *Southern History*, 1 (1979), 99–122; cf. D.MacCulloch, 'Kett's Rebellion in Context', *Past and Present*, 84 (1979), 36–59; Clark, *English Provincial Society*, pp. 78–80.

[37] D. M. Loades, *Mary Tudor* (Oxford, 1989), pp. 118–19, 331.

tomb of their sainted founder King Edward) and there was no official effort to create cults of modern Catholic martyrs such as More or Fisher – hardly surprisingly, when leading members of Mary's regime included such figures as Bishops Gardiner and Bonner who had been prominent supporters of the government which had caused their deaths.

As much as the cult of the saints, the houses of religion had been one of the cornerstones of England's religious system up to the 1530s. Although English monastic life had generally been, in the words of its greatest modern historian David Knowles, 'humanly speaking easier and less spiritually stimulating in 1530 than it had been a century earlier', recruit-ment had remained stable since the fourteenth-century crisis created by the Black Death, and certainly hardly any religious house had spon-taneously given up existence for lack of will to survive before the general dissolution.[38] However, when Mary came to restore the monastic life, her efforts were small-scale, and almost look like acts of filial piety, as she concentrated on houses like those of the Franciscan Observants or that at Sion which had been at the centre of her mother's circle of supporters. Her one other major monastic refoundation, Westminster Abbey, was later said, by one who had known it, to have established a life more like that of the fellowship of an Oxbridge College or of the Inns of Court than one of the medieval Benedictine houses which it sought to recreate.[39] Few others among the traditionalist elite showed any signs of following even the limited example set by the queen in monastic restoration; nor did the government make any noticeable effort to tap the springs of Continental revival in the religious life. The first representative in England of the Society of Jesus, which would do so much to turn the Protestant tide elsewhere in Europe over the next decades, arrived just in time to unpack and repack his bags in the month before the queen's death in 1558.

A beginning was indeed made in building on the battered conservatism of most of the population to recreate an informed Catholicism. Mary did recognise the vital role of education to transform the minds of the articulate and influential, leaving as much money in her will to the two universities as she did to her pet projects of restored monastic life at Sheen and Sion. Her government effectively purged at least the university of Oxford, and enthusiastic Catholics endowed a handful of university colleges and grammar schools. It is significant that the Marian govern-ment made no attempt to ban the English Bible; indeed, Parkyn the conservative Yorkshire parson included Bible-reading as part of his devotional rule for the Christian life. Here was one achievement of the English Reformation which the government was apparently prepared not

[38] D. Knowles, *The Religious Orders in England* (3 vols., Cambridge, 1948–59), III. 460.
[39] Knowles, *Religious Orders in England*, III. 431.

to challenge, but perhaps to attempt to redeploy for its own purposes, in the manner championed by Catholic humanists like Cardinal Pole.[40]

On a wider front across the country, the gradual rise in the number of traditionalist will preambles across the country registered the slow rebuilding of Catholic practice, but it is noticeable how quickly this trend was reversed on Elizabeth's accession. For many, the credibility of the old structure of prayer must have been shattered when Edward's officials and clergy had silenced the Mass and the monasteries and chantries had been closed without the Last Judgement arriving or the sky falling in. Along with an absence of Marian official initiatives at revival, the evidence of local records is that the cult of the saints and provision for souls in Purgatory were (in Dr Hutton's words) 'abiding casualties' of the work of Edwardian destruction; even the gilds, formerly vital outlets for popular lay piety, were not restored in any significant number, and many of those which were restored seem to have been little more than fund-raising bodies rather than centres of devotional and social life as in the past.[41]

Equally one cannot ignore the evidence of continuing Protestant vigour in the face of the apparent disaster of King Edward's death and Queen Jane's removal: for instance, the nearly 300 Protestant martyrs who would subsequently colour the memory of Mary's reign. Moreover, the distribution of martyrs distorts the map of Protestant survival because it reflects the enthusiasm of the persecuting classes, largely a few traditionalist gentry among the local magistracy most active in Sussex, the Home Counties, London and Suffolk. A slightly more representative picture of the geography of Protestant enthusiasm can be gained from analysing almost 800 individuals known to have gone into exile to the Continent under Mary: clergy, gentry and merchants representing an articulate and educated opposition. These included a substantial body of gentlemen from the south-west, Lancashire and Yorkshire, showing that the conservatism of the west and north was beginning to dissipate among those who were in closer contact with the Protestant heartland of south-east England.[42]

A still wider picture can be gained again from assuming that the views of the dying reflect those of the living and analysing will preambles (admittedly, varying by region) which either defiantly retain Protestant phraseology or show dumb insolence to Catholicism by adopting some

---

[40] On Mary and education, Loades, *Mary Tudor*, pp. 371–2, and cf. p. 331. On Parkyn, A. G. Dickens, 'The last medieval Englishman', in P. Newman Brooks (ed.), *Christian Spirituality: Essays in honour of Gordon Rupp* (London, 1975), p. 163.
[41] Hutton, 'Local Impact of the Tudor Reformations', p. 131; Whiting, 'Prayers for the Dead', 82–3.
[42] M. J. Kitch (ed.), *Studies in Sussex Church History* (Brighton, 1981), pp. 94–6; C. H. Garrett, *The Marian Exiles* (Cambridge, 1938).

neutral form of commending the testator's soul to God. Even in conservative Yorkshire, A. G. Dickens could find a quarter falling into these two categories during Mary's reign, and among the laity of Suffolk, the same figure was as much as 52 per cent, with 16 per cent continuing to use explicitly Protestant formulae. To remind us that the north–south divide was not the only measure for religious variation, it is worth noting that the comparable proportion for Protestant formulae in Sussex was only 10 per cent, but even this represented a daunting block of stubborn opinion.[43] In the short time available, not much could be done. For in the end, time and death proved cruel to Mary's hopes. After her illusions of pregnancy were exposed as pathetic wish-fulfilment, misreading her perpetually fragile health, she was struck by cancer, amid an epidemic of influenza which proved particularly virulent among the elderly clergy, aristocrats and gentlemen who were the mainstay of her regime. Her most faithful advisor, Cardinal Reginald Pole, died within a few hours of hearing that she was dead; the way was open for her half-sister Elizabeth to take up the policies of Reformation where Edward's government had left off.

SELECT BIBLIOGRAPHY

Aston, M. *England's Iconoclasts: 1, Laws against Images* (2 vols., Oxford, I, 1989).
Bowker, M. *The Henrician Reformation: the diocese of Lincoln under John Longland 1521–1547* (Cambridge, 1981).
Brigden, S. *London and the Reformation* (Oxford, 1989).
Clark, P. *English Provincial Society from the Reformation to the Revolution: Kent 1500–1640* (Hassocks, 1977).
Clebsch, W. *England's Earliest Protestants 1520–1535* (New Haven, 1964).
Cross, C. *Church and People 1450–1660* (London, 1976).
Davis, J. F. 'The trials of Thomas Bilney and the English Reformation', *HJ*, 24 (1981), 775–90.
   Heresy and Reformation in the South East of England 1520–1559 (London and New Jersey: Royal Historical Society Studies in History Series 34, 1983).
Dickens, A. G. *Lollards and Protestants in the Diocese of York 1509–1558* (New edn. London, 1982).
   'The early expansion of Protestantism in England 1520–1558', *ARG*, 78 (1987), 379–410.
   The English Reformation (2nd edn. 1989).
Elton, G. R. *Reform and Reformation* (London, 1977).
   The Tudor Constitution (London, 2nd edn., 1982).
Fletcher, A. *Tudor Rebellions* (London, 3rd edn. 1983).

---

[43] Dickens, *Lollards and Protestants*, pp. 220–1; Peet, 'Mid-sixteenth-century Parish Clergy', p. 223; Mayhew, 'Reformation in east Sussex', 46–7.

Fox, A. and Guy, J. *Reassessing the Henrician Age: Humanism, Politics and Reform 1500–1550* (Oxford, 1986).

Guy, J. *Tudor England* (Oxford, 1988).

Haigh, C. *Reformation and Resistance in Tudor Lancashire* (Cambridge, 1975).

(ed.), *The English Reformation Revised* (Cambridge, 1987).

Heal, F. and O'Day, R. (eds.). *Church and Society in England* (Basingstoke, 1977).

Hall, B. 'The early Rise and gradual Decline of Lutheranism in England (1520–1600)', in D. Baker (ed.), *Reform and Reformation: England and the Continent c. 1500–c. 1750* (London: SCH: Subsidia 2, 1979), pp. 103–31.

Horst, I. B. *The Radical Brethren: Anabaptism and the English Reformation to 1558* (Nieuwkoop, 1972).

Ives, E. W. *Anne Boleyn* (Oxford, 1986).

Knowles, D. *The Religious Orders in England: III: The Tudor Age* (Cambridge, 1971).

Kreider, A. *English Chantries: the road to dissolution* (Cambridge, Mass., 1979).

MacCulloch, D. *Suffolk and the Tudors: politics and religion in an English County 1500–1600* (Oxford, 1986).

Martin, J. W. *Religious Radicals in Tudor England* (London, 1989).

Palliser, D. *Tudor York* (Oxford, 1979).

Pettegree, A. *Foreign Protestant Communities in Sixteenth Century London* (Oxford, 1986).

Pogson, R. 'Revival and Reform in Mary Tudor's Church: a Question of Money', in Haigh (ed.), *The English Reformation Revised*; repr. from *JEH*, 25 (1974).

Redworth, G. *In Defence of the Church Catholic: the life of Stephen Gardiner* (Oxford, 1990).

Ridley, J. *Thomas Cranmer* (Oxford, 1962).

Rupp, E. G. *Studies in the making of the English Protestant Tradition* (Cambridge, 1947).

Smyth, C. *Cranmer and the Reformation under Edward VI* (London, 1985).

Starkey, D. *The Reign of Henry VII: Personalities and Politics* (London, 1985).

Whiting, R. *The Blind Devotion of the People* (Cambridge, 1989).

Williams, G. *Recovery, Reorientation and Reformation in Wales c. 1415–1642* (Oxford, 1987).

Youings, J. *The Dissolution of the Monasteries* (London, 1971).

9 Italy

Euan Cameron

At the outset of any discussion of the Reformation in Italy, the point needs to be stressed that Italians of all sorts and conditions were at least as susceptible to the intellectual and spiritual message of the European Reformation as the other peoples of the Continent. Until fairly recently Italy tended to be treated as a special case in Reformation history. Some historians, seeing early sixteenth-century Italian clerics espouse reforming church politics and Augustinian theology, seemed uncertain how to classify their views: as late medieval reformism, Renaissance humanism, precocious Counter-Reformation spirituality, or quite what. From this uncertainty was born the concept labelled (unhelpfully) as Italian 'Evangelism', which despite attempts to supplant it, retains a strong hold on the literature.[1] Such Evangelism was alleged to have been undogmatic and aristocratic: undogmatic, because those who discussed the cardinal Reformation doctrine of justification by faith did not use it as a weapon to attack the entire fabric of the church; rather they retreated into 'hazy, vague religiousness' and practised the traditional rites.[2] It was also claimed that some 'evangelicals', even when they appeared to teach doctrines identical to those of the Protestant reformers, did so after reaching their views independently, without deriving them directly from Luther or Calvin.[3] Secondly, the evangelicals were 'aristocratic', in that

---

[1] The term was first used in relation to Italy in H. Jedin, *Girolamo Seripando* (2 vols., Würzburg, 1937), II. 135, and soon taken up by D. Cantimori and others: see E.-M. Jung, 'On the Nature of Evangelism in Sixteenth-Century Italy', in *Journal of the History of Ideas*, XIV (1953), 511–12; see also P. Simoncelli, *Evangelismo italiano del Cinquecento: Questione religiosa e nicodemismo politico* (Rome, 1979), for continuing use of the term; and the review articles by E. G. Gleason, 'On the Nature of Sixteenth-Century Italian Evangelism: Scholarship, 1953–1978', in *Sixteenth Century Journal*, 9 (1978), 4–25; and A. J. Schutte, 'Periodization of Sixteenth-Century Italian Religious History: The Post-Cantimori Paradigm Shift', in *Journal of Modern History*, 61 (1989), 273–5.
[2] Jung, 'Nature of Evangelism', 520–3; cf. Simoncelli, *Evangelismo*, introduction, pp. vii–ix.
[3] See for example the conclusion to J. C. Nieto, *Juan de Valdés and the Origins of the Spanish and Italian Reformation* (Geneva, 1970); compare similar claims by P. G. J. M. Imbart de la Tour, *Les Origines de la Réforme* (Paris and Melun, 1914–48), in respect of Jacques Lefèvre d'Etaples, discussed by L. Febvre, 'Une question mal posée: les origines de la réforme française', in his *Au coeur religieux du XVIe siècle* (Paris, 1957), pp. 1–70.

they regarded their special doctrines and meditations simply as topics for
discussion in pious literary salons. They did not (so the argument goes)
take their arguments into the pulpits and streets to stir up religious
revolution as the reformers did. They did not expose their opinions to the
mob.[4] If those qualities of dogmatic vagueness and aristocratic pre-
ciousness are ascribed (as they can all too easily be) to the entire Italian
movement, it becomes easy to explain its failure: it 'did not protest'; it did
not wish, by the criteria of a reformed church, to succeed.[5]

However, the last quarter-century or so of scholarship has shown with
surprising uniformity how the undogmatic and aristocratic features of
Italy's engagement with the Reformation have been grossly overstated.
First of all, several of the key writings of evangelism have turned out to
contain large unacknowledged extracts from the major writings of the
leading Protestant reformers. Such leaders of the Italian reformed
thought as Piermartire Vermigli, Bernardino Ochino, Pier Paolo
Vergerio, or Girolamo Zanchi who went on to play leading roles in the
northern European Reformation can now be shown to have held views
explicitly dependent on the German or Swiss reformers for at least several
years before they took the route to exile.[6] Secondly, alongside the salons
and academies of 'delicate protonotaries' and aristocratic clergymen
whom Calvin satirised, evidence has emerged of numerous Protestant
cells composed of artisans, craftsmen, and other bourgeois.[7]

Since Italy can now be seen to resemble northern Europe more closely
than used to be thought, the question of why the Reformation failed in
Italy can be put more precisely. There were Italian Protestants, but there
was not an Italian Reformation. The subversive teachings and beliefs
remained in the air; they did not lead to outbursts of popular commitment, widespread iconoclastic riots, the demolition of monasteries or the

[4] Jung, 'Nature of Evangelism', 523–5.
[5] Jung, 'Nature of Evangelism', 525–7, adds the epithet 'transitory' to 'undogmatic and
aristocratic' in her list of attributes, the last following from the first two.
[6] See T. Bozza, *Nuovi studi sulla Riforma in Italia I: Il 'Beneficio di Cristo'* (Rome, 1976), and
as cited by P. McNair, *Peter Martyr in Italy: An Anatomy of Apostasy* (Oxford, 1967),
pp. 46–8, for the evidence that large parts of Benedetto di Mantova and Marc'Antonio
Flaminio, *Trattato utilissimo del Beneficio di Giesù Cristo Crocifisso* derived from Calvin's
Institutes; see also the edn. of the text by S. Caponetto, *Il Beneficio di Cristo* (Florence and
Chicago, 1972); for evidence that Juan de Valdés borrowed from Luther see the suggestions of McNair, *Peter Martyr*, pp. 45–7, and C. Gilly, 'Juan de Valdés: Übersetzer und
Bearbeiter von Luthers Schriften in seinem Dialogo de Doctrina', *ARG*, 74 (1983),
257–305.
[7] In his *Excuse à Messieurs les Nicodémites, sur la complaincte qu'ilz font de sa trop grand'
riguer*, cited by Jung, 'Nature of Evangelism', 519; cf. H. Heller, *The Conquest of Poverty:
The Calvinist Revolt in Sixteenth-Century France* (Leiden, 1985), pp. 111–41. Jung's whole
concept of 'Evangelism' was disputed by McNair, *Peter Martyr*, pp. 4–49, and is summarised, with qualifications, by D. Fenlon, *Heresy and Obedience in Tridentine Italy: Cardinal Pole and the Counter Reformation* (Cambridge, 1972), pp. 14–23.

confiscation and redistribution of church revenues. The old Mass continued to be said and heard almost everywhere. There was no erection of new community or state churches save on the very periphery of the Italian-speaking lands. Before 1520 no-one wished for such an upheaval; after about 1560 the apparatus of repression was nearly everywhere sufficiently well entrenched to nip any such attempt in the bud. Between those years the Italian Reformation movement missed its chance.

How far was this owing to its own qualities and limitations, and how far to the pressures of war, Habsburg imperialism, and papal politics? It will be suggested here that the rich diversity of early sixteenth-century Italian religious life fogged over the issues distinctive to the Reformation; until the early 1540s, the Reformation in Italy lacked the kind of militant, committed leadership which would have been essential if the old hierarchies were to be overthrown. In the crisis years of 1541–2 the really divisive questions came to the fore, but the hard-line Catholic zealots also made important political gains for Catholic orthodoxy. After that point most of the truly Protestant cells of clandestine believers took shape. Their confessional ambiguity was gone, but with it their opportunity to establish a reformed church within the communities or states of Italy had largely evaporated.

Religious life in early Renaissance Italy was rich and diverse: many different styles and types of spiritual movements jostled for attention. Though there are risks in analysing any pattern of religious life with hindsight, one must ask whether any discernible features of Italy's religious context made it either more or less susceptible than other countries to the challenges and blandishments of the Reformation.

It used to be fashionable to describe late medieval religious life almost entirely in terms of its decadence, the breaches of observance, the greed, ignorance, unchastity, or disorderly behaviour of clerics. Italy suffered from such failings in abundance; things were at least as bad as elsewhere in Europe, and occasionally worse.[8] However, what matters is not that there were failures of discipline, supervision and service; rather that they were recognised by all serious people as an unacceptable scandal. There was no debate as to whether reform of the church was desirable; but a great deal over which of the many possible forms it should take as an ideal.[9] At the level of the secular clergy the prevailing vision of reform concentrated on uncovering and redressing moral and disciplinary fail-

---

[8] See D. Hay, *The Church in Italy in the Fifteenth Century* (Cambridge, 1977), pp. 56 ff; cf. the complaints of Gian Pietro Caraffa, as in E. G. Gleason (ed.), *Reform Thought in Sixteenth-Century Italy* (Ann Arbor, 1981), 67–9, 71–4; and the *Consilium Delectorum Cardinalium* of 1537, *ibid.*, 88–94.

[9] See McNair, *Peter Martyr*, pp. 2 ff, for an interesting typology of different levels of reform in sixteenth-century thought.

ings among the parish priesthood. Such initiatives originated first and foremost from diocesan bishops like Niccolò Albergati of Bologna or Antonino Pierozzi of Florence in the fifteenth century, and Giammateo Giberti of Verona in the early sixteenth.[10] The means employed were the traditional pastoral visitation, whose ground rules had been established since the Fourth Lateran Council in 1215, and which was destined to be the continuing primary means of episcopal supervision.[11]

To the extent that the higher clergy took the lead in trying to remedy these recognised failings in the secular priesthood, the laity's contempt for disorderly priests would have been inhibited from exploding into violent anticlerical attacks on the priestly class as a whole.[12] Italian evidence, in fact, so far from demonstrating widespread lay alienation from the clergy, seems to suggest that the structures and rituals of late medieval civic religion bound lay people and ecclesiastics closer together in the joint and co-operative management of their church affairs.[13] The close-knit structure of the numerous lay confraternities, comprising both laity and clergy and including within their number (though not all in the same society) men and women, cleric and lay, and all social classes, could only have contributed further to strengthening the hold which the Catholic ritual and its practitioners held over the loyalties of lay citizens.[14] Some social historians have analysed the Reformation (for instance in the Baltic cities or Strasburg) by assuming rightly or wrongly that the populace excluded from political power and alienated from the official religion of civil oligarchs were specially likely to vent their class antagonisms in grievances against the church.[15] Whatever the merits of that argument, it does not seem likely to apply to Italian conditions, not least because the infinite diversity of Catholic religious forms offered something to almost everyone. However, it would be absurd to suppose that Italian civic politics were destined to operate according to entirely secular principles, or that the fusion of spiritual and political grievances was somehow unique to an atmosphere of German *Frömmigkeit*. The country which produced Savonarola had nothing to learn from northern Europe when it

[10] See some instances of reforming pastoral bishops cited in E. Cameron, *The European Reformation* (Oxford, 1991), p. 44.

[11] See U. Mazzone and A. Turchini, *Le Visite pastorali: analisi di una fonte* (Bologna, 1985), *passim*, but esp. pp. 25 ff.

[12] Compare northern European experience summarised in Cameron, *European Reformation*, pp. 56–61.

[13] See A. Olivieri, *La Riforma in Italia: Strutture e simboli, classi e potere* (Milan, 1979), pp. 36 ff; cf. the situation in Strasburg, as in T. A. Brady, *Ruling Class, Regime and Reformation at Strasbourg, 1520–1555* (Leiden, 1978), pp. 238–9.

[14] C. F. Black, *Italian Confraternities in the Sixteenth Century* (Cambridge, 1989), pp. 26–49.

[15] See the theories discussed in Cameron, *European Reformation*, pp. 240 ff, 297 ff, 302 ff.

came to finding spiritual endorsement for a programme of political change.[16]

The ignorance and crudity of lay believers used to figure as prominently in the old style of religious history as the disorderliness of their priests. If late sixteenth-century inquisitorial records may fairly be assumed to reflect earlier periods, lowland Italy seems to have been as prone to the attractions of charms, spells and folk-magic as any other part of rural Europe. In the 1590s the Inquisition in Modena regularly concerned itself with people who used church prayers as healing spells, or abused prayers, candles, or other religious objects for love-magic.[17] Before the Counter Reformation it is almost certain that such popular religion formed a seamless web, blending in with the conduct of services and the distribution of sacramentals, consecrated bread, holy water, candles and so forth which was the primary role of the secular priesthood in the fifteenth century.[18] This system in turn serviced a pattern of belief where spiritual goods were assigned to the believer as a quantitative reward for good works performed.[19] If the crudities of Italian popular religion were fairly typical of Europe as a whole, so were its refinements. The conventional piety of fifteenth-century Europe, mediated through the pulpit and the confessional, was developed and publicised in Italy, above all by the mendicant orders. Right up to the Reformation period Italian writers produced sermon-cycles, manuals for parish preachers, and encyclopedias on the art of hearing confessions. This literature was predominantly businesslike and stereotypical: it published the old standards of a penitential system and an administrative clergy, with greater efficiency, but little distinctive flavour or direction.[20] Indeed, if evidence were needed of how thoroughly Italian churchmen established the paradigms of late medieval religious behaviour, one need only cite the immense popularity which two encyclopedias on the art of hearing confessions, the *Sylvestrina* and the

[16] On the interplay of religious and civic ritual see above all R. C. Trexler, *Public Life in Renaissance Florence* (New York, 1980), *passim*, but esp. pp. 1–128; also D. Weinstein, *Savonarola and Florence: Prophecy and Patriotism in the Renaissance* (Princeton, 1970).

[17] See M. O'Neil, 'Magical Healing, Love Magic and the Inquisition in Late Sixteenth-Century Modena', in S. Haliczer (ed.), *Inquisition and Society in Early Modern Europe* (London, 1987), pp. 88–114.

[18] R. Rusconi, 'Dal pulpito alla confessione. Modelli di comportamento religioso in Italia tra 1470 circa e 1520 circa', in P. Prodi and P. Johanek (eds.), *Strutture ecclesiastiche in Italia e in Germania prima della Riforma* (Annali dell'Istituto storico italo-germanico, Quaderno 16, Bologna, 1984), pp. 280 ff; cf. R. W. Scribner, 'Cosmic Order and Daily Life: Sacred and Secular in Pre-Industrial German Society', in K. von Greyerz (ed.), *Religion and Society in Early Modern Europe, 1500–1800* (London, 1984), pp. 19–21.

[19] Rusconi, 'Dal pulpito alla confessione', 278–80; cf. J. Chiffoleau, *La comptabilité de l'au-delà: les hommes, la mort et la religion dans la région avignonnaise à la fin du moyen âge (1320–1480)* (Rome, 1980), pp. 211 ff, 323–56.

[20] Rusconi, 'Dal pulpito alla confessione', 289–304.

Summa Angelica, enjoyed right across Europe. It was ironic that the authors of these works, Silvestro Mazzolini of Priero and Angelo Carletti of Chivasso, were both natives of Piedmont, the one region of Italy which was also to see the nearest thing to a spontaneous territorial Protestant church.[21]

The slogans of reform, of course, affected the religious orders more than the secular priesthood and the laity. All the main forms of monasticism, Benedictine monks, Augustinians, and mendicants, produced in Italy an indigenous version of the movements for observant reform which restated the monastic ideal in the fifteenth century.[22] Since such orders sometimes chose to remain small and preserve their pristine enthusiasm rather than burgeoning out and embracing ill-trained or uncommitted converts, it would be misleading to regard their modest numbers (in any case impressive enough) as evidence of flagging enthusiasm. Possibly the most significant effect of the observant movement was its impact on the practice of granting monasteries *in commendam*. Under *commendam* the revenues were assigned to an absentee ecclesiastic not belonging to the order, or even to a layman, in the absence of an abbot or prior, leading to the depletion of a monastery's moral and material resources. In observant houses *commendam* was either abolished (since the headship of the house became a temporary rotating office which could not be poached by an outsider); or alternatively a potential abuse was turned to a religious purpose, since some monastic reformers actually began their work as commendators of demoralised abbeys.[23]

The reform of the religious orders did not just generate a simple, one-dimensional return to austerity and strict observance. In numerous cases it was associated with particular intellectual trends. Most obviously, it has been claimed that the Italian Augustinian orders fostered a tradition of neo-Augustinian theology which would in due course make such orders especially susceptible to Lutheran influences. Such a tradition dated back to the anti-Occamist writings of Gregory of Rimini in the fourteenth century, continued in the writings of Augustinians like Simone Fidati, Hugolino of Orvieto, or Agostino Favaroni (d. 1443).[24] Such

[21] On the success of confessors' manuals see esp. T. N. Tentler, *Sin and Confession on the Eve of the Reformation* (Princeton, 1977), *passim*, also e.g. L. Febvre and H.-J. Martin, *The Coming of the Book: The Impact of Printing, 1450–1800* (London, 1976), pp. 251 ff.
[22] The observant movement is summarised in Cameron, *European Reformation*, pp. 41–3.
[23] G. Zarri, 'Aspetti dello sviluppo degli ordini religiosi in Italia tra Quattro e Cinquecento. Studi e problemi', in Prodi and Johanek, *Strutture ecclesiastiche in Italia e in Germania prima della Riforma* (Annali dell'Istituto storico italo-germanico, Quaderno 16, Bologna, 1984), pp. 207–57 and esp. 224 ff, 242 ff.
[24] See the summary of this school of thought in D. C. Steinmetz, *Luther and Staupitz: An Essay in the Intellectual Origins of the Protestant Reformation* (Durham, NC, 1980), pp. 11–23; Cameron, *European Reformation*, p. 86.

intellectual movements should not be seen, moreover, as passive or derivative revivals of earlier traditions. Recent work on the Cassinese Benedictine Order has shown how their indigenous spiritual tradition, nourished by the Antiochene Fathers, not only prepared the Cassinese to take an interest in the Reformation; it also ensured that their response to it remained idiosyncratic. The Cassinese were to approach Lutheran ideas from such a distinctive viewpoint that their tradition contrived to attract accusations both of Crypto-Protestantism and Pelagianism.[25]

The impact of Renaissance humanism is one area where differences between Italy and northern Europe might be expected to emerge. Fifteenth-century Italy turned the rhetoric of Latinate scholars into a vehicle for secular political theory (whether republican or despotic) and classical literary criticism.[26] Yet, despite the piety of a Vittorino da Feltre or a Guarino of Verona, Italy did not produce a figure of the stature of Erasmus, embodying in equal measure humanist classicism and the call to religious sincerity and simplicity. Indeed, the Italian response to Erasmus illustrates one of the few clear differences between the two sides of the Alps. In the north Luther depended for many of his first supporters on those who had already read Erasmus and embraced his critiques of vulgar piety and scholasticism. In Italy the reverse was the case. From the 1520s onwards ecclesiastics like Aleander did their level best to assimilate Erasmus to Luther, alleging him to be not just a participant but the source of the trouble; thus the orthodox became prejudiced against him, while interest in Erasmus became more and more confined to those already interested in heterodoxy. Luther gave Erasmus notoriety in Italy, not the other way around.[27]

At least in the central and northern lowlands, on which any discussion of Italy Protestantism must focus, Italian religious life in the two generations before the Reformation thus reflected the same general tendencies found in other countries of western Europe, with its diocesan reform movements, confraternities, and observant reform, as well as its superstitions and moral failings. Even if significant deviations from the norm could be demonstrated, of course, no predetermined conclusions need have followed. Spiritual lethargy or irreligion could be claimed to prove either how much reform was needed, or how stony was the ground on which the Protestant gospel would fall. Unusual vigour and life in the church could portend a vibrant Catholicism well placed to resist the

---

[25] B. Collett, *Italian Benedictine Scholars and the Reformation: The Congregation of Santa Giustina of Padua* (Oxford, 1985), pp. 196–235.

[26] See e.g. Q. Skinner, *The Foundations of Modern Political Thought* (2 vols., Cambridge, 1978), vol. I., *passim*; C. Trinkaus, *The Scope of Renaissance Humanism* (Ann Arbor, 1983).

[27] S. Seidel Menchi, *Erasmo in Italia, 1520–1580* (Turin, 1987), pp. 41–72.

Lutheran threat, or, on the contrary, a thoughtful piety awake to new possibilities. To take the single example of confraternities: in 1540s Siena and 1550s Modena, some members of confraternities sought with Protestant arguments to dissuade their fellow-brethren from ritualistic good works and self-indulgent socialising alike. The confraternity was thus the object and the victim of Protestant critiques; but it was also the milieu and the forum in which they spread.[28] No less than elsewhere in Europe, the response of Italians to the Reformation message could never be taken for granted.

The European Reformation, as it grew from the writings and sermons of the first generation of reformers, took the form initially of religious discussion and debate. It did not lead its exponents forthwith to abandon traditional worship or to define new criteria of a true church. In this pristine, primitive form the Reformation reached Italy during the 1520s, and in this form it lasted for some fifteen years. At this stage the primary evangelical activity was undoubtedly the production, distribution and reading of books. Some of the earliest evidence for the impact of the Reformation consists of decrees forbidding the ownership and circulation of such tracts.[29] Censorship of works by German and Swiss reformers was effectively evaded by a variety of subterfuges. Names of notorious authors were translated into their (unknown) equivalents in another language, so that Melanchthon's *Common Places* circulated with the attribution 'Ippofilo da Terra Negra', and Bucer's *Exposition of the Psalms* as by 'Aretius Felinus'; or books were falsely attributed to an orthodox author, as when Luther's works circulated under the names of Erasmus or Federigo Fregoso.[30] Alternatively, anonymous compilations could be issued, of which one of the most influential was the *Sommario della Sacra Scrittura*, an abstract of various tracts by Luther apparently produced in the Low Countries in the 1520s and subsequently translated.[31] Meanwhile, native Italians began to produce their own texts: crucial to this development was the Florentine author and publisher Antonio Brucioli, who not only published his translation of the Bible in instalments until its completion in 1551, but also issued numerous

---

[28] V. Marchetti, *Gruppi ereticali senesi del cinquecento* (Florence, 1975), pp. 51 ff; S. Peyronel Rambaldi, *Speranze e crisi nel cinquecento modenese: Tensioni religiose e vita cittadina ai tempi di Giovanni Morone* (Milan, 1979), pp. 254–5.

[29] For examples see G. K. Brown, *Italy and the Reformation to 1550* (Oxford, 1933), pp. 67, 69, 80–2, 110, 121–3, 127–8, 160, 220; Collett, *Italian Benedictine Scholars*, pp. 77 ff, 87.

[30] Brown, *Italy and the Reformation*, pp. 120–3; U. Rozzo and S. Seidel Menchi, 'Livre et réforme en Italie', in J.-F. Gilmont (ed.), *La Réforme et le livre* (Paris, 1990), pp. 342 ff, 352 ff, 361.

[31] Peyronel Rambaldi, *Speranze e crisi*, pp. 256–61; Rozzo and Seidel Menchi, 'Livre et réforme en Italie', p. 356.

tracts.[32] Reading went hand in hand with discussion. Recent studies on literacy have demonstrated how private, silent reading was by no means the normal way for sixteenth-century people to use a book. Reading a text aloud, often in company, alternating discussion and exposition with simple recitation, both provided the social milieu for reforming propaganda and bridged the gap between literate and illiterate.[33]

Between 1524 and 1540, such reading and discussion of the issues and themes of the Reformation took root among a wide range of social classes and groups. The reformers' writings were first studied by their Italian equivalents, namely the ecclesiastical elite of regular clergy, academics and senior churchmen. The most famous such group clustered round the Venetian nobleman Gasparo Contarini, who in writing to the ascetic Paolo Giustiniani as early as 1523 had expressed a concern for justification, hinting at more than a little Lutheran influence.[34] By the early 1530s Contarini's associates at Venice and Padua included representatives of the most dynamic religious reform movements of the age: Marc'Antonio Flaminio, a member of the Oratory of Divine Love; Gregorio Cortese, a Cassinese Benedictine of the house of San Giorgio Maggiore; and the English exile Reginald Pole, like Contarini associated with the Oratory of Divine Love. Cortese, indeed, seems to have been formally licensed to read Lutheran works for the purpose of refuting them.[35] Several of the Cassinese Benedictines, most notably Teofilo Folengo, Isidoro Chiari, and Luciano degli Ottoni, responded to the Protestant challenge by writing works reaffirming the Pauline, but independent and indigenous, theological traditions of their order.[36] Reforming ideas were also current within the Capuchin order of reformed Franciscans: in 1551 the Anabaptist Pietro Manelfi was to attribute his first becoming 'Lutheran' eleven years earlier to the persuasion of a Capuchin at Ancona, while the general of the order, Bernardino Ochino, was to abandon his order for Protestant Switzerland notoriously and spectacularly in 1542.[37]

---

[32] Rozzo and Seidel Menchi, 'Livre et réforme en Italie', p. 363; D. Cantimori, *Eretici italiani del cinquecento: ricerche storiche* (Florence, 1939), pp. 22–3; Brown, *Italy and the Reformation*, pp. 172–3.

[33] J. Martin, 'Popular Culture and the Shaping of Popular Heresy in Renaissance Venice', in S. Haliczer (ed.), *Inquisition and Society in Early Modern Europe* (London, 1987), pp. 121–2; and the introduction to Gilmont (ed.), *La Réforme et le livre*.

[34] Fenlon, *Heresy and Obedience*, pp. 10–13, 16–18; text in Gleason (ed.), *Reform Thought*, 31–3.

[35] Fenlon, *Heresy and Obedience*, pp. 18–21, 29–44; McNair, *Peter Martyr*, pp. 10–15, A. Pastore, *Marcantonio Flaminio: Fortune e sfortune di un chierico nell'Italia del cinquecento* (Milan, 1981), pp. 51 ff, 94; Collett, *Italian Benedictine Scholars*, pp. 77–8.

[36] Collett, *Italian Benedictine Scholars*, pp. 81–6, 102–11, 121–37.

[37] C. Ginzburg (ed.), *I Costituti di Don Pietro Manelfi* (Florence and Chicago, 1970), 10, 31–2; on Ochino see also R. H. Bainton, *Bernardino Ochino, esule e riformatore senese*

The ecclesiastical elites soon broadened to embrace learned enthusiasts from the lay aristocracy of Italy. By far the most important of these aristocratic cliques was that which formed at Naples around the émigré Spanish humanist Juan de Valdés from 1535 until his death in 1541. He gathered such highly born followers as Giulia Gonzaga and Vittoria Colonna, and in 1536 was joined by the rising Capuchin friar Bernardino Ochino. In Lent 1536 Ochino preached a series of sermons whose contents, though unrecorded, seem to have had a catalytic effect on the thinking of the Valdés circle. In 1537 a reformed Augustinian of the order of Lateran Canons, Piermartire Vermigli, took up the abbacy of San Pietro ad Aram in the city and soon gravitated into the group; during 1539–40 he gave public lectures on I Corinthians which were probably influenced by its discussions.[38] 'Valdesianism', whose doctrinal content is as debatable as evangelism itself, did not remain confined to Naples. During 1538–41 two members of the Valdés circle, Ochino and Flaminio, made contacts and paid visits both to Siena and Florence; a third associate of the group, the protonotary Pietro Carnesecchi, ensured for Flaminio a welcome among the literati of the Medici court and especially from Caterina Cibo, duchess of Camerino. At Siena, a surviving manuscript of extracts from Valdés's works, including some writings otherwise unknown, testifies to his influence.[39]

These aristocratic movements represent the most famous foyers within which the Reformation's message was discussed, often with sympathy, before 1542. So impressive is the subtlety and moral prestige of the circles of Contarini and Valdés that it is all too tempting to regard these as though they were the Italian response to the Reformation. When leading members of the moderate reforming ecclesiastics (the so-called *spirituali*) such as Contarini, Pole, and Cortese were invited to help form Paul III's reforming commission in 1536, it might have seemed that the papal *Curia* itself had partly embraced their attitude of self-examination and self-criticism by the hierarchy. However, the commission ultimately submitted in 1537 a conventional proposal of administrative simplification and the abolition of abuses, representing the common denominator of the views of its disparate members.[40] The moral authority of the leading *spirituali* did undoubtedly play a major, and in a certain sense decisive, role in the

1487–1563 (Florence, 1940), and P. McNair and J. Tedeschi, 'New Light on Ochino', in *Bulletin d'Humanisme et Renaissance*, 35 (1973), 273–301.

[38] McNair, *Peter Martyr*, pp. 17–42, 147–72; Nieto, *Juan de Valdés*; P. Lopez, *Il Movimento valdesiano a Napoli* (Naples, 1976); M. Firpo, 'Juan de Valdés e l'evangelismo italiano: Appunti e problemi di una ricerca in corso', in *Studi Storici*, 4 (1985), 733–54.

[39] S. Caponetto, *Aonio Paleario (1503–1570) e la riforma protestante in Toscana* (Turin, 1979), pp. 41–50; Marchetti, *Gruppi eretticali senesi*, pp. 33 ff.

[40] McNair, *Peter Martyr*, pp. 131–8; text trans. in Gleason (ed.), *Reform Thought*, 81–100.

fate of the Reformation in Italy. However, clerics and aristocrats were by no means the only kinds of people to discuss the reformers' teachings. The wider social impact of the Reformation was in Italy, no less than elsewhere in Europe, chiefly confined to the cities.[41] Within those cities, above all in Tuscany, Lombardy and the Veneto, two sorts of people were specially likely to be affected. First, numerous literary and intellectual societies, mostly loose and informal, had grown up in the Renaissance to discuss secular literature and philosophical subjects, just like similar associations in Germany or Switzerland.[42] At Modena between around 1535 and 1545 the *Accademia*, a loose association of literate lawyers, doctors and merchants meeting at the house of the physician Giovanni Grillenzoni, became 'the cultural centre of the city'; and in that capacity introduced many heterodox ideas.[43] By the early 1540s the Sienese *Accademia degli intronati* circulated letters written by Ochino shortly after his apostasy; in the literary societies assembled in the environs of the city by Aonio Paleario at Colle Valdelsa and by the physician Achille Benvoglienti and the notary Fabio Cioni at Grosseto, these middle-class professionals shared ideas and texts and (discreetly) evangelised a few others less educated.[44] However, artisans and petty bourgeois were also able to discover the new and subversive ideas for themselves, and perhaps not just as the passive pupils of clerics and professional men. Already in Venice in the early 1530s a group of artisans led by a master carpenter called Antonio were listening to sermons on St Paul and vigorously denouncing the traditional pieties; Protestant sympathies were to be persistently expressed among professionals and artisans at Venice until the 1580s.[45] In Modena likewise, the artisan's workshop soon emerged as a normal location for religious debate, where initiates learned new ideas, and informers also heard compromising statements.[46]

How much of this activity, though, was actually Protestant? This question involves more than the simple question of whether such movements

41   See L. Donvito, 'La "religione cittadina" e le nuove prospettive sul cinquecento religioso italiano', in *Rivista di Storia e Letteratura Religiosa*, 19 (1983), 435 f; cf. some minor exceptions in Olivieri, *Riforma in Italia*, pp. 100 ff.
42   Compare the cliques described by L. W. Spitz, *The Religious Renaissance of the German Humanists* (Cambridge, Mass., 1963), *passim*, or by G. W. Locher, *Die zwinglische Reformation im Rahmen der europäischen Kirchengeschichte* (Göttingen and Zürich, 1979), pp. 45 ff.
43   Peyronel Rambaldi, *Speranze e crisi*, pp. 230–3.
44   Marchetti, *Gruppi ereticali senesi*, pp. 25–30, 46 ff, 69–81; also Caponetto, *Aonio Paleario*, pp. 33–9.
45   J. Martin, 'Salvation and Society in Sixteenth-Century Venice: Popular Evangelism in a Renaissance City', *Journal of Modern History*, 60 (1988), 207, 220–6; Martin, 'Popular Culture and the Shaping of Popular Heresy', in Haliczer (ed.), *Inquisition and Society*, pp. 116–19.
46   Peyronel Rambaldi, *Speranze e crisi*, pp. 233–4, 245–6, 261.

'protested' or not;[47] it also involves more than the issue of whether adherents of such opinions continued to worship as Catholics or not, and if so, for what reasons. For, just as in France or the Netherlands at the same period, the ideas of the leading reformers were only one set of ingredients in a varied spiritual and intellectual brew. Another ingredient, both in the early years before 1542 and in much later decades, was Erasmian humanism. At Modena in March 1541 a furore blew up over a young priest named Giovanni Bertari, who had been criticising mechanical, uncomprehending prayer (quite along the lines of Erasmus' *Enchiridion*) in the course of his expositions of St Paul. In 1542 an apothecary of Bologna named Girolamo Rainaldi asked a schoolmaster to read to his heterodox group Erasmus' edition of the New Testament; this experience led some members of the group to adopt simplified forms of prayer.[48] A second ingredient was the native Augustinian tradition, which could be invoked against 'Pelagians' in a way calculated to raise orthodox hackles. In February 1538 the preacher Agostino Museo of Treviso, invited to preach in Siena by the city council, drew a charge of heresy simply for preaching an Augustinian view of justification too trenchantly. The ensuing correspondence between Contarini, Flaminio, Girolamo Seripando, Lattanzio Tolomei and others revealed how uncertain the frontiers between different dogmas had become.[49]

A third component in the thought of the period, thrown into focus by recent research, was the neo-Antiochene theology of the restoration of fallen human nature taught by the Cassinese Benedictines. One of the most extraordinary ironies of the early Italian Reformation was that its most successful publication was, in its genesis, not Protestant at all. The *Trattato utilissimo del beneficio di Giesù Cristo crocifisso verso i cristiani*, published in Venice in the autumn of 1543, amalgamated themes and treatments drawn from a range of not always consistent traditions. Its first author, Benedetto di Mantova, seems to have written a piece setting out human salvation in terms of the renewal and healing of fallen human nature by the apprehension of divine grace and inner renewal. The work was then edited and substantially altered before publication by Marcantonio Flaminio, who both polished parts of the original text and added new material of his own. Since Flaminio was a disciple of Juan de Valdés, it has been traditional to examine the *Beneficio* for Valdesian influence. After the work of Tomasso Bozza revealed substantial unacknowledged quotations from Calvin's *Institutes*, most recent scholarship has explained the book in terms of three determining influences: late medieval

[47] Jung, 'Nature of Evangelism', 523–5, and as discussed by McNair, *Peter Martyr*, 48.
[48] Seidel Menchi, *Erasmo in Italia*, pp. 73 ff.
[49] Marchetti, *Gruppi ereticali senesi*, pp. 17–24.

Benedictine writing (from Dom Benedetto) on the one hand, and extracts or paraphrases from Valdés and Calvin on the other (added by Flaminio).[50] However, since there is now evidence that Valdés himself borrowed extensively from Luther, perhaps the work can be seen more simply as an attempt to harmonise Benedictine and classic Protestant teachings.[51] Yet the work was fervently recommended by such leading *spirituali* as Giovanni Morone, Gregorio Cortese, or Tommasso Badia.[52] That themes from Luther, Melanchthon and Calvin could merge so easily within one short text illustrates a final point: that Italy, like other countries in Europe where no confessional standards or church structures existed, could not maintain strict fidelity to one strand of reforming thought. Lutheran, Zwinglian and Calvinist themes jostled for attention, Calvinism only gradually coming to the fore, as in the Netherlands or Eastern Europe. Supremely indifferent to such nuances, Italian inquisitors invariably described as *luterani* any Protestants who were not actually Anabaptists.[53]

Many of the observations so far made about the Reformation in Italy, its stress on reading and discussion, its concentration among literate clergy, professionals and urban artisans, and its doctrinal eclecticism, could surely be applied equally convincingly to other countries where the establishment of reformed church structures had to wait until the second half of the sixteenth century. However, beyond this point important divergences become apparent. In Italy, haziness about doctrine, and delay in progressing from ideas to actions, was not an accidental consequence of an inchoate political situation: it was a deliberate policy chosen by the spiritual leaders of advanced Italian thought. For leading *spirituali* like Contarini, Morone, or Pole frequently acted as the spiritual patrons and mentors of reforming thinkers much more advanced than themselves.[54] The *spirituali* had long been convinced that, while the Protestant insight into the means of human justification was biblical and true, the truth of that insight must not be allowed to lead to the abandonment of traditional worship or to revolt from established hierarchical authority. They apparently regarded it as 'presumptuous' to draw such subversive practical conclusions from a theological doctrine.[55] They were, in short, trying to

[50] See Collett, *Italian Benedictine Scholars*, pp. 157–85, and the full references cited there; Benedetto da Mantova, *Il Beneficio di Cristo*, ed. S. Caponetto (Florence and Chicago, 1972); and the translation with notes and references in Gleason (ed.), *Reform Thought*, 103–61.
[51] Gilly, 'Juan de Valdés', as above, n. 6.   [52] Gleason (ed.), *Reform Thought*, 103.
[53] Donvito, 'La "religione cittadina"', 438; Peyronel Rambaldi, *Speranze e crisi*, p. 246; Martin, 'Salvation and Society in Sixteenth-Century Venice', 207 n.
[54] Pastore, *Marcantonio Flaminio*, pp. 127 ff.
[55] Fenlon, *Heresy and Obedience*, 65; for a similar reluctance to confront the logic of one's position see A. J. Schutte, *Pier Paolo Vergerio: The Making of an Italian Reformer* (Geneva, 1977), esp. pp. 118 ff, 132 ff, 201–15.

resist that logical and cultural drift which, everywhere else in Europe, pushed on from theological discussion to the reform of worship and the re-working of church structures.[56]

The effects of this attitude can be most clearly seen in Modena, one of the most advanced of Italian cities in its reception of Protestantism. By 1542 reforming preaching in the city had put its bishop, Cardinal Giovanni Morone, under pressure to respond effectively. Officially sponsored orthodox preachers were proving to be alarmingly unreliable, and by August 1542 there was a threat that the newly established Roman Inquisition might intervene. Morone, however, still regarded the issue as one which could be resolved by the work of a good resident bishop. He was unwilling to believe that so many senior clergy from his see and his circle of associates were in fact Protestants, and was still regarding Piermartire Vermigli as a reliable preacher, even as a possible future bishop, on the very eve of his defection and flight.[57] In September 1542 Morone submitted to the leading citizens of Modena a *Formulario di fede*, which offered the Modenese a chance to demonstrate their basic loyalty to the church and thereby ward off the intrusions of the nascent Inquisition. The *Formulario*, devised by Gasparo Contarini, was a compromise piece intended to placate and win over those in danger of converting to Protestantism. It repeatedly referred to the role of faith as the criterion of a true Christian, or as the means by which the sacraments worked. It implicitly denied the meritorious quality of good works. On the issue of the need for sacramental penance, the *Formulario* reflected a tortuous ongoing epistolary debate between Contarini and Pole, only terminated by the death of the former on 24 August 1542.[58] The position of Morone and Contarini was so uneasy that historians tend to dwell on its intellectual inconsistencies rather than on its political effects. Yet, in the short term, it worked for Modena. None of those to whom the *Formulario* was offered for subscription refused to sign it. As the historian of Modena's sixteenth-century religious experience has remarked, this was perhaps the only occasion in which the moral authority of the *spirituali* over Protestants was put to a decisive test.[59] In this case they acted (successfully) as the brakes rather than the motor of the Italian Reformation.

Events at Modena in the autumn of 1542 illustrate important features about the influence wielded by the *spirituali* over the would-be reformers

[56] Fenlon, *Heresy and Obedience*, pp. 62 ff; compare Cameron, *European Reformation*, pp. 132–5.
[57] McNair, *Peter Martyr*, p. 255.   [58] Fenlon, *Heresy and Obedience*, pp. 62–6.
[59] Peyronel Rambaldi, *Speranze e crisi*, pp. 263–8; on this episode see also M. Firpo, 'Gli "spirituali", l'Accademia di Modena e il formulario di fede del 1542: Controllo del dissenso religioso e nicodemismo', in *Rivista di Storia e Letteratura Religiosa*, 20 (1984), 40–111.

in Italy; they also form part of a larger crisis which overtook religious life from the end of the 1530s. After 1542 certain political choices had been made which decisively changed the prospects for Italian Protestantism; although, as some recent research has shown, this crisis was not an irrecoverable death-blow which settled the movement's fate once and for all.[60] The crisis had several aspects. First of all, within a short period it became clear that the enthusiasts for the Reformation in a number of cities were no longer willing to contain their utterances and their actions within the limits of even a tenuous respect for orthodoxy. Secondly, the promoters of the policy of restraint and reconciliation with the Protestant 'heretics', who had hitherto enjoyed great prestige within the *Curia*, were seriously discredited.

It is difficult to judge exactly when the tensions in the cities threw the movement into serious crisis. At Modena it was clearly full-blown by the summer of 1542; other cities saw similar strains around the same time. As early as 1539 famine and social tension brought matters to a head in Siena. In response to the subsistence crisis different confraternities organised themselves to provide poor-relief and to organise penitential exercises. Bartolomeo Garosi of Petroio, also known as Brandano, organised the mostly proletarian confraternity of St Antony Abbot in the Augustinian Church by preaching the all-sufficiency of Christ's merits and the need for repentance, criticising papal and bourgeois wealth alike. A rival group led by Giovanni Battista Cafarelli at the Observant Franciscans preached a pelagian doctrine of good works. During 1541–2 the city council protested to the ecclesiastical authorities that, despite appearances, it was making efforts to suppress the spread of heresy. Into the ensuing wrangle was drawn Aonio Paleario, who had been quietly debating with his followers at Colle Valdelsa: he was denounced to the archbishop and in December 1542 subjected to a theological investigation, which proved inconclusive.[61] The peak of such crypto-Protestant activity at Siena was to be reached during the evangelising efforts of Basilio Guerrieri and Lelio Sozzini in the middle to late 1540s.[62] More notorious and threatening were events at Lucca, where two Lateran canons under the influence of Piermartire Vermigli committed acts of, to say the least, gross rashness. Some time in the summer of 1542 Fra Girolamo da Pluvio celebrated a reformed Zwinglian Eucharist in his monastery of S Agostino. Early in August he was arrested by agents of the Roman Inquisition,

[60] A. J. Schutte, 'Periodization of Sixteenth-Century Italian Religious History: The Post-Cantimori Paradigm Shift', *Journal of Modern History*, 61 (1989), 269–84 and esp. 271–5; Martin, 'Salvation and Society in Sixteenth-Century Venice', 211–14.
[61] Marchetti, *Gruppi ereticali senesi*, pp. 37–50, 117 ff; Caponetto, *Aonio Paleario*, pp. 59 ff.
[62] Marchetti, *Gruppi ereticali senesi*, pp. 51–128.

only to be tumultuously liberated by some Lucchese citizens and then promptly re-arrested. About the same time Fra Costantino di Carrara made breathtakingly frank admissions of his disbelief in the powers of the Roman papacy to two Dominicans who visited his monastery of S Maria di Fregionaia. Matters were developing beyond simple preaching and lecturing: a layman named Mateo Gigli was holding religious conventicles at which it was rumoured that irregular Eucharists were celebrated.[63]

Events in the cities proceeded in tandem with political struggles within the *Curia* itself. The leaders of the *spirituali* had staked a great deal of political prestige on the attempt to find a doctrinal accord with the leaders of moderate German Protestantism at the religious conference at Regensburg in April–July 1541. The Regensburg drafts originated in irenic discussions held earlier between Bucer and Melanchthon and moderate German Catholics like Johannes Gropper and Julius Pflug.[64] However, Contarini's intimate involvement as the Pope's representative at the conference had a decisive impact on the Italian reformers. Late in April and early in May the protagonists reached an agreed form of words on the doctrine of justification; then their talks broke down over the Eucharist, penance and absolution, and the authority of church and Papacy. Following that breakdown both Luther and the Papacy disavowed the concessions already made in order to bring about the formula on justification.[65]Contarini and his allies were thus in the impossible position of having made politically dangerous concessions to the German Protestants, impaired their standing at Rome and confirmed the suspicions of the hardline orthodox that they were no better Catholics than the heretics with whom they were negotiating. In the following year they suffered a worse blow in the defection of two of the principal preachers on whom the *spirituali* had relied to retard the spread of heresy. Bernardino Ochino and Piermartire Vermigli, independently and almost simultaneously, decided in August 1542 to escape from Italy to Switzerland, apparently affording clear proof of the zealots' worst fears. It is now thought highly likely that the leaders of the *spirituali* had at least a very

[63] McNair, *Peter Martyr*, pp. 240–68; Donvito, 'La "religione cittadina"', 469, with ref. to M. Berengo, *Nobili e mercanti nella Lucca del cinquecento* (Turin, 1974), pp. 357–454; but see also S. Adorni-Braccesi, 'Libri e lettori a Lucca tra Riforma a Controriforma: Un'indagine in corso', in *Libri, idee e sentimenti religiosi nel cinquecento italiano* (Ferrara, 1987), pp. 39–46.
[64] On the background to these events in Germany see F. Lau and E. Bizer, *A History of the Reformation in Germany to 1555* (London, 1969), pp. 153–7, 161–5.
[65] Lau and Bizer, *Reformation in Germany*, pp. 165–71; Fenlon, *Heresy and Obedience*, pp. 45 ff; P. Matheson, *Cardinal Contarini at Regensburg* (Oxford, 1972), *passim*; documents on these events are in B. J. Kidd (ed.), *Documents Illustrative of the Continental Reformation* (Oxford, 1911), 341 ff.

good idea of their intentions before the reformers' flight, and connived at, or even abetted, it.[66]

The discredit brought on the *spirituali* by the failure of their German policy and the defection of their favourite preachers confirmed a political victory for the opposing *curial* faction, which was already being won by its leader Giovanni Pietro Caraffa, bishop of Chieti and leading Oratorian. The bull *Licet ab Initio* of 21 July 1542 established a papal, Roman Inquisition, under six inquisitors-General drawn from the College of Cardinals and led by Caraffa. The effect of this was to supersede the local inquisitions hitherto operated either by diocesan bishops or mendicants working under papal commissions in groups of provinces; its apparent intention to forestall inconsistent or lenient behaviour by the responsible authorities, in Italy above all.[67] This political crisis in Italian religious life divided the moderates from the extremists, helped to determine the future course of policies in the *Curia*, and brought into being the means by which deviations from orthodoxy might in future be identified and suppressed. Therefore, its effects on Italian Protestantism were complex. The equivocation and ambiguity which accommodated the reformers' theological affirmations while ignoring their heretical denials was no longer necessary. The heresy which the conventiclers espoused would henceforth be more blatant; the contexts in which they met had correspondingly to be much more discreet. However, the crisis of 1542 did not necessarily imply any immediate change in the typical behaviour of Italian reforming enthusiasts. There was no reason why the activities characteristic to the cells of Italian Protestants (reading and discussion) should change. In some cases and areas they persisted for another two decades.[68]

After 1542 Italians continued to meet and discuss the doctrines of the Reformation, in the same way and in many of the same places as they had done before. At Venice, the influence of reformers like Baldassare Altieri ensured that Protestant conventicles became more, rather than less, frequent during the later 1540s. The jeweller Alessandro Caravia remarked in 1546 that theology was routinely discussed by 'smiths, tailors, and barbers'. As well as discussion-groups, private devotional meetings were held, for instance at the *Fondaco dei Tedeschi* or on the

---

[66] McNair, *Peter Martyr*, 269 ff; Fenlon, *Heresy and Obedience*, 51 ff; G. Fragnito, 'Gli "spirituali" e la fuga di Bernardino Ochino', in her *Gasparo Contarini: un magistrato veneziano al servizio della Cristianità* (Biblioteca della Rivista di Storia e Letteratura Religiosa, Studi e Testi, IX, Florence, 1988), pp. 251–306; also in *Rivista Storica Italiana*, 84 (1972), 777–813.

[67] For the bull of foundation see Kidd, *Documents*, 346–50.

[68] Martin, 'Salvation and Society in Sixteenth-Century Venice', esp. 212 f and n. 11; Schutte, 'Periodization', 279 ff; note that Vergerio's crisis of conscience came several years later, in 1549: see Schutte, *Pier Paolo Vergerio*, pp. 238–65.

Isola San Giorgio, often through the organisation and persuasion of the physician Teofilo Panarelli, who was ultimately executed for heresy at Rome.[69] About 1549 the patrician Alessandro Trissino moved from Vicenza, where he had already met Calvinist teachings, to Padua: there he found a heterogeneous community of Cretans, Cypriots and natives of the Veneto and the Friuli amongst whom Protestant books were discussed exhaustively, and whose contacts he brought back with him to Vicenza. During a later stay at Venice around 1560 he encountered other vigorous talking-shops of the same type.[70]

Tuscany continued to be as susceptible as the Veneto. From exile Bernardino Ochino influenced his native Siena through his letter sent to the city Council in November 1543, which was cited extensively in a well-publicised Catholic rebuttal issued by Ambrogio Catarino. On All Saints' Eve 1544 the artisan Pier Antonio di Giovanni Battista aroused a debate over prayer to saints in the Confraternity of the Holy Trinity, claiming that Christ, not the saints, was the sole mediator. When he was interrogated it later emerged that Pier Antonio had been under the influence of Lelio Sozzini and above all the barber Basilio Guerrieri. Guerrieri evolved a technique of insinuating Calvinist ideas through the artisan confraternities as well as the existing noble or upper-bourgeois literary salons; one of his associates, Dionisia Rocchi, was also quietly subverting the Augustinian nuns in the convent of S Paolo.[71] Meanwhile on 28 July 1546 Aonio Paleario was appointed to teach the humanities in Lucca. The legacy of Piermartire Vermigli's teaching evidently persisted there; yet it gave little overt evidence of itself until 1555, when many Lucchese families emigrated to Geneva. Alongside an elegant Erasmian sentiment cultivated by townspeople, there grew up a movement of popular Calvinist preaching in the countryside of the Valle di Serchio.[72]

These examples were not unique. At Cremona in 1550 a probably long-standing clandestine Calvinist church came to light, which through the cleric Gerolamo Teggia may have influenced similar covert groups at Modena; other such cells of heterodox believers operated under the guidance of Pietro Bresciani at Casalmaggiore, Ulisse Aldovrandi at Bologna and (as already noted) of Achille Benvoglienti and Fabio Cioni

[69] Martin, 'Salvation and Society in Sixteenth-Century Venice', 212–20; Martin, 'Popular Culture and the Shaping of Popular Heresy', in Haliczer (ed.), *Inquisition and Society*, pp. 115 ff.
[70] A. Olivieri, 'Alessandro Trissino e il movimento calvinista vicentino del cinquecento', *Rivista di Storia della Chiesa in Italia*, 21 (1967), 54–62.
[71] Marchetti, *Gruppi ereticali senesi*, pp. 1–16, 51–67, 85–112; Caponetto, *Aonio Paleario*, pp. 85 ff.
[72] Caponetto, *Aonio Paleario*, pp. 77–85.

at Grosseto, near Siena.[73] However, the most striking feature of this activity is just how closely it does resemble the conventicle activity of the 1530s and early 1540s: Italian Protestantism did not, apparently, make what in northern Europe was the normal progress from 'evangelical teaching' to 'evangelical action'.[74] At most it might engage in semi-organised conventicles or some ritual act such as defiance of the Catholic Lenten fast.[75] While the *spirituali* still held out the prospect of integrating the reformers' insights into the Catholic tradition, this restraint was understandable. Afterwards, however, it constituted a serious self-imposed limitation on most of the reformed communities of lowland Italy; it distinguished them sharply from the equivalent movements under hostile regimes, for instance in France, the Low Countries, or the duchy of Savoy. The vital question, then, is just why did the Italian reformers, by now committed to a consciously heterodox and schismatic creed, prove unable to turn their spiritual movement into a 'Reformation from below' of the classic Calvinist type?

Private discussion, even private worship, could be carried on in secret; it allowed Protestant believers to avoid the trials of a political confrontation and the ensuing risks to property, conscience, or life. Nicodemism, the deliberate and persistent dissimulation of Protestant sentiment under the cover of Catholic observance, was of course prevalent amongst crypto-Protestant cells in France and the Low Countries as well as in Italy. Calvin's complaints about 'Messieurs les Nicodemites' were addressed as much to his own countrymen as to the Italians.[76] However, Italians continued to espouse Nicodemite attitudes with a perverse combination of intellectual sophistication and political naivety. On one hand Nicodemism could be justified with Erasmian arguments that the niceties of religious conviction need not be broadcast or debated in public. In particular, those like the Sozzini who questioned a whole range of credal formulae might find intellectual reasons for avoiding public affirmations.[77] On the other, would-be Protestants could continue to claim

[73] Peyronel Rambaldi, *Speranze e crisi*, pp. 240–6 and references.
[74] A remark made at a cities' assembly at Ulm in 1524; see H.-C. Rublack, *Die Einführung der Reformation in Konstanz* (Gütersloh, 1971), p. 31.
[75] Peyronel Rambaldi, *Speranze e crisi*, p. 248.   [76] See above, n. 7.
[77] On Italian Nicodemism see esp. D. Cantimori, 'Submission and Conformity: "Nicodemism" and the Expectations of a Conciliar Solution to the Religious Question', in E. Cochrane (ed.), *The Late Italian Renaissance 1525–1630* (London, 1970), pp. 244–65; A. Biondi, 'La Giustificazione della simulazione nel cinquecento', in L. Firpo and G. Spini (eds.), *Eresia e Riforma nell'Italia del cinquecento*, Biblioteca del 'Corpus Reformatorum Italicorum', Miscellanea I (Florence and Chicago, 1974), pp. 7–68; C. Ginzburg, *Il nicodemismo. Simulazione e dissimulazione religiosa nell'Europa del '500* (Turin, 1970); A. Rotondò, 'Atteggiamenti della vita morale del cinquecento, la pratica nicodemitica', *Rivista Storica Italiana*, 79 (1967), 991–1030; Donvito, 'La "religione cittadina"', 464–6; Peyronel Rambaldi, *Speranze e crisi*, p. 251.

that they were just waiting for the right moment to make public profession. Even in the 1570s it was still hoped that a rival Church Council,
or a triumph by the Huguenots in France, might grant the Italian
crypto-Protestants their wishes.[78] There was, then, a twofold argument
for doing nothing: first, that Nicodemism was morally and intellectually
defensible; secondly, that if one waited for external events the circumstances might improve and Protestantism might peacefully win civil
rights in any case.

A second reason why the Italian reformers failed must be that, for some
reason, they did not decisively engage and coalesce with any other social
and political opposition elements who shared their desire to overturn the
status of the church. Such coalitions, such political marriages of con-
venience, acted as indispensable midwives to the northern European civic
Reformations.[79] In Italy, despite the efforts of recent historians to find
such equivalent coalitions, the social dimension to Italian Protestantism
has proved surprisingly elusive. In fact, several different potential allies
for the nascent Protestant movement proved either hostile or at best
limited in their aid.

Aristocrats and patricians, for example, might have been expected, as
elsewhere, to protect those suspected of heterodoxy so as to spite ecclesiastical judges whom they disliked. At Lucca, Siena and Modena, there is
evidence that patrician households used their influence to inhibit ecclesiastical justice, or to impede the workings of the Inquisition.[80] However,
this was at best negative, provisional protection: it might safeguard the
persons of the reformers; it would not promote their programmes, nor
create a favourable context on its own. There was no Italian Princes' War:
the Italian nobility did not band together to defy the Habsburgs for the
sake of a Reformation.[81] Neither, of course, could that anti-Italian xeno-
phobia, which made the estates in the *Reichstag* echo or at least understand Luther's protests in the early 1520s, be exploited by the Italians
themselves.[82] By the time that the reformers tried to align themselves with
political resistance to the Habsburg–Medici threat to civic autonomy, for
instance in the strange plot of Altieri and other Venetians at Venice in
1546–7 or the anti-Spanish revolt at Siena in 1552, it was too late to

[78] See Olivieri, 'Alessandro Trissino', 63 ff, 72 ff; cf. also Martin, 'Salvation and Society in
Sixteenth-Century Venice', 231 ff; Cantimori, 'Submission and Conformity', as above.
[79] See e.g. the argument in Cameron, *European Reformation*, pp. 293–313.
[80] See Caponetto, *Aonio Paleario*, pp. 77 ff, Marchetti, *Gruppi ereticali senesi*, pp. 169 ff;
Peyronel Rambaldi, *Speranze e crisi*, p. 237.
[81] Cf. Peyronel Rambaldi, *Speranze e crisi*, pp. 239–40.
[82] See A. G. Dickens, *The German Nation and Martin Luther* (London, 1974), pp. 7–8, 28–9
and references.

mount more than a rearguard action for civic liberties or international Protestantism.[83]

Secondly, the Italian reformers seem to have had equal difficulty in aligning their programme with campaigns for bourgeois urban renewal. At times of economic hardship the classic north-European plan for confiscating church wealth and combining it in a civic common chest to support both poor relief and spiritual services ought to have seemed attractive.[84] There were stirrings in this direction at various stages in the story; but they failed to coalesce in a coherent, let alone an irresistible, policy.[85] No doubt the Italian Reformation did have a social dimension. All the same, Protestantism does seem to have acted as a distraction from political activity rather than a spur to it. It did not give its followers something to unite their protests and focus them on a shared goal.[86]

There are various other problems which can readily be identified with the Protestant movement in lowland Italy. Unlike France, Italy as a whole did not enjoy widespread support from Geneva for its missionary effort. The sole exception to this rule is the case of Piedmont-Savoy, where not only the Waldensian congregations of the upland valleys, but also the churches of the plains, received repeated nominations of pastors in the late 1550s and early 1560s.[87] Elsewhere, however, the primary contribution of Geneva was as a source of literary encouragement and as a place of refuge. Those Italians who escaped there were usually retrained for a ministry somewhere other than their place of origin: hence Scipione Lentolo from Naples was assigned first to Carignano in Piedmont, then to the Waldensian valleys; Alessandro Trissino went to serve the churches of the Valtelline.[88] It could even be argued that, while Italians faced the alternatives of Nicodemite secrecy or escape abroad, they were given yet another opportunity to evade the dangerous business of turning their beliefs into a public profession and a political campaign. Each time a

---

[83] Martin, 'Salvation and Society in Sixteenth-Century Venice', 217; Marchetti, *Gruppi ereticali senesi*, pp. 117 ff and 129 ff.

[84] Cf. Cameron, *European Reformation*, pp. 258–60.

[85] For possible instances see Marchetti, *Gruppi ereticali senesi*, pp. 37 ff, 40 ff; Seidel Menchi, *Erasmo in Italia*, 75; A. Olivieri, '"Eresie" e gruppi sociali nelle città italiane del '500', *Rivista di Storia e Letteratura Religiosa*, 17 (1961), 259 ff.

[86] Martin, 'Salvation and Society in Sixteenth-Century Venice', 225 ff; Martin, 'Popular Culture and the Shaping of Popular Heresy', in Haliczer (ed.), *Inquisition and Society*, pp. 117 ff; Olivieri, '"Eresie" e gruppi sociali', 264–5.

[87] E. Cameron, *The Reformation of the Heretics: The Waldenses of the Alps 1480–1580* (Oxford, 1984), pp. 157–9, 171–5; G. Jalla, *Storia della Riforma in Piemonte fino alla morte di Emanuele Filiberto, 1517–1580* (Florence, 1914), pp. 79–86.

[88] Cameron, *Reformation of the Heretics*, pp. 173–4; Olivieri, 'Alessandro Trissino', 64–9.

crisis loomed the nascent movement might be stripped of its leaders by flight.[89]

Since the Italian Protestant movement lacked firm credal formulae as well as institutional structures, there was nothing to constrain its exponents from following where the argument led. Owing to the enormous authority wielded by Delio Cantimori over the subject until recent times, the degree to which all Italian reforming thinkers indulged in rationalistic, undogmatic, unregulated free thought may have been slightly exaggerated. There were major figures in the movement who became notorious heretics to Protestants and Catholics alike: men such as Celio Secundo Curione, Camillo Renato and, above all, Lelio and Fausto Sozzini.[90] However, it is striking how often this drift towards free thought actually became most pronounced after the reformer in question had left Italy.[91] Within the peninsula itself the work of Camillo Renato at Modena or Lelio Sozzini at Siena, not to mention Bernardino Ochino, was directed first of all to promoting themes common to orthodox as well as heterodox Protestantism. Secondly, it was not just Christian heterodoxy in which the discussion-groups indulged. There is evidence that they broadened their discussions from religion into abstruse alchemical or magical speculations.[92] Finally, one should beware of assuming that there was some trait in the Italian religious temperament which made it unwilling to accept the constraints of a creed. It was Italians, above all Agostino Mainardi and Scipione Lentolo, who later in the sixteenth century worked hardest to contain their compatriots within bounds. At times their language could be positively inquisitorial in character.[93]

A major worry to northern European reformers was the frequently spectacular, though usually ephemeral, attraction which Anabaptism held for city populations. For a brief period around 1550 the distinctive Italian form of Anabaptism had a brief flowering in the Veneto, no doubt diverting energies from the mainstream Protestant movement at that critical juncture in the process. In October 1551 the secular priest Pietro

---

[89] Not only in the case of the preachers who left Italy in 1542; but also in such later instances as Giulio da Milano, Pier Paolo Vergerio, Camillo Renato, Lelio Sozzini, or Alessandro Trissino.

[90] On these figures, besides the classic work of Cantimori, *Eretici italiani del cinquecento*, G. H. Williams, *The Radical Reformation* (London, 1962), still provides basic information; see also J. A. Tedeschi (ed.), *Italian Reformation Studies in Honour of Laelius Socinus* (Florence, 1965).

[91] On this topic see esp. D. Caccamo, *Eretici Italiani in Moravia, Polonia, Transilvania (1558–1611): Studi e documenti* (Florence and Chicago, 1970), *passim*.

[92] Olivieri, '"Eresie" e gruppi sociali', 263 ff; Olivieri, 'Alessandro Trissino', 59 ff.

[93] The sources for this are found in T. Schiess (ed.), *Bullingers Korrespondenz mit den Graubündern* (3 vols., Quellen zur schweizer Geschichte, 23–5, Basle, 1904–6), II. 277–8; P. D. Rosius a Porta, *Historia Reformationis Ecclesiarum Raeticarum* (2 vols., Chur, 1771–7), I. pt. 2., 497–507.

Manelfi of San Vito was interrogated by a Dominican inquisitor at Bologna, and declared himself to be a penitent Anabaptist willing to disclose many details of the sectaries' locations and activities. In particular he gave details of an Anabaptist synod which had gathered in Venice in September or October 1550. Although a number of Manelfi's claims have since been doubted or actually discredited (he exaggerated the scale and significance of the synod), the picture of Italian Anabaptism which has finally emerged still suggests a brief but animated two years or so of extremist dissenting activity from 1549 to 1551, concentrated in the north-east from the Grisons and Friuli down to Ferrara.[94]

The closest parallels to the Italian political experience of the Reformation might, in fact, be thought to lie in areas such as south-eastern Germany or central Switzerland, where there were both major ecclesiastical principalities and secular lordships firmly and rigidly committed to the old church. In those areas which proved most fertile ground for Reformation ideas, especially Tuscany and the Romagna, Habsburg and Medici power was sufficiently well entrenched by the 1540s to make a religious revolt extremely dangerous; by 1559, with heavy Spanish presence in some cities, it was effectively irresistible.[95] In the one state which might have acted independently, namely Venice, the pursuit of an independent and often anti-papal policy did not exclude the city from becoming ever more intolerant and zealously Catholic as its civic Inquisition took hold from the 1550s onwards.[96] By the 1550s even the margins of Italy were not necessarily safe, as was shown by the experience of Locarno. There a small gathered church of several hundred townspeople, only set up in 1550, fell foul of the administrative powers wielded over the region by the Catholic cantons of Switzerland. After confrontation and disputation with the local Catholics the Protestants were simply ordered either to return to Catholicism or leave the town by 3 March 1555; some 200 of its members left and settled in Zürich, there to be ministered to by Bernardino Ochino.[97] Finally, although there are risks in passing judgement on an institution whose records are almost entirely inaccessible,[98]

94 U. Gastaldi, *Storia dell'Anabattismo* (2 vols., Turin, 1972–81), II. 531–77 and refs.; see esp. A. Stella, *Anabattismo e antitrinitarismo in Italia nel xvi. secolo* (Padua, 1969); C. Ginzburg (ed.), *I Costituti di Don Pietro Manelfi* (Florence and Chicago, 1970); cf. Donvito, 'La "religione cittadina"', 438 on sectarian divisions among Italian Protestants.
95 See for instance the combined pressure from the Medici and the Spanish in Siena, as in Marchetti, *Gruppi ereticali senesi*, 143 ff, 174 ff.
96 See the main conclusions of P. F. Grendler, *The Roman Inquisition and the Venetian Press, 1540–1605* (Princeton, NJ, 1977).
97 Cameron, *Reformation of the Heretics*, pp. 257–8, and the sources cited in n. 23.
98 Apart from dispersed scraps (some now collected in the Library of Trinity College, Dublin) the records of the Roman Inquisition remain stubbornly closed to scholars. See J. Tedeschi in G. Henningsen and J. Tedeschi (eds.), *The Inquisition in Early Modern*

the Roman Inquisition does seem to have been quite effective both as an investigating agency and (perhaps as importantly) as a deterrent to Protestant clergymen. Resident ministers were the lifeblood of any settled church: if the congregations could be rendered headless by the abduction, execution, or simply the frightening off of potential pastors, the Protestant movement could be prevented from growing out of control, as it had done in Germany in the 1520s or France in the later 1550s.[99]

The few regions of the Italian-speaking world where a Protestant Church was successfully established provide valuable control samples to test the hypotheses advanced so far. In Piedmont, the dukes of Savoy were able to crush religious dissent in the lowland towns by the later 1560s,[100] but could not prevent settled churches from being formed in the Alps and in the French protectorate of Saluzzo. In the Waldensian Alpine valleys the critical period fell between 1555 and 1565. From the spring of 1555 ministers from Geneva began to settle and evangelise the Alpine Waldenses, earlier contacts with associates of Guillaume Farel having been inconclusive. By the autumn of 1557 these churches had some two dozen ministers, including the former Capuchin and friend of Ochino, Giafredo Varaglia. By vigorous lobbying the Swiss Protestant churches managed to dissuade Henry II from carrying out a wholesale persecution, although many individuals were captured and executed. On being restored to his duchy in 1559 Duke Emanuele Filiberto wasted little time in passing the Edict of Nice of 15 February 1560, as a prologue to an armed attack. The military raid on the Waldenses failed: by the Treaty of Cavour of 5 June 1561 the duke was obliged to concede limited freedom of worship within very narrow boundaries to the heretics and their immigrant pastors. Not only that: the war seems to have brought about greater solidarity between the natives and the newcomers, as the Waldenses recognised the value of their pastors' leadership, and the pastors recognised the practicality of the heretics' traditions of violent and tenacious self-defence. In the following few years up to 1564 the synodal structure and Calvinist discipline of these churches was definitively established.[101]

The other main reformed district, the Milanese territories of

Europe: Studies on Sources and Methods (DeKalb, Ill., 1986), pp. 13–32; and refs. cited in Schutte, 'Periodization', 282–3.
[99] For attempts to abduct or assassinate Italian ministers in the Valtelline, see T. McCrie, *History of the Progress and Suppression of the Reformation in Italy* (2nd edn., Edinburgh and London, 1833), pp. 401–2; J. U. Campell, *Ulrici Campelli Historia Raetica*, ed. P. Plattner (2 vols., Quellen zur schweizer Geschichte, vols. 8–9, Basle, 1887–90), II. 462–8.
[100] Jalla, *Riforma in Piemonte*, pp. 209 ff, 265 ff.
[101] Cameron, *Reformation of the Heretics*, pp. 155–66, 171–5, 191–9, 213–15, 220–4.

Chiavenna, the Valtelline, and Bormio, had been administered from 1512 onwards by the Swiss Confederation, and more immediately by the three 'Grey Leagues' or Grisons. The Grisons had already allowed religious diversity in their own lands since the mid-1520s; but in the Valtelline it took until at least the 1540s before settled churches of Italian-speakers were set up, since the terms of the edicts of toleration required each community to approve the installation of a preacher individually.[102] By 1549, however, the churches of Chiavenna, Vicosoprano, Sondrio, Poschiavo and the Engadine had almost an embarrassment of ministerial riches. Talents as remarkable, diverse, and quarrelsome as Agostino Mainardi, Pier Paolo Vergerio, Giulio da Milano, Celso Martinenghi, Francesco Negri, Camillo Renato, or Lelio Sozzini exercised their skills on the peoples there. There is evidence that here, unlike Piedmont, Protestant conversions were concentrated among the better-off families, with 'rustic heretics', as a Catholic visitor described them, the exception rather than the rule.[103] After the departure of some of the worst troublemakers, Valtelline Protestantism matured into a remarkable coexistence of Catholic and Protestant until the ravages of Spanish troops put an end to it all in the 1620s.[104] In each of these cases two factors, weak central government and an abnormally powerful presence of ecclesiastical talent, aided in Piedmont by a long-standing social tradition of dissent, gave the Italian reformers a precarious and remote homeland in which to work.

Susanna Peyronel Rambaldi has demonstrated how, during the trial of Giovanni Morone, leaders of the *spirituali* were seen by the orthodox as responsible for the growth of a potent Protestant threat in the diocese of Modena. Convinced that the doctrine of justification by faith was inherently orthodox, they connived at the emergence of a movement which proved ultimately no less hostile to the principles and hierarchy of the visible Catholic Church than its northern counterpart.[105] The conclusion reached here, albeit a tentative one, is that Morone's judges were entirely mistaken. In the years between 1517 and 1521 the Roman hierarchy, and especially the Italian Dominicans, had fanned the flames of the Lutheran schism by responding to the sincere misgivings of an earnest Augustinian

---

[102] O. Vasella, 'Zur Entstehungsgeschichte des I. Ilanzer Artikelbriefs vom 4 April 1524 und des Eidgenössischen Glaubenskonkordates von 1525', *Zeitschrift für schweizerische Kirchengeschichte*, 34 (1940), 182–91; McCrie, *Reformation in Italy*, pp. 385–6, 393–4.

[103] See F. Ninguarda, *Atti della visita pastorale diocesana*, (2 vols., Como, Società Storica Comense, 1892–4), I. 281 ff, 285 f, 300, 306, 311, 330 ff, 334, 340 ff.

[104] Note the sharing of places of worship between Catholics and Protestants at Dubino, Caspano, and Brusio, in Ninguarda, *Atti*, I. 245, 280, 350; cf. also A. Pastore, *Nella Valtellina del tardo cinquecento: fede, cultura, società* (Milan, 1975).

[105] Peyronel Rambaldi, *Speranze e crisi*, pp. 265–71.

with the heavy-handed thunderbolts of crude theological positivism and unscrupulous manipulation of the church's judicial machinery. It is not too excessive a claim to make that Luther's opponents turned the Reformation into a revolt. Whatever else they did, the *spirituali* were not about to repeat that tragedy within Italy itself. On the contrary, they fostered and encouraged the belief that evangelism, ecumenism, or ultimately Nicodemism might still provide a painless and risk-free route to Reformation, long after such hopes had really become the purest self-delusion. Contarini, Pole and Morone served the cause of the Papacy better by their equivocations than ever did Caraffa with his thunderbolts; though the Roman Catholicism which they thus protected turned out very different from their hopes. Italian Evangelism was neither the Italian form of the Reformation, nor yet its covert ally: it was its subtlest and yet its most effective adversary.

SELECT BIBLIOGRAPHY

Benedetto da Mantova, O. S. B. *Il Beneficio di Cristo*, ed. S. Caponetto (Florence and Chicago, 1972).

Black, C. F. *Italian Confraternities in the Sixteenth Century* (Cambridge, 1989).

Brown, G. K. *Italy and the Reformation to 1550* (Oxford, 1933).

Caccamo, D. *Eretici Italiani in Moravia, Polonia, Transilvania (1558–1611): Studi e documenti* (Florence and Chicago, 1970).

Cameron, E. *The Reformation of the Heretics: The Waldenses of the Alps, 1480–1580* (Oxford, 1984).

Cantimori, D. *Eretici italiani del Cinquecento: Ricerche storiche* (Florence, 1939). *Prospettive di storia ereticale italiana del Cinquecento* (Bari, 1960).

Caponetto, S. *Aonio Paleario (1503–1570) e la Riforma protestante in Toscana* (Turin, 1979).

Church, F. C. *The Italian Reformers, 1534–1564* (New York, 1932).

Cochrane, E. (ed.), *The Late Italian Renaissance* (London, 1970).

Collett, B. *Italian Benedictine Scholars and the Reformation: The Congregation of Santa Giustina of Padua* (Oxford, 1985).

Donvito, L. 'La "religione cittadina" e le nuove prospettive sul Cinquecento religioso italiano', *Rivista di Storia e Letteratura Religiosa*, 19 (1983), 431–74.

Eresia e riforma nell'Italia del Cinquecento: Miscellanea I del Corpus Reformatorum Italicorum (Florence and Chicago, 1974).

Fenlon, D. *Heresy and Obedience in Tridentine Italy: Cardinal Pole and the Counter Reformation* (Cambridge, 1972).

Fragnito, G. *Gasparo Contarini: Un magistrato veneziano al servizio della Cristianità* (Biblioteca della Rivista di Storia e Letteratura Religiosa, Studi e Testi, IX, Florence, 1988).

Ginzburg, G. *Il nicodemismo: Simulazione e dissimulazione religiosa nell' Europa del '500* (Turin, 1970).

Gleason, E. G. (ed.), *Reform Thought in Sixteenth-Century Italy*, American Academy of Religion, Texts and Translations, 4 (Ann Arbor, 1981).

214   Euan Cameron

Grendler, P. F. *The Roman Inquisition and the Venetian Press, 1540–1605* (Princeton, 1977).

Hay, D. *The Church in Italy in the Fifteenth Century* (Cambridge, 1977).

Jalla, G. *La Riforma in Piemonte fino alla morte di Emanuele Filiberto, 1517–1580* (Florence, 1914).

Jung, E.-M. 'On the Nature of Evangelism in Sixteenth-Century Italy', *Journal of the History of Ideas*, 14 (1953), 511–27.

McNair, P. *Peter Martyr in Italy: An Anatomy of Apostasy* (Oxford, 1967).

Marchetti, V. *Gruppi ereticali senesi del Cinquecento* (Florence, 1975).

Martin, J. 'Popular Culture and the Shaping of Popular Heresy in Renaissance Venice', in S. Haliczer (ed.), *Inquisition and Society in Early Modern Europe* (London, 1987), pp. 115–28.

'Salvation and Society in Sixteenth-Century Venice: Popular Evangelism in a Renaissance City', *Journal of Modern History*, 60 (1988), 205–33.

Matheson, P. *Cardinal Contarini at Regensburg* (Oxford, 1972).

Nieto, J. C. *Juan de Valdés and the Origins of the Spanish and Italian Reformation* (Geneva, 1970).

Olivieri, A. 'Alessandro Trissino e il movimento calvinista vicentino del Cinquecento', *Rivista di storia della Chiesa in Italia*, 21 (1967), 54–117.

La Riforma in Italia: Strutture e simboli, classi e potere (Milan, 1979).

'"Eresie" e gruppi sociali nelle città italiane del '500', *Rivista di Storia e Letteratura Religiosa*, 17 (1981), 253–66.

Pastore, A. *Marcantonio Flaminio: Fortune e sfortune di un chierico nell' Italia del Cinquecento* (Milan, 1981).

Peyronel Rambaldi, S. *Speranze e crisi nel Cinquecento modenese: Tensioni religiose e vita cittadini ai tempi di Giovanni Morone* (Milan, 1979).

Prodi, P. and P. Johanek (eds.), *Strutture ecclesiastiche in Italia e in Germania prima della Riforma* (Bologna, 1984).

Schutte, A. J. *Pier Paolo Vergerio: The Making of an Italian Reformer* (Geneva, 1977).

Printed Italian Vernacular Religious Books, 1465–1550: A Finding List (Geneva, 1983).

'Periodization of Sixteenth-Century Italian Religious History: The Post-Cantimori Paradigm Shift', *Journal of Modern History*, 61 (1989), 269–84.

Seidel Menchi, S. *Erasmo in Italia* (Turin, 1987).

Simoncelli, P. *Evangelismo italiano del Cinquecento: Questione religiosa e nicodemismo politico* (Rome, 1979).

Stella, A. *Anabattismo e antitrinitarismo in Italia nel XVI secolo* (Padua, 1969).

Tedeschi, J. A. (ed.), *Italian Reformation Studies in Honor of Laelius Socinus* (Florence, 1965).

Welti, M. *Kleine Geschichte der italienischen Reformation* (Gütersloh, 1985); Italian edn. by A. Rizzi, *Breve storia della Riforma italiana* (Casale Monferrato, 1985).

10   Spain

A. Gordon Kinder

Contrary to the prevailing belief, the Reformation did not entirely bypass Spain, although its progress there was uncertain, its demise swift and so thoroughly effected that it left little abiding monument. The claim is often made that the reforms of the Spanish Church instituted by Cardinal Francisco Ximénez de Cisneros around the turn of the century made unnecessary, even impossible, any movement of Protestant reform in the country.[1] It is therefore worth emphasising that, while these measures did to some extent sharpen morals, deepen piety and strengthen ecclesiastical discipline, they left untouched the structure of the church and its doctrines, which were two main preoccupations of the reformers. Indeed, to some extent, Cisneros' provision of devotional literature may well have contributed to producing a climate favourable to Protestant ideas. And, however successful his reforms, they still left room in the country for a ready response to Erasmian satire against hypocrisy and low standards amongst secular and regular clergy, particularly the mendicant orders. Although in retrospect the ecclesiastical situation in Spain at the beginning of the Reformation may seem to have been untroubled and static, it needs to be borne in mind that the country was not cut off from the cross-currents of religious ideas in Europe during the first half of the sixteenth century, and the assertion that there was no demand at all for a reform of the Protestant kind is made without reference to the ruthless operation of the Inquisition.

In addition, it is as well to recognise that during the 700 years leading up to the Reformation, Spain had had a very different experience from the rest of Western Europe. Spanish culture and intellectual life were to a large extent formed by the experience of that long process of military

---

[1] Works mentioned in the appended bibliography are given in abbreviated form in the notes. M. Menéndez Pelayo, *Heterodoxos españoles* (Madrid, 1965), I, 46; A. Huerga, 'Erasmismo y Alumbradismo', in M. Revuelta Sañudo and C. Morón Arroyo (eds.), *Erasmo y España, El Erasmismo en España* (Santender, 1986), 339–56; M. Andrés Martín, 'The Common Denominator of Alumbrados, Erasmians, "Lutherans", and Mystics: the Risk of a More "Intimate" Spirituality', in A. Alcalá (ed.), *The Spanish Inquisition and the Inquisitorial Mind*, Columbia University Press, 1987, 457–94.

struggle by which control of the Iberian peninsula was wrested back from the Moorish invader. Before that, there had been many centuries of Muslim supremacy over parts of the country: with the Muslim invaders had come a substantial number of Jews, and in both Christian and Muslim realms in Spain all three religions had lived together in varying degrees of tolerance.[2] The final victory of the Christians came only with the fall of Granada in 1492, an event that heralded a new era of Christian triumphalism, which replaced *convivencia* by an official policy of intolerance. Immediately after the conquest of Granada the Jews were given an ultimatum amounting to an order to convert to Christianity or leave the country. Similar moves were taken against the Muslims in due course. Although massive emigration took place, there were mass baptisms too, resulting in large numbers of so-called New Christians, who were not properly integrated for many years. As unassimilated groups, the former Jews (*conversos* or *judeoconversos*) and Muslims (*moriscos*), were perceived as a threat to the unity of the state. The problem they posed was used to persuade Ferdinand and Isabella of the need to set up the Spanish Inquisition, which was established in 1478 as an ecclesiastical court directly responsible to the Crown, and reorganised in 1492. This differed in certain respects from the medieval inquisition, since its main function, at least at first, was to supervise the converts produced by various coercive measures. The result was a well-organised council of state, such as no other nation in Europe possessed (except Portugal from 1536), with the ability to produce sufficient resources to run a legal system with its own prisons, parallel to the civil and ecclesiastical courts, to guard the ports and frontiers, and to censor books when printed. Although frequently overstretched, and not efficient by modern standards, it managed to make its presence felt throughout Spanish territories. The view taken was that, once baptism had been accepted, even under threat, the obligations of Christian observance could be enforced on the New Christians, many of whom continued the clandestine practice of their old faith. More importantly from the point of view of the Reformation, the machinery of the Inquisition could be brought to bear against heresy wherever it was suspected. It was ideal for combating the early manifestations of Protestantism, and it was soon being used against Old and New Christians alike.

How the intellectual and spiritual life of Spain would have developed without the Inquisition is a matter for conjecture. What is clear is that by the early 1560s it had succeeded in imposing an outward conformity on the country; even from the beginning of the sixteenth century writers had

---

[2] *Convivencia* is the term used to denote the generally peaceful co-existence of the three religions in medieval Spain.

to be circumspect about how they expressed themselves, and increasingly so as the century advanced. The imposition of ever narrower standards meant that some works that had originally passed the censor were destroyed, to disappear without trace.[3] This makes the task of assessing the impact of the Reformation through a scrutiny of surviving books extremely difficult, since often the only evidence of a book's existence is that provided by notarial and inquisitorial records, and these are frequently vague, and survive only in a haphazard fashion; all too often even these have been lost. The first Spanish *Index of Prohibited Books* was published by the Council of State in 1551,[4] after which it was constantly updated and reissued. It prohibited many editions of Bibles, and the Inquisition ordered an examination of all Bibles in 1552, which resulted in the publication of an expurgatory *Censura generalis contra errores, quibus recentes haeretici Sacram scripturam asperserunt ...* (Valladolid, 1554).[5] Inquisition records and the various editions of the *Index* reveal how aware the authorities were of developments in intellectual fashions and ideas, and how thorough a control they attempted.

None the less, reformist ideas were not discouraged by the measures adopted up to this point. Several factors helped the growth and the spread of evangelical views in Spain. First, the invention of printing from movable type meant that, in Spain as elsewhere, books could be produced in greater numbers than manuscripts, and thus ideas could spread more quickly. Second, there was a growing interest in the Bible, epitomised by the initiative of Cisneros, who gathered together in the University of Alcalá de Henares – founded by himself and functioning from *c.* 1508 – the humanist expertise and the necessary manuscripts for the compilation of the Complutensian Polyglot, printed between 1514 and 1517.[6] Thirdly, and more broadly, when Charles V ascended the Imperial throne Spain was intimately linked into the general European scene in a way that had not been the case for many centuries. Courtiers, soldiers and others from northern Europe visited Spain, and Spaniards went to the Emperor's lands in Flanders, Germany and Austria. And finally, Spain's Atlantic

[3] See V. Pinto Crespo, *Inquisición y control ideológico en la España del siglo XVI* (Madrid, 1983); and his 'Censorship: a System of Control and an Instrument of Action', in *The Spanish Inquisition and the Inquisitorial Mind*, 303–20.
[4] Reproduced in facsimile in J. M. de Bujanda (ed.), *Index de livres interdits*, V *Index de l'Inquisition espagnole 1551, 1554, 1559* (Geneva, 1984), 595–686.
[5] J. I. Tellechea, 'Biblias publicadas fuera de España secuestradas por la Inquisición de Sevilla', *Bulletin Hispanique*, 64 (1962), 236–47; and his 'La censura inquisicional de Biblias de 1554', *Anthologica Annua*, 10 (1962), 89–142.
[6] The Latin name for Alcalá de Henares is Complutum. Ambitious by any standards, the folio edition contained the original Hebrew, Chaldean and Aramaic of the OT, the Septuagint, the original Greek of the NT, the Vulgate, and a recently made Latin translation.

ports controlled the trade with the newly discovered Americas, attracting shipping from northern Europe, carrying books and people with new ideas.

Erasmus himself was invited by Cisneros to participate in the production of the Polyglot, but declined. The enterprise was upstaged by Erasmus' own Greek New Testament of 1516, which received a four-year Imperial privilege. This probably delayed the Polyglot's official publication till after the receipt of the papal privilege in 1520. Erasmus' work was not only first on the market, but was more accessibly priced. Other Latin works of Erasmus began to reach Spain soon after they were published. They quickly created an Erasmian movement amongst sections of the educated classes, centred on the University of Alcalá. Erasmus became even better known as his works were published in Spanish versions, although these were rarely exact translations, and the ideas of Erasmus conveyed by them were modified by what the various translators felt would prove acceptable to the authorities. The first of these, *Tratado o sermon del niño Jesus* ... (Seville, 1516), was probably the first translation into any vernacular of a work by Erasmus. The university printer brought out a whole series of Erasmus' works in both Latin and Spanish between 1525 and 1529, and there was a veritable explosion of Spanish translations of Erasmian works, printed and reprinted in Spain and Antwerp. By far the most popular of these was the *Enchiridion*, which achieved something like best-seller status, and was actually dedicated to the Inquisitor General. It has been stated that Erasmus enjoyed a popularity in Spain such as in no other country.[7] If this was so, the success was of short duration. There had been opposition from the first, and ultimately the anti-Erasmians triumphed at a gathering in Valladolid in 1527 called to examine Erasmus' works, and these became targets of the Inquisition, in spite of modified support for Erasmus from Charles V.

A movement clearly influenced by both Erasmian writings and works commissioned by Cisneros, usually referred to as the Alumbrados or Illuminists, arose during the early part of the century in the region roughly bounded by Toledo, Salamanca and Alcalá. The initial impulse seems to have come from the preaching of a certain 'friar Melchor', who went about urging reform on Franciscan houses, which he considered to be lacking in real Christianity, and he gained a strong following among both friars and lay-people, particularly *conversos*, and pious women known as *beatas*. The reading of various works of piety helped to develop their beliefs; this included what was available of the Bible in Spanish at the

7 M. Bataillon, *Erasmo y España* (1966), 314.

time,[8] besides works mentioned above, and others, amongst which figured prominently Thomas à Kempis' *Imitation of Christ*. The term, 'Alumbrado' appears to have been used originally within the movement as a codeword denoting membership of the group, but it quickly became current outside this circle and was employed to refer to them by others, including the Inquisition.[9] Two types began to emerge: the *recogidos* (who practised 'recollection') and the *dexados* (who 'abandoned' themselves to the love of God); of which the former were approved and the latter eventually suppressed by authority. There was interaction between the two, cross-fertilisation amongst the various groups that sprang up, rivalry and friendships between their leaders. It is apparent that local groupings were not identical with each other, and that Alumbrado beliefs did not remain fixed, but developed as time went on.

A question of central importance is whether the origin of this movement owed anything directly to the northern reform; but the answer remains enigmatic. Authorities have put forward a wide variety of suggestions on this point, which range from the downright fantastic to several feasible but conflicting hypotheses.[10] Giving evidence at his trial in Toledo in 1524, the Alumbrado Pedro Ruiz declared that Isabel de la Cruz had been his teacher 'since before 1512', a statement which would appear to rule out any prior knowledge on his part of Luther and his writings. The Alumbrados then would be a peculiarly Spanish product of the general spiritual ferment which was experienced all over Western Europe in the later fifteenth and early sixteenth centuries. Nevertheless, the Inquisition soon began indifferently to accuse those brought before it of being 'Alumbrado, Erasmian, and Lutheran',[11] and, even though the absolute origins of the movement may have antedated Luther, it is quite evident that, as time went on, the Alumbrados were at least acquainted with Luther's ideas;[12] and it seems likely that the Alumbrados themselves, as they became aware of the new evangelical teaching, saw some close similarity between it and their own views.

[8] This comprised compilations of the church lectionary, such as *Evangelios e Epistolas, siquier liciones de los domingos e fiestas solemnes de todo el año e de los santos*, trans. Gonzalo de Santa María (Saragossa, 1485), and Ludolf of Saxony *Vita Christi*, trans. Ambrosio Montesino (Alcalá, 1502).

[9] Significantly, the first page of an early Spanish edition of the *Imitation of Christ* (Burgos, 1495) contains the words 'Si queremos verdaderamente ser alumbrados y librados de toda ceguedad del coraçon'.

[10] The fantastic include early Christian Gnosticism (A. Márquez) and Muslim *shadilíes* (M. Asín Palacios); the feasible include strong assertions in favour of native reform unaffected from outside (J. C. Nieto) and equally firm claims that Protestant reform was the cause (M. Menédez Pelayo). None offers incontrovertible proof.

[11] In the sixteenth century in Spain the word *luterano* was used indifferently to denote all forms of Protestant.

[12] There seems to be no certain evidence that they actually read any of his books.

The movement seems to have begun in Pastrana, where Isabel de la Cruz gathered around herself a group of friars and lay-people which included Gaspar Bedoya and Pedro Ruiz de Alcaraz. She was revered for her knowledge of the Bible, and for her skill in expounding it. Isabel's influence was eclipsed by Francisca Hernández who operated in and around Salamanca. Her circle was attended by Antonio de Medrano, Bernardino de Tovar, his half-brother Juan de Vergara, Gil López, and the Franciscan guardian of Escalona, Fray Juan de Olmillos. She also spent some time in Valladolid, where she added to her following Pedro de Cazalla, Bishop Juan de Cazalla and his sister María, and Fray Francisco Ortiz. María de Cazalla went on to create her own group in Guadalajara, besides keeping in contact with those in Pastrana. Alcaraz moved to Escalona, where he acted as a lay-preacher. In the same town there was a group in the Franciscan convent of Cifuentes, directed by Francisco de Ocaña. Another group existed in Toledo, led by Petronila de Lucena in the home of her brother, Juan del Castillo. Another brother, Gaspar de Lucena, was an adept, along with Luis de Beteta. The inquisitorial trial of the latter group is the only occasion when books by Reformers are specifically mentioned in connection with the Alumbrados. The movement spread to some extent amongst the academics at the University of Alcalá, some of whom were proposed for inclusion in the group of 'twelve apostles' mentioned below. It is extremely difficult to separate unequivocally the elements of Erasmianism, illuminism and even Protestantism amongst the evangelicals in Alcalá, but there were well documented connections between them and the principal Alumbrados and their centres of activity.[13]

The patronage of the nobility was a crucial factor in the growth of this movement. Isabel de la Cruz was a dressmaker and Pedro Ruiz de Alcaraz a book-keeper employed in the household of the Mendoza Duke of the Infantado, and Alcaraz was later in the service of the Marquess of Villena at Escalona at the same time as Juan de Valdés, a man who has been described, perhaps not entirely accurately, as 'the theologian of the Alumbrados'.[14] Even after his trial and punishment, Antonio de Medrano was protected by the Dukes of Nájera, and no less a person than Fadrique Enríquez, the Admiral of Castile, kept open house in Medina del Ríoseco for Alumbrados, even being persuaded in 1525 by the Basque priest, Juan López de Celaín, into supporting a scheme of recruiting 'twelve apostles'

13 There were similar connections with Ignatius Loyola, who was tried for illuminism. See Fidel Fita, 'Los dos procesos de San Ignacio de Loyola', *Boletín de la Real Academia de la Historia*, 33 (1898), 431–3; Luis Fernández, 'Iñigo de Loyola y los alumbrados', *Hispania Sacra*, 35 (1983), 585–680.
14 Antonio Márquez, 'Juan de Valdés, teólogo de los alumbrados', *La Ciudad de Dios*, 184 (1971), 150–67.

to evangelise his estates, to become a base for a much more ambitious campaign, linking up with Germany.

A frequently quoted Alumbrado tenet is that the love of God in man is God, which appears to mean that by abandoning oneself to this love, one's soul can be divinised. Some take the view that this abandonment has merely the moral purpose of revealing the inability of unaided human nature to perform good works, and ensuring one's obedience to the Commandments and loving one's neighbour. This comes near to the idea of justification by faith, without using that form of words. They asserted that they experienced the presence of God through his love in a manner more immediate than that claimed for the real presence in the sacrament. This illumination by the Holy Spirit working directly in the individual's mind and heart gave them a great independence of institutionalised means of grace; they clearly preferred their own conventicles to the services of the church, and they rejected outward ceremonies in favour of an inward piety. But it is very difficult to pin down the exact beliefs of adherents, because much of the information we have comes either from cautious statements made by some of them under investigation by the Inquisition or from the Inquisition's own assessments, often made on the basis of previous known heresies. Research into the Alumbrados is hampered by the fact that nothing they wrote in total freedom has survived, and they seem to have printed nothing. The movement was condemned by an edict promulgated in Toledo on 23 September 1525, and a systematic prosecution of its leaders by the Inquisition ensued, although for the most part their punishments were relatively mild.[15] Unconcealed Protestantism seems to explain the fate of the few who were put to death: Juan del Castillo, fray Diego de Barreda, Juan Ramírez, and Garzón.

The fate of these individuals, clearly touched by Protestant teaching, suggests that Spanish evangelicals had access to Protestant works from an early date. And indeed, entry into Spain of foreign editions of such material is well documented. Pope Leo X issued briefs on 21 March 1521 to the Regents of Castile, requiring them to adopt measures to prevent the introduction into Spain of the writings of Luther and his sympathisers. The grandees of Spain pointed out to Charles soon after his accession in the same year, that 'tares' were being sown amongst the 'wheat' of Spain. And the Royal Council sent a letter in similar vein to him from Burgos.[16] These missives make it clear that 'Lutheran' works were being translated

---

[15] A. Márquez, *Los Alumbrados*, 273–83.
[16] T. McCrie, *Reformation in Spain*, 61; A. Redondo, 'Luther et l'Espagne', 122; J. Simón Díaz, *El libro español antiguo: análisis de su estructura, Texto* [sic] *del Siglio de oro, Bibliografías y Catálogos*, (Cassel, 1983), I, 23.

into Spanish and introduced into Spain, although unfortunately none of these seems to have survived. Later that year the Headquarters or *Suprema* of the Inquisition alerted its branches to the danger of such infiltration, and a letter of 27 September commended the Inquisition of Valencia for having detected and burnt 'Lutheran' books. In 1523, the Inquisition of Navarre was thanked for its vigilance in the ports and along the border with France. Books were seized and destroyed in Aragon too. In February 1525, Charles V was informed that three Venetian galleys loaded with 'Lutheran' books had been detected in a port of Granada. The books mentioned in trials for heresy are often difficult to identify, but it is clear that Protestant works produced abroad in Spanish did achieve a certain dissemination. There are various claims that books by Protestant authors were even published in Spain in Spanish versions: that, for instance, Luther's *Commentary on Galatians* was translated into Spanish in 1520, and that Calvin's *Institutes* were published in Saragossa.[17] Alarm was expressed in 1532 when it was suggested that a 'Lutheran' book had been printed in Valencia.[18] As no precise documentation was included, it is difficult to substantiate such allegations about books which have not survived, and, for that reason, even harder to assess how far the native movements were influenced by Protestantism.

The difficulties in disentangling the threads of influence are evident in the careers of Alfonso and Juan de Valdés. The elder brother, Alfonso, a correspondent of Erasmus and Melanchthon, wrote two works, *Dialogo de las cosas acaecidas en Roma* ... and *Dialogo de Mercurio y Caron* ..., that praise Erasmus and are critical of the failings of the church and of many of its practices, although their main purpose was to argue that the Pope rather than Charles V was responsible for the Sack of Rome in 1527, alleging papal immorality and widespread failure of the clergy to act in accordance with the principles of the Gospel (by their requiring payment for the church's ministrations, encouraging idolatrous devotion to saints and relics, conducting wars and so on). Each puts much the same strongly Erasmian argument, verging on the Protestant. Five anonymous editions were published in Spanish of these two works together, besides translations. Alfonso accompanied the imperial court in June 1529, and his death from plague in Vienna shortly afterwards probably saved him from the Inquisition's attentions so that his orthodoxy was never tested, but there have been suggestions that the strictures against Luther in his books

---

[17] J. Stoughton, *The Spanish Reformers* (London, 1883), 36; *Colección de documentos para la historia de España*, V, 400.

[18] R. García Cárcel, *Herejía y sociedad en el siglo XVI. La Inquisición en Valencia 1530–1609* (Barcelona, 1980), 22–5.

were there merely to strengthen the impression of Erasmianism, at a time when Erasmus was still acceptable.[19] Juan de Valdés was one of a number of Spaniards who went into self-imposed exile to escape the threat posed by the Inquisition investigations. In 1530, he went to Rome with Mateo Pascual, the rector of the Trilingual College of Alcalá. Miguel de Torres, the vice-rector, Manuel Miona (later a companion of Ignatius Loyola) and Juan del Castillo all fled to Paris – although Castillo was eventually to join those in Rome, and was teaching Greek in Bologna in 1533 when he was apprehended by the authorities and returned to Spain to face trial. It was whilst he was in the service of the Marquess of Villena that Juan de Valdés came into contact with an Alumbrado leader, Pedro Ruiz de Alcaraz. Bataillon's dictum was long accepted without question that Valdés youthful *Dialogo de doctrina Christiana* (Alcalá, 1529), was an Erasmian work in which there was no influence from Protestant sources. Recently, however, the possibility of such influence has been mooted: there seem to be connections in terms of verbal parallels with texts of Luther, Oecolampadius, and Melanchthon, and the publication dates do not preclude the possibility.[20] Valdés' Protestantism was not, however, overt, so that when the *Dialogo* was officially examined it was approved. It is significant that later every one of the censors involved was brought before the Inquisition, as was its printer.

Juan stayed only briefly in Rome, and then settled in Naples, where he gathered round himself a group of spiritual reformers, who included Bernardino Ochino, Peter Martyr Vermigli, Marcantonio Flaminio, and Pietro Carnesecchi. The honour of being the first to translate from the original languages into modern Spanish whole books of both the Old and the New Testaments seems to belong to Juan de Valdés, but these were not published in his lifetime, and indeed only two were published at all in the sixteenth century. Juan Pérez de Pineda brought out in Geneva (with the false imprint of Venice) Valdés' commentaries on Romans and on I Corinthians, both of which contain full translations.[21] There is evidence that these circulated in Spain.[22] Both were amongst the books carried to Seville by Julián Hernández in 1557. Valdés' versions of the Psalms and of

---

[19] J. C. Nieto, 'Luther's Ghost and Erasmus's Masks in Spain', *BHR*, 36 (1974), 253–72.

[20] This was published anonymously, but its authorship was never in doubt. See C. Gilly, 'Juan de Valdés: Übersetzer und Bearbeiter von Luthers Schriften in seinem *Diálogo de Doctrina*', *ARG*, 74 (1983), 257–306.

[21] *Comentario, o declaracion breve, y compendiosa sobre la epistola de San Paulo apostol a los Romanos, muy saludable para todo Christiano* (1556), and *Comentario o declaracion familiar, y compendiosa sobre la primera epistola de San Paulo apostol a los Corinthios, muy util para todos los amadores de la piedad Christiana* (1557).

[22] Both titles are listed amongst books seized in Seville and Valladolid, and they occur in inventories of private libraries in Spain at the time.

Matthew's Gospel remained unnoticed in manuscript for several centuries before their publication.[23] Juan wrote a number of other works in Italian: *Alphabeto christiano* with *In che maniera il christiano ha di studiare ...* (first published 1545); *Modo che si deve tenere nel'insegnare et predicare ...* (first published 1545); *Le cento e dieci divine considerationi* (first published 1550); *Qual maniera si devrebbe tenere a informare ... i figliuoli de christiani delle cose della religione* (first published before 1549); and others; these influenced the progress of the Reformation in Italy and beyond.[24] The *Beneficio de Cristo* was produced from within his circle. A good number of his followers emigrated to the north and joined up with mainstream Protestantism.

Valdés was one Spaniard whose influence was felt beyond his homeland. Inevitably the Spanish evangelical movement also threw up more maverick individuals: one such was Michael Servetus.[25] It is not always realised that Servetus was a Spaniard. He stands out as a solitary figure both intellectually and theologically. Geographer, physician, astrologer, editor, theologian, he stands in the great humanist tradition, widely read in Scripture, the Koran, classical and patristic works. Although circumstances caused him to be put to death in Protestant Geneva in 1553, he had escaped from a French prison and was on the Spanish Inquisition's wanted list. In his youth he went into the service of the prelate Juan de Quintana, and soon obtained leave to study in Toulouse, never returning to Spain. He clearly encountered both Alumbrado and Anabaptist beliefs early in his life. His theology had more of a Protestant cast than a Catholic one, but, although his scholarship was solidly Bible-based, he was too radical for the magisterial reformers, since, besides his more notorious (though often misunderstood) ideas concerning the Trinity, he put forward a number that were Anabaptist (e.g., delaying baptism till adulthood, a monophysite belief in the spiritual flesh of Christ and teaching that the aim of faith is to divinise humanity). It is striking to note how he manages to bring religious considerations into most of his publications.[26] Thus, even in his defence of the physician Fuchs in 1536, he attacks the Lutheran interpretation of justification by

[23] E. Boehmer (ed.) *El Salterio traduzido del hebreo en romance castellano por Juan de Valdés, ahora por primera vez impreso* (Bonn, 1880); T. Fliedner (ed.) *El evangelio de San Mateo declarado por Juan de Valdés, ahora por primera vez publicado* (Madrid, 1880).

[24] Valdés's *One Hundred and Ten Considerations* was particularly popular in sixteenth-century France and seventeenth-century England (see lists of editions in Kinder, 'Juan de Valdés', *Bibliotheca Dissidentium*, IX (Baden-Baden, Koerner, 1988), 176–9).

[25] Probably the best general work in English on Servetus is R. H. Bainton, *Hunted Heretic*. See also J. Friedman, *Michael Servetus: a Case-Study in Total Heresy* (Geneva, Droz, 1978) and Kinder, *Servetus* (Bibliotheca Dissidentium, X).

[26] The reverse is also true; he used medical ideas to illustrate his theology: hence his well-known use of the circulation of the blood to that end.

faith. In his edition of Ptolemy's Geography (1535) he says Spain is a country rife with religious superstition; he deplores the miserable lives of the peasants whose revolt was condemned by Luther, and mourns their defeat; he observes that Palestine was not the land of milk and honey described by the Bible, a statement that earned him Calvin's disdainful comments. But it was his works intended as pure theology that led him finally to the stake. The first two of these, *De Trinitatis erroribus libri septem* (1531) and *Dialogorum de Trinitate libri duo* (1532), printed in Hagenau, caused a scandal which obliged him to go into hiding for a while. In the end it was his third such work, *Restitutio Christianismi* (Vienne, 1553), which brought about his martyrdom in the following year. His stated aim in writing on the Trinity was not to overthrow the doctrine, but to make it more acceptable to Jews and Muslims, clearly a legacy of his Spanish origins. His apparent denial of the Trinity and his rejection of infant baptism were the main accusations against him. The destruction of copies of the *Restitutio* was so thorough that only three now survive, plus a few in manuscript.[27]

Although the Inquisition aspired to strict control of thought, the sporadic nature of persecution before 1540 meant that evangelicals did not feel overwhelmingly threatened. Against the odds, native activity began again. A number of theologians trained at Alcalá University migrated to Seville and gave rise to an evangelical movement there in the 1540s and 1550s. Francisco de Vargas seems to have been of some importance, but he apparently wrote nothing, and died without having to face the Inquisition, although he was apparently marked for investigation. His library reveals a fair amount of biblical material and works by Erasmus, but nothing by Protestant reformers.[28] The sermons of the cathedral preacher, Juan Gil (alias Dr Egidio), appointed in 1537, gave rise to conventicles in the city, and eventually led to his being brought before the Inquisition and required to retract in 1552.[29] At this time there did not seem to have been any general pursuit of others with similar ideas. Nevertheless, Gaspar Zapata, a printer, and three priests connected with the orphanage called the Colegio de los Niños de la Doctrina felt it was prudent to leave Seville: Juan Pérez de Pineda, Luis Hernández del Castillo, and Diego de la Cruz. The three made for Paris, where they

[27] The printed copies are to be found in Edinburgh University Library, the Bibliothèque National in Paris, and the Österreichisches Nationalbibliothek in Vienna. Three of the MSS are in the Bibliothèque Nationale, another is also in Paris in the Library of the Société de l'Histoire du Protestantisme Français, and one is in East Berlin Staatsbibliothek.

[28] K. Wagner, 'La biblioteca del doctor Francisco de Vargas', *Bulletin Hispanique*, 78 (1976), 313–24.

[29] Text in German in Schäfer, *Beiträge*, II, 342–53.

joined forces with Juan Morillo, an Aragonese who had shortly before been a Catholic theologian working with Cardinal Reginald Pole at the Council of Trent. They held open house for Spaniards with reformist views.[30] It does not seem that Egidio ever published anything, although it is reported that at his death there existed manuscripts written by him of commentaries on various books of the Bible, but which have since disappeared. He died in 1556 shortly after he had returned from an exhausting journey to confer with Agustín Cazalla, the leader of the evangelical conventicle in Valladolid. Four years later, however, Egidio's followers were being harassed, he himself was tried and condemned posthumously, and his bones were disinterred and burnt with his effigy. He was succeeded in his office of cathedral preacher in 1556 by Constantino Ponce de la Fuente, who continued the same trend.

Constantino had become a correspondent of Erasmus in 1530 when he wrote a reply (apparently not printed) to Luis de Carvajal's anti-Erasmian *Dulcoratio*. He had already had an earlier period of service at Seville cathedral from 1533 to 1548, followed by a tour of duty with the court as a royal chaplain, and had written a number of works. His *Summa de doctrina christiana en que se contiene todo lo principal y necessario que el hombre christiano deve saber y obrar* came out in Seville in 1543, with his *Sermon de Christo nuestro Redemptor en el Monte* appended. It is in the form of a dialogue, and draws heavily on Juan de Valdés' *Dialogo*.[31] There were several other editions printed in Seville and Antwerp. In 1546 he published in Seville *Exposicion del primer Psalmo de David cuyo principio es Beatus vir, dividida en seis sermones*, which likewise had other editions in Seville and Antwerp. Constantino's *Catecismo* came out in Seville in 1547, where also appeared a year later his *Doctrina christiana ... Parte primera. De los articulos de la fe*, and *Confission delante de Jesu Christo redemptor y juez de los hombres*. In the inquisitional censure of the *Doctrina*, certain passages are condemned as 'Alumbrado doctrine'. Besides writing and preaching, Constantino lectured on the Bible in the same boys' orphanage of Seville from which three teachers had earlier fled. Already under investigation by the Inquisition, he was thrown into prison when the general hue and cry against Protestants was raised in Seville in 1558, and died before coming to trial. A large number of other writings of his were discovered in the home of a woman follower, also imprisoned. These were destroyed, and there is now no way of knowing

[30] J. I. Tellechea, 'Españoles en Lovaina 1551–58', *Revista Española de Teología* 23 (1963), 21–45; A. G. Kinder, 'Juan Morillo: Catholic Theologian at Trent, Calvinist Elder in Frankfurt', *BHR*, 38 (1976), 345–50 (for 'elder' read 'minister').

[31] See M. Bataillon, introduction to his edition of J. de Valdés, *Diálogo de doctrina christiana* (Coimbra, University, 1925), 198, 234, 237, 260, 265–6, 269–70, 296, 309–13.

exactly what they were, but Inquisition records indicate that they were of a more definitely Protestant nature than published works. There was some promise in 1567 that these documents, or others of a similar nature, were to be published in Germany, but this seems never to have happened.[32] In 1550 there was published in Geneva a Spanish version of Calvin's Catechism, by an unknown translator who apologises for the standard of his Spanish because of his long residence outside Spain. Copies of these were sent in sealed envelopes to various important Spaniards, including the Admiral of Castile, with no noticeable effect save consternation amongst the Spanish authorities.[33]

By this time, the movement in Seville had moved on from Erasmianism to become a series of conventicles preaching arguably Protestant doctrines. Egidio's former followers had increased and acquired new leaders. At the height of their activity their number was perhaps as many as 800, from all levels of society in and around the city. They obtained books by various Protestant authors, some of which they procured from the Inquisition itself through the contact of a member, the monk Antonio del Corro, whose uncle was an Inquisitor of the same name. When these were finally confiscated by the Inquisition, they made an impressive list, and included works by all the major Reformers, and many by less well known ones.[34] The movement seems to have taken a Protestant turn when a layman named Rodrigo Valer underwent evangelical conversion and challenged the leaders to deepen their faith and understanding. Cristobal de Losada, a physician, was another layman who became a director of this group. The nunneries of Santa Paula and Santa Isabel and the Dominican monastery inside the city, and the Observant Hieronymite monasteries of San Isidoro at Santiponce (four miles outside) and Nuestra Señora at Écija were strongly affected. The influence came into San Isidoro by the prior García Arias, who allowed the monks to abandon the regular offices in favour of reading the Bible, then reversed his instructions, only to return to rejection of the offices. Thereafter he remained constant to the evangelical practice and perished in flames in 1562. One monk Casiodoro de Reina, is categorised as a 'dogmatiser' in the Inquisition records.[35] Meantime a parallel movement was developing in Valladolid amongst a smaller and socially more elevated group led by the royal chaplain, Agustín Cazalla. They maintained contacts with those in Seville. We have

---

[32] Reginaldus Gonsalvius Montanus, *Sanctae Inquisitionis Hispanicae Artes* (Heidelberg, 1567), 283–4.
[33] Bataillon, *Erasmo y España* (1966), 704.
[34] A list of these is given in Schäfer, II, 392–400. They range from Luther, Calvin and other leading reformers, through to less well known to those on the edges of orthodoxy, such as Servetus, Ochino, Borrhaus and Postel.
[35] In the trial of María de Bohorques, 1558 (Schäfer, *Beiträge*, II, 278).

the Inquisition's list of the beliefs of this group, which contains many undeniably Protestant ideas,[36] although they do not seem to have had such a wide selection of Protestant works at their disposal as their Seville counterparts.

Until recently, accounts of the Reformation in sixteenth-century Spain have stated that only in these two centres, Seville and Valladolid, was the influence of Protestantism discernible in these years. The rest of the country has been seen as having no more than scattered individuals, mainly found in the ports and in regions not too far from the Pyrenees. Recently, however, it has been discovered that there was in addition a small nucleus of convinced evangelicals in Aragon, which came to the attention of the authorities at the same time as the larger centres.[37] The discovery of the Seville circle in fact revealed a fairly sophisticated network of evangelical contacts. But it was vulnerable to just such a fatal lapse of security as in fact occurred. In 1557 Julián Hernández made one of his periodic visits overland to Spain taking letters for sympathisers still in Seville, and on this occasion copies of the works printed in recent years in Geneva carefully concealed inside more innocent merchandise. When he began to deliver his material in Seville, unfortunately, one packet, containing the strongly anti-papal *Imagen del Antechristo*, fell into the wrong hands, and the authorities were informed. This triggered the Inquisition into action, initially in Seville, and then all over Spain. In the calm before the storm, the monks of San Isidoro and nearby Nuestra Señora in Écija got wind of the situation – perhaps from Antonio del Corro's uncle – and with some lay-people about a dozen of them fled to safety abroad. A large number of the rest, with many other people, were taken into the Inquisition's prisons to await investigation. The Emperor was informed, and almost his last instructions to his son Philip II were for the imposition of an exemplary crackdown on this movement. The poor unfortunates in land-locked Valladolid were not favourably placed. All fugitives were apprehended in flight before they reached the border. The group in Aragon was revealed by investigations into the rector of the *colegio mayor* of Saragossa, Miguel Monterde, who had been corresponding with Protestant Spaniards abroad, and by the foolhardy return to the area of Jayme Sánchez, who had been sent to Paris at the age of twelve to be brought up in the Protestant faith by Juan Morillo and company. His name had been revealed during the interrogation of others, and the efficient Inquisition filing system recognised it when he made an

---

[36] J. I. Tellechea has published the document containing over 150 statements of belief taken from members under interrogation, 'Perfil teológico del protestantismo castellano del siglo XVI', *Cuadernos de Investigación Histórica*, 7 (1983), 79–111.

[37] See Kinder, 'Protestants in Aragon'.

unprompted false confession, hoping to avoid serious trouble by admitting part, but not the whole, of his past.[38]

The vigilance of the Inquisition led to protracted interrogations, trials and a series of spectacular *autos de fe*. Those celebrated in Valladolid on 21 May and 8 October 1559, and Seville on 24 September 1559, 22 December 1560, and 26 April and 28 October 1562 were attended by royalty. A good number were burnt at the stake, the effigies of some who had escaped were burnt with them; others were subjected to a whole gamut of other punishments, designed to degrade those straying from the orthodox path and discipline them back into it. A surprising side-effect of the action against Protestantism in Valladolid in 1559 led to the arrest there on charges of heresy of the Primate of Spain, the Archbishop of Toledo, Bartolomé Carranza de Miranda. This move was politically motivated and was carried out at an opportune time during the king's absence, but once the Inquisition's wheels had been set in motion it was difficult to stop them. Although there was probably no foundation for the accusation, Carranza had had some interesting, not to say suspect, associates and had read some compromising material. Mountains of paper had been used in interrogations before the Pope stepped in and transferred the case to Rome, where Carranza died after seventeen years of confinement.[39]

As a result of this series of blows to Spain's religious integrity, a number of measures were taken. Students attending foreign universities were recalled (although the ban was never totally effective). Extreme vigilance was imposed on borders and ports to keep out prohibited books. The Inquisition's savage treatment of the merest hint of Protestantism had stamped out all overt doctrinal dissent. This was backed up by a concerted effort to convince people by all possible means that a Spaniard is naturally a Roman Catholic. After a brief period of openness, the country had retreated behind its ideological frontiers. From then on in Spain 'Lutheran' was a bogeyman to be raised against all forms of dissent quite unconnected with genuine Protestantism.

This was a watershed. There was no room for Protestantism in the homogeneous society now being imposed with what on the surface seemed to be widespread public approval. Nevertheless, Spanish Protestantism was kept alive by those in exile. Before long there was quite a 'family' of *émigrés* in northern Europe: Switzerland, Germany, the Netherlands and England. One of the earliest of these was the important figure, Francisco de Enzinas (usually known outside Spain by his learned

[38] *Ibid.*, pp. 148–56. It is pleasant to note that after his trial Sánchez managed to escape and disappear.
[39] On this, see the many publications of J. I. Tellechea.

name of Dryander), who was from a noble Burgos family.[40] He and his brother Jaime were educated at Louvain, where they seem to have become Protestants earlier than most other Spaniards. Francisco published pseudonymously in 1540 a small work which turns out to be a compilation from Luther and Calvin, with his own introduction, *Breve y compendiosa instituçion de la religion Christiana* . . .,[41] and Jaime published a Spanish catechism in Antwerp in 1541, all trace of which has since been lost. In October 1541 Francisco stayed some time in Wittenberg at the home of Melanchthon whilst attending the university and making the first version from Greek into modern Spanish of the complete New Testament, which he took to Antwerp in 1543 to be printed.[42] It was dedicated and presented personally to Charles V. After it was examined, the translator found himself imprisoned in Brussels, but managed to escape and flee back to Wittenberg, where he wrote a Latin account later published in French, *Histoire de l'état du Pais Bas, et de la religion d'Espagne*, ('Ste Marie' [=Strasburg], 1558). This gave the earliest account of a fellow native of Burgos, Francisco de San Román, who was converted in Bremen and taken prisoner by the Emperor in Regensburg, from where he was hauled to Valladolid for trial, being burnt at the stake and becoming Spain's first unequivocally Protestant martyr in 1542.[43] Dryander published in Basle in 1546 a commentary on the proceedings of the Council of Trent. In 1548 he was appointed to teach Greek in Cambridge. Two years later he went to Strasburg to have some books printed and did not return to England, dying of plague in 1552. Meantime his brother Jaime had been ill-advised enough to go to Rome, where he

40 The best works on Enzinas is still that in E. Boehmer, *Bibliotheca Wiffeniana*, I, 131–84, but see also J. L. Nelson, 'The Nature and Authority of Scripture in Four Spanish Protestant Reformers of the Sixteenth Century: Francisco de Enzinas, Juan Pérez, Casiodoro de Reina, Cipriano de Valera' (Unpublished MA thesis, Wheaton College, Illinois, 1987), which concentrates on Enzinas.

41 He used a Hebrew form of his name, 'Elao', to disguise the authorship, and 'Topeia' as the place of printing. The introduction was reprinted by Bataillon: *El hispanismo y los problemas de la historia de la espiritualidad española (al propósito de un libro protestante olvidado)* (Madrid, FUE, 1977).

42 *El nuevo testamento de nuestro Redemptor y Salvador Jesu Christo, traduzido de Griego en lengua Castellana, por Francisco de Enzinas, dedicado a la Cesarea Magestad*; the colophon states that it was printed in Antwerp by Stephen Mierdmann on 25 October 1543, although the arrangements had been made with the printer Mattheus Crom, who had died before finishing the work. See H. F. Wijnman, 'The mysterious sixteenth-century printer Niclaes van Oldenborch: Antwerp or Emden?', in *Studia Bibliographica in Honorem Herman de la Fontaine Verwey* (Amsterdam, 1966), 461–3.

43 This has twice been reprinted in modern French in Brussels, 1862–3, and 1963, and once in Spanish (Buenos Aires, 1943). The original Latin MS is in the Vatican Library (Fond. Palatin., Cod. lat. 1853). The account about San Román received documentary confirmation only recently; see J. I. Tellechea Idígoras, 'Francisco de San Román: un mártir protestante burgalés (1542)', *Cuadernos de Investigación Histórica*, 8 (1984), 233–60.

was tried and burnt at the stake in 1547. An associate of Enzinas, Juan Díaz from Cuenca, wrote *Christianae religionis summa* (Neuburg, 1546).[44] Díaz's murder for sectarian reasons by his own brother in the same year, gave rise to several books, not however by Spaniards.

In 1556 another Spaniard flirting with Protestantism in the Low Countries, Fadrique Furió Ceriol, published *Bononia, sive de libris sacris in vernaculam linguam convertendis* (Basle, 1556). Documents make it clear that Furió had manuscripts of other books of a similar or more Protestant slant, which he handed over to the authorities as part of a deal enabling him to return to Spain. One of Furió's associates, Felipe de la Torre, seems to have gone even so far as to accept ordination as a Protestant minister. He too negotiated his return to Spain, where thereafter he, like Furió, enjoyed a distinguished career.[45] Another who was persuaded to go back was Gaspar Zapata, who had been a member of Reina's congregation in London. On the other hand, the latter may have been an *agent provocateur* acting in league with Francisco de Abrego (who certainly was) to bring about Reina's capture and return to Spain for trial.[46] Not that Abrego had much joy of it, for as soon as he arrived in Spain an Inquisition warrant was out for his arrest. The spy network directed from the Spanish Netherlands was constantly active in its efforts to apprehend Spanish heretics, not without some success.[47] Juan de León, a San Isidoro monk, was caught in Strasburg. A Cistercian, Julián de Tudela, who had acted as a go-between amongst scattered Spanish heretics, died in Germany before he could be caught. Another Cistercian, Andrés Muñoz, on his way to London, was taken, as were Dr Andrés Bustamante Farias, and Antonio Dávalos. Others were more fortunate. Agostino Boazio, a Genoese from Cadiz who had already been in the hands of the Mexican Inquisition and escaped from the ship taking him to Spain, managed to use a legal ploy to get out of prison in Flanders and took refuge in England. After his operations in Paris, Juan Morillo moved on to Antwerp, where he too was ordained Protestant minister of an exiled French-speaking congregation, leading them in search of a permanent home first to Wesel, then to Frankfurt. Here he linked up with his former associates Luis del Castillo and Diego de la Cruz in the already estab-

---

[44] Reprinted in *Reformistas antiguos Españoles*, vol. 21, 99–110.
[45] See Kinder, 'Protestants in Aragon', 137–8; R. W. Truman (ed.), Introduction to Felipe de la Torre, *Institución de un rey Christiano* (Antwerp 1556) (Exeter, University, 1979); id., 'Felipe de la Torre and his *Institución de un rey Christiano*' (Antwerp, 1556): the Protestant connections of a Spanish Royal Chaplain', *BHR*, 46 (1984), 83–93.
[46] See Kinder, *Casiodoro de Reina*, 28–37. More information on this episode is available and will appear in the second (Spanish) edition now in preparation.
[47] See R. W. Truman and A. G. Kinder, 'The pursuit of Spanish heretics in the Low Counties'.

lished French Church, but soon Pier Paolo Vergerio reported to Henry Bullinger that he had been poisoned by Inquisition agents.[48] When they came to Frankfurt, the English Marian exiles declared that the other two Spaniards were very helpful to them.[49]

It was hardly prudent to publish overtly Protestant material inside Spain, but the other *émigré* Spanish writers certainly produced wholly Protestant works, some of them violently anti-papal. Antonio del Corro, writing in Antwerp in 1567, is adamant that he and his companions left their monasteries to preserve their definitely Protestant views. A similar point is made by the unidentified Reginaldus Gonsalvius and by Cipriano de Valera.[50] Since Enzinas' Spanish translation of the New Testament had not managed to circulate widely, another one, also from the original Greek, was produced by the already mentioned Juan Pérez, who by then was the pastor of a small Spanish Protestant congregation in Geneva, and printed in that city by Crespin in 1556. It is not clear how much use he made of Enzinas' New Testament to make his own version. A year later, Pérez's version of the Psalms was published by the same Geneva printer. Both were hidden beneath the same false imprint as Pérez's editions of Valdés. Juan Pérez also produced several other books in Spanish in Geneva: an adaptation of Calvin's Catechism, *Sumario breve de la doctrina Christiana* (1556); *Carta embiada a ... Philippe, Rey d'España* (1558); an adaptation of a work by Sleidanus, *Dos informaciones muy utiles, la una dirigida a la Magestad del emperador Carlos quinto ... la otra a los Estados del Imperio ... con una suplicacion a la Magestad del rey*; a Spanish translation of Calvin's Catechism (1559) (differing in many respects from the previous anonymous version of 1550 sent to many Spanish notables); an expanded free translation of Urbanus Rhegius' Latin *Novae doctrinae ad veterem collatio* (Augsburg, 1526), bearing the title *Breve tratado de la doctrina antigua de Dios y de la nueva de los hombres* (1560); and *Epistola para consolar a los fieles de Jesu Christo, que padecen persecucion* (1560).[51]

It is not entirely clear just how much connection Juan Pérez had with the translation of a pamphlet, *Breve summario de indulgencias y gracias*, without place, printer or date, produced at this time in Geneva; there were

[48] Letter published in Kinder, 'Protestants in sixteenth-century Aragon', 146.

[49] W. Whittingham, *A brieff discourse of the troubles begun at Frankfort in the year 1554 about the Book of Common Prayer and ceremonies* reprinted from the 1575 edition (London, 1846), v–vi.

[50] Corro, *Lettre envoyée au roi*, A4^r, A5^r–B1^r; R. Gonsalvius Montanus, *Sanctae Inquisitionis hispanicae artes*, 173–297; Cipriano de Valera, *Dos tratados ...* (London, 1588), 246–53.

[51] An English version by John Daniel appeared ten years later: *An Excelent Comfort to all Christians against all Kinde of Calamities: no lesse Comfortable then Pleasant, Pithy, & Profitable ...* (London, 1576).

after all other Spaniards in Geneva. Printed to look like an indulgence of the traditional Roman Catholic kind, but carrying a strongly Protestant message, it is very much in his style. Still less clear is which Spaniard was responsible for the fateful illustrated pamphlet *Imagen del Antechristo*, not in Pérez's style at all, translated from the Italian of Bernardino Ochino by an unidentified 'Alonso de Peñafuerte'. Copies of both these pamphlets were carried overland to Spain by Julián Hernández, together with all Pérez's books; and Peter Veller of Antwerp had been engaged in the shipment of quantities of them to Seville. This flurry of activity in mid-century was in all likelihood connected with the resistance to Spanish domination in the Netherlands, where many publications were produced to stir up hatred of things Spanish. The attempt to plant evangelical books in Spain seems to have been part of a move to carry the battle into the enemy camp, in which England, as second in line, also took part.[52] There is no evidence that more than the occasional copy of any of these books, other than Inquisition 'file-copies', ever got through to Spain, although there are records of concerted efforts at this time to introduce Calvin's *Institutes* in quantity, perhaps as part of the endeavour of French Protestants to replant evangelical Christianity in Spain, and/or of the ideological side of the Dutch struggle for independence.[53]

One of the most notable of the Spanish *émigrés*, Casiodoro de Reina, a monk of San Isidoro, fled first to Geneva, arriving when circumstances were occurring concerning the treatment of Valentin Gentile, similar to those which led to the death of Servetus. Reacting to this evidence of Protestant intolerance, reminiscent of the Spanish Inquisition, he quickly set to work persuading several of his companions to seek refuge in England, where Elizabeth's accession had opened the way. In London, he gathered a congregation of Spaniards, and was granted a church and an income. A confession of faith he composed so that his church might be received as one of the so-called Strangers' Churches is still extant. It reveals an independent mind, not willing to be totally bound by Calvinist orthodoxy.[54] Reina was the translator–compiler of the first complete Spanish Bible (including the books of the Apocrypha), produced

[52] This anti-Spanish offensive was responsible for the creation of the Black Legend. Various works by Spanish Protestants were used to this end: besides that by Gonsalvius Montanus, others by Corro and Valera. On the latter, see A. G., Kinder, 'Religious Literature as an offensive weapon: Cipriano de Valera's part in England's war with Spain', *SCJ*, 19 (1988), 223–35.

[53] J. A. Goris, *Étude sur les colonies marchandes méridionales (Portugais, Espagnols, Italiens) à Anvers de 1488 à 1567* (Louvain, 1925), 583–5.

[54] This remained in MS till Casiodoro published it in Frankfurt in 1577; one sole copy has survived (in the British Library). A recent edition has been published: A. G. Kinder (ed). *Confesión de fe christiana. The Spanish Protestant Confession of Faith (London, 1560/61)* (Exeter: University of Exeter, 1988).

remarkably speedily considering the vicissitudes of his own life. He had to leave England precipitately when Spanish *agents provocateurs* made life difficult, and went into hiding in Antwerp, then crossed France to confer with fellow-exiles, before joining his wife in Frankfurt to earn his living trading in books and silk. He had hoped to have his Bible printed in Geneva, but the inconveniences of distance, politics and Reina's personal circumstances prevented this. In the end, its printing was begun in Basle by Oporinus, whose death complicated matters, and it was finally completed by Biener for Guarin in 1569. Reina made use of Pérez's New Testament in the closing stages. He would have preferred to have obtained a copy of the new edition that Pérez had been producing. Pérez had left Geneva for France in 1560, and, after a short period as a parish minister in Blois, he had been taken into the service of Renée de France as a chaplain together with Antonio del Corro, who had been obliged to leave his post as a minister in Béarn. Pérez died in Paris in 1566 as his work was being produced, and shortly afterwards the King of France ordered the seizure and destruction of the whole printing.

The antagonism of Calvinists pushed Casiodoro ultimately into the Lutheran camp, and, he finished his days as pastor to a French-speaking Lutheran Church in Antwerp and Frankfurt. He wrote several theological works in Latin, and it is clear from the records of Strasburg City Council that he had something to do with the production of the widely translated work by the unidentified Spanish writer Reginaldus Gonsalvius Montanus entitled *Sanctae Inquisitionis hispanicae artes detectae ac palam traductae* (Heidelberg, 1567), a much translated book instrumental in the growth of the so-called Black Legend. This work is an account of the rise and suppression of Protestant beliefs in Spain, evidently written by an eye-witness of Inquisition activity who had lived in Seville.

Antonio del Corro, having served a restless ministry in Béarn, was rescued from the political situation by Renée de France and taken to Montargis to be one of her domestic chaplains. In late 1566 he answered a call to Antwerp, where again the political situation obliged him to move on. He had time to publish two books there in French in 1567: his *Lettre envoyée à la Maiesté du Roy des Espaignes* ... is an open letter to Philip II explaining his reasons for leaving the Roman Church and arguing strongly for religious toleration in the king's domains; the *Epistre et amiable remonstrance* ... *aux pasteurs de l'église flamengue d'Anvers* ... is an exhortation to the Lutheran and Reformed ministers in Antwerp to take a more tolerant attitude to one another. He went to England, where two years later he issued a doctrinal broadsheet, *Tableau de L'œuvre de Dieu*, which he revised and reissued in Latin. This, in the cavilling spirit of the day, got him into trouble as a latitudinarian with hints of anti-trinitarianism. He published the correspondence occasioned by the dispute in *Acta consistorii ecclesiae Londinogallicae cum responsio Antonii Corrani* (London, 1571). None of his writings were in Spanish, which indicates that they were not intended for evangelisation in Spain.

Another notable Spanish exile was Cipriano de Valera, who accompanied Reina to London, but was soon in Cambridge, where he was appointed fellow of Magdalene College in 1560; he was one of a number of foreign Calvinists brought in to strengthen the Protestant presence in the universities. After eight years, he went to London, attending the Italian Church, and reportedly working as a teacher and preacher. He had several influential patrons, who doubtless provided the funds for the strongly anti-Catholic works he began to produce in the year of the Armada, which can be seen as an ideological component in the hostilities with Spain.

Yet the fact that these leading figures made successful careers in England and Germany was itself significant: with the passing of its first and only generation the memory of any genuine Spanish Protestantism had begun to fade. Inside Spain, however, the idea of *luteranismo* 'became a permanent spectre ... which was made to "collaborate" in the task of stabilizing a feudal, aristocratic, and authoritarian social order. Never was an enemy made use of so profitably.'[55] Continually reminded of the supposed dangers of Protestantism, and of the real danger of being a Protestant in Spain, Spaniards became solidly Roman Catholic for the next four centuries.

[55] J. Contreras, 'Impact of Protestantism', 62.

SELECT BIBLIOGRAPHY

Boehmer, Eduard, *Bibliotheca Wiffeniana: Spanish Protestants of Two Centuries*, (3 vols., London, Trübner, 1874–1904).
Menéndez y Pelayo, Marcelini, *Historia de los heterodoxos españoles*, (3 vols., Madrid, V. Suárez, 1880–1).
Schäfer, Ernst H. J., *Beiträge zue Geschichte des spanischen Protestantismus im sechzehnten Jahrhundert* (3 vols., Gütersloh, Bertelsmann, 1902).

The above three nineteenth-century works are basic, but unfortunately they are even nowadays used all too extensively. Texts of works written by Spanish reformers are very rare in their originals. Many were edited by Luis de Usoz y Río and Benjamin B. Wiffen and republished last century in a series called Reformistas Antiguos Españoles (now itself rare), a facsimile edition of which was issued in 1981 in Barcelona by the Libreria Diego Gómez Flores.
Aspe Ansa, María Paz, *Constantino Ponce de la Fuente: el hombre y su lenguaje* (Madrid, FUE, 1975).

Bainton, Herbert E. *Hunted Heretic. The Life and Death of Michael Servetus* (Boston, Mass., Beacon, 1953), 2nd edn. 1972.

Bataillon, Marcel, *Erasmo y España: estudios sobre la historia espiritual del siglo XVI*, trans. Antonio Alatorre, 3rd edn. (Mexico City, FCE, 1966), and several reprints. The earlier editions: French (Paris, Droz, 1937) and Spanish (Mexico City, FCE, 1950) are useful, as is a fourth edition (Geneva, Droz, 1991).

Contreras, Jaime, 'The Impact of Protestantism in Spain 1520–1600', in Stephen Haliczer (ed.), *Inquisition and Society in Early Modern Europe* (London, Croom Helm, 1986), 47–63.

Kinder, A. Gordon. 'Cipriano de Valera, Spanish Reformer', *Bulletin of Hispanic Studies*, 46 (1969), 109–19.

Casiodoro de Reina, Spanish Reformer of the Sixteenth Century (London, Tamesis, 1975).

'Juan Pérez de Pineda (Pierius): a Spanish Calvinist Minister of the Gospel in sixteenth-century Geneva', *BHR*, 53 (1976), 83–300.

Spanish Protestants and Reformers in the Sixteenth Century: a Bibliography, Research Bibliographies and Checklists, vol. 39 (London, Grant and Cutler, 1983).

'A hitherto Unknown Group of Protestants in sixteenth-century Aragon', *Cuadernos de Historia Jerónimo Zurita*, 51–52 (1985), 131–60.

'Juan de Valdés', *Bibliotheca Dissidentium*, vol. 9, 111–95 (Baden-Baden, Koerner, 1988).

Servetus, Bibliotheca Dissidentium, vol. 10 (Baden-Baden, Koerner, 1989).

Longhurst, John E. 'The Alumbrados of Toledo: Juan del Castillo and the Lucenas', *ARG* 45 (1954), 233–53.

Erasmus and the Spanish Inquisition: the case of Juan de Valdés, (Albuquerque, University of New Mexico Press, 1950).

Luther and the Spanish Inquisition: the case of Diego de Uceda 1528–1529, (Albuquerque, University of New Mexico Press, 1953).

Luther's Ghost in Spain (Lawrence, Kansas, Coronado, 1969).

McCrie, Thomas, *History of the Progress and Suppression of the Reformation in Spain in the sixteenth century* (Edinburgh, Blackwood, 1827).

Márquez, Antonio, *Los Alumbrados. Orígenes y filosofía 1525–1559* (Madrid, Taurus, 1972), 2nd edn., 1980.

Nieto, José C. *Juan de Valdés and the Origins of the Spanish and Italian Reformations* (Geneva, Droz, 1970).

Redondo, A. 'Luther et l'Espagne de 1530 à 1536', *Mélanges de la Casa de Velázquez*, 1 (1965), 109–65.

Tellechea Idígoras, José Ignacio. *El arzobispo Carranza y su tiempo* (Madrid, Guadarrama, 1968).

'Don Carlos de Seso y el Arzobispo Carranza: un veronés introductor del protestantismo en España', in Raffaele Belvedere (ed.), *Miscellanea Card. Giuseppe Siri* (Genoa, 1973), 62–124.

Tiempos recios: inquisición y heterodoxias (Salamanca, Sígueme, 1977).

Melanchthon y Carranza: préstamos y afinidades, (Salamanca, Universidad Pontificia, 1979).

Truman, Ronald W. 'Fadrique Furió Ceriol's return to Spain from the Netherlands in 1564: further Information on its Circumstances', *BHR*, 41 (1979),
359–66.

Truman, Ronald W. and A. G. Kinder, 'The Pursuit of Spanish Heretics in the
Low Countries: the Activities of Alonso del Canto 1561–1564', *JEH*, 30
(1979), 65–93.

Index

barbes 121
Bardejov 59–60, 65
Barreda, Diego de 221
Barry, Jean de, seigneur de la Renaudie
   137
Bascouter, Georgius die 148
Basle 4, 38, 63, 74, 78, 79, 80, 81, 83, 85,
   89, 90, 145 n., 159, 160
   Council of (1436) 27–8
   diocese 73
   Peace of (1499) 72
   printing 75, 230, 231, 234
   Reformation in 70, 77, 82, 87–8
   university 74, 87
Batenburg, Jan van 158
Batenburgers 158–9, 160
Baumheckel, George 56
Bazas 134
Béarn 120, 136, 234
Beaupas, François de 135
Bebek, Francis 61
Bedoya, Gaspar 220
Beheim, Bernhard 58
Béla 61
Bellay, Guillaume du 127
Bellay, Jean du 127
Bellay, René du 125, 127
Benedictines 184, 193, 194, 196, 199
Benkner, Paul 63
Benvoglienti, Achille 198, 205
Berne 72, 75, 80, 81, 83, 84, 85, 174
   Disputation (1528), 81, 86
   Reformation in 70, 77, 81–2, 86–7
   relations with Zurich 72, 86
   Synod (1532) 86
   and Geneva 89–90
Bernhard, Simon 57
Berquin, Louis de 125
Bertari, Giovanni 199
Beteta, Luis de 220
Biberach 84
Bibles, Bible study 150–2, 217, 220, 227
Bible translations
   Complutensian Polyglot 217–8
   Czech 39 n.
   Danish 97
   English 171, 181, 184
   Hungarian 65
   Italian 195
   Spanish 218–9, 223–4, 230, 232, 233–4
   Swedish 113
Bijns, Anna 148, 152
Bille, Torbern 105
Billom 138
Bilney, Thomas 173
Binder, Matthew 59

Biró, Matthias Dévai 60, 65, 66
Bistrita 63
Black Death 178, 184
Blekinge 97
Blois 234
Boazio, Agostino 231
Bocher, Joan 175
Bogbinder, Ambrosius 110
Bogner, Balthomew 61
Bohemia 2, 19, 23–37, 38, 39, 40, 43, 46,
   47, 49, 51, 53, 56, 59
Bohemian Brethren (*Unitas Fratrum*) 26,
   31–2, 34–5, 37, 39, 40, 42, 46
Bohemicus, George 64
Bökman, Hans 114
Boleyn, Anne 167
Bologna 55, 191, 199, 205, 210, 223
Bolsec, Hieronymous 91
Bonner, Edmund 184
books, *see* printing
Bordeaux 128
Bormio 212
Borrhaus, Martin 227 n.
Boysonné, Jean du 127
Bozza, Tomasso 199
Brabant 12, 144, 145, 146, 147
Brandenburg 31
Brask, Hans 108, 112, 113, 115
Brassó 61–3
Bratislava 51, 55, 67
   Treaty of (1491) 49
Braunschweig 102
Bremen 99, 230
Bremgarten 85
Brennwald, Heinrich 75
Bresciani, Pietro 205
Briceño, Doña 91
Briçonnet, Guillaume 123–5, 139, 140
Brie 137
Bristol 12, 177, 178
Brittany 136
Brucioli, Antonio 195
Brünn 24, 38, 41
   Diet of (1550) 42
Brunner, Fridolin 77
Brunner, George 77
Brus von Müglitz, Anton 37
Brussels 144, 146, 147, 148, 230
   evangelical activity 149–50, 152
Bucer, Martin 4, 7, 19, 22, 32, 84, 86, 88,
   154 n., 173–4, 195, 203
Buda 55, 57–8, 65
Bugenhagen, Johannes 103, 110, 111
Bullinger, Heinrich 66, 70, 85–6, 88, 90, 91,
   92, 232
Buren 146

Burgos 221, 230
Buscoducensis, Nicolaus 145 n.
Bustamente Farias, Andres 231

Cadiz 231
Cafarelli, Giovanni Battista 202
Cahera, Havel 30
Calais 180
Calixtines, *see* Utraquists
Calvin, Jean 22, 32, 70, 87, 88, 89–90, 92,
    129, 174, 188, 189, 206, 225
    Institutes 129, 189 n., 199–200, 222, 233
    other works 189 n., 227, 230, 232
Calvinism 37, 65, 129, 130, 161, 205, 235
    and France 129–30, 133–40
    and The Netherlands 148 n., 163
    and Waldensians 211
Cambridge 4, 22, 169, 170, 171, 173, 174,
    230, 235
Campeggio, Lorenzo Cardinal 58
Campen, Jacob van 157
Campo Rakos 58
Capito, Wolfgang 84, 86
Capuchins 196, 197, 211
Caracciolo, Antonio 139, 140
Caraffa, Giovanni Pietro 204, 213
Caravia, Alessandro 204
Carignono 208
Carletti, Angelo 193
Carmelites 96, 105, 108, 109, 144
Carnesecchi, Pietro 197, 223
Caroli, Pierre 124
Carraca, Constantino di 203
Carranza de Miranda, Cardinal
    Bartholomé 229
Carvajal, Luis de 226
Casalmaggiore 205
Castellio, Sébastien 88, 135
Castile 221
Castillo, Juan del 220, 221, 223
Castillo, Luis del 231
Catarino, Ambrogio 205
catechisms 18, 20–1, 227, 230, 232
Catherine de Medici 127, 139
Catholic League 131
Cavour, Treaty of (1561) 211
Cazalla, Augustin 226, 227
Cazalla, Juan de 220
Cazalla, María de 220
Cazalla, Pedro de 220
Celtis, Conrad 55
Cenalis, Robert 125
Cévennes 129, 136
chambre ardente 122
Champagne 134, 137
chantries 146, 176, 178, 181, 185

Charles V, Emperor 6, 8, 13, 14, 21, 46, 58,
    83, 160, 171, 173, 230
    and Denmark 97
    and The Netherlands 144–6, 157, 163
    and Spain 217–8, 221–2, 228
Châteaubriand, Edict of (1551) 122
Chiari, Isidoro 196
Chiavenna 212
Chieti 204
Chinon 134
Christian II, King of Denmark 14, 94,
    96–7, 104, 110, 112, 114, 115, 117, 145
Christian III, King of Denmark 111, 117
    while Duke of Haderslev/Tønning
    97–100, 102, 104
Christian Civic Union 84–5, 86, 88
Chur 73
Cibo, Caterino, duchess of Camerino
    197
Cioni, Fabio 198, 205
Cisneros, Cardinal Francisco Ximénez de
    215, 217
cistercians 231
Claesz, Jan 161
Cleves 160
Cluj 63
Coligny, Gaspard de 136
colleges, in France 127–8, 135, 138; *see also*
    schools
Cologne 4, 21, 160
Colonna, Vittoria 197
colporteurs 126
communion in both kinds 15, 28, 40, 46,
    153 n.; *see also* Eucharist
Condé, Louis de 136, 137
Confessio Pentapolitana 60
confession 159, 192–3
confraternities 109, 138, 194–5, 202, 205
Consensus Tigurinus 88, 90
Constance 29, 73, 85
consubstantiation 103
Contarini, Gasparo 196, 197, 199, 200, 201,
    203, 213
conventicles, 147–53, 162, 206, 221, 225,
    226, 227
Copenhagen 12, 96, 104–11, 112, 117
    Reformation 109–10
    university 96, 105, 109
Cordatus, Conrad 57–9
Cornwall 180, 182
Corpus Christi 133
Corro, Antonio del 227, 228, 231, 234
Cortese, Gregorio 196, 197, 200
Corvinus, *see* Matthias
Council, *see* Basle, Trent
    of Troubles 147

242   *Index*